Napoleon's Prisoner of War

Napoleon's Prisoner of War
Experiences of a British Officer during the Napoleonic Wars in Spain and France

Andrew Thomas Blayney

LEONAUR

Napoleon's Prisoner of War
*Experiences of a British Officer during
the Napoleonic Wars in Spain and France*
by Andrew Thomas Blayney

First published under the titles
*Narrative of a Forced
Journey Through
Spain and France
as a Prisoner of War
in the Years 1810 to 1814
in two Volumes*

Leonaur is an imprint
of Oakpast Ltd

Copyright in this form © 2009 Oakpast Ltd

ISBN: 978-1-84677-770-7 (hardcover)
ISBN: 978-1-84677-769-1 (softcover)

http://www.leonaur.com

Publisher's Notes

In the interests of authenticity, the spellings, grammar and place names used have been retained from the original editions.

The opinions of the authors represent a view of events in which he was a participant related from his own perspective, as such the text is relevant as an historical document.

The views expressed in this book are not necessarily those of the publisher.

Contents

Preface	9
Embarkation of the Troops	11
Continuation of the Operations Against Fiangerolla	19
Brutality of the Polish Commandant	27
Malaga	33
March from Malaga to Grenada	37
Spanish and French Repasts	43
Praises of Buonaparte	51
Sebastiani's Birthday	59
Escape of Spanish Prisoners	69
Disagreeable Spanish Custom	77
Surrender of Dupont's Army	83
Effects of the French Invasion	88
Convoy from France	96
Campaign in Flanders	105
From Toledo to Madrid	112
Treatment of the Prisoners	116
Spanish Generosity	122
French Over-Civility	130
Madrid	134
Made a Close Prisoner in the Retiro	141
From Madrid to Burgos	148
From Segovia to Valladolid	159
The Cid	164
From Burgos to Mendragon	170
From Mendragon to St. Jean de Luz	177
Route to Bourdeaux	184

Bourdeaux	191
Masquerade	200
Conscription	208
Execution of Four Gentlemen	221
Field of Battle	231
Amboise	241
Birth of the King of Rome	251
Palace of Luxembourg	261
Column of the Grand Army	268
Arrival at Verdun	278
Sketch of its History	285
Arrest and Confinement	293
Excursion to Clermont	301
Excursion from Verdun to Metz and Nancy	304
Spanish *Renegadoes*	308
Death of the Commandant	316
Russian and Cossack Officers	327
Evacuation of the Depôts of Metz	337
French Officers' Abuse of Napoleon	345
A French Acquaintance	356
Passage of Prisoners	361
Russian Prisoners	370
Department of the Creuse	382
Departure of English Prisoners	391
English at Paris	396
England	407
Appendix	419

To His Royal Highness
The Duke of York.

Sir,

In presuming to solicit Your Royal Highness's protection for the following pages, I at once gratify two of the first feelings of my heart; the expression of profound reverence for Your Royal Highness's illustrious person, and the most perfect devotion to the service at the head of which Your Royal Highness presides with such distinguished honour. To whom indeed can a soldier dedicate his work with so much propriety as to a Prince who by the unanimous suffrage of the British Army is hailed by the glorious title of "The Soldier's Friend?"

I can only regret that these volumes are not more worthy the patronage with which Your Royal Highness has been pleased to honour them, by deigning to accept their dedication; but whatever they may want in interest, from the confined opportunities of a prisoner, I trust they will be found to contain the expression of the patriotic feelings of a British officer, who glories in his unalterable (attachment to Your Royal Highness's August House, as well as in the devotion and respect with which he has the honour to be,

    Sir,
    Your Royal Highness's
        Most obedient
    And most faithful humble servant,
        Blayney.

Preface

It is the common custom of travellers to publish their *Journals* with a prefatory apology for their literary faults, on the ground of their not having been intended for publication; but although the author of the following pages is truly entitled to plead this excuse in bar of severe criticism, he waves that right, convinced that it can neither add to the merit of the work nor efficiently apologize for its defects. He begs the reader, however, to bear in mind, that though the peculiar situation in which he was placed frequently deprived him of the opportunity of immediately putting pen to paper, yet he has endeavoured from recollection to supply that deficiency though perhaps at some distance of time after the circumstances happened. This, he trusts, will excuse any inaccuracies that may be met with; for, without affectation, he must declare that he had not originally any idea of offering this narrative to public notice.

Nor is it his intention to enter into the circumstances, which from enemies united Great Britain and Spain in one common cause, the glorious one of Justice, Humanity, and the Independence of all Europe. It is sufficient to say, that the sympathising generosity of the English nation could not contemplate the freedom of a gallant people, in danger of being annihilated, without affording its assistance to snatch them from the abyss.

The system of operations laid down for the conduct of the war in Spain, at the time this *Narrative* commences, being to distract the enemy's attention by calling it towards as many distant points as possible, the author was of consequence appointed to the command of a detachment of British and foreign troops in the English service, and a Spanish regiment, intended to make a diversion on the coast of Andalusia; and thought this object failed, owing to circumstances which he could not provide against, he dares assert, with confidence, that no blame can be attached to himself, or to the officers in general who served under him; and therefore he feels comparatively happy in the consolatory reflexion that though he could not "command success," he endeavoured to "deserve it," which was all that depended on himself.

Although a prisoner, the author's rank entitled him to a degree of personal liberty while travelling, and procured him a familiar intercourse with the first classes of society, both French and Spanish, which afforded him opportunities of observation that could scarcely have occurred to an officer of inferior rank. The result of these observations the author now presumes to offer to the public; and though he is far from expecting that his work will entirely satisfy those who seek for instruction alone, he hopes it will not be found destitute of reflections, interesting to the politician and the patriot, and that it will also afford to the most numerous class of readers, that amusement which they principally look for in works of this nature.

Chapter 1

Embarkation of the Troops

1810.

Cadiz being closely invested by the army of the Duc de Bellune, it appeared from the geographical position of the neighbouring country, that the most effectual mode of interrupting the siege, and harassing the enemy, would be to send detachments to various parts of the Spanish coast; which, by occupying their attention, would oblige them to weaken the besieging army, in order to succour the points menaced with attack.

It was also at this time of the utmost moment to support and keep alive the animosity of the peasantry, by affording them every possible assistance; without which, their exertions would certainly grow weaker; and it was even to be feared that they might ultimately surrender themselves to the French in despair. Besides, the French army before Cadiz drawing its supplies chiefly from Seville, the *seranos* (or mountaineers) of the Sierra de Xeres, and of the chain of mountains extending from Ronda Xeres, and from hence in a southeast direction by Mijas and Fiangerolla, were particularly to be encouraged, in order to induce them to act with vigour in cutting off the enemy's supplies.

To these circumstances must also be added, that in the beginning of October, information was received at Gibraltar, through various channels, that at Ronda the enemy's force consisted of only nine hundred men, *viz.* one company of grenadiers, one off riflemen, and eighty dragoons, in all two hundred and forty French; the remaining six hundred and sixty being composed

PORTRAIT OF A FRENCH OFFICER

of Germans, Poles, &c. upon whom little dependence could be placed. The same information stated that at Fiangerolla the enemy had but two hundred men, at Mijas but forty, and at Ronda one hundred, chiefly dragoons; while the country surrounding these ports, was said to be in the possession of a body of well armed, fierce, and exasperated mountaineers, nearly capable of keeping the French in check, having already obliged them several times to abandon St. Roque and Algeziras, with considerable loss.

The vicinity of these mountaineers, as well as the extreme badness of the road between Ronda and Fiangerolla, appeared to render it very difficult, if not impossible, for the enemy to send any reinforcement from the former to the latter place; while at the same time it was understood that much dissatisfaction reigned in Malaga, and that the inhabitants would readily unite their efforts with any force that might be sent to assist them in driving the French out of the town. Such was the situation of the enemy's detached forces, while they were carrying on the siege of Cadiz with vigour, having completed several batteries opposite the town, from whence, by means of very large mortars, they threw shells much farther than the usual distance, and thereby rendered the anchorage of our shipping very insecure.

The most certain means of checking the progress of the siege, was, as I have already observed, to call the attention of the enemy to other points; and, with this idea, several expeditions had been already sent to various places with different degrees of success. In furtherance of this principle; and after a communication between the Lieutenant-Governor of Gibraltar and the Spanish Government at Cadiz, it was determined to send a force from the former place against the ports already named, as well as to co-operate with the loyalist party in Malaga.

His Excellency Lieutenant-General Campbell did me the honour of confiding to me the conduct of this expedition; and on the 10th of October I accordingly received orders to prepare for secret service, and to take under my command four companies of His Majesty's 89th regiment, amounting to three hundred rank and file, together with five hundred German, Polish, and Italian deserters. With this force I was directed to proceed to Ceuta, where it was to be increased by the Spanish regiment of Toledo. As dispatch was an object of the first consequence, not a moment was lost, and the whole detachment was clothed, accoutred, and embarked on the same day; and as soon as I received my final instructions, I repaired on board His Majesty's ship *Topaze*, from whence I issued the necessary orders and instructions, and also prepared an address to the people of Malaga, which will be found in the Appendix.

Early in the morning of the 11th October, the squadron weighed and stood across for Ceuta; but light airs preventing our anchoring there until a late hour in the evening, I was obliged to defer going on shore till the morning. That no time might however be lost, I acquainted Major-General Frazer of my arrival by letter, and requested him to expedite the embarkation of the Spanish regiment. The following morning I proceeded on shore, and breakfasted with the General, but found it impossible to prevail on him to interfere in any manner, with respect to the object of my orders; and I was therefore under the necessity of applying personally to the Spanish Governor, who received me most politely, and cheerfully assured me of every assistance in his power. I must here observe, that the Spaniards of Ceuta looked on the English with the most jealous suspicion, and though General Frazer's force consisted of but one weak regiment (the Second battalion of the Fourth), the guns of the citadel, in which it was quartered, and which commands the town, had been all removed.

The embarkation of the Spanish troops being completed in the forenoon, I visited several of the transports, and in some of them found the Spaniards much dissatisfied with the nature of their provisions, owing entirely to the masters adhering literally to their instructions, and issuing meat on a *maigre* day, when common sense should have pointed out to them, the propriety of serving out other species in lieu. Indeed, I have frequently observed that foreign soldiers are dissatisfied with the species of provisions they receive on board our ships; and as these complaints could be so easily remedied, it seems extraordinary that no attention has been hitherto paid to then).

The regiment of Toledo being better cloathed, and apparently composed of a more orderly set of men than the generality of Spanish soldiers at this time, I paid their colonel some compliments on their appearance, and requested to be informed if they were compleat in every respect, which he assured me they were. Aware, however, of the astonishing neglect which pervaded every part of the Spanish military affairs, I did not choose to put implicit confidence in this assertion; and on enquiring minutely into the state of their arms and ammunition, I found a deficiency of one hundred and forty-eight firelocks, and that they had embarked literally without a single round of ammunition. I immediately wrote to the Spanish Governor, stating the impossibility of my supplying the latter, as our cartridges would not fit the Spanish arms. He returned a very polite answer, and the necessary ammunition was immediately sent off: the deficiency of muskets I supplied, together, with one hundred cartridges for each.

Having delivered the Spanish colonel his instructions, the squadron weighed and stood for the coast of Spain. The lightness of the wind rendered our passage tedious, and in the night of the 13th Captain Hall of the navy, commanding a detachment of gunboats under my orders, came on board from Gibraltar, with letters from his Excellency the Lieutenant-Governor. Captain Hall expressed himself very sanguinely as to the possibility of carrying Malaga by a *coup de main*, and founded his opinion on information received at Gibraltar, that the guns on the mole had been removed; he therefore proposed that the troops should occupy the enemy's attention on the land side, while the ships bombarded the town to the eastward, and that the boats should at the same time push for the mole, and throw a party into the town, to favour and assist an insurrection of the inhabitants.

To this plan I found it impossible to give my approbation, well assured that no intelligence received from the Spaniards was to be depended on; and besides there being an extensive plain between the Rio Grande and Malaga, in which a large body of cavalry could act to the greatest advantage: and as I had every reason to believe that the enemy could immediately collect a force of this description, it seemed to me highly imprudent to *risque* encountering it, with the motley troop of foreigners that composed two-thirds of my detachment.

These reasons induced me to determine on proceeding to the Calle de la Moralle, a small bay, one league east of Marabella and two west of Fiangerolla, with the intention of attacking the latter fortress, the possession of which would be of the greatest consequence to my future proceedings, as affording the means of receiving regular and certain information, as well as of organizing the peasantry, and commanding the neighbouring country. On the morning of the 14th the *Sparrowhawk* joined the squadron, and I was informed that arms had been distributed to the peasants, pursuant to orders which I had previously given. At nine o'clock the squadron anchored in the bay of Calle de la Moralle, and the signals were immediately made to prepare for landing the troops, and for the boats to assemble alongside the *Topaze*.

The shoalness of the water preventing the larger vessels from approaching the shore so as to cover the landing, the gunboats only were employed in that service; and having taken their station, at half past ten, the boats pushed for the shore, and the troops landed without accident or opposition on a fine sandy beach: indeed there did not appear to be any preparation whatever made by the enemy to oppose us. As soon as the troops were all formed on shore, I issued regulating orders for their movements, calculated to prevent the confusion that might arise from such a mixture of nations as composed my small force, there being English, French, Italians, Spaniards, Poles and Germans. I therefore directed that all movements should be carried into execution by the sound of the bugle, and restricted the sounds to four.

When tolerably perfect in this exercise, I gave orders to advance, but found the country so very mountainous, and without any road, that it was impossible the artillery could accompany us and it was therefore of necessity sent by water.

Previous to marching I had some conversation with Captain Miller of the 95th regiment, who, with several other officers, had been latterly employed in organizing the Spanish peasants. He informed me that a considerable quantity of arms and ammunition had been distributed amongst them, and consequently that I might expect a number to join me immediately; in this however I was entirely disappointed, not more than ten or twelve making their appearance.

One Spaniard I am, however, bound to notice, with the praise he deserves for the loyalty and fidelity with which he has always served the cause of his country; he is well known at Gibraltar, but at the present moment it would be improper and imprudent to name him. His loyalty was entirely disinterested, and indeed it is but doing justice to the Spaniards in general to observe that their zeal seems to proceed from real patriotism, without any hope or expectation of pecuniary emolument.

The services rendered to the cause by the person above alluded to, certainly entitled him to a considerable reward from the English, yet his sole request was to be permitted to wear a sash similar to that of our officers, which of course was granted, and from it he seemed to derive no small share of consequence in the eyes of his countrymen. Indeed, when I observed the delight expressed by the Spaniards at receiving the smallest honorary distinction, I was surprised that the Spanish loyal government had not created a military order of merit, to reward those who might be most active and enterprising in the cause; the hope of acquiring such a distinction from their legal rulers, would not only increase emulation, but diminish the value of the distinctions conferred by the French on their *partisans*.

The desire of chivalric distinctions is indeed universal throughout all Christian Europe: the cold phlegmatic German receives them with pleasure, and the Italian, burning with the ardour of a more genial climate, with delight; but it is in France, above all other countries, that they are sought after with the greatest avidity, and where they inspire their possessors with the greatest degree of vanity and self-consequence, as well as of military ardour, and the hopes of the *croix d'honneur* is perhaps the most powerful stimulant to the courage of the French soldier. When we reflect on this general feeling, we cannot account for the Junta's and Regency's having hitherto neglected the establishment of so certain and so cheap a mode of attaching the people to their cause.

Chapter 2

Continuation of the Operations Against Fiangerolla

The mountains and ravines which occupy the entire space between the Calle de la Moralle and Fiangerolla, rendered our march extremely fatiguing and tedious, so that we did not get sight of the fortress till two o'clock in the afternoon; when I immediately sent in a flag of truce with a summons, which was rejected. A projecting point of land to the westward of the castle, for some time covered the gunboats in their course along shore, but on passing this point, they became exposed to the guns of the castle, from which a heavy fire was immediately commenced on them.

I now advanced close to the work with the foreign riflemen, supported by the four companies of the 89th, when a brisk fire commenced on both sides; ours being confined to musketry, while the enemy had the advantage of firing grape from their artillery, by which Major Grant of the 89th was mortally wounded, while receiving my directions to take possession of a small ridge of hills, which extending to the beach would have afforded cover to the regiment. I felt severely the loss of this worthy officer, who after serving the best part of his life in the 86th regiment in the East-Indies, had returned in hopes of spending the remainder of his days in his native country; but finding it still required his services, he disdained to remain in idleness.

He just lived to be landed at Gibraltar, where he was buried with all military honours; the whole garrison attending his funeral, and paying the last melancholy tribute of respect to his remains. The fire from the castle continued on the gunboats, of which one was sunk, and several persons killed and wounded in the others; the troops, however, drawing a considerable part of the enemy's attention (which indeed was my motive for advancing so close), the boats were at last enabled to take their stations.

The castle I found to be infinitely stronger than it had been represented, consisting of a large square fort, situated on a hillock, of which it occupies the entire summit. Circumstanced as we were, and having information of a large body of the enemy being on its march towards as, it would have been decidedly the most advisable plan, to have attempted an escalade, had there been any tolerable hopes of success; but, after a mature consideration of the subject, I was obliged to relinquish this idea, not only from its apparent impracticability, but also from the certain great loss of men that must have attended even its success, and which would have rendered me incapable of defending the conquest, or of any further operations.

Having succeeded in silencing the guns of the castle for a short time, I withdrew part of the troops that were too much exposed, and at the same time directed the Spanish regiment to occupy a good position on the summit of a rough commanding hill, with a difficult ravine in front, which, in the opinion of Captain Harding of the engineers and myself, was a sufficient protection from a sudden attack. The Spanish colonel, however, now started an unexpected difficulty, namely that it was Sunday, and that it was not their custom to fight on the Sabbath,[1] I found also that there, was much discontent amongst the men of this regiment, from the want of a clergyman to perform divine service.

This circumstance I could only lament, and would have cheerfully offered to officiate, had I thought myself equal to the task. Here I must observe, that during the considerable period

---

1. The same occurrence took place at Talavera.

that I have commanded either a regiment or detachment in His Majesty's service, I have always been extremely, particular in enforcing a due observance of the Sabbath, not only from religious motives, but also because I have found it gradually create an orderly and proper deportment in the soldiers, which prevents the necessity of frequent punishment.

On the present occasion I was, however, obliged to leave the church to pray for our success; and this I did with no small degree of confidence, when I reflected that the contest we were engaged in, was for the preservation of order, religion and liberty to a whole nation, against the unprovoked attacks of a people, whose constant aim and end, for the last twenty years, had been to complete their overthrow.

The vicinity of Mijas, which is but five English miles from, and in sight of Fiangerolla, making it necessary to endeavour to cut off the communication between them so as to prevent assistance being sent from the former to the latter, I therefore prevailed on the Spanish commandant to detach four companies of his regiment, together with one hundred Germans, to execute this service, by occupying the angle where the roads or pathways meet, about half a mile from Mijas, and by which the enemy must pass, there being no other road, and the rocks on each side inaccessible. Captain Mullins, my brigade major, volunteered conducting this service, and though I gave him positive orders to act only on the defensive, the importunities of the Spaniards led him to exceed these orders and to make an attack on the town, where he met a most vigorous and unexpected resistance, that obliged him to fall back rapidly on the main body of the troops.

Mijas is a small town, containing about one thousand inhabitants, and the approach to it is so difficult, that a very small force may defend it against a very large one. It is situated on the declivity of a rocky hill, the side of which, facing Fiangerolla, is inaccessible, except by a narrow and winding pathway, skirted on one side by a deep rocky ravine. A river runs at the foot of the hill, which divides into two branches, and at the point of separation is crossed by an inconvenient bridge.

The castle of Fiangerolla commanding every point of the beach where boats could put on shore, the landing of the artillery was obliged to be postponed till night, when it was accomplished in a thunder storm, accompanied by heavy rain, which continued to pour down the whole night, and increased every rivulet to the magnitude of a river. Neither difficulty nor danger could however depress the persevering ardour of the soldiers and sailors, who before day broke had compleated a battery of two twelve-pounders and a howitzer, at the distance of three hundred and fifty yards from the castle, and oh the summit of a rocky hill, the ascent to which is difficult even to an unincumbered individual. Another battery was also compleated on the beach with one thirty-two pound carronade.

The whole of the detachment suffered severely during this dreadful night, neither officers or men having shelter or rest; those only who have been accustomed to tropical rains can form am adequate, idea of the torrents that poured down.

October 15. A little before daylight the advanced piquets were called in; and as soon as we could see each other, a heavy fire commenced on each side. A shell from our battery bursting killed most of the men at one of the enemy's guns, and silenced it for some time; our shot also destroyed part of the parapet of the castle, and left the people much exposed to our musketry, which evidently did great execution. The walls, were, however, so solid, that our small artillery could make but little impression. on them; and, indeed, it would have required twenty-four pounders to make a practicable breach; nevertheless, from the supposed smallness of the garrison, as at first represented, I hoped that our shells and musketry alone would soon oblige it to surrender, unless it received very speedy reinforcements.

I was therefore greatly mortified at learning that these reinforcements had been received previous to our arrival, and as I had therefore every reason to expect that a sortie would be made, my first object was to place the troops so as to meet it with the greatest possible advantage. At the same time I received information that General Sebastiani was marching from Malaga with a large force, and though again contradicted, this intelligence was soon positively confirmed.

Lieutenant-Colonel Basset, formerly of the 5th regiment, Lieutenant-Colonel Warrington, and one or two other officers joined us from the Sierras, where they had been employed in an attempt to organize the peasants, the plan of which had been suggested to the British Government by the Duke of Infantado; and its advantages would in all probability have been extremely great, had proper attention been paid to the selection of the officers.

An officer entrusted with a service of this delicate nature, should not only possess an enterprising and active disposition, a knowledge of mankind, and a perfect acquaintance with the language of the country, but his circumstances should also be such as to make him totally dependent on his talents and exertions for advancement. Such persons would have been invaluable in Spain, and many such might doubtless have been found in London, languishing in involuntary idleness, who would have been happy to accept such an employment, and by whose exertions the peasantry might have been better organized, and roused to a more efficient resistance, which must have ultimately succeeded in delivering their country from its lawless and cruel invaders.

The expulsion of the Moors affords the Spaniards a grand example of what their nation is capable of performing; and this example is deeply impressed on the minds of all classes. In that contest, as well as in the present, the Spaniards were at first defeated; but the loss of a battle served only to inspire fresh energy, while it taught them to correct their military faults, and the most perfect success crowned their perseverance.

I cannot quit this subject, which perhaps has led me into too long a digression, without doing justice to Captain Miller of the 95th regiment, who being perfectly acquainted with the Spanish language, had been of the utmost service in uniting the peasantry, and had acquired an extended knowledge of the country in general and of the strong passes of the mountains in particular. The reports of this officer; which I have had different opportunities of seeing, appeared to be very judicious:

Another circumstance, in some measure connected with the above observation, should not be passed over, namely, the large sums advanced by England for the Spanish cause, and over the expenditure of which no efficient control has been hitherto established, whence it is at least possible they may not be always applied to the intended purposes. When I was at Gibraltar a person named Moretti resided there, who assumed the title of general, and who was entrusted with the distribution of large sums, in which employment he contrived to enrich himself, until arousing the jealousy or suspicion of the Spanish Government, he was recalled to Cadiz, to undergo an enquiry, of the result of which I am ignorant.

This *soi-disant* general I had formerly seen at Palermo, where he was one of the principal performers in the orchestra of the opera, and an excellent musician. I must do him the justice to say that he appeared to be active and intelligent in his new employment, and his musical talents rendered him peculiarly agreeable to the Spanish ladies, who are great admirers of that art. Here I must claim a general indulgence for the digressions I may be occasionally led into in the course of this narrative, which though not always immediately connected with the main subject, I trust will tend to enliven the otherwise dry recital of military operations.

On the certain confirmation of the intelligence that Sebastiani was marching against us with a large force, I considered the best means of opposing a successful resistance with my small and badly composed detachment. I therefore, in company with Captain Harding, minutely examined the ground; in doing which we were several times exposed to a heavy fire of musketry from the castle. I found that the position we occupied was well suited for operations against the latter, but not so for defence against such a superior force as I had reason to expect, and which my intelligence stated to be four thousand seven hundred infantry, eight hundred cavalry, and sixteen pieces of artillery, commanded by General Sebastiani in person; while my whole force now amounted only to fourteen hundred infantry, and three pieces of artillery.

The reason already assigned for not leading the artillery by daylight, namely, the exposure of the beach to the guns of the castle, operated in like manner to prevent its re-embarkation; and being determined not to abandon it, nothing was left but to make preparations for receiving the enemy in the best manner possible; for this purpose I intended to have made some alterations in our position by occupying a ruined tower, capable of containing about fifty men, having a ridge of hills extending on its right and the sea close behind it; time was not however allowed me to accomplish this intention.

At this moment His Majesty's ship *Rodney*, with a Spanish line of battle ship, appeared off the coast, and I learnt that they had on board the 82nd regiment, one thousand strong, which had been sent from Gibraltar to reinforce me; my anxiety to receive them was of course very great; and boats were immediately sent off to assist in landing them.

My principal fear was that the enemy's cavalry would charge on the beach and gain our rear; to prevent which, if possible, I went with Captain Hall in a gunboat, with the intention of placing two boats on each flank so as to rake the beach; these boats were so close to the shore that I could have gone and returned in five minutes. During this arrangement, a desperate sortie was made from the castle by about six hundred and fifty infantry and sixty cavalry, and entirely directed to the left, where the Spanish and other foreign troops were posted, who fled with scarce any resistance, and abandoned the artillery to the enemy.

At this moment I observed the boats with the troops had pushed off from the ships, and were fast approaching the shore, which gave me hopes of being still able to retrieve the day, both from the strength of our position, and from my confidence in the 82nd regiment; I therefore immediately formed the 89th, and, though consisting of only two hundred and eighty men, retook the guns by the bayonet. In advancing to the charge my horse was wounded, and soon after killed by a second shot, so that I was obliged to charge on foot After a short but very severe contest, the enemy wheeled and fled; at the same moment a strong body came running across us in front, drest precisely similar to the Spanish troops, and a cry of "they are Spaniards!" at the same time took place.

I therefore ceased firing for a few minutes, both in order to form the troops more regularly, and to ascertain whether this body was really Spaniards or French, as well as to economize the, ammunition which began to fall short. Unfortunately I was not supported by the artillery, now again in our possession, and the enemy had only blown up a part of the, ammunition, leaving several loose rounds of grape in the battery, which, had they been employed, must have done great execution. Being dismounted I could not go to the left sufficiently quick to ascertain whether the approaching body were French or Spaniards:

I soon, however, observed a column close in from the left, on whose caps I perceived the number 4 with an eagle, and which proved to be the *Qatrième* Polonois. The troops with me, after firing a few rounds, charged this column, and a very severe conflict ensued, which unfortunately ended in my being made prisoner, having but nine men remaining of those that advanced with me.

Those only who have suffered a similar fate can form any idea of my sensations at being thus obliged to surrender to a ferocious *banditti*, who loaded me with every vile epithet, but in whose outrageous violence I in great measure found my personal safety, for they crowded so thick on me that they had not room to give force to their blows; They tore my cloaths, rifled my pockets, and attempted to pull off my epaulets, and the resistance I made to this last indignity procured me several blows from the butt ends of their muskets, that covered me with contusions. I was indeed probably indebted for my life to a Lieutenant Petit; of the Polish regiment, who opportunely came up on horseback; he was the only French, officer in the corps, and his humane and gentlemanly conduct did honour to his country.

CHAPTER 3

Brutality of the Polish Commandant

On entering the castle I was met by Captain Makosovitz, a Pole, who commanded, accompanied by several other officers; the former accosted me in the most brutal language, demanding "if it was I who had the insolence to send him in a flag of truce, and who had caused so much bloodshed," at the same time pointing to three houses in which the dead bodies were collected.

To this I replied, "that it was to prevent the effusion of blood that I had sent in a flag of truce, and that he would indeed have had reason to complain had I not done so."

The scene that presented itself at this moment can never be effaced from my memory; both officers and soldiers had all the appearance of those desperate *banditti* described in romances; their long *moustachios*, their faces blackened by smoke and gunpowder, and their bloody and torn cloths, giving to their whole appearance a degree of indescribable ferocity. Makosovitz conducted me upstairs with the other officers made prisoners, and the scene here was worse than that below, the surgeons being employed in dressing the officers, of whom scarce one escaped without a wound or contusion.

More melancholy from the thoughts of my captivity than from the pain of my bruises, which was however sufficiently acute, I went on the rampart, from whence I had a full view of the shipping. The fort was still firing at the *Rodney*, and at the boats with the troops, which approached close to the shore. A few minutes would have brought them to my assistance, and they would certainly have changed the fortune of the day in my favour; but fate ordered it otherwise. While thus absorbed in my own melancholy reflections, I could not help exclaiming, as I looked on the *Rodney* and *Topaze*, there is the ship where a few days since I dined in social friendship, and there the frigate which brought me to this shore, rejoicing in the sanguine hope of serving my country; all on board them are free, while I am doomed to pass an indefinite period in captivity, deprived of the society of all those who are dear to me in the world!

What, thought I, will my country say of my failure, or how will it appreciate my conduct in this unfortunate day? Will not the people, who too often estimate merit by success, will they not overlook the insurmountable difficulties I bad to encounter, and consider want of success as want of merit: although hitherto fortunate in every enterprise with which I have been charged, and thought worthy the approbation of my superior officers, will not these successes be sunk in oblivion, while my present failure is alone remembered?

From the indulgence of this melancholy soliloquy I was roused by the Polish commandant slapping me violently on the shoulder, and addressing me with, "*Allons, camarade, venez boire un coup d'eau de vie; vous n'êtes pas chez vous!*"—Indeed this observation was too literally true, for I never felt less at home in my life. I accompanied him however to a room, in which everything was in disorder, and where officers and soldiers were promiscuously helping themselves to *agua ardiente*, from jars, while a succession of ruffians was every moment entering and displaying the spoils taken from our unfortunate soldiers made prisoners, or drest in the clothes and accoutrements stripped from the dead; the entrance of each of these plunderers was loudly applauded by bravos from the whole assembly. In order to shew their good fellowship, someone or other of this *banditti* would every moment slap me on the back, crying, "*Allons, camarade, buvons, buvons!*"

The torment I suffered from my bruises, which produced a spitting of blood, was much increased by these acts of manual kindness; nevertheless, knowing I should meet no commiseration, I concealed my feelings and suffered in silence; and accepted some *agua ardiente* and water, which was the first thing I had tasted for twenty-four hours.

As soon as an opportunity occurred of conversing with my fellow prisoners, we naturally began to enquire into the causes of our capture; when I learned that most of the Germans had deserted to the enemy. Having rested nearly two hours in the castle, I was, with the rest of the prisoners, ordered to Mijas, and after being paraded, we set off with a strong escort of cavalry and infantry; Ensign Hopper and the rest of the wounded remaining in the castle. Lieutenant Petit, of whom I have before spoken [9] provided me with a horse, and the other officers were furnished with mules or asses.

On our arrival at Mijas the officers were sent to a public house, and the soldiers confined in the prison. I was particularly honoured by having four centinels placed over me, besides a Polish officer for a companion. The good people of the house in which I was billeted, were all kindness and humanity; they immediately brought we some vinegar to wash my contusons, and drest me some eggs, Whenever the Polish officer quitted the room, the mother and daughter would enter, and sympathising in my misfortune, would lament it with tears in their eyes.

Here I passed the first part of a miserable night; for at three o'clock in the morning (October 16), I was called up to return to Fiangerolla to meet General Sebastians. Though in the greatest pain I was obliged to mount a horse, and was escorted by one hundred dragoons, and several officers, while the rest of the prisoners were ordered to proceed direct to Malaga.

On approaching Fiangerolla, I observed the general surrounded by a large body of troops, and was immediately presented to him. After the first salutation, he enquired what had become of my sword, and on my answering that I supposed some of the officers or soldiers had it in their possession, General Milhaw instantly took off his own and presented it to me, saying, "*Monsieur le Général,* here is one which has been employed in all the campaigns against the Austrians, Russians, and Prussians, and it is now much at your service."

This speech, though tinctured with the vanity natural to a Frenchman, was applauded by the bravos of both officers and soldiers who were within hearing; I accepted the sword, and indeed felt somewhat gratified at being paid such a public compliment by an enemy.

I begged permission of the General to visit the scene of action, which was readily granted, and two. of his *aides de camp*, one of whom was his brother, were directed to accompany me. The scene was such as a recent field of battle usually exhibits; it was strewed with the naked and terribly mangled bodies of the soldiers of both parties. Such a scene would probably have lost much of its effect on my feelings, had fortune, favoured instead of deserting me; but now the melancholy reflections on my situation, almost made me regret not having shared the fate of the gallant fellows that had fallen around me. On my return from the field I entered into conversation with the general, who, as well as his *aides de camp*, soon recollected me as having served in Egypt; and their attentions from this time were redoubled.

Quitting Fiangerolla we passed through a very mountainous country, and by a rugged pathway, not deserving the name of road, and which skirting the sea,. I had still the mortification of contemplating our shipping cruising in the offing, and observed that they had been joined by the *Circe* frigate. The manner in which the French conveyed their artillery through this mountainous track is worthy of notice; two light pieces balancing each other are slung one on each side of a mule, their carriages are carried in like manner on another, and the ammunition boxes which are moveable on a third.

After passing through the romantic village of Belameda, we arrived at Torre a Molinas, a small town with about fifteen hundred inhabitants. Here we put up at the house of a priest, in which we found everything clean and comfortable, and the general staff and some other officers, in all thirty-six persons, sat down to an excellent breakfast of cold and hot meats, pies, &c.

At this place the detachment from Mijas joined us, and the officers signed a parole; this, however, seemed to be a very useless formality, for they were escorted by a strong detachment, in the centre of which they were placed; a necessary precaution, as it was affirmed, to prevent their falling into the bands of the brigands, whose parties were represented as formidable in this part of the country.

Their concern lest I should straggle, and fall in with any of these bands was so great, that although I had also given my parole I was always attended by an officer, who repeatedly assured me that he accompanied me solely from this apprehension, it is easy to conceive how much I differed from him on this subject, for though I was well treated by the general and his staff, no condemned culprit ever looked with more anxiety to a rescue, than I did to the appearance of a formidable body of brigands coming to my relief.

Discretion, however, directed me to conceal my hopes and wishes, and although I did not believe a word of my companion's assurances, I replied to them all with a "*Monsieur, vous êtes bien bon!*" and on his repeating his expressions of care and tenderness for my safety, I could only change the note to "*Monsieur, vous êtes bien aimable!*" at which it was impossible for him to forbear smiling, while he persisted in his absurd declamations. However it may be with their other qualities, we must cede to the French the palm of dissimulation, in which indeed they are perfect masters; they not only justify and glory in the grossest deceit, but often gain the approbation of the spectators, by glossing it over with the name of finesse.

Within a few leagues of Malaga the country totally changed its appearance. Instead of the rugged mountains and barren rocks over which we had hitherto passed, we now entered a most luxuriant and highly cultivated plain, covered with gardens and vineyards, and dotted with handsome villas, of which the *façades* having generally a colonnade gave them a rich and, at the same time, a rural appearance.

We crossed the Rio Guadajo by a ford, where the water was

up to our saddle skirts, though at times it is nearly dry, being like all streams in the vicinity of mountains subject to very sudden rises and falls. At this river it was that Captain Hall proposed leading the troops to attack Malaga by a *coup de main*; I now found that my objections to this plan had been perfectly well founded, for here is an extensive plain in which cavalry could act to the greatest advantage, and the enemy had in and about Malaga, a large and well appointed force of that description.

Chapter 4

Malaga

We entered Malaga amidst a great concourse of people, by a wide and handsome street, that leads to the mole and harbour. Our cavalcade passing through the stress had an imposing appearance, which could not but annoy me. Circumstanced as the French are in Spain, every species of military parade is politic, and besides it costs them nothing, for the inhabitants are obliged to defray all expenses of this nature, and indeed the contributions levied on the people of Malaga were at this time enormous and loudly complained of.

The disagreeable sensation of being gazed at by the multitude, increased by observing that the general seemed to wish to exhibit the prisoners, for the mere gratification of his vanity, made me anxious to get under cover, and I would indeed have given any thing to have been allowed to retire quietly and indulge my melancholy reflections, as well as to procure the rest and tranquillity necessary to the state of my health.

These consolations were, however, denied me, for on entering the house appropriated to the general, we found it filled with public functionaries, waiting to pay their respects to him. I was obliged to submit to the fatigue and plague of a ceremonious introduction to this assembly, and afterwards to sit down with a large party to dinner, which, according to the French custom, was very short, not exceeding three quarters of an hour at table.

In this respect the French and English differ greatly:—the

short dinners of the former are far from being to the taste of the latter when in health and spirits. Amongst the guests wits Mr. Kilpatrick, a Scotch gentleman, of excellent character, who had long been established here in a commercial line, and acted as American Consul. After dinner I accompanied this gentleman to his house, where I found a large party, or *converzatione*, assembled, and the solicitations of my host obliged me to remain and partake of an elegant supper, at which thirty persons sat down.

The following morning (October 17), I rose early, being anxious to see the state of the fortifications towards the sea, and for that purpose I proceeded to the mole, and found that, instead of the guns having been removed from it, it had a formidable battery of fourteen twenty-four pounders in excellent order, with furnaces for heating shot; and the mole not being more than the height of a frigate's quarter-deck above the water, I am convinced no fleet could hope for success in attacking it; and beyond all doubt the little squadron from which I landed would have ran the risk of almost certain destruction in the attempt, I felt therefore happy that I had resisted the proposals to that effect.

From the mole I walked to a spot from whence I had a good view of the citadel, a very strong work, well situated on an eminence, though said to be commanded, which, together with its supposed defenceless state as reported by persons who had long resided here, led to the general belief at Gibraltar that little difficulty would be met with in its reduction; on the contrary, however, the citadel was in the most perfect state, mounting thirty-six pieces of heavy ordnance, six twelve pounders, and four mortars, with military stores and provisions for a garrison of two thousand men for two or three months; besides, the eminence which commands it is distant fourteen hundred yards. In short, it was at this time capable of holding out against an army thrice the number of its garrison for a considerable time.

From this specimen we may judge of the little dependence to be placed on the information received from the Spaniards; and this inaccuracy it the less easy to be accounted for, when we recollect that the inhabitants of the country being generally loyalists their reports may reasonably be supposed worthy of credit) the contrary has, however, been too generally the case, as is evident from the experience of Sir John Moore, and indeed of every person who has been connected with the Spaniards during the present struggle, It appears but justice to attribute this effect rather to the ten hasty judgments of an over ardent zeal, than to any intention to mislead, for though the Spaniards may have many faults as a people, they possess a distinguished place among modern nations for honour, and a strict adherence to truth.

Having finished my promenade, I went by invitation to breakfast with the Governor, whom I found to be a Frenchman, and not behind any of his compatriots in volubility of speech, or rather incessant rattle. By the general's permission, in the course of the forenoon, I sent on board the squadron for my baggage; for hitherto I had been dependant on the general for changes of linen, having with me only the suit of cloaths in which I was made prisoner. I also took this opportunity of detailing our situation by letter. A numerous party were invited to meet me at dinner at Mr. Kilpatrick's, and though I wished for quietness, yet politeness and propriety obliged me to join a party assembled on my account.

On the morning of the 19th I received a notification to prepare to proceed immediately to Grenada with General Sebastiani, a journey which I endeavoured to get excused from on account of my ill health, but without success; the general in the politest manner stating the impossibility of my remaining at Malaga, and offering me a carriage if I found myself unable to ride. Our short stay at Malaga afforded me little opportunity of gaining information respecting it: I observed, however, that the favourable impression of its beauty received on entering it, by the handsome street I have mentioned, is soon done away, the greater part of the other: streets being narrow and crooked.

The Plaza Mayor itself is by no means worthy of its name;— it has, however, in the centre a handsome marble fountain. The cathedral and custom-house are worthy of the traveller's notice; the latter is a new edifice on an extensive and noble plan. The antiquary will find in this town the remains of a Roman temple:

The population of Malaga is between thirty and forty thousand souls, and though it still retains some external appearance of its former prosperity, it is but the unsubstantial shadow of departed reality, the total cessation of commerce, and the losses consequent on the war; have produced innumerable bankruptcies and universal distress; the port, which is daily growing shallower from the mud carried into it by the Gua del Medina, has lost all appearance of commercial life, some fishing boats alone being seen in movement, while a few *polacres, feluccas*, and other smaller vessels are laid up rotting.

What a contrast with the former flourishing commerce of this city, whose annual exports were valued at near half a million sterling in wines, brandy, oil, fruits, anchovies, and some silks. Its imports, which consisted in woollens, hardware, cheese, butter, and salt fish, did not exceed half the value of its exports. Such have been the desolating effects of the unprovoked and unjustifiable invasion of the French, which, if successful, must shake the throne of every legitimate prince of Europe; for who shall then dare setting bounds to the ambition of Buonaparte, or say to him, "thus far shalt thou go, and no farther?"

CHAPTER 5

March from Malaga to Grenada

The wounded, having been provided for, the prisoners were marched off from Malaga early in the morning, and at half past ten o'clock a body of one thousand cavalry, composed of the 16th Dragoons, a regiment of *Lanciers Polonois* and detachments of other corps were paraded, and a number of carriages and baggage-wagons drawn out for departure. Having no desire to exhibit myself in this pageant, I requested and received permission to proceed through a different part of the town, half a league outside of which I was to join the general. Monsieur Lavoisteen, one of his *aides-de-camp*, with an escort, was ordered to accompany me, and we joined him at the appointed place.

To my surprise I found the road equal to any turnpike road in England, contrary to our information at Gibraltar, which stated it to be generally broken up by the brigands, who were said to be in such force as to keep the French in continual alarm. In fact, the country being extremely mountainous and the passes difficult, even an irregular body of this nature might have resisted all the attempts of the French, and have kept possession of the country, had they taken the necessary precaution to destroy the bridges and break up the roads, neither of which they seem to have thought of.

A few horsemen appearing on the summit of a hill, a detachment of the *Lanciers Polonois* was ordered to reconnoitre them, while the convoy halted to take some refreshment at a small house on the road side. The Poles ascended the hill with great rapidity, and soon returned with five horses, reporting that they belonged to the brigands, of whom they had killed seven. The general with an air of triumph bid me observe the cattle on which our allies were mounted, while some of his suite, taking their tone from him, observed, "*Voilà les Alliés de l'Angleterre!*"

These animals were indeed most wretched, and a kind of pad on which the country people convey their things to market served for saddles, From this, as well as other, circumstances, I firmly believe that these brigands were in reality nothing more than a party of inoffensive peasants, whom the Poles had robbed of their horses, in order to corroborate the detail of their prowess; besides it was considered as a sufficient proof of brigandage for the peasants to be found in the smallest number at any distance from their villages.

The escort was augmented by a detachment of the 10th Dragoons near Antequera, where we arrived so late in the evening that the general's cooks had not time to exert their abilities to the full, and we were obliged to content ourselves with a scanty repast. I could not help remarking the distance at which the general kept the inferior officers, whose stomachs even he appeared to have reduced to discipline; for though about twenty-six of them sat down to supper at the same time, not one of them touched anything until the general officers had done.

During this repast the *alcaide* and principal persons of the town paid their respects to the general, who received them with the greatest affability, and informed them of the heavy contributions it would be necessary to lay them under, with such grace and good humour, that they seemed to depart perfectly satisfied. The manner of the general, indeed, afforded an excellent lesson in the art of levying contributions.

The distance between Malaga and Antequera is eight Spanish leagues, or about thirty-six English miles; the road ascends the whole way, and is skirted with vineyards, which afford the well known Malaga wine. The scenery is extremely romantic, being diversified by steep rocks cloathed with wood, fertile and well cultivated valleys, with abundance of fruit trees, particularly almonds, and extensive fields of melons. Within a league of Antequera the mountains afford a most singular appearance: rocks of various forms are seen as if shaped by art to represent a town, with its streets, churches, towers, houses, fountains, &c. together with men, women, and animals, particularly camels; from the clefts of these rocks shoot out various shrubs and plants, which compleat the extraordinary aspect of this spot, called, I believe, Torcal, and celebrated for its beautiful marble.

Antequera, probably the Anticaria of the Romans, and by some supposed to be built on the ruins of the ancient Sirigilis, is one of the most ancient towns of Spain. It is situated on the declivity of a hill, and is divided into the upper and lower town; through the latter runs the rivulets of La Villa and Guadalorce, which turn many mills near the town, and also supply it with water from several handsome fountains.

On the summit of the hill is a Moorish castle, commanding the town, and which the French have put into a respectable state of defence. Antequera contains between thirteen and fourteen thousand inhabitants; it has given birth to some celebrated men, particularly Antonio Mohedano, a painter, and Solano Loque, a physician, who made some important discoveries in medicine in the last century.

My quarters here were at the house of an old priest whose sister and her family resided with him, from all of whom I received the greatest attention and considerable information. I was indeed glad to get away from the general's society as soon as possible after dinner, in order to enjoy a *segar* in quietness, together with the conversation of the family on which I was billeted; and as I was never accompanied by any Frenchman, I was always certain of being received with kindness and without reserve.

My desire of retiring from the general's society was not, however, from any want of attention on his part; on the contrary, I met with every politeness, both from him and his suite, and after leaving Malaga my restraint was merely nominal. These attentions I probably owed to my acquaintance with many of the ancient French *noblesse*, of whom Sebastiani, and indeed all other

Frenchmen high in station whom I have lately met with, speak with the greatest respect, and are happy when they can trace any relationship to them. The general's staff was generally of this order, and their manners were so engaging and their attentions so polite, that I found myself perfectly at ease amongst them, and came ultimately to be considered as one of the establishment, with the character of a *parfaitement bon garçon*.

Du Cogni, one of the *aides-de-camp* (of the family of the celebrated Marshal Du Cogni), to whose sister Sebastiani is married, in particular deserves my warmest remembrance for the liberality of his sentiments and conduct, so different from the herd of modern *parvenus*. To the Adjutant-Général de Bouillé I was also indebted, for much civility; with this officer I had formerly been acquainted, when he commanded the *Hulans Britanniques*, in the campaigns of Holland in 1794 and 1795, the events of which afforded us much matter of conversation.

Leaving Antequera early in the morning (Oct. 19) we passed through a generally level country, with a few scattered hills, the whole fertile and well cultivated, and arrived at a narrow defile, formed by a high mountain on the left and a lesser one on the right: the former is named Sierra de los Amaraos, or the Lover's Mountain, from a traditional tale that a Moorish prince precipitated himself from its summit in despair, at being prohibited by his religion from marrying a Christian Princess, with whom he had fallen in love. However this may be, the defile would form an excellent military post for a small detachment.

In the course of this day's march I chiefly attached myself to General Milhaud, who had distinguished himself during the revolution as a cavalry officer. Our conversation now, however, chiefly turned on the subject of good living, for the general appeared to be a *bon vivant* in the utmost extent of the term, and expressed the greatest delight when I happened to hit on a good dish, or made an *à propos* quotation from the *Journal des Gourmands*, the bible of French epicures.

At Archidona we halted to breakfast, which, since leaving Malaga, has always been as substantial a repast as dinner, consisting of rich *ragoûts* and other made dishes, with all the fruits of the season, but more particularly melons. The wine we have met with on the road has, however, been much inferior to the eatables, but the French seem to have little discrimination in this respect, and therefore swallow it without complaining. A great concourse of people assembled to view our cavalcade, among whom were a number of women, conspicuous for their fine countenances and simple dress. At breakfast we were attended by four extremely pretty girls, whom the French officers, to shew their gallantry, pinched and pulled about, until the poor girls were afraid to approach the table, and although I did not join in tormenting them, I suffered as if I had, and was obliged to assist myself.

Archidona, as well as most of the towns in the Grenadines, is romantically situated at the foot of a hill, whose summit is crowned with a Moorish castle. These places, which compleatly command the towns and overawe the inhabitants, have all been repaired and put into a state of defence by the French. The neglect of the Spaniards, in not occupying the castle at the commencement of the invasion, is totally unaccountable, being from their situations defensible by very small garrisons, and the possession of them would have enabled the loyalists to annoy the French by that harassing and desultory warfare, by which they suffer more than by pitched battles. Archidona was formerly the property of the Duke d'Assuyne, but the French Emperor has been graciously pleased to appropriate it to himself, and the inhabitants have the peculiar blessing of enjoying the immediate protection of Napoleon-le-Grand.

"*Ces gens sont assez heureux en appartenant particulièrement à l'Empereur*" added Sebastiani, after informing me of this circumstance.

"*Quel bonheur!*" replied I, and left him to put his own construction on the ambiguous exclamation.

From Archidona to Loxa, where we arrived in the evening, the road was indifferent, passing through extensive groves of olive trees; oil, together with saffron, being the principal productions of this part of the country. Loxa is situated on a hill rising from the banks of the Xenil, or Genil; it contains nothing worth notice, except some extensive saltpetre and copper works.

We commenced our march from Loxa early in the morning of the 20th (October), and I availed myself of the polite offer of Major Grotowski, commanding the 9th Polonois, to take a seat in his carriage, a great unwieldy machine drawn by eight mules. Besides the Major and two other persons, we had the company of a Signor Chevarial, a Spaniard, holding a situation under the invading government. There being a pack of cards in the carriage, we played at *Trente et Quarante* till we reached Lachao, where we halted to breakfast. This village had been totally destroyed by the French, and the greater part of the inhabitants massacred, but was now partly rebuilt. The surrounding country is fertile and well watered by the Xenil, which falls into the Guadalquivir at Seville.

From Lachao our next stage was Santa Fé, a strong town, where we were joined by Generals Purmurent and Roison, with the 12th regiment of Dragoons, in order to render Sebastiani's entrance into Grenada more imposing.

CHAPTER 6

Spanish and French Repasts

Our entry into Grenada was conducted with the greatest parade. After passing through several streets we arrived at the Plaza di Triompha, in which a great concourse of people was assembled, to witness a scene very different from what the name of the place would seem to denote. In the centre of the square is a large gallows, with a staircase to ascend by, and on the right a *garrote*, the mode of execution by which deserves notice.

On a platform are placed a number of stools, with a perpendicular post behind each; the criminal being seated on the stool, an iron collar is placed round his neck, and the executioner by the turn of a screw puts an end to his existence in a moment. This is an old Spanish punishment, and seems to be one of the easiest kinds of death. Scarce a day passes without several similar executions, the sufferers being mostly those whom the French stigmatize with the names of rebels and brigands, but to whom the page of history will accord those of loyalists and patriots.

Passing from the Plaza di Triompha through some narrow streets, followed by the stupid mob, shouting *viva! viva!* we reached the palace, a large uncomfortable building, formerly the royal residence when the Court visited Grenada, but now occupied by Sebastiani. The arrangement of the apartments in this edifice, as well indeed as in most Spanish mansions, is exceedingly inconvenient. Long suites of rooms leading through each other, without any secondary outlet, obliges you to pass through the whole range to reach the innermost; indeed, the Spaniards have great pride in throwing open all the doors, and affording their visitors an uninterrupted view of a range of saloons.

Though the winters are sometimes severe in this part of Spain, the luxury of a fire-side is still unknown, the apartments being warmed by braziers, or large brass pans, two-thirds filled with hot ashes and charcoal, the smell of which is extremely disagreeable, and the effects injurious to the health; besides, the degree of heat they afford is but just sufficient to create a wish for more,

Immediately after our arrival at the palace, Sebastian! was waited on by the chief civil and military authorities, and I was conducted to lodgings assigned me at the house of M. Millones, collector of the contributions for the French, whose wife and family received me with civility, and hoped (in the common complimentary style) that I would consider everything in their house entirely at my disposal. With respect to their table there was little danger of my presuming much on their invitation, for Spanish repasts are little suited to an Englishman's palate, being chiefly composed of meats swimming in rancid oil, and of luscious and cloying sweetmeats, so that even the French, whose stomachs are much more accommodating than ours, (and who, although *ils sont des braves gens,* are not conspicuous for modesty in declining invitations in general,) excuse themselves from those of the Spaniards.

Having dressed myself as well as the circumstances of my wardrobe would admit, I proceeded to dine at the palace, where I was certain of finding a repast very different from that of my host's, the general's cooks being masters of their art, and so necessary are their services deemed, that three of them always travel in his suite. Indeed, in every respect the general's establishment is superb, and well calculated, not only to acquire the respect of the Spaniards, but also to maintain the dignity of his elevated situation with his own troops.

He had brought some English cheese and porter from Malaga, as he thought proper to say, for me; but it appeared that the French officers were at least equal amateurs of the latter, and those who tasted it, (for there was not sufficient for all), exclaimed, "*Dieu, qu'elle est bonne, la bierre porterre!*" After dinner I accompanied the general to the theatre; an old building wretchedly fitted up, but which is to be replaced by a magnificent one erected by the French, and which it was intended to open on Sebastiani's birthday.

The attention of the general to me was here greater than I could have wished, for he insisted on placing me in a crimson and gold chair, peculiarly destined for himself, while he occupied a common rush bottom one by me; but the splendour of my seat formed much too great a contrast with my old regimental coat, which had suffered greatly when I was made prisoner. This marked attention to me was, however, probably more political than sincere; for the French general who had preceded Sebastiani at Grenada, having treated the Spanish prisoners with the most barbarous severity, Sebastiani now hoped to soften the recollection of these atrocities, by proving that all the officers of his nation did not treat prisoners with the same inhumanity.

The piece performed this evening was a long farce, the humour of which, though it would not have saved it from certain damnation on the poorest country stage of England, gave the greatest delight to the Spanish audience. A countryman enters a barber's shop, and bargains with the master to take off his beard and that of his companion for six *quarts*.[1]

The barber, however, desires to see this companion before he commences on the countryman, but this the latter slyly avoids, and the barber proceeds and finishes the operation. The countryman then goes out to seek his companion, and immediately returns with an ass, which put the audience into an ecstasy of delight: the barber hesitates at first to fulfil his bargain, but, sooner than lose his money, at last fixes his shaving cloth under the animal's chin, and is about to commence, when another traveller enters and interrupts him, &c.

A judgment may be formed of the Spanish comedies in general from this specimen, few of them having a more rational plot

---

1. A copper coin not quite the value of a halfpenny.

to recommend them. The house was miserably lighted, but as the chief motive of a number of the spectators for frequenting it seemed to be founded on gallantry, this darkness visible was convenient. From the theatre I retired immediately to bed, and rested well in spite of damp sheets and bugs: I had indeed of late been so much accustomed to companions of this description, that I should now have almost felt myself solitary without them.

The following morning I felt, much pain, and was seized with a spitting of blood, caused by the exercise of riding in my bruised state. I was not, however, allowed to remain quiet, being expected to breakfast at the general's, where a large company always assembled at eleven o'clock, and this repast, which was almost as substantial as the dinner, was at noon. These *déjeûnés à la fourchette*, which are now universal among the French, have the disagreeable consequence of making those unused to them heavy and incapable of exertion during the rest of the day.

After breakfast the general proposed a ride to the Alhambra, a palace of the Moorish kings, of which I had heard and read so much that I was very anxious to visit it. It is situated on the summit of a hill which entirely commands the town, and whose foot is washed, by the rivers Darro and Xenil. The sides of the hill are covered with wood, and the ascent is so steep, that it has been necessary to form a winding road up to the palace.

The entrance to this vast pile is through a Moorish archway, surmounted by a square tower, which is called the gate of judgment: over the gate is a key in marble, and above it at a little distance a hand, the meaning of which device is said to be that the fortress will be taken by the enemy when the hand takes hold of the key.

The first apartments we entered were the chambers of audience and of justice, neither of which are so large as might have been expected from the purposes to which they were assigned. The floors are composed of a kind of mosaic, and from the ceilings project a variety of fantastic figures. We next entered; a gallery of an oblong form but not large, containing several pictures of the Moorish and Christian kings of Spain; and from hence we proceeded to the apartments of the royal family, in each of which, in an alcove, is a fountain for water, and near the alcove an elevation of curious workmanship in porcelain, on which the bed was placed. The queen's dressing room is almost singular apartment, and affords great scope for conjecture respecting the dress and ornaments of the Moorish princesses.

In this cabinet is a marble urn, pierced with small apertures to emit the vapours of the perfumes that were kept continually burning in it. To this suite of apartments are attached three baths, the king's, queen's, and royal children's, and a music hall, surrounded by an elevated gallery, in which I suppose the audience sat while the orchestra was placed in the centre. From these apartments we descended into an oblong court paved with white marble, and surrounded by a gallery supported by marble columns. The walls and ceiling of the gallery are covered with mosaic, grotesque paintings, and figures of stucco in relief of delicate workmanship, intermixed with Arabic sentences from the Koran.

The middle of this court is occupied by a large bason of running water deep enough to swim in, and which served as a bath for the royal household. It is surrounded by orange trees and flowers. Descending a few steps from this court we entered another, on one side of which is the chamber of execution,. having in the middle a marble bason about three feet deep, sloping gradually inwards, on the edge of which the victims Were decapitated, and the blood received into the bason.

Some of the apartments have been fitted up in the modern style by Sebastiani, which certainly is no proof of his good taste, for a Parisian *salon* or *boudoir* in a Moorish palace five hundred years old, is almost as absurd as dressing an antique statue in the .costume of a modern *petit maître*. We next visited the garden, which is well stocked with a variety of fruit trees:—it was now putting into order, having been neglected since the disturbances in the country. Crossing the court on our return from the garden, I observed at some distance the statues of Ferdinand and

Isabella,

The Alhambra is surrounded by a high wall, flanked with towers and a kind of bastions, in which the cannon are mounted, pointing towards the city, to overawe the inhabitants into tranquillity. Looking over the parapet of the wall, a view of the whole town and of the neighbouring country, which is highly cultivated, and pleasingly diversified with hills and valleys, presents itself, while the villages seen on every side with their churches give a lively appearance to the whole landscape.

Near to the Alhambra is a magnificent modern palace, commenced by Charles the Fifth, but still unfinished. It occupies a considerable extent of ground with no other buildings near it, except a few temporary erections for the accommodation of the workmen. Its figure is nearly a perfect square, each face having a superb entrance differently ornamented. On that which fronts the south-west are three large oval bronze plates, the one on the right representing the labours of Hercules, and the other two ancient battles. The windows are bordered with black marble, and the key-stones represent eagles' heads.

Round the whole building, at equal distances, are heads of lions, with an immense bronze ring in the mouth of each. The Cour des Lions is an oblong square, one hundred feet by fifty. It is surrounded by a gallery supported on slender columns of white marble, coupled two and two, and of very delicate workmanship. The walls of the gallery are covered with arabesque painting and gilding, in stucco, elegantly executed, which have received some injury.

A handsome *cupola*, fifteen or sixteen feet each way, is placed at both ends of this court, and in the centre is a large bason, in the middle of which is a beautiful cupola of alabaster six feet high, supported by several lions of marble, and surmounted by a lesser cupola, from which issues a superb *jet d'eau*. Several other *jets d'eau* throw up columns of water to considerable heights. In short, the whole plan of this palace is magnificent, and well worthy the elevated ideas of the monarch by whom it was commenced. We have, however, to regret that it is not only left unfinished, but is also suffering daily injury from total neglect.

Above the Alhambra the French have formed a strong and tolerably extensive field work, which commands the whole summit of the hill.

On our return from the Alhambra I found the prisoners taken with me had arrived; they spoke in the highest terms of the treatment they met with from the officers of their escort belonging to the 32nd -and 58th regiments, who always ceded to them the place of honour at table, and shewed them every other mark of polite attention. These regiments had been warmly engaged at the battle of Talavera, and with the greatest liberality of sentiment did ample justice to the gallant conduct of our troops on that memorable day.

I had, indeed, many opportunities of observing, on our march, the superior liberality of the French officers and soldiers, to the Germans and Spaniards in the French service; both of the latter conducting themselves towards their prisoners with the most unmanly brutality, while the former treated the soldiers with humanity, and the officers with politeness and attention.

Doubtless, these mercenary Germans and rebel Spaniards hope to recommend themselves to their French masters, by the ferocity of their behaviour to their defenceless prisoners; no such effect, however, was produced, at least on the officers of our escort, who expressed a sovereign contempt both for the Germans and Spaniards, but more particularly for the former.

Our officers were at first granted their parole, but in a day or two they were again deprived of it, and confined in the Alhambra with the soldiers and seamen, by order of Marshal Soult; for my own part, I enjoyed perfect liberty to employ my time as I thought proper. The evenings I usually passed at the Duchess of Goa's *tertulias*, or routs, which were always well attended, and the play tolerably deep. General Sebastiani, in particular, staked high, but apparently more from ostentation than any love of play.

The most usual games were Pharo, at which the deal went round, Bouillotte and Monté. Madame d'Aguillac, whose husband holds a lucrative place under the French Government in

Spain, also saw company in the evenings, and I frequently made one of her party.

Chapter 7

Praises of Buonaparte

Grenada is delightfully situated on two hills, at the extremity of a beautiful plain, called the Vega de Grenada. The rivers Darro and Xenil, which fertilize the plain, run through the town; they are both mountain streams, fordable almost everywhere in summer, but subject to sudden rises, which often carry away the bridges and do other damage. The plain is about thirty leagues in circumference, and is surrounded by mountains, whose summits, capped with snow throughout the year, are seen at twenty leagues distance from land in the Mediterranean. To seamen these mountains are generally known by the name of the Grenadines.

Besides the two rivers already mentioned, the plain has three others, named the Diler, the Vogro, and the Monachil: this abundance of water and the gentle declivity of the ground enables the inhabitants to carry irrigation to perfection, the result of which is a perpetual vegetation and verdure, and a most exuberant production of grapes, olives, mulberries, lemons, oranges, and the sugar-cane. The climate of Andalusia is peculiarly favourable to the cultivation of the latter, and is equally calculated for the production of other tropical vegetables. The sugar made from the canes of this province is of the best quality, and near Malaga and at other places are considerable sugar works.

The quantity of colonial produce which may be derived from Andalusia, is in itself a sufficient motive for our using every exertion to prevent its remaining under the power of France; for there can be no doubt that it would in a very short time become a most formidable rival to our West India colonies, if that power was to enjoy the quiet possession of it. Possessing an extensive coast both on the Ocean and Mediterranean, with many good harbours, or safe roads for shipping, the facility of export would reduce the price of its produce to foreign merchants, while by inland navigation it would be conveyed to the interior with equal advantage, and safe from the danger of being intercepted by our cruisers.

While at Grenada I occasionally breakfasted with Major Growtowski of the 9th Polonois, with whom I had formed an intimacy, as well as with some other officers of the same corps, who were in general persons of rank and property in Poland, and whose polite manners had procured them a favourable reception at Grenada. The conversation between the major and myself often turned on politics, and whenever I expressed my surprise that a warlike nation, with a population of fifteen millions, a large army of hardy troops, and a compact territory, capable by its nature, of an easy defence, should submit to a foreign dominion, his answer always was;

> that of two evils the Poles chose the least; for that if they were not allies of France, they would probably become the slaves of Russia; that they were under obligations to the former, for having in some measure restored them their country; and finally that every Pole, abhorring the unjust partition of their kingdom, naturally felt the most implacable hatred for the sharers in the spoils, and therefore thought any alternative better than subjection to them.

These sentiments I could, however, easily perceive, proceeded from the temporary impression made on the major by constantly hearing extolled the grandeur of the French Empire, and the munificence of its sovereign. Indeed, nothing could be more tiresome than the eternal praises of the Emperor, which formed the chief topic of conversation at Sebastiani's parties. With a solemnity of countenance and a measured tone, so conspicuous in French oratory, the general would every day at table treat us with a panegyric on the virtues and exploits of his master, of which the following was usually the burthen;

Messieurs, l'Empereur est un homme sans défaut, c'est le seul homme au monde avec lant de pouvoir à qui personne ne peut faire la moindre reproche.

Or,

Messieurs, l'Empereur est le plus grand homme, le plus grand héros qui a jamais paru;

and then he would draw a comparison with Cesar or Alexander, both of whom, of course, were *imbéciles* to Napoleon. At length I got so disgusted with this nonsense, that finding no hero in. Grecian or Roman history equal to Buonaparte, I sought to match him in more remote antiquity, and compared him to Nimrod, who was a mighty one on the earth, and a mighty, hunter before the Lord. The ridicule which this comparison threw on the subject produced the effect I wished, in preventing a repetition of such fulsome panegyrics, both in the general's societies and in the other circles where his suite retailed his oratorical declamations respecting the French monarch.

Hitherto the whole of the prisoners were confined in the Alhambra, and the Germans and other foreigners being much more numerous than the English, frequent quarrels arose, which usually terminating in battles, induced me to apply for. their separation, which was granted without difficulty.

The, return of the spitting of blood and an oppression in my chest, obliging me to seek for medical assistance, I applied to Major Growtowski for his surgeon, a Pole, who accordingly visited me, and endeavoured to make himself understood in a mixed jargon of French, Spanish, Hungarian, and Polish. I soon discovered that little dependence was to be placed upon his skill. I, however, allowed him to bleed me, but prescribed for myself some cooling medicines. and a low diet, which in a few days produced a: considerable amendment in my health and spirits.

When sufficiently recovered, Madame Milliones, my landlady, was obliging enough to give a grand ball on my account, a civility I could have gladly dispensed with; but as she would not listen to such a proposition, I was obliged to submit to suffer her kindness. There were several Polish officers at this ball, but not one Frenchman; and the former being all violin players, each took it in turn to act as fiddler, there being no regular musicians. Waltzes and English country dances chiefly prevailed; but the Spanish tunes are so different from ours, that it was scarcely possible to adapt any figure to them; besides, the ladies being at our gentlemen's side of the dance, made it exceedingly awkward to me, for my landlady would not even excuse me from dancing, and as the figures were called English, the company naturally looked to me for instruction.

When the dances were over, I was in hopes I should be allowed to remain quiet; but, on the contrary, blindman's buff commenced, in which I was also obliged to join, to prevent myself being eternally importuned by the ladies. This diversion differs something from ours of the same name; the person blindfolded has a cane in his hand, with which he endeavours to touch one of the company who dance round him, and when he has succeeded, all stand still, and he guesses the name of the person touched; if right, this person takes his place.

Another amusement of the evening was mewing like cats; and between the acts of blindman's buff, a solemn looking old gentleman several times pushed open the door from outside, made a short speech, with a variety of ridiculous grimaces; and ran out again, every time receiving the loudest applause from the company. This kind of childish nonsense, indeed, pervades all the domestic diversions of the Spaniards, and has often made me heartily, tired of their parties. The entertainment was given in my apartments, and when the company were about to retire, at three o'clock in the morning, and I was in hopes of getting some repose, a violent thunder storm commenced, and detained them an hour longer.

The following day (October 24) I was introduced by the

intendant chevalier to Madame Quesada and her amiable daughter; this lady's husband had been Governor of Minorca, when it was taken by Sir Charles Stewart. She asked me many questions respecting the island, and having been there some time, I was enabled to answer to her satisfaction. I often visited this interesting family afterwards, and the young lady obligingly undertook to improve me in the Spanish language.

In my intercourse with Spanish families, I could not help remarking the listless indolence in which the females doze away their lives; never have I seen a book or a needle in their hands, and their sole occupation seems to be playing with pet animals, particularly cats and dogs. Besides a monkey, several parrots and some pigeons, my landlady had four little curs, whose barking and snarling made them complete nuisances; she had also a large and a small cat, for each of which a proportionate sized hole was cut in the bottom of every door, not recollecting, I suppose, that the small cat could pass through the large hole; however this might be, the current of air that these holes admitted counterbalanced the effects of the *brasier*, and made the apartments most uncomfortable.

During my stay at Grenada, I often rode about the environs with the general, who was always attended by a numerous suite and a strong, guard, many straggling Frenchmen having been lately murdered close to the town. On these occasions the whole cavalcade always passed through the villages at full gallop, in order to strike the inhabitants with astonishment and awe. In one excursion we visited a convent of Chartreux about a mile from Grenada, of which the monks, twenty-five in number, had been either massacred or expelled.

This edifice is beautifully situated, commanding an extensive view, and contains several spacious reception rooms, in one of which were now collected several statues of Saints, some valuable pictures, chiefly of Spagnioletto and Murilla, and a quantity of church plate, the plunder of other religious buildings. These objects as well as the edifice are in charge of Monsieur d'Aguillar, who resides in elegant apartments in the building, and to whose handsome wife the general was said to be partial.

The *sacristie* of this content is particularly worthy of notice, from its light and elegant appearance, and the good taste it exhibits. The tables which surround it are of the most valuable marbles, and of exquisite workmanship, and the whole are said to be the performance of one man.

While viewing the valuable articles of church furniture collected here, Sebastiani declaimed on the oppressive taxes the Spaniards must have borne, to furnish religious ornaments alone, and the advantages that must result from the abolition of monastic institutions. Here I could not help reflecting, that if plundering the churches was for the good of the country, the French had certainly taken a most lively interest in its welfare. This idea I however kept to myself, as well as most others that did not coincide with those of the general, whose *amour-propre* would have made it very difficult to convince him he was mistaken, and more particularly so as his *ipse dixit* was always received as an immutable truth by everyone around him.

One of my daily promenades was to the Carera, where, when the weather is fine, an immense concourse of people assemble at three o'clock in the afternoon. This walk is formed by a long street, which had lately been widened and ornamented, and at its extremity is a wood, intersected by pleasant alleys. However the present contest may terminate, it must be admitted that the Spaniards will be indebted to the French for many works both of utility and ornament, which under their old lethargic government would probably have never been thought of.

Among other public works commenced by the French at Grenada, are a bridge of a single arch over the Xenil, and a theatre, on which a vast number of workmen were now employed, in order to finish it before the general's birthday, on which, as I have before said, it is to be opened. The contrast between this edifice and the old theatre is striking, the latter being a heavy and gloomy building, without ornaments either external or internal, while the former is light and airy, with decorations approaching to the tawdry; one reminds us of the sober seriousness of the

Spaniard, the other of the gay flippancy of the Frenchman. The orchestra in the French theatre is. constructed on a new principle, apparently well calculated for the diffusion of sound.

The boxes are gaudily painted, and on the fronts alternately is a gilt eagle and an N. which reminded me of the pun of a Frenchman, who, on visiting the Thuilleries, and observing this letter on every side, exclaimed, "*Ma foi, il a des N. mis partaut!*" An Englishman is satisfied with the government while he can grumble out his constitutional discontent without control or restraint; a Frenchman, on the contrary, consoles himself in every stage of oppression with a pun or *bon mot*; and in this respect his language is peculiarly happy, but whether from its perfection or imperfection I will not pretend to determine.

In the evening of October 25, I accompanied my landlady and her daughter to a *tertulia* at Madame Caracaos, where we found a number of old ladies crowded round a *brasier* in an apartment just sufficiently lighted to make darkness visible. On our arrival a play was commenced resembling our Hunt the Slipper, to which succeeded a dance, and in both of which I was obliged to join, having the young lady of the house for my partner in the dance.

There was not a Frenchman present, nor have I met one of them at any Spanish house, except the Duchess of Goa's. The exercise of the evening brought on a return of my complaint, and obliged me to have recourse again to the Polish doctor's lancet, which,, together with the application of a strong blister and quiet living for a day or two, once more gave me relief.

October 30, being able to quit the house, I visited the cathedral, a fine building, with a superb dome supported by twelve large columns, the ceiling well pointed and ornamented with several gilt figures. Over the colonnade are two rows of balconies richly gilt, and behind the grand altar a chapel, with several monuments, particularly those of Ferdinand and Isabella, and of Philip the First and his queen.

The *sacristie* is very rich, the altar being of valuable marble, and the tables of scarce and curious dark coloured woods, inlaid with gold and ivory, which has a fine effect. Among the valuables collected in this apartment are the crowns of Ferdinand and Isabella, and a considerable quantity of rich church plate and ornaments, which however formed but a portion of what it formerly possessed, the French having considerably stripped it ; and indeed it is probable that what remains has been only left not too far to outrage the feelings of the people, and that they will be carried off at some other opportunity.

The same morning I was invited to accompany General Sebastiani to breakfast with General Purmerent, who informed me that this repast should be entirely *à la Provencale*, and he kept his word so minutely that I never desire to partake of such another; every dish, whatever might be its other ingredients, contained such an abominable mixture of garlic and rancid oil, that those of the company who could command their stomachs so far as to get some of them down, were ill for several days after; indeed the general and his *aide-de-camp* seemed alone to relish the breakfast. This general had been ambassador to the United States, where he picked up a few words of English; amongst which, "G— d— your eyes, how do you do?" was the most expressive, and his usual salutation to me.

CHAPTER 8

Sebastiani's Birthday

November 1. Though the conversation at General Sebastiani's usually turned on the military operations of the day, and though aware that a Frenchman is a most restless animal, whether he has any cause or not for movement, I had for some days observed a more than usual bustle among the staff, and a mysterious manner, that led me to suppose some serious movement of the army was intended; which was soon confirmed by the arrival of Colonel Grouvel; commanding the 16th Légère, with a report from the advanced posts.

The conversation between this officer and Sebastian! was, on the part of the latter, peremptory and warm, and some reply of the colonel's called forth such a reprimand from the general as struck him speechless. This colonel was indeed so compleat a caricature of. a French soldier, that I could not resist the temptation of taking a sketch of him, which I have given as a frontispiece.

This cavalier treatment of an officer of rank by the general, leads me to offer a few observations on the discipline of the French army, which is certainly preserved in a surprising manner, amongst the variety of temptations and provocations to insubordination. Although ill cloathed, badly paid, and often scantily fed, the soldier performs his duty with alacrity and cheerfulness, and is seldom missing when called upon: but, on the contrary, is generally at the appointed rendezvous before the specified time, which saves the non-commissioned officers a world of trouble.

The external appearance of the soldiers being deemed of little moment, they have no dress parades, but their arms they keep in good order for their own preservation, and are careful of their ammunition for the same reason.

The conscripts are perfectly drilled at a depôt before they are sent to join their regiments, and this instruction seems to be so impressed upon them that they never forget it. In their regimental manoeuvres there is often an appearance of disorder and confusion which surprises an English officer, but from which, however, the intention is finally accomplished; such, for instance, is the case in wheeling a column, when the pivots are always moveable; when broken they act on no fixed principle, and it would seem impossible that they could be again formed by the manoeuvres they adopt.

I have however seen this accomplished with great rapidity, even under a heavy fire. Indeed, instead of mere automatons put in motion by a power of whose principles they are ignorant, every French soldier reasons on the movements of the army he belongs to, and says what he would have done in such a case. I have been often surprised at the shrewd observations and theoretical knowledge of some of the private men, which often seemed to place them above their officers.

But though the want of fixed principles of action may not perhaps be of much consequence in an army of veteran soldiers, amongst raw ones it must often be fatal, and probably this will shortly be proved in Spain, where the veterans who composed the first invading armies are mostly "killed off," and two-thirds of the present are conscripts, and mostly boys, and all of them without practical experience, which might make up for the want of theory. It is said that Buonaparte expresses his preference of young soldiers; however, in this respect, I doubt if he does not resemble the spendthrift, whose extravagance obliging him to cut down an ancient wood, told his friend he did so because he preferred young trees.

The confidence in their own judgment which forms a part of the general French character, is perhaps one of the causes which prevents Frenchmen from making good seamen, for a ship must be very badly manoeuvred, where every one of her crew pretends to have an opinion of his own. Conversing with some merchants at Bayonne concerned in privateers, they assured me that one-third of this description of vessels were either upset at sea, or run on shore, from the self-sufficient confidence of the men.

To conclude my observations on French soldiers; I must do them the justice to say that I have never found them mercenary, but, on the contrary, that I have often received civilities from them without their asking or appearing to expect any pecuniary reward: I must also observe that their share of plunder is usually very trifling, the superior officers taking care not to forget themselves in the division.

I at length learnt (November 3) that the unusual bustle I had observed at the general's was in consequence of a movement made by Blake, who was at this time at Baza near Lorca, with twelve thousand men; that the French troops were all in motion, and that Sebastiani was. to set out the next morning to take the command.

On consulting the map I found that the French army was so distributed, that in twenty-four hours a considerable force could be assembled in any point menaced with attack. At dinner the general informed me of all the circumstances of Blake's movement, and on rising from table he received a dispatch from Marshal Soult, detailing the proceedings before Cadiz, the meeting of the Cortes, the nature of their deliberations, and the dismission of the Duc d'Orleans from the isle of Leon by their order. From the manner in which Sebastiani spoke of the proceedings of this assembly, it was evident that its proceedings was by no means agreeable to the French interests.

In the course of the evening I entered into conversation with Monsieur Cussini, chief of the engineer department, who expressed much surprise at our not having possessed ourselves of the coast of the Mediterranean, to enable us to land small detachments at different points, by which the French must be much harassed, as in the state of the country it was impossible for them to be guarded everywhere.

These observations in fact were perfectly just, for with a Levant wind a squadron could run down from Cape de Gata to Malaga in a few hours, the distance being but about thirty-five leagues; the troops embarked on board might be landed at Motril or Almunecar, at which latter place there was but a very trifling force, and no artillery; nor could the French immediately assemble any considerable force in that neighbourhood, while any troops Sebastiani might be able to spare would have to march upwards of one hundred miles through a mountainous country, scarcely practicable for heavy artillery, and subject continually to the attacks of the numerous bands of guerrillas who occupied these mountains. Thus a respectable force being once established on any part of the coast near Malaga, would be able to maintain itself against any detachments that could at this time have been sent against it. Had I been fortunate enough to have been joined by the 82nd regiment, it was my intention to have acted on this plan.

November 4, according to arrangement, General Sebastiani set off for Baza early in the morning of the fourth, leaving his *aide-de-camp* Lavoisteen to keep me company, and with orders to his servants to furnish our table as usual; this day, however, I was engaged to dine with General Dufour, Governor of the city, who though he has not the character of being a great general, is a most respectable old gentleman of the ancient *régime*. After dinner information was received of the total defeat of Blake's army, of which I shall have occasion to speak more fully hereafter,

The next morning (November 5) I breakfasted with Lavoisteen, when it was agreed that we should dine *tête à tête* during the general's absence. In the evening I visited the Alhambra, and directed each of our soldiers confined there to be furnished with a shirt and pair of shoes; for though, on my previous demand, I had been assured that they should be immediately supplied with the cloathing they might require by the French Government, I now found that no steps had been taken for that purpose. From the Alhambra I rode to a village three miles from Grenada, situated in a fertile plain, where I observed their manner of separating the corn from the ear. The corn is placed on a paved circular spot, round which two mares are driven, as we ring horses, and who tread out the corn. I have observed that in Spain, in Egypt, South America, and the Cape of Good Hope, mares are kept for this purpose and for breeding alone, never being used for the saddle or draft, while in France mares are seen employed for these uses, the horses being all bought up for the armies.

The valley which called forth these observations is well irrigated, and indeed this seems to be the only part of husbandry in which the Spaniards take any pains, Their farming utensils in particular are most wretched, the harrow being furnished with wooden pins only, and is often drawn by an ass and a goat, while it is very common to see a plough worked by two mules or bullocks only, with tackling of cow hide and rope mixed, and no pains being taken to make the animals step together, they fatigue themselves and do scarce any work.

In France, where agriculture is carried to much higher perfection, I have often seen a mixture of animals yoked to the plough, such as two half-starved horses at the wheels, two bullocks in the middle, and two asses as leaders; or else the bullocks at the wheels and the horses in the centre: for I never remember to have seen the bullocks as leaders, though, from being the slowest animals of the three, this arrangement would certainly be the best, as it is the leaders that regulate the pace.

On returning from my ride I found Growtowski, whose regiment had marched but a short distance when it received orders to return. He shook me very cordially by the band, and, forgetting himself I suppose, congratulated me on the recent victory, as if I had been a Frenchman, According to agreement Lavoisteen and I dined *tête à tête, à l'Angloise*, over a good fire, to which, as well as to our customs in general and our countrymen, he pretended to be very partial. This gentleman's knowledge, as is the case with most Frenchmen, is very, multifarious, but superficial, and his quotations from Voltaire and other philosophic writers were so rapid, and often so unconnected, that there was no answering his arguments; but although I do not pretend to a profound knowledge of history, I found that even in quoting from Voltaire's historical works I had the advantage in correctness, which my talkative companion was obliged to acknowledge.

On the 6th I received a trunk of cloaths from Gibraltar, and at the same time learnt that the moment my servants heard of my being made prisoner, they plundered everything they could get at. I felt the more sensibly this ingratitude, as I had treated them with more than common kindness, and even studied to make them comfortable.

On the following day (November 7) a Polish officer arrived who had been wounded in the late action, and from whose account it would, have appeared that the victory was entirely owing to his individual prowess; he also informed us that Sebastiani had gone on to Baza, and would not return to Grenada for five or six days. The arrival of several other officers gave me an opportunity of enquiring by what mismanagement the army of Blake had been defeated by a force so very inferior; for it appeared that of the French army the 5th Dragoons, one regiment of Polish *lanciers*, and an inconsiderable detachment of infantry, had alone been engaged.

I learnt that the Spanish army was composed principally of recruits totally ignorant of the use of their arms, and it was crowded into a plain without any protection in front, nor did they even take possession of some broken ground, or form *trous de loup* as a defence against cavalry; so that on the first charge the army was broken, and the men throwing down their arms cried for quarter. About eighteen hundred were said to be killed, and upwards of eleven hundred, including forty-seven officers, made prisoners.

I had seen General Blake at Gibraltar, when on his way from Cadiz to Carthagena to take the command of this army; he had the appearance of a good honest farmer, but nothing in his countenance or manners that denoted superior talents. His staff was wretchedly made up, and, it was said, set the example of seeking safety in flight.

The Spanish prisoners arrived on the 8th, and were marched through the Plaza de Triompha, which was crowded with the inhabitants. The officers seemed to have been all wounded by the sabre: one-third of the privates were half naked, and half starved boys from fourteen to sixteen; another third infirm old men, just able to crawl, for those who could not get on were charitably shot on the road by their escort; the last third were composed of men of a tolerable appearance, and could alone have opposed any efficient resistance to the French,

The next morning (November 9) I accompanied Lavoisteen to meet the general: we had a pleasant ride of three leagues, through a most romantic country, the appearance of which seemed to denote its having undergone some great natural convulsion. At a short distance on our right rose the Sierras de Grenada, a mountainous ridge of considerable elevation, at the foot of which stretches an extensive plain, reckoned one of the most fertile tracts of the kingdom. This ridge is inhabited by a brave and warlike people, so well protected by the natural strength of the country, that while they continue to defend their fortresses it must be impossible to subdue them; nor indeed have the French yet been able to retain the positions they have occasionally occupied among them.

About three leagues from Grenada we met General Sebastiani, escorted by the *Lanciers Polonois* and a detachment of cavalry: the 12th Dragoons also joined near Grenada, to render his entrance more imposing. The Plaza de Triompha was, as usual, crowded with spectators to view the triumph of their invaders. Having, however, seen the miserable wretches the French had to contend with, I could give them but little credit for their victory; nevertheless, according to their usual gasconade, every individual had encountered a host and destroyed legions.

In the evening I went to a concert at Mr. Galway's, an Irish merchant, married to an agreeable Spanish lady; in their sitting room was a chimney, the comforts of which were so well, appreciated by the lady, that she assured me she seldom quitted the fireside. The 10th was employed by the general in making arrangements for the security of the prisoners, but the succeeding morning he proposed a ride to the village of Robach, two leagues from Grenada; the country between is richly cultivated, and the village a very good one. We alighted at the house of a respectable priest, who possessed a tolerable library and a collection of pictures.

While walking with him through his garden, which was in neat order, he told me that he had belonged to the household of Charles the Third, and indeed I soon found that he united the polish of the court to the knowledge of the scholar. Feeling that he had no occasion for reserve with me, he described what his flock had suffered from the invaders, with the tenderness of a parent, whilst unaffected benevolence was marked in his countenance. When his eyes filled with tears, as he drew the picture of the horrors he had witnessed, I could not help exclaiming:

> *Merciful Heaven!*
> *Thou rather with thy sharp and sulphurous Bolt*
> *Splits the unwedgeable and gnarled Oak,*
> *Than the soft Myrtle:—O, but Man! proud Man,*
> *Drest in a little brief Authority,*
> *Plays such fantastic Tricks before high Heaven*
> *As makes the Angels weep!—*

On our return from the garden the good priest led us into a small chapel, adorned with some pictures and images, and taking down one of the latter of gold, offered it to the general, who declined accepting it. Several *alcaides* and priests waited on him here, and were received with the greatest politeness, while in their own language, which he speaks with purity, he recommended to them a strict attention to the morality of the rising generation, and to encourage industry and orderly habits, among the peasantry of their respective villages. His audience bowed with reverence, and put on the outward signs of a satisfaction it is almost impossible they could really feel. In our return to

Grenada we made a circuit of some miles, and passed through several charming villages. On approaching the city I had a good view of the field works constructing above the Alhambra; they were four in number, palisaded round, mount thirty-six pieces of heavy ordnance, and serve, as a cavalier to the Alhambra.

On our arrival in the town the general abruptly informed me that the prisoners were to be sent off the next day, and that I must prepare to accompany them: I, however, procured a day's delay for myself, in order to provide the necessary conveyance for my baggage; and this being the general's birthday (November 12), I had an opportunity of being present at the fête given on the occasion.

In the morning, before breakfast, he received the compliments of the staff, of the garrison, and the officers of corps, presented by their respective commandants; to these succeeded the civil staff of the army and the civil authorities of the city. This ceremony concluded, breakfast was served, during which an officer entered with a verbal report of some deserters being retaken: "*Qu'on les pend tout de suite!*" replied the general, without altering a feature, or saying another word on the subject, and the officer bowed and retired. Such are the steps deemed requisite under these circumstances.

After breakfast Sebastiani proceeded to church, attended by all the authorities, in the greatest pomp, and as the procession was crossing the Plaza de Triompha, the eleven hundred prisoners of Blake's army appeared under a large escort. Whether this rencontre was accidental or premeditated, I cannot say, but should rather suppose the latter, and that the general meant by it to remind the gaping multitude that he united the hero and the Christian. I could not help reflecting, that probably at this very moment another multitude was assembled in a different part of the town, to witness the execution of the unhappy wretches whom the unjustifiable invasion of Spain by France deemed a necessary sacrifice.

A ball, fireworks, and illuminations closed the day's rejoicing; but the former was rather meagre, there being few attractive females. Waltzes and what were called English country dances chiefly prevailed, one set only performing French country dances, in which the men far excelled the women. There was also deep play at Trente et Quarante and Pharo. An elegant supper was served after the ball, and the whole evening's entertainment was in a stile of magnificence and cheerfulness that precluded *ennui*.

Chapter 9

Escape of Spanish Prisoners

November 13. Having purchased two mules and made all the necessary preparations for departure, in the morning I took leave of the general, who politely begged my acceptance of a horse, completely caparisoned; he also gave me several open letters of recommendation, both general add particular, desiring that I might be paid every attention to. The officers of his staff also individually took leave of me as if I had been their dearest friend, and furnished me with letters for their relations in France. The attention both of the General and his staff will never be effaced from my memory.

I hired a French servant to conduct the mules, on one of which I placed two trunks, inside purposely for this mode of conveyance, containing my clothes, and on the other two similar ones, filled with provisions for a week, such as hams, for which Granada is famous, pies, and other good things together with a small barrel of wine; in short, having neglected nothing to make me independent of inns on the road. I quitted Grenada, escorted by a detachment of twelve dragoons, and accompanied by Colonel Marshall and Monsieur de Billi, who were directed by the general to provide me with suitable quarters, while we remained together, and in every other respect to attend to my comfort. In spite, however, of all these attentions, the prospect of a three months journey at this inclement season was by no means exhilarating.

The country we passed through for some miles is flat, and

cultivated as well as the Spanish system of agriculture admits. At a small village, called Pixor, where we .bated the cattle, the country assumes a quite different appearance, being generally hilly and rocky, with considerable woods, which formerly reached quite to the road; but the trees for about four hundred yards in depth on each side had been recently cut down, to deprive the brigands of the cover they afforded, to conceal themselves and shoot at the straggling parties of French. The abrupt inequalities of this tract of country would lead one to suppose it had undergone the effects of earthquake. The summits of several of the hills are crowned by small Moorish towers, which seem to have served for making signals.

Having separated a little distance from the body of the escort, I entered into conversation with a dragoon, whose manners and address bespoke his superior education. I found that his parents had been respectable people, but that his having been drawn for the conscription had so affected his mother, as to deprive her of her intellects, and that his father had in consequence disposed of his property, and removed from his former residence to he knew not whither. This simple tale he delivered with a feeling and modesty that could not fail of making a strong impression, and certainly it did so on me.

A heavy storm of rain and wind coming on before we could reach Alcala Reale, we entered that town wet and uncomfortable, and I had no change of clothes, having been obliged to leave the mules in the rear, to come on with a return escort. Colonel Marshall, who commanded at Alcala Reale, had, like most of the French superior officers, formed a temporary connexion with a Spanish lady, from whom I met great civility, and spent the evening pleasantly with the colonel over a pipe and some hot brandy and water; for the wine was execrable. Here I met a Portuguese officer in the French service, who spoke good English; he appeared to be much interested in the fate of his country, and lamented that circumstances obliged him to remain in the service of her enemy.

Alcala Reale is a considerable town of about eight to nine

thousand inhabitants; it is in Andalusia, nearly on the borders of Grenada, and is situated on an elevated plain. It is commanded by a strong Moorish castle, and has been considerably improved by the French, particularly by the formation of public walks.

November 14. While at breakfast with Colonel Marshall, the officer charged with escorting the prisoners arrived, and reported that some Spanish officers bad escaped, at the same time proposing that the person at whose house they were billeted should be arrested and punished; but the colonel very properly demanded if a centinel had been placed over them? and being answered in the affirmative, replied, that the officer of the guard or the centinel was to blame, and not the Spaniard; a very unusual instance of considerate justice in a French officer in Spain, for in general the unfortunate Spaniards are punished for the negligence of the French officers and soldiers charged with the prisoners.

The main body of the escort having quitted Alcala Reale early in the morning, after breakfast I took advantage of a detachment of cavalry to rejoin it. The road skirted a ravine, which forms some strong passes, formerly crossed by bridges, but all now broken down, to obstruct the passage of the French; the road was also broken up in several places, and certainly had the Spaniards defended these passes with common resolution, the enemy could never have penetrated into the country with heavy artillery. The feet, however, is, that at the commencement the Spaniards were lukewarm in their own cause, and would probably have still remained so, had not the cruelties and excesses of the French roused them to resistance and revenge.

Our escort, which originally consisted of nineteen hundred infantry and one hundred cavalry, to guard eleven hundred Spaniards and about one hundred and forty English and Germans, was continually increased by numbers of travellers, who availed themselves of the safety it offered them. The curious vehicles of these travellers, the mixture of animals by which they were drawn, and the dresses of the passengers, formed an amusing sight.

With respect to the latter, few of them paid much attention to externals, a dirty red night cap usually covering their heads, which, had I not known that they have no such word, and are even ignorant of its meaning, I might have thought they intended for comfort.

After four hours march we reached Alcaudete, an insignificant town, on irregular ground, with narrow and badly paved streets. Here we slept, and resuming our journey next morning (November 15), passed over a tract covered with beautiful turf, interspersed with clumps of evergreen oaks, and in every respect resembling a highly drest English park. The escort usually halted between the stages on the brink of some rivulet to take refreshment, and this as much from necessity as choice, for we seldom met an isolated house in a day's match.

The Countess of Superonda and her daughter, who were among the travellers that joined the escort, when we halted, politely invited me to partake of their repast. This lady travelled in a large coach, drawn by seven mules, and filled with feather beds, live poultry, and drest provisions; she was accompanied by an intelligent priest, and attended by several domestics, mounted on asses. She informed me that the greater part of a considerable property which she possessed near Malaga, had been confiscated by the French, add that she was now going to Madrid to endeavour to arrange for the reception of the part which, at the commencement of the troubles, she had taken the precaution to make over to a friend in that city.

Before we reached Martos we were met by a Monsieur Saul, a German, who, though but a lieutenant, commanded in the town. He immediately introduced himself to me, and did not leave me long in doubt as to his character's being that of a ferocious *braggadocio*, which I suppose was his chief recommendation to a command in this unhappy country. Among other stories equally marvellous, he had singly attacked forty armed Spaniards, of whom he killed thirteen and made the rest prisoners; which reminded me of the story of the Irish soldier, who on bringing several prisoners before his commander, and being asked how he singly could have managed to take so many, answered, "by my soul, I surrounded them, to be sure!"

As we approached Martos this ruffian pointed out to me two poor wretches hanging at a tree, who had recently been executed by his order, observing with an infernal smile, "that was the way to subdue Spain"

To which I could not help replying, "that it would require a vast deal of rope and a great many hangmen to execute eleven millions of people, and that if one only remained, revenge would be his motto."

Clenching his fist, knitting his diabolical brows, and curling his bushy *mustachios*, he swore a terrible oath, that, "if it depended on him he would not leave one Spaniard in existence!" Determined to glut me with sights of horror, on arriving at the *Plaza* in the town, he desired me to remark a marble seat covered with the blood and brains of victims recently butchered; then suddenly changing the subject invited me to dine with him, an honour which I declined with little appearance of politeness, so much was I shocked with the bloodthirsty character of this monster.

At Martos I was billeted at the house of an old officer of the Walloon Guards, who had served forty-six years, and whose prepossessing appearance singularly contrasted with that of the ferocious Saul. This respectable old gentleman led me over his house, which had been the family mansion for centuries, and shewed me an apartment in which he exultingly informed me that Charles the Third had once deigned to pass the night, and which he requested me to occupy as the greatest honour he could then do an English officer of distinction. In this apartment was a splendid altar with several figures of saints, and the good old lady of the mansion who accompanied us, informed me that I could there perform my never dreaming that I was a heretic, nor was there any necessity for my enlightening her on the subject.

These good people prepared me a comfortable dinner with six covers, to which I invited our officers and Monsieur de Billi.

During a part of our repast our hosts sat and conversed with us, and though they seemed to be really rejoiced at being able to treat us with hospitality, they could not help expressing their surprise at the quantity of wine we drank; and as we several times declined coffee, they concluded Englishmen had a general aversion to it, which was also a matter of astonishment.

November 16. Quitting Martos at an early hour, our road lay over a rich, well cultivated, and seemingly more populous country than I had yet observed, for we passed through two large villages before we arrived at Jaen, on entering which I was accosted by the Major de Place, a genteel voting man who was raising a Spanish regiment for the French service, and who accompanied me to Colonel Schoumalu, the commandant, residing in the bishop's palace. From this gentleman I met an extremely civil reception, and accepted his invitation to dinner.

Jaen is a middling sized town with a population of between eight and ten thousand inhabitants. It is situated on very uneven ground, with narrow, crooked and steep streets, and is surrounded by an old Moorish wall and commanded by a castle. The cathedral which I visited before dinner, accompanied by the commandant and dean, stands in the *Plaza* and opposite the bishop's palace. It is a superb edifice: the correct Corinthian order is preserved throughout, with the exception of the columns in the inside, which are rather .heavy in proportion to the rest of the building. It had formerly four hundred canons or dignitaries, but is now much reduced.

Among the pictures particularly worthy of notice were a Virgin by Mesci, a St. Jerome by Spagnoletto, and the Martyrdom of St. Chrysostom. The *sacristie* is well proportioned and elegant, and the grand altar magnificent, being supported by columns of a marble found in the neighbourhood, resembling *lapis lazuli*. In many houses on the road I had observed a head of Christ, engraved in a singular manner, and I now found that they were copies from a painting in this cathedral, which on my requesting to.see, the dean politely prepared to gratify my curiosity. Having retired for some minutes he returned drest in his canonicals, accompanied by twelve priests bearing lighted wax tapers in large golden candlesticks: after a mass had been said, two small folding doors were thrown open with great devotion, and by the light of tome candles I observed in a niche a dark representation of the head and neck of our Saviour, so inimitably executed that I was struck with an awful sensation sot to be described.

The eyes appeared to penetrate the inmost recesses of the soul, and the whole had so much the appearance of life, that if anything could excuse the superstitious worship of the material representation of the divinity, it would certainly be this picture. The crown of the head is covered with a veil, and the picture is placed in a frame of solid gold, set with diamonds and emeralds of immense value. The miraculous history of this *santa farsa* is, that on old woman is said to have placed a handkerchief thrice folded on the face of our Saviour, on his descent from the cross, and when taken off each fold was found to have received an exact impression of the countenance; one is preserved at Madrid, a second at Toledo, and the third is that at Jaen,

According to invitation I proceeded to dine with the commandant, where a party of about thirty was assembled, and amongst them the dean, with whom I had much pleasing and instructive conversation in Spanish, which he spoke with such elegance that I much regretted not being able to spend some days in his society to improve myself in that language. The commandant I also found to be a most respectable character, with a degree of sincerity and frankness in his manners and conversation seldom met with in modern Frenchmen.

While at dinner I learnt that Major Ropach had been sent with a detachment to destroy a village about twelve miles distant, where some French soldiers had been murdered the preceding night; for it is a general order, that the inhabitants of the place where such a crime is committed, are to be put to the sword, without exception of age or sex, and their habitations burned to the ground; nor is any enquiry ever made into the provocation that may have occasioned these excesses.

By this system of terror and extermination the French have

created the bands, which they name brigands; for the inhabitants of a village who are fortunate enough to escape from these military executions, having no place of refuge, join the first armed party they meet, and urged by revenge and desperation, commit the greatest cruelties on the enemies that fall into their hands: in short, such is the horrid manner of conducting the war in Spain, that the French have every individual Spaniard against them in his heart; and as to the ultimate result of the contest I can only observe, that the subjection of a civilized and powerful nation, united in the common defence of its liberty, religion and property, by a foreign army, would be an event hitherto unprecedented in history.

After dinner the commandant politely saw me to my lodgings, where I received an invitation from my host and his wife to accompany them to a *tertulia*, which however I declined. I observed that the inhabitants were obliged by order to keep a candle burning in every window throughout the night, by which the streets are lighted in a cheap and easy manner.

CHAPTER 10

Disagreeable Spanish Custom

November 16, quitting Jaen early, we passed over a flat country to Andujar, where I found excellent quarters had been secured for me at the house of the Marquis de Contadura, in consequence of a notification from General Sebastiani to General Blondeau. The latter invited me to dinner the day of our arrival; but I preferred a quiet one at my lodgings, to which I invited our officers; the greatest part of the dinner I drest myself, rather than be poisoned by Spanish cookery. The next morning (November 17) I learnt that we were to remain at Andujar for four or five days, to be joined by a convoy expected from Seville and Cadiz, and also proceeding to Madrid.

Andujar is one of the principal towns of Andalusia, containing about fourteen thousand inhabitants. The streets are wide, and kept tolerably clean, and many of the houses have an appearance that denotes the easy circumstances of their proprietors. The Guadalquivir, after serpentizing through an agreeable valley, passes by the walls of the town, where it is crossed by a stone bridge of several arches.

By this river, which is navigable for vessels of burthen from St. Lucar at its mouth in the Bay of Cadiz to Seville, the French convey the artillery made in this last city, to supply their batteries against Cadiz. In the foundry at Seville, the French have cast mortars of such a size as will throw the shells much beyond the usual distance. A great quantity of grain and provisions are also conveyed down the Guadalquivir. The plain in which Andujar is situated produces wine, oil, and honey in abundance; and in the vicinity of the town is a very white argillaceous clay, of which earthenware of a good quality is manufactured to a considerable extent, and the town has besides extensive silk manufactures.

Here the English and Spanish prisoners were confined in the same convent, but in separate parts; the Spanish officers, and men were indiscriminately crowded into the chapel, for since the desertion of the officers at Alcala Reale no distinction had been made. After breakfast (November 18) I paid my respects to General Blondeau, who received me in the most polite manner, doubtless chiefly owing to the flattering letters of recommendation from General Sebastiani, and gave me a general invitation to his table while we remained at Andujar.

This day the dinner party consisted of above eighteen persons, besides the general's staff; amongst the strangers were the Marquis de Contadura, and the Polish major commanding the convoy, with whom I had some words on the road respecting, the treatment of the prisoners; but we afterwards became good friends, on his changing the measures I complained of.—General Blondeau has all the appearance of a plain honest farmer, both in his dress and address, so that I felt perfectly at home in his company, and on his asking me to give my opinion of the dinner, I candidly recommended a less proportion of garlic and grease, and that the dishes should be sent warm to table.

These observations produced an invitation to dinner the next day, and the cook was sent for and ordered to take my directions. The general at the same time informed me, the neighbouring country abounded with hares, and that the next morning he would mount me on his cream coloured charger, take out his fifteen greyhounds, and we should have a fine morning's coursing, while he would also send out a *chasseur* with his gun, to procure a variety of game.

After dinner, when the rest of the party had withdrawn, he politely invited me to partake of a bowl of punch and smoke a pipe over a good fire in his cabinet, and we accordingly retired to this recess of sociability, when he at full entertained me with the history of his campaigns, and, like his countrymen,

> *Fought all his battles o'er again......*
> *And thrice he slew the slain.*

As this subject was most uninteresting to me, I soon changed it to a disquisition on the female sex, and particularly French and Spanish women, to the latter of whom the general adjudged the palm of beauty; an opinion in which not finding me inclined to coincide, he determined to support it by ocular demonstration, and ringing the bell, it was answered by a beautiful Spanish girl of about eighteen, whose elegant shape, perfect head and bosom, shaded by the most beautiful hair falling in graceful ringlets over her shoulders, might have entitled her to sit for the picture of Venus.

This interesting young creature, the general told me, had thrown herself on his protection to escape the brutality of the brigands, and that she officiated as his housekeeper. Without ceremony she drew a chair, seated herself beside me, and fitted my glass with excellent punch, which she told me was of her own making. The general absenting himself for some time, the fair Spaniard related her interesting story in elegant Spanish, and with a simplicity and modesty that gave it additional interest.

Having emptied our bowl of punch, the general insisted on seeing me to my lodgings, where I prevailed on him to partake of a glass of grog, and a *segar*, which kept us up till four o'clock, when it became my turn to see him home.

Next morning (November 19) being mounted on the general's cream coloured horse, which, though shewy, I soon found had neither speed nor bottom, we proceeded in search of the promised sport, attended *en prince* by about one hundred dragoons. Our pack was composed of several greyhounds, who all ran by the nose, which the French consider a perfection, and were much surprised, when I told them that in England this quality would cause them to be hanged for lurchers.

Our party was numerous, and consisted entirely of French officers, except the Marquis de Contadura, a Spanish nobleman, who had deserted his country's cause and joined its invaders, while the other members of his family, and even his wife, remained steady in their loyalty; indeed this lady informed, me, that his former friends had ceased all correspondence with him, although he was one of the most distinguished Hidalgos of Spain. Our sport consisted in a few tolerable gallops, which completely knocked up my charger, and the produce of our three hours course was eighteen hares, the dragoons forming a line and beating across the fields, to put up the animals.

As I had promised to instruct the general's cook in making hare soup, on our return I repaired to the kitchen, where I found four brace of partridges, brought in by the *chasseur*, as well as some wild ducks, and knowing that the French roast game to a cinder, I with much difficulty persuaded the cook to dress the ducks simply *à la broche*, and to serve them up with the sauce I should compose, taking care to specify particularly, that they were not to be put to the fire until the first course was served up.

Although the cook and his assistants were diverted with the *bizarrerie* of the *cuisine Anglois*, I had the satisfaction to find at dinner that my hare soup was universally relished, and the ducks declared to be delicious. After dinner I retired with the general to his cabinet, where we played a party at piquet, while his charming housekeeper kept our glasses replenished with excellent punch, and proclaimed to bring her sister to be of our party the following evening. Thirty-six Spanish prisoners made their escape this night.

In the morning (November 20) I strolled about the immediate environs of the town, and even for this short distance I was obliged to have an escort, so great was the dread of the brigands. At dinner at the general's I met a party of ten, one of whom was a clergyman, who spoke his political opinions with a freedom that surprised me, in a French military society, where such kind of discussions are considered as little less than treason; a point in which the French differ entirely from us, who are taught to believe, that truth is most certainly to be attained through the medium of argument.

On retiring to the general's cabinet, we found the fair housekeeper had not forgot her promise of introducing her sister, whose charms were equal to her own; and whose conversation made the evening pass with additional pleasure.

Neat day (November 21), a convoy being expected to arrive from Seville, I went out to meet it, accompanied by Monsieur de Billi, and by some, of our officers. Before we fell in with, the convoy we met with three Irishmen, without any escort, who pretended they were prisoners taken at Cadiz, ,but who in reality were deserters from the 87th regiment. There were also with them some English sailors, and among them a young lad named Archibald Lindsey, belonging to the *Thames* frigate, who told me that he had been constantly kept in irons, and treated with the greatest cruelty, to oblige him to enter into the French service.

We at last met the convoy, which was not very considerable, the number of prisoners in it being only fifty, among whom were a few English soldiers and sailors. I dined as usual with the General, but this day most uncomfortably, from a custom prevalent among the people of condition in Spain, than which nothing can be more contrary to an Englishman's habits and ideas, that of making complimentary visits during dinner.

Just as we had sat down to table, the Countess of Superonda and her daughter paid one of those *mal à propos* visits to a Madame Benedicio, who had arrived with the convoy from Seville, and dined with the general. "*Place aux dames*" was of course a necessary civility, and I was obliged to retire my chair a yard from the table, which made my situation most disagreeable; and, what was still worse, while the ladies were thus annoying me, as much as if they had studied a week before how to do so, they cried out every moment, "*Monsieur, ne dérangez-vous pas, je vous en prie.*"

Unfortunately, neither these polite requests, nor their frivolous chit-chat, consoled me for the almost entire loss of my dinner; and I could not help reflecting, that what one people regards as the height of politeness, another considers as the very extreme of rudeness.

After returning to the *salon* for a short time, and joining in the public conversation, I took leave of the good general, whose kind attention I cannot easily forget; and on this occasion I must observe, that I have always found the well educated French extremely attentive to, and apparently interested in an Englishman, as if there was something extraordinary in him that called forth their admiration.

While we remained in the *salon*, M. Huet and M. Cavällos, the former paymaster of the 9th Corps, and the latter paymaster-general of the army of Portugal, attached themselves to me, and laughed heartily at my description of the annoyance I suffered at dinner, from the intrusion of Madame Superonda, who I observed was not badly named; for the enormous rotundity of her person frightened me from entering the lists with her against such dreadful odds, and I thought it therefore most prudent to draw back my chair, even at the expense of my dinner. These observations called forth a number of sarcastic remarks from the Frenchmen on the Countess's embonpoint; and the levity of manner of her handsome daughter gave occasion to others not less cutting, but of a different nature. I could not decline the invitation of my facetious companions to sup with them, and we did not part till four o'clock in the morning.

Chapter 11

Surrender of Dupont's Army

At six o'clock in the morning of November 22nd, we began our march from Andujar, with an escort of one thousand infantry and two hundred cavalry; this force being thought necessary to protect six million of *reals* in specie going to Madrid. In passing the place where the prisoners had been confined, I observed a poor wretch with his brains knocked out, and covered with stabs; and on enquiring of the Polish major who commanded the escort *en second*, I learnt that it was a Spaniard who had attempted to escape; and, continued the major with a sardonic grin, "*le sentinelle l'a joliment tué!*" Though shocked by the unfeeling levity of the expression, I made no reply.

The country, which near Andujar is level and rich, soon became poor and rocky, and continued so to Baylen; an insignificant town four leagues from Andujar, where we arrived at an early hour, and found wretched accommodation; it having suffered greatly from the French, who at this time occupied a large and strong Moorish castle on the left entering the town.

Here the army of Dupont, consisting of eight thousand men, laid down their arms to the Spaniards, commanded by Castanos, Reding and Venagas. This check caused Buonaparte to send a fresh army of two hundred thousand veterans into Spain, to ensure its conquest; an event which, at the moment I am writing this, is certainly as far distant as ever, after the loss of half a million of French soldiers: and, indeed, it requires little penetration to discover, that the exterminating system of warfare adopted by France, although it might succeed in a country where the inhabitants could be hemmed into a little space, must inevitably fail in one so extensive and so naturally strong as Spain.

Cruelty, therefore, serves only to exasperate the whole nation, of which, while one individual remains, the remembrance will never be obliterated. The assembly of the Cortes has infused a new spirit into the Spanish people, who look with confidence to the wisdom of this august body, for the salvation of their country and the preservation of their liberty. It was a similar confidence in their Congress that carried the Americans through every difficulty to final success, and similar causes produce similar effects.

Quitting Baylen early in the morning of the 23rd, we passed through Guaraman, the first of a chain of villages built by Charles the Third, for the reception of a colony of Germans, which he established in the Sierra Morena. This village is regularly built, and the houses exactly alike, but they were now totally deserted, in consequence of the French invasion. Indeed the colony never arrived at any great prosperity; and perhaps it may be admitted as an axiom in politics, that the mere will of the sovereign is totally inadequate for forcing the progress of industry, commerce, or manufactures, and more particularly the latter, whose birth is in general spontaneous, and their growth the effect of local causes and circumstances.

From Guaraman we approached the colonial town of Carolina by a fine shaded alley, with rich gardens on each side. This town, as well as fire others which we passed through in the Sierra, is surrounded by a wall, with loop holes, and has been regularly fortified by the French, by whom, however, several of the houses have been burnt, and most of the inhabitants had fled. In short, the cruelty and exactions of the invaders have caused this tract of country to be nearly deserted, and hence the grounds remaining uncultivated, the French find it extremely difficult to subsist themselves j thus, in every respect, their exterminating system injures their cause.

At Carolina we put up at a large inn built with cut stone,

which however did not afford a single convenience, not even shelter from the weather; for the windows and doors had been burnt and the roof destroyed, so that the wind and sleet found a free entrance into every apartment: it is not therefore surprising that we were anxious to quit this scene of desolation, and at break of day (November 24), resumed our route over a most barren tract, and through two colonial villages, both destroyed, and arrived at St. Helena, six leagues from Carolina, and similar to it.

This is the last of the colonial towns, it is situated at the foot of the Sierra, and is now totally abandoned. Here we received information that the brigands meditated an attack on the convoy; and the troops in consequence bivouacked round the town, and other precautions were taken. In a council of war, composed of the principal officers of the escort, it was determined that the Spanish prisoners should be indiscriminately put to death at the moment of attack, and they were accordingly tied two and two, to wait their fate. With this resolution I was made acquainted the following morning by Monsieur Garnier, who added, that

"it had been determined to spare the English prisoners, because they were sure they would join in repelling the brigands."

My only acknowledgment of this favour was by replying,

that we had six Frenchmen at least in England for one Englishman in the power of the French, and that certainly any violence perpetrated on an individual subject of England, would be severely retaliated; that for my own part, I had no fears either for my personal safety or for that of any one of my countrymen, fellow prisoners; and I was sure the commander of the convoy must reflect, that any atrocity of this nature would not only subject him to the execration of mankind, but that he would also be answerable to his own nation for sallying its honour, and to the whole civilized world, for a violation of the laws of war, as well as of the principles of humanity.

I immediately retired, and put on my uniform.

Towards the foot of the Sierra, among a profusion of romantic views, are many defiles, in passing which the convoy might certainly have been attacked to the greatest advantage: and indeed the expectation of it was so great, that every preparation was made for it; the individuals of the civil part of the escort arming themselves according to their fancy, with guns, swords, or pistols, and some with all three, while their martial appearance was increased by an immense cocked hat, generally stuck on over a red night cap.

At length we reached the famous Penon de los Peros, a tremendous rocky precipice, from the sides of which a great variety of large trees and shrubs grew out in such a manner, as, on a cursory view, to create astonishment how they could vegetate amidst such barrenness; but a nearer examination shews that the rock is split in every direction, and the cavities filled with rich and humid mould, in which the trees strike their roots, while the rock, which is calcareous, affords a prolific warmth that renders the vegetation extremely luxuriant.

At the foot of the precipice flows a river, which was now much swollen by recent rains, and increased the romantic effect of the landscape, Near the precipice is a drawbridge, and on the left of the latter some elevated batteries, commanding others beneath them, the possession of which, had the brigands attempted an attack, would have been of much consequence to the convoy. Farther in advance were the remains of several other batteries, all commanding this formidable pass, which it was expected in England would have prevented the penetration of the French army into Andalusia.

Accompanied by General Briott and several French officers, I visited this pass, and found that, like most defiles, its appearance of strength is very deceitful; but even the Spaniards did not know how, or neglected, to make the most of its natural advantages. The sites of their batteries were ill chosen, being commanded on all sides by musketry, and therefore at the mercy of an enemy who might gain the heights in their rear, or turn their flanks; both of which the French succeeded in. In the passage of the French army, Joseph Buonaparte commanded the centre, with Marshal Soult and General Desolles. Marshal Victor's corps proceeded to the right three days before the movement of the centre, and entered the Sierra nearly opposite Cordova, advancing in the rear of the Spaniards, with the intention of turning their left; while Sebastiani's corps advanced on the left, in order to turn their right; and thus the Spanish army being flanked and commanded on every side, fled in all directions, with scarce any resistance, and left the French an undisputed passage into the heart of Andalusia.

This unexpected misfortune was attempted to be accounted for in various ways, and many persons attributed it to treachery; but this idea, when the nature of the pass, and the force of the Spaniards are considered, must be abandoned; for, first, there was no natural protection for either of the flanks, such as a swamp or river; and, secondly, the Spanish army was barely sufficient to defend the road by which it was to be presumed the French would attempt to pass; as the latter had several other points open to them, by which they might cross the mountains, whose extent is so great, that their general defence requires a force greatly superior to what Spain and her allies could at this time have spared for the purpose.

The less the event was expected, the greater was the consternation on its arrival, and the Junto of Seville, who had placed entire confidence in this Thermopylæ of Spain, was cautiously and tediously proceeding in its deliberations, without having once thought of providing against a disaster, which it had not the most distant idea could ever arrive.

CHAPTER 12

Effects of the French Invasion

Before I quit Andalusia, I trust my Madera will not find uninteresting or misplaced, the few observations my mode of travelling permitted me to make on that kingdom, the chief seat of the war in Spain at the time of my passing through it. I have already cursorily observed, that the soil and climate of this part of Spain are eminently calculated to afford the same vegetable productions as the tropical colonies, and that therefore its possession by France would render those colonies almost unnecessary to her.

Like all mountainous region, Andalusia offers the most romantic; scenery to the picturesque traveller, while the agriculturist admires the richness of its rallies, which aided by a genial climate, yield in the same extent of surface nearly double the quantity of wine, oil, and com, produced in any other part of Europe: and hence it has deservedly acquired the title of "the wine cellar and granary of Spain." Even the mountains, which in most other countries are unproductive, are here a source of riches, in the great variety of marbles they contain, valuable both for the fineness of grain and the mixture of colours.

The extensive forests of Andalusia, and particularly those of evergreen oak, constitute an object of national riches. These trees attain a magnitude that would in other countries be considered with astonishment; nor, indeed, have I ever seen any of the vegetable reign arrive at such immensity, except those of Brazil, where several species of trees grow to a size that entitle them to the name of giants of the forest.

The population and industry of Andalusia have never recovered the blow they received by the expulsion of the Moors, at which epoch an immense number of towns and villages were seated on the banks of the Guadalquivir alone, and the population of the kingdom was estimated at seven millions, of which Grenada contained three millions. According to the most recent estimation, the number of inhabitants is new but two millions, of which it is said one fourth at least are useless to society by their religious vows.

Here I cannot help observing that, whatever may be the event of the present contest, the Spanish nation will derive an inestimable benefit from the invasion of the French, in getting rid of such legions of monks, who not only, like drones in a hive, hang a dead weight on the industry of the community, but, what is still worse, are the great obstacles to all national improvement, by the gross ignorance in which it is their interest to keep the people; for we can scarcely suppose it possible that, should the French be finally driven out of Spain, the Spanish Government or nation will be so lost to common sense, as to restore the monastic orders.

The observation that, *where nature is most bountiful, the people are most indolent*, is nowhere more completely verified than in Andalusia. Even the olive trees, which constitute a considerable portion not only of .the wealth, but of the very subsistence of the people, are so neglected, that generally nine out of ten are half decayed, or the vegetation only preserved by a single narrow strip of bark, while all the rest of the trunk is naked; nevertheless, such is the fertility of the soil, that a tree thus deprived of nine-tenths of its bark, is seen loaded with fruit.

But though in general agriculture is little understood in Andalusia, it is more advanced in some districts than in others, which is probably to be ascribed to the different direction of leases. In many parts, the tenant holds only for three years, in others for five; but neither term is sufficient to induce the farmer to go to any expense in improvement: on the contrary, it is evidently his interest to get the most he can out of the soil, at the least possible expense. Such, however, is the richness of the soil, the abundance of water consequent to a mountainous country, and the equal temperature of the climate, that the lands retain their fertility almost undiminished, in spite of the vicious system of agriculture.

The *mesta*, or ancient custom of driving vast flocks of sheep from one end of the kingdom to the ether for pasture, which is protected by the Government, is also extremely unfavourable to the improvement as well as to the extension of cultivation.

The valley through which the Guadalquivir winds its course, is supereminently fertile, and from it the French armies derive the greatest part of their forage and provisions. The sides of the mountains to the north of Cordova are covered with vineyards and gardens, interspersed with groves, of lemons and orange trees; in short, the territory of Fernan Nunez, about four leagues from Cordova, is but one continued beautiful garden for many miles.

The provinces of Seville and Grenada are the most fruitful in barley and maize; the former, mixed with a chopped straw, is the general food of the horses, for giving them barley alone is said to produce disease. The neighbourhood of Seville, Cordova, and Andujar produce abundance of wheat, and the quantity of this grain raised in the whole. of Andalusia, is said to be double its consumption. The crops particularly near the coast are, however; very uncertain, the Levant wind often destroying them, as well as the *Solano*, which blows in scorching blasts from the coast of Africa, and. produces a similar effect to the blight. . The coasts of Grenada are most exposed to this baneful wind, and here, therefore, the cultivation of hemp is preferred, this plant receiving no injury from it.

Amongst Spanish, wines those of Andalusia are the most esteemed, and particularly those of Grenada. The wines of the territory of Malaga are highly celebrated, and of which there are twenty to thirty varieties; those of Pietro Zimenes, the Muscatel, and the Tierno are of superior quality. Farther west dry wines are chiefly produced, of which the most esteemed are those of Rota and Xeres: of the latter, known by the name of sherry, fifty thousand *quintals* [1] are exported annually, chiefly by the port of Malaga, from which was also exported three hundred thousand *quintals* of raisins, the grapes of this district being of a very superior quality, and requiring no other preparation than merely hanging to dry in the sun.

The wine named Montella, produced in the vicinity of Cordova, is the most esteemed in the country. The olives of the territory of Seville are reckoned of a superior quality, but the oil made from them is generally rancid, owing, doubtless, to the negligent manner of preparing it

The Andalusian horses are deservedly considered the best of Spain, and this superiority they owe to the facility of crossing . then with those of Barbary, by the constant intercourse between the coasts.

The manufactures of Andalusia, which were formerly very considerable, particularly those of Seville, have constantly declined since the beginning of the seventeenth century. The silk manufactures of Cordova, Grenada, Seville, and Malaga, are, however, still flourishing, and those of Xeres and Puerto de Santa Maria respectable, Coarse woollens are also manufactured to a considerable extent in several towns. From the royal tobacco manufactory at Seville issues an immense quantity of *segars* and snuff, the latter named *polvillis*. At Velez Malaga is a manufactory of playing cards, the only one I believe in Spain, and which supplies both the whole kingdom and the colonies. Besides the sugar works at Malaga, there are some respectable ones at Motril.

The general commerce of Andalusia, though much declined from its ancient splendour, was still considerable at the period of the present invasion, the chief trading ports being Almeria, Malaga, and Cadiz. Almeria was, during the Moorish dominion, one of the most commercial cities of Europe, which it owed principally to the goodness of its port, at the head of a gulf,

---

1. A *quintal* in weight is one hundred pounds English; in liquid measure twelve gallons.

sheltered from the Levant winds by the promontory of Cape de Gata. A pestilential disease, which desolated the city in the fourteenth century, gave the first blow to its commerce, and the expulsion of the Moors totally annihilated it; nor have two centuries been able to restore it.

The commerce of Malaga, as I have before observed, has been totally destroyed by French fraternity or invasion, words synonymous in their effects; and this example ought to warn every nation to guard as cautiously against the one as the other. The exports from Malaga formerly amounted to upwards; of three millions of *piastres*, of which oil alone furnished one million, while the imports did not amount to two millions. Cadiz, until 1776, enjoyed the sole trade of the colonies, and though this commerce has been opened, to all the principal ports of Spain, it still retained two-thirds of the whole.

The wars with England, however, reduced it to a cipher, before the French invasion. In 1791 this port sent one hundred and seventy-seven ships to the colonies, and in 1801 only twenty cleared out from all the ports of Spain; no other proof need be adduced, how greatly it is the interest of Spain to be on good terms with England, who can thus in a moment annihilate the most valuable branch of her commerce, and upon which the very existence of her government, in the present state of the country, depends.

The French invasion, and the vast efforts made by England to support Spanish independence, will doubtless unite .the two nations more closely than ever, and, therefore, even in a commercial view (supposing France to fail in the subjection of the country, which I think is not problematic), she must lose considerably by the mistaken ambition of Buonaparte, for Spain will certainly procure hereafter from the British islands many of the articles which she formerly received from France, and other nations now subject to her.

Thus Irish have already superseded those of Holland, and if the colonies should succeed in their efforts for independence, another consequence of the French invasion they will certainly receive the manufactured objects they require from England, rather than from France. The exports of woollens alone from Marseilles to Spain, chiefly for the use of the colonies, was estimated at twelve millions of *francs*.

At the head of the distinguished characters to whom Andalusia has given birth, must be placed Seneca, the great waster of sententious morality. During the Moorish dominion the arts and sciences were highly cultivated, and rose to a great degree of perfection; particularly astronomy, mathematics, and medicine, in the last of which the Moors made vast improvements, and introduced a new system of physiology, which superseded that of the Greeks, and which was first adopted in France, from whence it found its way into the rest of Europe.

Andalusia has produced some poets of eminence of both sexes. Among the men Ferdinand de Herrera is the most esteemed, and among the females Aischa of Cordova, and Maria Alpharsati, surnamed the Sappho of Spain, whose picture I observed in several of the first collections.

This kingdom has also the honour of giving birth to several eminent painters, at the head of whom may be placed Paul Cespides, who was a universal genius, excelling equally in painting, engraving, architecture and poetry. Antonio Murillo deserves the second place. The Spaniards being extremely fond of music, this art has of course made considerable progress among them, but the national music is still far inferior to that of Italy or France. Malaga has produced some good botanists and chemists, whose works are to be found in the public libraries.

It is justly a matter of surprise, that during such a contest as the present, not a single Spaniard of superior talents or abilities has appeared on the great theatre of action, while the French revolution has brought forth geniuses of almost every description. Perhaps paucity of talent among the Spaniards is owing to the influence of the clergy not being yet sufficiently weakened, to permit the general adoption of a more liberal system of education, which can alone produce the desired revolution in the moral habits of the nation. In fact, what energy of action can be expected from a people, who trust more to a patron saint for protection than to their, own courage.

The soldier, who places his sole confidence in a relic suspended on his breast, may go into battle with the appearance of valour, but will surely turn his back the moment he thinks his saint has forsaken him. The inquisitorial prohibition of all books containing, liberal sentiments on religion, morality, natural philosophy, or politics, still exists, and a list of such books is seen hung up in every church. In some of the public libraries, however, these books are allowed a separate place, over which is inscribed *Books of Reference*, to denote that they are for the use of the learned alone, and not to be read by all persons indiscriminately, although in general they are the only books worth reading in the collections.

The Andalusians are distinguished front the natives of the other provinces of Spain by a peculiarity of costume and manners; the former they seem to have preserved from a very early period, and the *montero* cap is still universally worn by the peasantry, whose common dress is a light jacket with three close rows of oval buttons, and two of loops and tassels. Buttons indeed seem to be their favourite ornament, for to each knee of the breeches, they have usually twenty to thirty hung to silver chains, and two rows to the waistcoat fixed in a similar manner. Their shoes are out of measure long quartered, and as well as the knee bands fastened by enormous silver buckles.

The men plait their hair in a neat manner and fasten it at the extremity with a black ribbon, tied in a bow, which hangs half way down the back. The Andalusian prides himself on his country, and is seriously offended at being mistaken for a native of any other province, even though it should be of Castile itself. The *Bullero* and *Fandango* with castanets are the favourite dances of the Andalusians, and they usually accompany them with a popular song, which greatly adds to their effect.

The number of *Gustanos* or gypsies, scattered over this province is very considerable; their women, though their complexions are very dark, have in general fine features and brilliant eyes; these vagabonds were formerly protected by the nobles, in return for which, their *stiletto* was always at their patron's service, to revenge his injuries on his enemies, or satisfy his jealousy of a rival. In travelling through Spain the idea of assassination is every moment recalled to the mind, by the crosses erected to mark the spots where this crime has been committed, and the number of these *ecce-signa* proves the astonishing prevalence of this cowardly species of revenge.

Even a sketch of the natural history of Andalusia would lead me far beyond the limits I have prescribed to myself in this *journal*; I cannot however forbear mentioning the mines of gold and silver, which during the Roman dominion were celebrated for their richness, but which are at present not worth the working. Amongst the most noted are those of Linarez in the province of Jaen, which were worked by the Carthaginians, and were the property of the beautiful Himila, wife of Asdrubal.

They were still productive in the time of the Romans, and are described as being two thousand feet deep, and having several galleries. There are some rich copper mines on the banks of the Tinto, not far from Cordova. The kingdom of Grenada has several warm mineral springs chiefly sulphurous, of which the most celebrated are those of Albania at Grenada, and one within two miles of Antequera, famous for the cure of gravel complaints. To such of my readers as may wish for a detailed account of the mineral waters of this province, I can recommend a treatise on them by Don Juan de Dios Aguda, a copy of which was lent me at Andujar by the good priest I have already mentioned.

CHAPTER 13

Convoy from France

On entering La Mancha from Andalusia the traveller is forcibly struck by the great contrast both in the face of the country, the architecture of the buildings, and the costume of the people, which are as different from those of Andalusia, as if the two provinces formed distinct nations. Andalusia is covered with chains or groups of mountains, while La Mancha is but one immense plain, the soil a deep clay, highly cultivated and extremely productive. The stile of architecture and the arrangement of the apartments in Andalusia are light and cheerful, in La Mancha both are heavy and sombre.

Though the roads of Spain are in general horribly bad, that by which we entered La Mancha is an exception, being sixty feet wide, and in excellent order, so that we advanced rapidly, and reached Santa Cruz, from St. Helena, in the evening of November 24. Santa Cruz is the first town of La Mancha, towards the Sierra Morena, and has nothing worthy of note. The streets are narrow and badly paved, and the houses, built of clay or of dirty coloured bricks, there being no stone in the neighbourhood, are entered by a large court yard, round which are the stables and other out offices.

The naturally uncheerful look of the town was now increased by the ravages of war, the French having recently destroyed nearly one half of it, and the description my hosts gave me of their own deplorable situation and of the general misery, by no means tended to chase away the melancholy feelings inspired by this scene of wanton cruelty. The invaders, however, while they destroyed the houses of the defenceless inhabitants, had taken care to repair and garrison a castle close to the town.

November 25. Early in the morning we resumed our journey towards Toledo by a very bad cross road, the roughness of which was however in some measure compensated by the beauty of the country, which presented a series of luxuriant meadows, covered with the finest turf, watered by numerous rivulets, and clotted with clumps of majestic evergreen oaks, under which vast herds of cattle formerly sought shelter from the wind and rain in winter, and which doubtless in summer afforded them a shaded retreat from the ardour of the sun.

But this beautiful tract was now a desert, without peasants to cultivate it, or cattle to crop the herb. The numerous villages and hamlets which formerly afforded the traveller the cheerful appearance of rural comfort, were now laid in ashes, the inhabitants either massacred or fled, and nought, to be seen around but the desolation of an exterminating warfare. In short, the painter of landscape could in no part of the world find more beautiful scenery to occupy his pencil, nor the poet more affecting objects to employ his pen.

In the course of this day's march we had to cross a piece of water and wind round a small hill, which offers an excellent defensive position for an army, the pass not being above twelve feet wide, and its flank guarded by a deep river. We halted for a short time at the village of Val de Penas, midway, between Santa Cruz and Manzanares, and which is celebrated for a wine made in the vicinity resembling Port, but not so strong. We were not obliged to content ourselves with that of the last vintage, the French troops in their passage having exhausted all the old; but the *alcade* of the village kindly filled my little barrel with the best that remained, and which I calculated would serve me and my companion to Toledo.

At Val de Penas our escort was increased by six hundred infantry of the regiment of Nassau, and two hundred hussars of the same corps; the battalion of infantry of this regiment was now twelve hundred strong, and remarkably well appointed. Instead of our cumbersome tin canteens, which are continually wanting repair, each man had a skin bottle with a wooden or bone mouth piece, and holding about five pints; the older these vessels are, the more valuable.

Among the officers of this corps I recognized a Mr. Stelms, who had deserted from the French to us, and afterwards re-deserted back again to the French. This double deserter was received by the French officers with the greatest apparent cordiality, and a serjeant and some soldiers who had followed his example were as graciously received by their comrades, which induced me to ask one of the officers if they really considered this total want of honour as meritorious?

To which he made no other reply than, the usual one of a Frenchman when he does not know what to answer, a shrug of the shoulders. Mr. Stelms remained with his corps; but the serjeant, who had all the appearance of a perfect ruffian, was marched onward, and I had the pleasure of seeing him put in irons at Madrid.

Outside of Val de Penas we met a large convoy from France going into Andalusia, many of the persons in which could not refrain from loudly expressing their joy at seeing a few English prisoners, as if the fate of the war depended on our freedom or captivity. In this convoy I observed several carriages built on the model of English *post chaises*, but incapable of supporting a comparison as to the finish.

With respect to the French convoys, care is taken that two shall not meet at the same village; but this is doubtless more for their own sakes, to prevent a scarcity of provisions and quarters, than from any regard to the Spaniards. In the present case however this precaution was unnecessary, for we found provisions abundant, even to profusion, at Val de Penas.

Between this village and Manzanares we passed through or near several ruined villages. On approaching Manzanares, we were met by several Polish officers and gentlemen of the town, amongst whom I was surprised to see a certain Marquis de

Salinas,[1] whom I had formerly met at Lord Nelson's and Sir William Hamilton's houses at Palermo. At that time he was the holder of a Pharo bank, and besides collected modern antiques for travelling gentlemen, who wished to acquire the reputation of *cognoscenti*.

As the Marquis always produced his acquisitions of this nature in company, with a long harangue on their inestimable value, and the low price they were to be sold for, he generally disposed of them with ease, and I, among others, took some off his hands, which, though certainly more antique now than when I bought them, I would willingly spare under prime cost. Long absence, we are told, weakens friendship; and with respect to the Italian Marquis, I found that it weakens shame also, for though he was obliged to quit Palermo precipitately, in consequence of being openly detected cheating at play at Sir William Hamilton's, in my presence, and was afterwards turned out of the English fleet by Lord Keith, on violent suspicion of being a spy of the French, he now accosted me with an air of perfect composure, expressed his happiness at meeting me, and insisted on escorting me to my quarters.

Knowing him to be an entertaining fellow, from whom I might derive both information and amusement. I determined to look over the slight blemish of being a professed swindler; and, indeed, he seemed himself to think this no blot in his character, for he adverted to the transaction at Palermo, and treated it as a mere *bagatelle*.

The story he now related of himself was, that, expecting the French to become masters of Sicily, he thought it the best policy to secure his property there by espousing their cause; that he therefore quitted that island for Spain, and being married to a Spanish lady, who possessed property at Manzanares, he had just come from Madrid to take possession of it, but found that a French general had been beforehand with him, and now oc-

---

1. Lord Blayney was prosecuted by the Duke de Sorentino (formerly Marquis de Salinas) for this libel as it was the Count of Salinas Lord Blayney met not the Marquis.

cupied his house by military tenure; at the same time, that his Spanish tenants were unable to pay their rents, from the disturbed and distressed state of the country, and, that being disappointed in his expectations of the French becoming masters of Sicily, he could draw no succours from thence.

The noble Marquis found in me a Job's comforter; for, instead of condoling with him, I related the several unsuccessful attempts of the French on Sicily, and assured him that they had now seemingly given up the idea, as hopeless, while the English retained their superiority at sea.

November 25. As the convoy were to halt for the day at Manzanares, in the morning I walked out of the town over a fine plain, and entered into conversation with some country people, who, when they understood I was an English officer, told me all their sufferings from the tyranny of the French, and assured me, that if any of the English officers wished to escape, they should be provided that night with horses, money, and guides. This was not the first by many offers of the same nature that I had received; but even had I not been on parole, the liberality of General Sebastiani's conduct to me had been such, that I should have felt it impossible to take advantage of them.

On my return to the town, I waited on General Loye, who received me politely, invited me to dinner, and in the mean time asked me to accompany him to see a bullfight. This diversion, which took place in the public square, was, however, wretched in the extreme, the animals, except one, being mere calves, which the squibs and darts thrown at them by some men and boys on foot (for there were no cavaliers) could not irritate; the old one was less patient, and soon cleared the square.

The general gave me an excellent dinner with a good fire, and many of the guests being officers of the old school, and consequently of gentlemanly manners, the evening passed pleasantly, and was closed with a dance, at which all the ladies of the town were assembled; in whose persons, dress, or manners, I saw little to admire. One lady and gentleman danced a *Fandango* with castanets in a very good stile. In all the large towns occupied by the French, it is customary for the Governor to give a dance to the inhabitants every Sunday evening, the expense of which is either defrayed by the Government, or certain emoluments are granted the Governor in lieu.

November 26. Early in the morning we resumed our march, and in the evening reached Villa Robeda, or Rubia, only worthy of notice from its vicinity to the source of the Guadiamar. On the following day (November 27), after passing through a level tract of country, formerly producing a great quantity of corn, we arrived at Consuegra. In this day's march, a hare starting up close to us: I followed it with Monsieur Garnier, who had a greyhound, but we were soon obliged to halt, on coming in sight of some brigands' *vedettes*, who had kept on our flanks for the last two days, and gave us continual alarm. Consuegra is the best town we had yet seen in La Mancha, but has suffered greatly from the war, and more particularly, as I learnt, from the German troops, who in the act of desolation excel even the French.

Our present escort being entirely composed of these demi savages, the prisoners felt the full extent of their brutality, a blow with the butt end of a musket being the only answer to any complaint. Witnessing a fact of this nature myself, I remonstrated with the commanding officer in the strongest terms, and positively refused to march another step, even though death was to be the consequence unless the ruffian was punished, and he was accordingly marched on as a prisoner.

At Consuegra is a Moorish castle, capable of receiving a garrison of four thousand men. It is in good repair, and almost inaccessible, so that the Spaniards must have been infatuated, not to have seen the great advantage of occupying it at the commencement of the war.

On the following day (November 27), we reached Mora, a miserable village, where we halted, to wait for a reinforcement; it being reported that *Il Medico* was in possession of the castle of Almunaire, on the route to Toledo, and that he had a considerable force. *Il Medico* (the name which the French have, in derision of his profession of physician, given to this chief) is properly called Martinez. He was forced into his present situation by the cruelties of the French, who not only confiscated his property, but personally ill treated himself and his family, which rendering him desperate, he joined a body of the patriots, and was declared their chief. His force at this time was said to be eight hundred infantry and four hundred cavalry, with which he was extremely successful in harassing the French, and cutting off their convoys. His acts of personal courage have been also so daring, that his name alone strikes terror.

The two expresses dispatched successively to Toledo for a reinforcement having fallen into the hands of the patriots, we were obliged to halt a second day at Mora (November 28), and to kill time, a *partie de chasse* was proposed. From the preparations of hawking bags, powder and shot, flasks, and other sporting apparatus, as well as from the conversation on the subject, I anticipated an excellent day's sport: but a sportsman only can conceive my disappointment, when I found that the game was confined to larks and sparrows; nor did my companions expect to meet any other than these last poor birds.

We in four hours killed a couple of dozen, who were tranquilly picking up the scattered grains of corn in the yard of a corn mill, which, together with half a dozen larks, a couple of tomtits, a robin redbreast, and a wren, constituted our day's sport. In this true Cockney shooting party we were accompanied by a hundred cavalry and infantry.

On our return, I was invited to dine with Monsieur Denia at six o'clock; the dinner was not, however, served till past eight, and was as cold as the weather, which was extremely severe, and kept me in a shivering fit, though seated next to Madame Benedicio, whose rotundity of waist and ruddiness of countenance would have entitled her to be drawn as the emblem of the rising sup. The produce of our day's sport, roasted on wooden skewers, were served up as head and foot dishes, and afforded as animated a conversation on shooting, as if we had been grouse or deer-shooting in the Highlands of Scotland. Our wine was little better than vinegar, and as I could not get a drop of brandy to qualify it, I was obliged to accept a glass of *agua ardiente* from a soldier's canteen.

On my return to my quarters, I found a French officer had put his baggage into my apartment, which I did not much relish at first; but he soon waited on me, and apologised so politely for his intrusion, that I could not be angry. He greatly resembled the pictures I have seen of Charles the Twelfth, having a long beard and bald head. He assured me that these had been his regular quarters for the last three months, whenever he was allowed to sleep in a bed; but added, that not having his boots off for three weeks, one night more would make no difference, and he insisted on not deranging me.

Of course I repaid his politeness, by expressing my satisfaction at the accident that led to our acquaintance. As I found he had served in Egypt, we passed a part of the night conversing on the military and civil proceedings of the French in that country, over a bowl of punch and a *segar*.

November 29. Early in the morning we set out on our last day's march for Toledo, leaving on our right the strong castle of Almunaire, near which a battle was fought the preceding year, between the French and Spaniards, the former commanded by Sebastiani. Colonel Watalais, of the engineers, who was in our convoy, had been present at this affair, and pointed out to me the plain on which the Spaniards were drawn up, without any protection either to their front or flanks.

He acknowledged that the French deserved little credit for the defeat of a mere set of peasants, hastily collected, badly armed, and without discipline or commanders, or even confidence in each other; so that the line being once broken, it was impossible to reform it, and a total rout and dreadful carnage took place. The town of Almunaire had been reduced to ashes, as well as that of Arano, between it and Toledo, where another battle was fought with equal ill success on the part of the Spaniards.

In this affair the infantry was commanded by Soult and Mortier, and the cavalry by Sebastiani, who is, however, but a general of infantry; .but the French often make these transpositions, every Frenchman being supposed to possess universal genius.

On approaching Toledo, the country becomes mountainous and less fertile; and the road by which the town is entered, is absolutely dangerous for carriages, from its steep and rocky declivity, and its bad state. It leads to a bridge across the Tagus, from which the view is romantically wild.

CHAPTER 14

Campaign in Flanders

We entered Toledo by the gate of St. Martin, near which the first object that attracts notice is the tomb of Caba, daughter of Count St. Julian, whose violation by Roger the First, King of the Goths, was the cause of the invasion of Spain by the Moors. When this crime was perpetrated, St. Julian, who was of the blood royal of Spain, was Governor of Ceuta, on the coast of Barbary, and determining to revenge the affront offered to his family in the person of his daughter, solicited the assistance of the Caliph of Bagdad, whom in return he promised to aid in the conquest of Spain, which could not be difficult, the Spaniards detesting the yoke of the Goths.

The Caliph accordingly sent ten thousand men, under the command of a general named Tariff,[1] who landed at Gibraltar, and met with little difficulty in the conquest of Andalusia, so that the Caliph the following year sent forty thousand men, under Mufa, who subdued the peninsula with the exception of Asturias, and founded the empire of the Moors in Spain.

The *patricide* St. Julian retired to Bagdad, where it is supposed he was poisoned, and his daughter dying at Toledo, the capital of the kingdom of Andalusia, under the Moors, the tomb I have mentioned was erected over her remains.

Immediately on my arrival at my quarters, I received an invitation to dinner from General Lavoiser, and, *en attendant*, I ac-

---

1. Tariffa, now so conspicuous, near Gibraltar, for the defence lately made by Colonel Skerrett and the 47th regiment, was so called from Tariff's landing there.

companied him to visit the cathedral. It being the fête, of St. Andrew, high mass was celebrating, so that we were obliged to wait until it was finished, to see the church more circumstantially.

We visited the cloisters, the walls of which are finely painted in imitation of *bas relief*, by Francisco Bayeu, a modern artist, the painting not being twenty years old, and who certainly merits greater celebrity than he has acquired. The most striking picture represents the inside of a prison, the figures being the natural size, and the relief so perfect, that it is scarcely possible to avoid believing one's self in the company of living captives, insomuch that one instantaneously looks round for a way to escape, which seems to be prevented by iron bars and surrounding naked walls.

In short, this representation is, in painting, what Sterne's picture of Captivity is in writing. Another of the paintings represents mendicants receiving alms, at the bottom of the staircase of a great house; over the banisters of which two persons are leaning and giving them money; a third is the figure of a woman in the middle of a passage, soliciting charity; her outstretched arm and open hand, her doleful countenance, tattered garments, and appearance of superlative wretchedness, so compleatly deceived me for the moment, that I involuntarily put my hand into my pocket to relieve her.

There are also some paintings in the same style by Morelli, but so inferior, as only to serve as foils to those of Bayeu. At one end of the cloister is a column, with a Latin inscription denoting the consecration of the church in 630, and in the first year of the reign of the Gothic King, Flavius Recoredo. It is as follows:

In nomina Deii consecra
Ia eclesia Scta. Maria
In Catolico dio primo .
Idus Aprilis anno felicitur primo regni Domini
Nostri gloriosissimmi Fl. Recaredi regis era.
DCXXX.

This cathedral was converted into a mosque by the Moors,

but they were obliged to restore it to the Christians by Queen Constance, who dispossessed them of it by an armed force. It was rebuilt by Ferdinand in 1227. The inside is three hundred and forty-eight feet long by one hundred and sixty-four wide.

The *sacristie* is supported by a great number of white marble columns, and the pavement is of large alternate squares of white and black marble. The numerous secondary altars are richly ornamented with sculpture, and have some valuable paintings. Round the aisle are several monuments of the archbishops, and other dignitaries of the cathedral, and a great number of white marble statues of saints, *patriarchs*, and prophets in niches. Among the pictures, one of the Transfiguration is esteemed of the highest value. In the sanctuary are many interesting historical statues, particularly one of the shepherd, who guided King Alfonzo the Eighth at the battle of *las* Nieva de Tolosa, and one of the Moorish king Alfaqui.

In the *sacristie* are also the tombs of Alfonzo the Seventh, and of the Cardinal Pedro de Mendoza; the latter consists of several figures, of which an evangelist at each of the four corners, in *bas relief*, are inimitably executed: this monument is surrounded by an iron railing.

Of the numerous chapels within the cathedral, that of St. Peter is most worthy of notice; it was rebuilt in 1791, and now serves as a parish church. The architecture is gothic, and the altars and tables are composed of the most scarce and valuable marbles; the principal picture in it is St. Peter curing the lame at the gate of the Temple, by Vallego. The chapel de los Reges Nuovos, or New King's Chapel, contains the tombs of many of the sovereigns and princes of Spain, particularly those of John, eldest son of Henry the Second, and his wife Eleanor; of Catherine, wife of Henry the Third, with a statue of John the Second, whose, remains are at Mirapalous, near Burgos. This chapel has also a large picture of the birth of Christ.

In the chapel of St. James, among other objects of merit, are the magnificent tombs of Fereguolo, Archbishop of Toledo, who died in 1742, and that of Alvarez de Luna, Grand Master of the

Order of St. James, and Constable of Castile, the favourite and prime minister of John this Second, but who lost his head by order of that sovereign at Valladolid, in 1452. At each corner of this monument is a figure the size of life, kneeling with the strongest expression of sorrow, and it has besides many fine *bas reliefs*.

Passing the chapel of St. Ildefonso, in which there are some things worthy of notice, that of Nuestra Senoria del Sacrario most forcibly calls the attention. It consists of three distinct chapels; one, from its octagon shape, is called the Octravo; the second is square, and immensely rich, the floor and pillars being of the most beautiful marbles, and the ceiling finely painted by Carducho; and the third is also an octagon, and equally rich, having several golden urns set with diamonds and placed in niches, and an image of the infant Jesus, a foot high, of solid gold, ornamented with precious stones. On a throne of massive silver formerly rested an image of the Virgin, but both throne and image have vanished; a large silver *brasiero*, however, still remains, doubtless to form, with the other valuables, a *bonne bouche* for the French on a future day. The image of the Virgin in this chapel is of the most exquisite workmanship.

The *vestriano*, which adjoins the *sacristie*, as well is another adjacent apartment, still contains some rich church furniture, though the French have taken care of the most valuable. Amongst those which remain are a dress of the Virgin, covered with pearls, and the archbishop's robes of the richest embroidered stuffs. In this apartment are, also emblematical representations of the four quarters of the world.

The *sacristie* is finely ornamented, the dome painted by Jordan, the tables of beautiful yellow marble, and the numerous pictures encased in frames of gold, bronze, and different marbles. The most valuable paintings are a Samaritan by Reubens, the Deluge by Bassan, an Assumption, I believe, by d'Onento, the Division of Christ's Garments by the same artist, and a St. Augustine. The tabernacle is of the most superb workmanship; and the library contains a very large collection of books, and above seven thousand manuscripts.

Before the grand gate of the cathedral is a small terrace, enclosed by an iron railing, with six columns of white marble, each surmounted by a lion of the same material. The gate itself, and the architecture round it, are ornamented with a variety of sculptured figures, but rather too much crowded, and some good statues.

Having amply satisfied my curiosity in the cathedral, we next visited the archiepiscopal palace, now occupied by a French general. It is a large uncomfortable building, remarkable for nothing but a library, in which are some scarce books and manuscripts.

From this place I proceeded to the general's, where I found a large party had been invited to meet me. The moment we sat down the general informed me, that he had purposely provided a treat of roast beef and plum pudding, both of which he assured me were drest *à l'Anglaise*; and carving an immense slice, which proved to be scarcely warmed, he exclaimed triumphantly, "*du moins je crois que cela doit être à votre goût!*"

This exclamation drew on me the eyes of the whole company, who seemingly expected, with anxious curiosity, to see me devour this raw and tough carrion; and as I could not with politeness send, it away untouched, I forced myself to swallow a few mouthfuls, which a glass of brandy assisted me to keep down. The plum pudding was then served up, and could only be equalled in execrableness by the beef, being a solid lump of half-boiled dough, that would have required the powers of an ostrich to digest.

Added to these little *désagrémens*, the general was most tiresomely civil, particularly with his hands, which were scarce a moment off my shoulders. He also wearied me with the history of his achievements, when commanding a body of cavalry under General Pichegru, in Holland and Flanders; and when he learnt that I had been, in the same campaign, he entered into some particulars which were not uninteresting to me.

He, I found, commanded the cavalry at Boxtel, near Bois-le-Duc, at the affair of Michael Ghastel's Bridge, where I was engaged, under General Dœering, and where the Hesse Darmstadt troops were severely cut up, losing in killed, wounded, and prisoners, nineteen hundred men, out of two thousand five hundred, while the 89th regiment, which I commanded, successfully resisted the same force of the enemy; though not without considerable loss.

To whatever cause the destruction of the Hesse Darmstadt troops was owing, General Dœering felt it so severely, I understand, that he shot himself shortly after the action; and my regiment, in consequence of its loss, was ordered to fall back on a detachment commanded by Sir William Erskine, at Middleroad. The following morning detachments of the Guards, and of the 12th and 33rd regiments, under the command of Sir Ralph Abercrombie, marched to attack the enemy, but finding them considerably reinforced by Pichegru himself, the British were obliged to fall back, and the retreat of the whole army followed.

This military conversation being only interesting to the general and myself, I endeavoured to render it more general, by questioning a well informed priest respecting Toledo, and other subjects. The general, who is certainly one of the vainest of Frenchmen, although in all respects a *bon garçon*, soon interrupted our conversation by a long eulogium on his snuffbox, which on my praising he insisted on my accepting, with, "*c'est bien à votre service, et je votes prie de la garder comme un souvenir,*" and on my repeated rejection, it was "*mettez-la dans votre poche, je vous en prie,*" at the same time squeezing my hand with such warmth, that at one time I could have really thought him sincere.

But *à propos* of snuffboxes and sincerity: I remember in Sicily a Highland quarter master, a rough diamond, who taking a Sicilian marquis at his word, quietly pocketed a snuffbox thus pressed on him; but nothing being farther from the marquis's intention or expectation, he complained to me, as commanding officer, that he had been robbed of his snuffbox.

On enquiry I found, from the testimony of all the officers present, that the marquis had really pressed the box on the quarter master, who deeming his right to keep it undoubted, regarded not my representations, that such offers made by foreigners were considered by them as mere words of course. The value of the box, which he had nicely estimated, as well as the advice of the junior officers, who wished to see some fun, made him resolute in his determination, and it was with a good deal of difficulty that I at last persuaded him to return it.

On enquiring if he was under any other obligation to the marquis, he replied, that he recollected none except for a glass of water, And that he would repay it, when, calling for a tumbler of water, he presented it to the marquis, saying, "Now, *Mynheer*, we are quits;" for having served in Holland, where he discovered that *mynheer* signified sir, he concluded it was the same in every other foreign country.

But to return to the general's. After dinner several visitors arriving, be proposed retiring up stairs, where were prepared a good fire, plenty of punch, and cards. After a sober rubber at whist, the punch beginning to mount, *Trente et Quarante* was introduced; but as my purse was rather low, I told the general I could not play deep, when he produced a heap of gold and begged me to help myself. At first I had a run of extreme bad luck, and became considerably in debt, but fortune changing, I at last rose a winner to the amount of four hundred pounds.

Chapter 15

From Toledo to Madrid

November 30. It being daylight before I could get away from the general, I found the convoy in motion, and consequently was obliged to mount my house, without having been in bed. We passed through the city from end to end, and through a highly ornamented gate, outside of which is a fine promenade.

The Tagus surrounds about two-thirds of Toledo, and was navigable from this city to the sea in 1588. The quay, at which the boats loaded and discharged, is still to be seen, and is called the Plaza de los Barces. The town is built on hills, the streets in general are very narrow, and many of the houses in ruin; the whole presenting the appearance of poverty and decline.

Though the general had united me to partake of a sumptuous breakfast, I preferred a crust of ration bread and a glass of spirits in the open air, to the necessity of submitting a second time to his great attention.

I was somewhat surprised at finding General Lavoisier in the convoy, for though he swore to me that his friendship was so great that he would accompany me to Madrid, I put no more faith in his sincerity in this respect, than I had done in that of the snuffbox. He insisted that I should live with him during the journey; but as I did not admire this plan, I begged to decline his polite offer.

A part of our escort consisted of a detachment of the Hesse Darmstadt regiment, in garrison at Toledo, and among the officers were several who had served in the British pay in Holland.

A Spanish regiment also guarded us; and it would be difficult to say which, the Spaniards or Germans, were most brutal in their conduct to the prisoners.

On the march I was addressed by a soldier, who at first pretended to be a Spaniard; but on observing to him that his broad brogue denoted the green isle of his nativity too plainly to admit of his deceiving me, he acknowledged that he had deserted from the 87th regiment, he recounted the misery to which the French troops in Spain are often reduced, and said that he had suffered so much since his desertion, that he would willingly undergo any punishment, short of death, to be once more restored to his country. I listened to him with the more satisfaction, as he was overheard by some of our soldiers, who had shewn symptoms of an intention of entering the French service.

We passed through a country, of which the soil is a deep clay, retaining the marks of cultivation though it now lays waste, and arrived at the miserable village of Allascas, which, as well as others in the neighbourhood, were more than half destroyed by the French. Here, there being no quarters whatever for our officers, they were obliged to take part of mine, which were very little better than a stable.

On the 1st of December, the convoy set out at daylight for Madrid, but my mules not being ready I walked on with the rearguard, composed of a detachment of the 18th Légère, a regiment I was well acquainted with, from its having been continually opposed to us in Egypt. On quitting the village I was witness to the cruel treatment of a poor old Spaniard, whom the French soldiers not only robbed of the things he was carrying to market, but also beat most unmercifully. My own safety I perceived rendered silence prudent, for had I remonstrated, it was very probable these ruffians would have murdered me without hesitation.

As my mules were still behind, I entered into conversation with a dragoon who led his horse, and who entertained me with the feats of arms he had achieved, particularly in the campaign of Portugal. He passed the highest eulogium on Massena, who he had no doubt would chase the English into the sea; a prophecy which has however turned out as false as that of his imperial master, on the same subject. In order to get rid of this fellow's tiresome babble, I quitted the road for the fields, where, putting up a hare and some partridges, my attention was entirely drawn to them, and the mules passed me on the road without my observing them.

On returning to the road and not seeing them, I supposed they were still behind, and walked back nearly three miles to meet them, but not doing so I began to fear some accident, particularly as the people I met on the road had all the appearance of brigands. I therefore returned towards the convoy, and soon perceived my servant galloping towards me.

As we were now approaching Madrid, the general mounted his charger, and put on his full uniform, which is superb in the extreme, and consequently calculated to inspire respect in the soldiery, though the hat, edged with feathers, certainly too much resembled that of a drum-major, and reminded me of the anecdote of a cockney sportsman, who in the confusion of a first essay, seeing some feathers waving over a hedge, instantly fired, and lo, shot off the head of a recruiting serjeant.

On our right was pointed out to us a ruined chapel in which one of the general's *aides-de-camp*, with four other officers and sixty men, were attacked a few days before by the brigands, who set the chapel on fire and burnt every soul of the party. We rode to examine this ensanguined spot, in which were still seen the half consumed carcases of these victims of retaliation, who had been intercepted by a party of *Il Medico's* band on their return from Madrid, whither they had escorted a convoy. This sight seemed to shock the general and his officers, who could not help, expressing their detestation of the barbarous manner of carrying on the war.

The general being excessively vain, both of his horse and horsemanship, in order to shew them off, set out on a full gallop in the deepest part of the road; though on a miserable Spanish hack, I was determined to shew off too, and getting my beast into a prancing canter, I soon passed the general, who putting spurs to his horse, at the same time that he slacked the reins, and the animal being knee deep in mud, came down, as might be expected, and rolled over his rider.

The *aide-de-camp* and some *chasseurs* immediately ran to his assistance, but the miserable pickle he was in, and his ludicrous grimaces, almost discomposed their gravity, and they could scarce refrain from laughing aloud at the bedaubed face and uniform of their general, Such is the force of national pride even in trifles, that while I pitied the general's plight, I congratulated myself on having proved my superior horsemanship, for the honour of Old England; and my satisfaction was increased by reflecting, that had the same accident happened to me, the whole detachment would have triumphed both at the expense of my country and myself.

A short halt was the consequence of the general's mishap, and when he was rubbed down tolerably clean, we proceeded towards Madrid over a flat and well cultivated country, but with much fewer villages, or inhabitants, than might have been expected so near the metropolis; these few however were much superior in appearance to those we had hitherto met with.

CHAPTER 16

Treatment of the Prisoners

Previous to entering Madrid we crossed a superb bridge of several elliptical arches, with a beautiful marble balustrade surmounted by marble statues. The gate of Toledo, by which we entered, is also very handsome, and creates a favourable prepossession of the general elegance of the city After riding through a great number of streets at full gallop, over a very slippery pavement, at the risk of breaking our necks, or being trampled to death if our horses came down, merely to gratify the absurd vanity of the French general, who wished to create astonishment, we arrived at a wretched *posada*,[1] where I was immediately visited by Messrs. Boulard and Cassadevant, merchants of respectability, who informed me that they had received notice from Mr. Kilpatrick at Malaga to furnish me with money.

General Lavoisier invited me to dine with him at General Beliard's; this honour I declined until I had presented my letters from General Sebastiani, which I did in the course of the day, and was received with great politeness, but was not a little surprised at learning, that by King Joseph's express order, I was to take up my quarters in the Retiro; to soften the harshness of which, however, the general said he would particularly recommend me to the commandant of that citadel.

I also delivered a letter from Monsieur Chevariere to his father, who immediately offered me the use of his house, and of everything in it; but when I only requested he would allow my

---
1. A public-house.

horse to be put in his empty stable out of the rain, the difficulties were so numerous that I begged he would give himself no trouble about it. Being at a loss where to seek for a dinner, I asked the advice of Monsieur Cassadevant, who shewed me to a dirty house, kept by Messrs. Briere and Colignon, where I got some good soup and a cutlet, and not without difficulty a bottle of Val de Penes, the other wines being execrable.

At an early hour I repaired to my quarters in the Retiro, to pass a most uncomfortable night on a hard bed swarming with vermin, and in the morning (December 2) was called up soon after daylight by the *adjutant de place*, who informed me in a most dictatorial manner that I was to accompany him to breakfast with General Beliard. While I was dressing he entered the room several times, exclaiming, "*allons donc, depechez-vous, le général vous attend.*"

At length he so tired my patience, that I told him, "if he was to accompany me, he might return to the general and inform him, I preferred staying where I was to having such an attendant," which sent him off grumbling. I however was following him, when to my great surprise the centinel at the gate stopped me, presenting his bayonet to my breast; I of course returned, and finding out the adjutant enquired if it was by the general's orders, I was thus made a close prisoner, or if the centinel acted from his orders only?

He replied, that the centinel received his orders, from the officers of the guard, of whom I immediately demanded by what authority he acted, and found, that in fact the orders originated with the adjutant; to this latter, I therefore stated, that the general having invited me to breakfast the evening before, could not be so inconsistent as to order my being prevented from accepting his invitation; that therefore I would again proceed, and if stopped would write to the general for an explanation.

This savage I suppose finding that he would be likely to get into a scrape, walked with me to the gate, and with much *nonchalance* ordered the centinel to let me pass; I had not however walked many paces before I found him close by my side, and as

I did not think it worthwhile to be angry with so insignificant a fellow, I entered into conversation with him. "*Apparemment, Monsieur est quelque temps adjutant de place.*"

"*Oui, parbleu, depuis le commencemeut*"

"*Monsieur est entré donc avec l'armée lorsqu'elle a pris possession de la ville.*"

"*Oui, parbleu!*"

He then told me, that he commanded a detachment of grenadiers; pointed out as we passed the beautiful gate d'Alcala, the principal point of attack at the angle of the Calle d'Alcala, and described the massacre of the inhabitants with such energetic marks of delight, that he seemed to fancy himself at the, moment in the act of perpetrating the horrors he recounted. I could not refrain from ejaculating an involuntary sigh of pity for those who should ever be in, the power of this wretch; and this feeling was not diminished by the recollection that I was myself at the moment thus situated.

These melancholy reflections were however dissipated by the cheerful elegance of the Prado which we were crossing: the immense number of statues, the numerous, fountains, pouring out streams of the purest water, the superb Calle d'Alcala, terminated by the Plaza de Sol, a perfect circus, with streets branching from it like rays from the sun, all united to fix entirely the attention.

On my arrival at General Belian's, I found several officers in the anti-room, and among them a Mr. Walsh, one of the general's *aides-de-camp*, who had formerly served in our 9th regiment of Infantry. Though this person seemed to wish to be extremely civil to me, I met his advances with; the greatest coolness; or rather with that contempt which every loyal man feels for the traitor to his country and king, when he considers the total dereliction of principle which must be the attendant of this species of crime; for even the wretch who hesitates not at robbing on the highway, feels for the glory of his country, and will resent the disrespectful mention of it as a personal insult; how low, therefore, must the man of family and education be degraded, before he can join the standard of his country's enemies!

After some time the general made his appearance; his little round figure was enveloped in a uniform covered with lace and embroidery. We immediately sat down to an excellent breakfast, in company with Generals Lavoisier, Buchot, and other officers. The general knew I had served in Egypt, where indeed I had rendered his countrymen an essential service, on war taking possession of Grand Cairo; for being there attached to the Grand *Vizier's* army, in a detachment commanded by Colonel Stuart, it was only by our strongest exertions that we were able to prevent the Turks from massacring all the French and their adherents that fell in their way.

The conversation, in consequence of our mutual recognition, turned on the affairs in Egypt after the French had quitted it; and on my relating the massacre of the *Beys*, the general observed that the evacuation of the country by the French was a real misfortune to its inhabitants, in which I could not help concurring. Indeed it would have been better, in the eye of humanity, had they remained, for the power of the Turks and Mamelukes being so equally balanced that neither of them can acquire a lasting superiority, the country suffers all the misery and desolation of an endless civil war.

The general informed me, on taking leave, that I was only to lodge in the Retiro until a *billet de logement* could be procured for me in better quarters.

In the course of the day I visited the Puerto del Sol, from which some of the principal streets of the city branch off, namely, the Calle de la Montera, de los Carrelas, d'Alcala, Mayor, la Carrera de St. Jeronimo, &c. The Plaza del Sol is open and cheerful, with a superb fountain in the middle, and surrounded by lofty elegant buildings; from its central situation it is the principal promenade of the loungers of Madrid, and the rendezvous of the merchants.

In the Plaza Mayor is the chief vegetable market; it is of an oval figure, three hundred and fifty to four hundred feet long, and three hundred wide; the houses are all of five stories, well built, and each has a *portico* of hewn stone, balconies, and an iron railing before the windows. The centre house on one side of the *Plaza* is called la Casa de la Panadeira; and was appropriated formerly to receive the royal family, during public spectacles of bullfights, fireworks, &c. which were exhibited in this place. I entered the court of this building, which presented nothing but dirt and neglect, except that in its centre still remained a marble statue of Diana. This edifice was burnt down in 1672 and 1790, and after the last conflagration rebuilt with superior magnificence.

The greater number of the streets leading from the Plaza Mayor by no means correspond with it, being narrow, dirty, and generally ill built. There are, however, a few worthy of the metropolis of a great kingdom, particularly the Calle de Toledo, la Carrera de St. Jeronimo de Antiocha, del Prado, Calle Mayor, and Calle d'Alcala, which latter is inferior to none in Europe, for width and elegant termination.

After having amused myself in this promenade I visited General Lavoisier, who invited me to dinner, and recapitulated his bill of fare, which was sumptuous; he also proposed a plan for spending the evenings, by first attending the theatre, and then visiting some ladies of his acquaintance, where we should find an elegant *petit souper*, which was too agreeable to my wishes not to be immediately acceded to. The officers having represented the situation of the men as extremely bad, I enquired into the subject, and found several English and Maltese sailors confined with a considerable number of Germans in a small dungeon, where the air could not be renewed, and that the only provisions they received were black bread and water.

I remonstrated with the *adjutant de place* on this treatment, which must inevitably send many of the prisoners to die hospital, if not to the grave; and received, as I expected, a surly and evasive answer: indeed there could not exist a more unfeeling brute, nor one whose manners and appearance more clearly indicated a proper instrument for the perpetration of the most heinous acts. My remonstrances were, therefore, at this time in vain, nor could I even procure permission for the prisoners to visit the fresh air once a day under a guard.

At the dinner hour I repaired to General Lavoisier, feasting in imagination on the sumptuous repast he had announced to me; but was rather disappointed to find he had forgot to say he dined at home, and consequently that no dinner was prepared; I therefore, after waiting him a note to tell him I had waited on him according to his invitation, ordered dinner at Briere and Collignon's, which, though it wanted all the good things, I expected to find at the general's, had at least the, comfort of not laying me under, an obligation.

In the evening I received a visit from a Monsieur Longeau, a French merchant, who offered me his services with great civility. Knowing, however, that we were perfect strangers, and particularly as people are seldom so polite without some sinister view, I was cautious in my conversation with this gentleman, and more particularly as his first subject was very suspicious, for he entered fully into the situation of the French at Madrid, as well as into the characters of Generals Beliard and Lavoisier, and, from the anecdotes he related of the latter, I found that I ought not to be surprised at his forgetting having invited me to dinner.

I however related the circumstance, adding that I was rejoiced at the general's forgetfulness, as it had procured me the acquaintance *d'un homme d'esprit tel que monsieur*, in return for which compliment he launched into an encomium on England and the English. Our conversation next turned on the history of Spain, and I could not help losing sight for a moment of my prudential reserve, when I recollected the glorious epoch of Ferdinand and Isabella, and compared it with the present moment. The Frenchman abused the whole conduct of his government with such virulence, that my suspicions of him were increased, and I changed the conversation to the objects worthy of a stranger's notice in Madrid, with which he seemed to be well acquainted, and offered to accompany me in my perambulations, a civility which I accepted.

Chapter 17

Spanish Generosity

During the time I remained at Madrid, I amused myself with visiting the edifices most worthy of notice, and of which I shall endeavour to give my readers an idea; without attending to the particular days on which I saw them. My first visit was to the Cabinet of Natural History, whither I was accompanied by Monsieur Longeau, who proved an excellent Cicerone. The apartments of this building, which is situated in the Calle d'Alcala, are by no means prepossessing; but I found the objects they contained well worthy of attention: indeed, no country has had greater facilities of forming a collection of this nature than Spain, from her vast foreign possessions. I shall, however, confine myself to mentioning those which are esteemed the most rare and valuable.

>1. A specimen of crystal, named *Pietras figuratos espata calcareo*, which doubles the images presented to it. It came from Biscay.
>2. An extensive and fine collection of Spanish marbles, the most beautiful of which are from Loja and Xenil.
>3. Some specimens of rich silver ore from the mines of Almeria.
>4. A lump of virgin gold, as taken out of the mine, weighing 16 lb. 8 oz.
>5. A lump of virgin silver, weighing 265 lb. 3 oz.
>6. Several specimens of crystallized antimony, sulphur, iron, &c.

7. Several agates and other stones.
8. A large collection of sponges.
9. A human skull, with a pair of horns sprouting from it. On enquiry, I found it belonged to a Spaniard, but could not learn whether he was married or not!
10. Many specimens of petrified woods.
11. A mummy, very perfect.
12. A Mexican about to be pounded to death in a mortar.
13. A beautiful striped eagle, called the Imperial.

In the second apartment I noticed,

1. The skeleton of an animal, exceeding the mammoth in bulk, whose teeth denote it to have been carnivorous; but its family is unknown. Found in the Rio de la Plata.
2. Some Egyptian figures, taken in the *Flora* frigate.
3. The bark of some curious trees.
4. Several ornaments of teeth worn round the body and head.
5. The representation of some Spanish arms in shell work.

In the third apartment:

1. A dinner and desert service in jasper, onyx, and agate, said to be four hundred years older than the Christian era.
2. A singularly shaped beautiful shell, for which we were told that nine millions of *reals* had been offered.
3. Several topaz cups and a bowl of *lapis lazuli*.
4. A black topaz.
5. A service of plate, presented by Louis XIV.
6. The (Conquest of Mexico in Mosaic.
7. A dress of the Emperor of China.
8. Some American paintings.

The fourth apartment, named the *Salle de la Junto*, chiefly contains pictures, of which several are very valuable, particularly;

A group of Bacchanals, by Reubens.
A St. Jeronimo, by Murillo.
A Virgin, copied from Raphael.
A Woman and Child, by Murillo, peculiarly fine.
A Transfiguration, by Raphael.
An Assumption, by Cespedes.
An Ave, by Raphael.

In the fifth apartment are some well executed bronze figures.

A Venus, by Titian.
A Model of the Ruins of Saguntum.
Statues of Achilles and Patrocles.
A Statue of Venus.
The Battle of the Horatii and Curiatii, in relief.

Having detained my companion a whole day in taking only a cursory view of this museum, I invited him to dine with me at Briere and Colignon's, and was entertained by his volubility; though it was with him, as with most of his countrymen, *vox et pretœrea nihil.*—After dinner I received a visit from, an officer of the 26th Chasseurs à Cheval, to request my company at a Masonic meeting. The forms of admission were very serious; but I went through them sufficiently well, and received a warm welcome from the brethren, particularly from Colonel Vial, commanding the 26th Chasseurs, who was master of the lodge, and who invited me to supper and to dinner the next day.

At supper, when the punch began to mount, each played some ridiculous trick to divert the company; one making hideous grimaces; another taking off a priest in his robe, by means of a towel: on his fingers; a third-shaped mice out of the parings of apples, &c. &c. Indeed, I must do the French the justice to acknowledge that they far excel us in the art of making fools of themselves *pour passer le temps.*

On rising one morning I learnt, as I had foretold, that several of the prisoners had been obliged to be sent to the hospital, and that some serious quarrels had taken place between the English and Germans; finding also that the only provision yet supplied them was bread and water, I made enquiry whether the Government really allowed nothing more, and found that it contracted for half a pound of meat per man *per diem,* and consequently that there was a gross imposition somewhere. I therefore again addressed myself to the *adjutant de place,* who, as usual, fell into a passion, and endeavoured to bully me into silence; but finding me determined not to remain a tame spectator of the cruel and fraudulent treatment of those, for whom both duty and humanity called upon me to interfere, his passion knew no bounds, and he was about to draw his sword on me, though unarmed and a prisoner, when I told him that I had but one life to lose, and that I would cheerfully lay it down for the satisfaction of chastising such a ruffian, and procuring justice for my countrymen mid fellow sufferers; that if he attempted to draw his sword, he should mark the consequence; and that at all events I would write to General Beliard on the subject of the prisoners, for I was well assured that it was with his (the adjutant's) connivance that they were thus shamefully cheated of their provisions. This I immediately did, and meat was in consequence afterwards issued.

The condition of the prisoners while their allowance was thus withheld, would have been truly deplorable, had not the Spanish inhabitants generously assisted them; and it was not uncommon to see women of respectability conveying to them not only victuals but clothes, though they were repeatedly repulsed by the guards, who were also sometimes softened by the charms of the females employed in those acts of humanity. As I had gained my point in the article of meat, I thought it better to drop all appearance of animosity towards the adjutant; and one day, when a beautiful girl solicited permission to, deliver some victuals to the prisoners in his presence, and was refused, I addressed him with "*Monsieur est François?*"

To which he replied, "*Parbleu, oui!*"

I then continued,

formerly the French were conspicuous above all the nations of the world for their gallantry and complaisance towards the fair sex, and I cannot conceive it possible that so great a change has taken place in their manners, that a Frenchman can deny the request of a charming girl, to be permitted to do a benevolent action, in succouring the distressed prisoner!

This address had the desired effect in softening the adjutant, who admitted not only the girl in question, but several others, to converse with the prisoners, and bring them provisions, shirts, and other necessaries.

While at dinner one day with Colonel Vial, I was waited on by a Monsieur Guillet, who, with a profusion of compliments, informed me that he had prepared apartments for me in his house, concluding in like usual style of French sincerity, "*disposez de moi en tout ce que pouvez vous faire plaisir*"

On enquiring into the character of this person, I found it was not one of the best; but being aware that the French, as well as the Irish, abuse each other without cause, I paid little attention to the report; besides I had no alternative but to remain uncomfortably at the Retiro, or to accept his offer; and though I strongly suspected that he was intended to be placed as a spy over me, I prepared to take up my quarters in his house; besides, I learnt that he was a connoisseur in paintings, and received a salary from King Joseph, to collect the most valuable pictures. I therefore hoped to receive much information from him on this subject; and on my making my wishes known to him, he offered to accompany me the following day to view the best collections.

In our way to the palace, we crossed the Prado, which I have already mentioned as probably the most superb promenade in the world, and being almost the only one at Madrid, it is crowded with people, whose dresses and equipages cannot fail to amuse the stranger. In both respects the Spaniards are at least a century behind the English or French.

Here we see a coachman with a bag wig, a livery covered with gold lace, and an enormous cocked hat, all appearing to have served several generations, awkwardly driving at a snail's pace, a pair of mules in harness of crimson velvet, covered with a profusion of gilt buckles and plates, their manes platted with various coloured ribbands, falling in large bowknots, and attached to a heavy carriage, carved and gilded all over, through the glasses of which is seen an ancient *Grandee*, in full dress; but while admiring his serious air, you are roused from your reverie by the rattle of wheels, and on turning, observe a modern Hidalgo, or *parvenu*, of French fabric, galloping over the pavement in a light carriage, drawn by six or seven mules, and with several running footmen or outriders, in the most tawdry and ridiculous liveries. The pedestrians form a no less strange contrast in the mixture of French officers, Spanish merchants and citizens, all laughing at each other's costume, and each unconscious of what is ridiculous in his own; for it is plainly perceptible that the *toilette* has occupied the minds of all. in the preparation for exhibition on the Prado.

The Prado commences at the, ancient convent of Antiocha, at this time converted into an hospital, and extends to the Calle d'Alcala, at the entrance of which is a magnificent fountain, representing the goddess Cybele in the centre of a white marble bason, and in a chariot drawn by lions; she holds in her hand a key, the emblem of her attributes, as the goddess of cities and garrisons. The whole is in white marble inimitably executed.

The only fault in the Calle d'Alcala: is a small bend, which considerably injures the effect that would he produced if it was perfectly straight. The Puerta d'Alcala, which terminates it, consists of three superb arches, of which the middle is considerably the largest, being about thirty feet high and fourteen broad. The gates are iron richly worked, and the pillars white marble of the Ionic order. Besides the three great arches, destined for carriages and horsemen, on the east side is a lesser one for pedestrians. The total elevation of the gate is sixty feet, and the architrave is ornamented with lions' heads, &c.

Towards the end of the Calle d'Alcala is a fountain, representing Neptune and his queen, whom the god embraces round the waist; they are standing in a scallop shell, drawn by Hippopotami and attended by Nereids. A marble bason receives the water. This street contains also several other pieces of sculpture, and on one side of it is a botanic garden founded by Charles the Third, where a course of lectures are given *gratis*.

On the right in ascending the street is an unfinished palace, named Buonavista, built by the Prince of Peace; it is very extensive, but not free from faults, particularly in the windows, which are out of all proportion small. It however boasts a good collection of pictures by Murillo, Reubens, Bayeu, Velasquez, &c. amongst which the Marriage of the Adriatic, a pug dog by Velasquez, and a Virgin by Murillo, are peculiarly excellent. In one of the apartments is a bronze statue of Charles the Fifth, which takes to pieces; and it would seem that turning is a favourite amusement of princes, for in another room is a lathe, and all the implements employed in that art.

This palace has been several times on fire, and indeed accidents of this nature are surprisingly common throughout Spain, where the houses have not one-third of the timber employed in those of England and France. The principal apartments of this building were now filled with corn and wool.

The palace of the Duke of Medina Sidonia occupies a considerable portion of the Calle d'Alcala, and has one of its fronts towards the Prado; after having been compleatly plundered, it was taken possession of by Monsieur Demo, commissary general of the French army. The duke on the entry of the French fled so precipitately, that he did not carry off even his diamonds, which fell into the hands of the invaders.

After viewing these buildings I dined with my officers at the Fonda St Martin, which, though it has a high reputation, I found wretched enough; indeed the *traiteurs* in Spain at this time labour under one great *désagrément*, which renders them little anxious to please, for the great majority of their guests being French officers, who often in their hurry forget to settle their bills, those who have more correct memories are obliged, not only to make up the *deficit*, but also suffer in the quality and manner of their entertainment.

A party of French officers was this day dining at an adjoining table, most of whom retired after a very short repast. Amongst the few who remained was a respectable looking elderly man, with whom I entered into conversation, and found him a pleasant and well informed person, very different from those who had withdrawn, whose conversation turned solely on their achievements in love and war. One of those *braggadocios* had seated himself at our table, and attempted to join in conversation, but I suppose being *ennuyé* with English taciturnity, he soon left us and returned to his own table, where, to shew his spite, he wantonly broke several plates and glasses. In this frolic I encouraged him, from the pleasure, malicious I allow, of his increasing his bill under the article of breakages.

CHAPTER 18

French Over-Civility

Having shifted my quarters to the house of Mr. Guillet, I accepted his invitation to, dinner; but though it was good in itself, so annoying was the super-attention of my host and hostess, that I determined not to be a second time surfeited by it, and to avoid all *eclaircissement* I removed my things secretly back to the Retiro, preferring even a prison to the abominable tiresomeness of the civility with which these people overwhelmed me. Their ideas of politeness led them to think they ought not to leave me a moment alone; consequently I was tormented to death with their insipid company. While at dinner, because I could not eat like a ploughman, the lady every instant hoped I was not indisposed, or feared that there was nothing to my liking. Perhaps I carry my dislike of ceremonious manners farther than is strictly just, for nothing can annoy me more than wishing me a formal good morning at the end of a visit, or pressing me to sit down at its commencement.

The Retiro, which I thus preferred to my new quarters, and which was now full of prisoners, consists of a large square, with a smaller one on the left, and one side of another on the right The buildings are very irregular, and without ornaments. When the occasional residence of the Spanish monarchs, there was a theatre in the centre of the great court, which was now demolishing to employ the materials somewhere else. The menagerie is an octagon, with pens round it for the animals, and a gallery above, from which they could be looked down upon with safety;

the only beast now remaining was a bear, blind with old age. The gardens, as well as the buildings, were entirely neglected: the *jets d'eau* no longer acted, and the basins, which were filled by engines, the site of the Retiro being higher than the town, were entirely empty. The gardens were strewed with fragments of sculpture and mutilated statues; that of Narcissus alone remaining perfect, because it was out of the immediate reach of the destroyers. In short, the whole edifice presented the appearance of the devastations of the Goths and Vandals, rather than the visit of the encouragers and protectors of the arts, as the French stile themselves.

In one of the squares however still remained an equestrian statue of Philip the Second, in bronze, weighing 18,000 lb and which is fixed in the pedestal by the hind legs of the horse only. There are also a few other statues entire, particularly that of Charles the First, with a laurel wreath; and in a small apartment, with marble columns, those of Philip the Second and Mary Queen of Hungary.

In a small separate garden are also those of Ferdinand and Isabella. This palace had formerly one of the best collections of pictures to be found in Europe, containing several *chefs d'oeuvre* of Reubens, Titian, Poussin, Jordan, Ricci, Zarborea, Carte, and other masters; all of which have been removed. Several royal manufactures were established within the walls, particularly of tapestry and porcelain, which were established by Charles the Third, but have declined since his death, and have now entirely ceased. In fact, the only manufactures that Madrid still possesses to employ its numerous population, are some very insignificant ones, of coarse woollens, hats and paper.

As I found the English prisoners ware suffering much from the inclemency of the weather and the want of warm clothing, I directed each man to be supplied with a pair of woollen pantaloons, a shirt and pair of stockings. For the two first articles I procured the cloth and gave it the men to make for themselves, so that in the course of a day or two I had the satisfaction of seeing the poor fellows comparatively comfortable; and in doing this, it certainly cost me nothing but a little personal trouble, as I drew bills for the amount on account of the soldiers arrears. When it is thus easy to relieve the wants of the distressed, be must be entirely destitute of humanity who neglects doing so.

Several Spanish officers were confined in the Retiro, and were supplied by their country women with provisions and clothes; for I had occasion to observe, that whatever part the husbands take, the females adhere to the loyal side, and consider those who suffer in the cause as martyrs for their religion and their country. Besides the Spanish prisoners taken in arms, several persons of respectability were also confined in the same prison, because they could not or would not pay the heavy contributions demanded by the French.

With these I often entered into conversation, and found them animated by the most inveterate hatred of their invaders, and with the perfect confidence that they would ultimately not only be driven out of the country, but that a Spanish and English army would cross the Pyrenees, and retaliate in the heart of France the miseries they were suffering.

Learning that Mr. Coosfeld, one of the partners off Hope's house at Amsterdam, and whom I had formerly, known, was at Madrid, I called on him. He was not a little surprised at finding me a prisoner in the capital of Spain; but for my own part, I have had so many extraordinary and unexpected rencounters in the course, of my life, that nothing of this kind seems strange to me, and I felt more pleasure than surprise at this meeting. Mr. C. told me that his business at Madrid was to endeavour to recover large sums of money lent by his house to the late government; and I have since learnt, what indeed was only to have been expected, that his mission was entirely unsuccessful.

In the evening of the same day, after haying dined with some French officers, I accompanied them to the theatre, called Canons del Peral, and found both the house and performance equally wretched; the former being inconvenient, filthy and ill lighted, and the latter a miserable attempt at opera, which was barbarously murdered. The French, who swallow their dinner in a moment and content themselves with a few glasses of common wine while eating, find in the playhouse, however bad it may be, a resource against the *ennui* of a long and idle evening.

There were formerly two other theatres at Madrid, but both were now shut. Indeed, since the death of Ferdinand the Sixth, the Spanish theatre is said to have declined, and the French invasion has reduced it still lower. The performers' emoluments are in Spain, as well as in Italy and Portugal, very trifling; but the favourite singers and musicians used formerly to derive considerable revenues from the nobility, who though totally ignorant of everything that, according to our ideas, constitutes comfort, and though they deny themselves almost the necessaries of life, hesitate not to give a hundred, or a hundred and fifty guineas to a celebrated performer for a night's private entertainment in music or singing.

Being informed one morning that in the preceding night a fray had taken place between the English and German prisoners, I on enquiry found it had originated with an English sailor, who being a powerful bruiser, thought proper to have a round with some of the foreigners, and a gigantic serjeant, who was the bully of the prison! seeming a proper subject, he attacked him *secundum artem*, and soon demolished him: then taking out two others, he gave them such desperate beatings, that they were obliged to be sent to the hospital, and the tar was acknowledged by all sides to be the best man. The foreigners however not relishing this British amusement, requested and obtained a separation; and I at the same time procured permission for one in ten of our men to go out and wash the clothes of the rest, this necessary indulgence having been hitherto denied them.

CHAPTER 19

Madrid

Having obtained permission to visit the palace while the king was abroad, I went thither one afternoon, accompanied by some French gentlemen, and found a great number of workmen demolishing and clearing away a convent and several houses, which pressed so close on the front of the palace as considerably to injure its effect. The guards on duty were all Spaniards, with rich blue uniforms, cocked hats, and very large red feathers. Fine feathers, it is said, make fine birds; but notwithstanding the richness of their dress, and all the arts used to attach them, I believe there are but very few Spaniards in the French service friends in their hearts to the invaders.

This palace was built in the eleventh century, and was scarcely finished when it was taken by assault and plundered by the Moore. It was also nearly destroyed by an earthquake in the reign of Peter the Cruel, and rebuilt by his successor, Henry II. After being greatly improved and richly decorated by Charles the First, Philip II. and their successors, it was reduced to ashes in 1734, and rebuilt by Philip V and Ferdinand VI. The shape of the edifice is rather an oblong square, the two longest sides being about four hundred feet, and the others somewhat less; the elevation I suppose to be about eighty to ninety feet.

The first view of the exterior conveys an idea of magnificence, but on approaching, the smallness of the windows greatly diminishes this idea, and the filthy state of the courts, &c. entirely destroys it. On entering, the staircase is immediately observed to be much too small; it is, however, supported by fine marble pillars of the composite order, but which the Goths have most unaccountably whitewashed, so that without a close inspection, they appear no better than common stone.

The interior of the building compensates for the external faults, being excelled by no palace in Europe, in splendour and elegance. The first apartment we entered is small, but handsome, with some good pictures by Reubens and Jordan, particularly a Sabine Queen visiting the Temple, the Judgment of Solomon, and Delilah cutting Samson's hair, by the latter artist; a Magdalene by Spagnoletto, and a Spanish evening, are also very fine. This apartment and some others adjoining were occupied by the Princesses, and thence are called the Princesses' apartments.

Those of the Queen, which we next entered, are on a much grander scale, extending the whole length of the palace, and communicating with each other, so that when the folding doors are thrown open, the eye is almost dazzled by the splendid elegance of a long suite of magnificent saloons. In the centre of the first apartment is a superb golden *brasiero*,[1] a table of elegant workmanship, and a very handsome service of Seve porcelain; besides several good pictures, particularly a Centurion, by Tintoretti.

In the centre of the reception room is a fine marble table, and the ceiling is elegantly painted by Francisco Baliega. In this apartment is also a good Centurion, by Paul Veronese, and St. George and the Dragon, by Reubens, remarkable for colouring and effect. From the windows is a delightful view of the Guadarama mountains, the Casa del Campo, and the Escurial, with the river Manganaris running beneath.

The third apartment contains some old china and other handsome ornaments; the ceiling painted in an elegant and chaste style by Baliego, and the four Phases of the Moon by Mengs. In each apartment is a very rich clock; that in the fourth

---

1. A golden *brasier* may seem bordering, on a bull; but these kind of stoves are named *brasiero*, of whatever metal they may be composed.

is peculiarly superb, representing Atlas supporting the world. In this room is a good picture of Philip II by Titian, and the Family of Philip IV. by Velasquez. The ceiling is painted by Baliego, and represents the taking of Grenada from the Moors. It has likewise two superb vases of Seve porcelain, and several highly ornamented tables.

In short, everything is so magnificent, as to shut out all idea of comfort: the eye is dazzled, the mind struck with admiration, but neither is pleased. For my own part, the reflection I made was, how miserable I should be if forced to inhabit these superb apartments! for I am so unambitious as to prefer a well polished, snug mahogany table, a good fire, and the society of a few friends, to grandeur accompanied by ceremony and formality, which must have been always the case here; as none ever entered these apartments but in full dress, and with a feeling of their own inferiority.

The ceiling of the fifth *salon* represents Columbus presenting the new world to Ferdinand and Isabella, with its treasures and uncommon productions. In this apartment are also the celebrated pictures of the Virgin de la Pinto, and the Madona del Pace, by Raphael, some ceiling figures by Mengs, and some beautiful china. The porcelain *salon* contains various handsome articles of that kind, together with a steel clock on a fine pedestal; and the ceiling, painted by Mengs, represents the Triumph of Religion, Adjoining this apartment is a small elegantly fitted up library, the books of which are so superbly bound, and so nicety arranged, that one is almost afraid to touch them.

On the left of the library is. a small apartment with a white marble bath; two sides of this room are lined with looking glasses of a single piece, and the ceiling is finely painted. In a cabinet, communicating with it, is a bed to repose on after bathing. The dinner room, which looks towards the west, contains some valuable paintings by Jordan, but a portrait of Buonaparte by David by no means corresponds wish the celebrity of that artist. The ceiling is well painted, and in the room are some rich mosaic tables.

The succeeding apartment has several pictures by Reubens, particularly a St. Andrew much admired; the ceiling represents the death of Hercules, by Velasquez. In another spacious apartment is a handsome large musical clock, and several pictures by Reubens and Titian, of which the finest are an Adam and Eve by each of these masters, which are placed on either side of a window, and both so exquisite that it is impossible, to give either a preference; the other most valuable pictures are the discovery of the purple dye by the Phenician and his dog; and a Titus and Syriphus, both by Titian; the ceiling is painted by Mengs.

The apartment containing the throne is magnificent; the ceiling represents the costume of the different provinces of Spain, finely painted by a young Italian artist, named Philip Kehulo, previously scarcely known, and the walls are covered with the largest plate glasses in the world. On each side of the throne is a very large gilt figure of a lion. This apartment also contains some bronze figures from Rome, and a bronze statue of Philip the Second, much admired. In the blue room are pictures of this same prince and of Philip the Fourth by Velasquez, of Charles the Fifth by Titian, and of Fernandez, his father, by Reubens, besides ten others by Titian, and one by Reubens; also some antique vases, a handsome clock, and a lion in bronze, greatly admired for the expression of the eyes.

I have already observed, that in my visit to the palace I was accompanied by some French gentlemen. Amongst them was a Monsieur Demoland, a fat and consequential personage, who had-amassed £150,000 by privateering against the English, chiefly from St. Sebastian. He was attended by a most curious fellow, an Irishman, who had been once at sea, and was afterwards servant to an English dragoon officer, who when made prisoner left him to shift for himself.

This reprehensible neglect respecting their servants is indeed by far too common amongst our officers, and has been the cause of many good soldiers being lost to the service and the country; for being thus left without succour to enable them to go comfortably to a depot, where they would he found on an exchange, they enter into the service of the first Frenchman that will hire them.

The morning after my visit to the palace, I accompanied Colonel Vial and some other French officers to the village of Lyanos, about two leagues from Madrid, whither we were escorted by a detachment of the colonel's *chasseurs*. From hence we hastened back to be present at a bullfight, which is certainly the most entertaining spectacle that Spain offers to a stranger. The amphitheatre, which might hold one thousand persons, was filled by well drest people, waiting in a kind of awful suspense for the appearance of the animal, while a band of music played a slow and solemn tune.

When everything was ready, a man magnificently drest came forward, and after sounding a trumpet addressed the *corregidor*. Then appeared two cavaliers named *picadors*, one drest in a jacket of white satin and green pantaloons, and the other in a purple jacket and blue pantaloons, the sleeves of the jackets notched with crimson and gold, and the pantaloons covered with gold lace; their half-boots were of morocco, with immense gold tassels, and round their broad brimmed white hats was a gold band. They were, however, miserably mounted, for a bull sometimes killing fifteen or twenty horses, it would be expensive to bring forward good ones; and besides they are so sumptuously caparisoned, that their defects are scarcely visible.

The *picador* is armed with a lance, and when the bull has been goaded to fury outside of the arena, a door is opened and he rushes forward, his tail in the air, and instantly attacks one of the *picadors*, who receives him on his lance. The sensation I felt at this moment is not to be described, but it partook both of delight and apprehension.

The bull soon killed one of the horses, and the *picador* not being able to extricate himself readily, a *banderilla* or footman came to his assistance, and presenting a handkerchief to the animal, amused him with it, turning on one side as the bull charged him, until the second *picador* came forward and attacked him; the dexterity of the men, as well as the exertions of the bull, are loudly applauded by the spectators, who make the amphitheatre re-echo with their acclamations.

When this part of the entertainment had lasted some time, two *banderillas* came forward, each with a dart, to which are attached pieces of coloured paper and a handkerchief: the animal charges the handkerchief, which gives way, and the *banderilla* pricks him with the dart until he becomes perfectly furious; at other times they drive him mad with crackers and fireworks.

When King Joseph, who was present, thought that this second act had lasted long enough, he ordered the *matador* to appear, who accordingly came forward on foot, richly drest, and armed with a small sword only; the bull instantly rushed on him, and was received on the point of the sword, which entered the spine at the back of the neck, and the animal dropped lifeless at the feet of the triumphant *matador*, who held up the reeking sword, and received the loudest applause from the spectators: and certainly his courage and dexterity were equally great, for had he missed the vital spot, which is not larger than a sixpence, his life would most probably have paid the forfeit of his awkwardness.

The *matador* is however stimulated, by the knowledge that his courage and success will gain him the plaudits of the fair sex, who contend for the preference in his good graces. A second bull was dispatched in the same manner, but not until he had killed two horses, one of whom supported a second charge with his bowels trailing on the ground. Several other bulls were afterwards brought forward, but with their horns muffled, and a number of amateurs entered the lists with them, and shewed their dexterity by receiving them on their handkerchiefs. Certainly there is no spectacle in Spain so well worth seeing as a good bullfight.

The pleasure derived from it must, however, be allowed to be at the expense of humanity, for men, as well as horses and bulls, often lose their lives in this sport. These fights had been discontinued for some years, but on the arrival of the French were permitted to be renewed. The summer and autumn are the most common seasons for these spectacles, particularly the latter, when the bulls are more fierce; they seldom take place in winter, and the present one was in consequence of the feast of Christmas.

Chapter 20
Made a Close Prisoner in the Retiro

Some days after the bullfight I accompanied the colonel of the 26th Chasseurs and some of his officers on a coursing party to Lyanos. The colonel had the politeness to mount me on an English mare, taken at Talavera; and after partaking of a sumptuous breakfast, prepared for us at Lyanos, we set out, escorted by a strong body of dragoons and Polish lancers. We found hares extremely numerous, and having sixteen greyhounds all let loose at once, and some of whom run by the nose, it was to be expected that we should do much execution; however, by taking advantage of several spots of brushwood and fern, most of the hares escaped, and we killed only four out of fourteen courses.

As there were some fears that the brigands or peasants might attempt to carry me off, a curious fellow, of the name of Oliver, with a number of dragoons, were ordered to protect me; but though they used every endeavour to keep close to me, as I happened to be better mounted, and, I may add without much vanity, a better horseman, I frequently left them far behind, and made them blow several of their horses.

This Oliver was quite a mountebank, and the butt of the colonel, whom he amused with his grimaces and buffoonery; and indeed, in most French regiments there is a person of this description, on whom the officers expend their gross witticisms. Oliver was notwithstanding standing a good soldier, who had risen front the ranks, but had no pretensions to gentility.

He entertained me with an account of his being encamped

at Boulogne, and employed in patrolling the coast to prevent smuggling; yet he candidly acknowledged that he was not always incorruptible, and that the smugglers often found the means of engaging him to alter his intended *patrole*. Thus, a smuggler asking him in what quarter he intended going his rounds, if he answered to the south, the other replied, that the north was by far the most pleasant, and accompanying his advice with a *douceur*, the business was decided.

On our return from coursing, we found an abundant dinner prepared, at which presided two ladies, one of whom was the *bonne amie* of the colonel, The evening passed so pleasantly with music, singing, and plentiful libations of punch, that before we recollected we had to return to Madrid, it was past the hour of shutting the gates, and we were therefore obliged to remain. As no beds could be procured, cards were called for, and we spent the night at Bouillot. I played with various success, but was latterly a considerable loser, when one lucky bit brought me nearly home.

We left off at six o'clock, and after refreshing myself by washing my face, I played a few games of billiards, but was unsuccessful, from too soon exposing my play. My loss in cash I regretted much less than that of a gold broach, representing a pointer dog, finely executed. These kind of trinkets were so uncommon among the French and Spaniards, that all the company mistook it for an order, and made many enquiries respecting it. I did not think proper to undeceive them, and they were ashamed to be. too inquisitive, lest they should expose their ignorance on a subject, with which their *amour-propre* led them to conceive they should be acquainted. The broach was in my shirt on sitting down to dinner; but one of the ladies amusing herself with an innocent game of romps, it disappeared!

An inspector of review being expected to examine some horses, the colonel was obliged to wait his arrival; and as I could not return to Madrid without ,an escort, I was also obliged to wait till the review was over, which was not till three o'clock, when after a *déjeûné à la fourchette*, we set out, and reached Madrid late in the evening. On my return to the Retiro, I found that our absence had given rise to several stories, some asserting that the party was cut to pieces, and that I was carried off by the brigands, while others were as confident that I had deserted. King Joseph being informed of our absence, a search was ordered to be made in every direction.

Had I had the most distant idea of the consequences, I should certainly have returned the same night; but the fact was, I was so well amused, that neither King Joseph, General Beliard, the commandant of the Retiro, or my being a prisoner, ever once entered my head. A certain *insouciance* of character is occasionally a blessing, for it not only prevents us from poisoning our pleasures, by anticipating evils, but it also enables us to support them when they arrive; and had I not possessed a portion of this happy indifference, I should probably have sunk under the various difficulties I at times have had to encounter.

The morning after my return, the *adjutant de place* called on me with the information that King Joseph had ordered me to be closely confined. As I had no doubt but that this order originated with the general himself, I wrote him an explanatory letter on the subject of my last day's absence. I soon however discovered, that had I not stirred from Madrid, I should have been equally made a close prisoner, from the apprehensions entertained of an insurrection of the inhabitants, in which it appeared that I was denounced as intending to take an active part.

Five centinels were at first placed over me, and two more were afterwards added. During the day I received several visits from my friends in the city, and found that I had acquired their esteem; probably from never talking seriously, but confining myself to chit chat, or *bagatelle*, when in French society. The officers confined with me, namely, Captain Annesley, Lieutenant Sheetry, and Ensigns Watts and Moulson, all of the 89th, were entirely disposed to cheerfulness: my confinement therefore wais not so disagreeable as it would otherwise have been; and, indeed, I determined on appearing perfectly indifferent on the subject, not to give my enemies the satisfaction of believing they could annoy me.

Happening to have with me *White's Veterinary*, and knowing the French and Spanish ignorance of the treatment of horses, I, in order to amuse myself, proposed giving lectures on the subject, and treating the horses of my friends *gratis*. This was no sooner known, than sick and lame horses came from all quarters. The first I took in hand was an English mare of Monsieur de Billi, who had received a severe blow in the eye, and was pronounced incurable. By frequent steeping I succeeded in reducing the inflammation; I then applied finely pounded sugar, and lastly, Goulard's extract of Saturn, made weak, which produced a perfect cure.

The horse of a general officer was next brought me, which I was told the General highly esteemed, and had tried everything to restore, The animal had not been able to put one of his feet to the ground for nine months. I immediately perceived that he had picked up a nail, which produced a great inflammation and suppuration. Taking the horse's foot between my legs, (which surprised the attendants, as in France and Spain one man holds up the leg while another puts on the shoe, or performs any other operation[1]) I pared down the foot near the heel with a penknife, and soon perceived a small stump of a nail; on extracting which, a considerable discharge took place, and on letting down the foot, the animal walked with great firmness, to the great astonishment of the spectators, who could not be persuaded but that I had acted by some charm.

My fame as a horse doctor was now spread throughout Madrid, and I had so much practice, that had I taken fees, I should have made a handsome livelihood. In consequence of this, I was allowed to go to the stables and the forge, both within the walls. I had often in foreign countries, as well as when hunting, experienced the inconvenience of not being able to make and put on a horse-shoe, I therefore at once applied seriously, and soon made myself expert in the business. My particular friends now considered it as the highest favour to have a horse shod by me,

---

1. In the Low Countries, the horse's foot is raised by an iron chain.

and shewed him about in all directions, with no small vanity; for although I might not be considered as a first-rate blacksmith in England, both my shoes and shoeing wore infinitely superior to those of the Spaniards.

During the course of the French revolution, I frequently reflected in what manner I could gain a livelihood if my country was in similar circumstances, and felt a certain confidence in my knowledge of the treatment of horses. In another respect I was also at ease, that was in cookery; having often found the necessity of being my own cook while on campaigns, or grousing parties, I learnt to excel particularly in the dressing of four dishes. Indeed I cooked my own dinner almost the entire journey from Grenada to Madrid; for being allowed six rations of meat and bread, with a proportion of wine per day, I usually prepared dinner at my quarters, which afforded me an opportunity of inviting the officers of the 89th. As I was also allowed barley and chopped straw for the mules, the only articles I had to purchase were a few onions and other vegetables; and in fact there was seldom anything else to be bought, so that my whole expenses from Grenada to Madrid, for living and faring very well, did not exceed twelve *francs*, though the distance is above three hundred miles.

In spite of my resolution to appear indifferent, I soon found the want of liberty become insupportable, and more particularly to as I was under the charge of a brutish lieutenant of the 43rd infantry, who, conceiving I had treated him with contempt, placed two additional centinels over me, and greatly diminished the limits I had been allowed to walk in. The conduct of this fellow was indeed as illiberal as that of the lowest ruffian, but had no other effect on my treatment of him, than causing me to express the most sovereign contempt both for his mind and person. The sarcasms I threw out on the latter in particular, made him furious; for though a deformed little monster, he had the highest opinion of his personal beauty. In this respect, nature occasionally compensates her stinginess, by giving to such kind of animals a more than common share of conceit and vanity.

Among my visitors were some Spanish ladies, who sung and played, so that with the assistance of my male friends, I was enabled to produce an occasional and tolerable concert. Before I was thus closely confined, I used to attend concerts at Monsieur Denia's three or four times a week, where there were always assembled some first rate performers; particularly Monsieur Garnier, who is ranked among the first *hautboys* in Europe. At Monsieur Crochard's, who was an excellent violin, we used also to have some pleasant dinner parties and evening concerts.

December 25. In spite of all my attempts to render captivity less galling, the time passed on but heavily, and I had abundant proof that nothing can compensate the loss of liberty, wanting which, *even virtue mourns and looks round for happiness in vain.* At length Christmas Day arrived, and as I am one of those old fashioned persons, who think that the good old customs of our forefathers are not *better kept in the breach than in the observance*, I invited some of my friends, among whom were General Briott and Messrs. Cavallos and Hervot, to dinner, which they accepted.

Our repast was tolerably good, but most exorbitantly dear; the French *traiteur* (residing in the Retiro) who furnished it, doubtless thinking he had a right to make me pay doubly, for the double title by which he addressed me, of My Lord *Général Anglois*. I had however some reason to suppose, that the *adjutant de place* shared in his profits, from his always highly praising him. This officer latterly became good-humoured, and I once invited him to dinner, when he swallowed our anecdotes bordering on romance as greedily as he did his wine, of which he took a good allowance.

Indeed the character which the French have acquired of great sobriety, is only merited when they pay for. their wine, for I have always found them ready to do justice to the bottle when at others expense. But to return to our Christmas dinner. In the midst of our conviviality, at nine o'clock, the lieutenant of the 43rd entered, with two of the guard, and ordered us to disperse, in such an insolent manner, that I asked him, "if this brutal stile was natural to him, or if he had received orders to use such uncouth language?" adding, "that if he would try the experiment, he would find that a gentlemanly manner would be much more certain of producing a ready compliance." We therefore determined that he should use force to disperse us; but this extremity he did not choose, and at last retired with his soldiers.

The arrival of troops from various quarters, and of disabled soldiers about to return to France to receive their discharge, indicated that we were likely to march soon, to the no small joy of our officers and soldiers, as well as of many French officers, who were either to compose our escort, at were returning to France for various causes. General Beliard often inspected them in the court of the Retiro, but I never spoke to him: and on the 27th December, when it was notified to us that we were to march on the 29th, I received a polite note from him requesting my company to dinner, which I refused.

Indeed, his conduct had been entirely unbecoming an officer and gentleman, not only to myself, but to every English officer at Madrid; for though they were nominally on parole, they were confined in the Retiro; or when occasionally permitted to go into the town, were always accompanied by some subaltern officer, whose appearance and manners denoted anything but a gentleman.

For my own part, I refused to quit the Retiro with such an attendant, who I was sure would misrepresent everything he heard me say, and give a false and garbled account of my conduct to the general; and I know that such misrepresentation had been made. The general paid no attention to the complaints made by the officers of the studied insults they received. It is however but justice to the generality of the French superior officers that I have had occasion to meet in Spain, to acknowledge, that their conduct formed a striking contrast to that of General Beliard, and indeed they all spoke in the most indignant terms of his behaviour.

CHAPTER 21

From Madrid to Burgos

Early on the morning of the 29th December a very large convoy, collected from various parts of Spain, quitted Madrid for France. Instead of passing through the streets we made the circuit on the outside of the city, round which there is an excellent road, until we reached the Puerta de St. Vincent, where we halted, and the officers who had accompanied their friends bade them *adieu*; not without envy, for there were very few who were not heartily sick of the campaigns in Spain.

After passing along a beautiful road for a mile and a half, we went through the handsome gate of Segovia, and crossed the Guadarama by a superb bridge of that name. The distance from Madrid to the village of Guadarama is nine long Spanish leagues, so that on arriving there the convoy was greatly fatigued; and particularly the prisoners, after their long confinement The road was, however, tolerably good, and the single row of trees on each side relieving the eye, made it appear shorter; the country also seemed to be well cultivated. The village of Guadarama, situated at the foot of the mountains of the same name, was in a wretched state, from the constant passage of French troops to or from Madrid; there being no other place of accommodation near; it. It was formerly celebrated for its cheeses; the houses were now heaps of ruins, and the inhabitants deserted or destroyed.

Our convoy consisted of several carriages, and about two thousand six hundred persons, including the Spanish prisoners. who had been retained at Madrid at hard labour in the public works, in order to force them to enter King Joseph's service; a service from which they are sure to desert as soon as possible, with their arms and accoutrements. I was billeted in a wretched house, half destroyed, where not one single accommodation was to be found.

With difficulty we at last made a fire, and prepared a bed of heath, of which, however, we were dispossessed by a French officer and his wife (the most frightful gorgon I ever beheld), who on entering the apartment placed their things on our bed, *sans cérémonie*, and took possession of the fire; and some soldiers returning home on leave also coming in, we dared neither produce our provisions, or insist on our right to the fire and bed we had been at the trouble of making: we had therefore no alternative but that of taking up our lodging in the stable with the mules, where we past, the night cold, wet, and hungry.

December 30. In the morning, stiff and unrefreshed, we quitted the village of Guadarama, to cross the mountains which separate the New and Old Castiles. Here, as usual, when we came to any difficult pass, nothing but *brigands* was in the mouths of the French officers, whose apprehensions were plainly visible in their looks and conversation: and yet these were the *braggadocios* who, according to their own accounts, had encountered hosts. I observed that the greatest ruffians among them were the most apprehensive; and, indeed, I believe it will be always found, that persons of mild and liberal manners encounter danger with more fortitude than bullying and blustering fellows.

We halted some time on the summit of the ridge of mountains, from whence we had a fine view of the Escurial, though at too great a distance to give a circumstantial description of it from my own observations; I trust, therefore, my readers will not be displeased at my presenting them with some details taken from other travellers. This palace is considered as the eighth wonder of the world by the Spaniards, who in speaking of it use an emphatic ardour peculiar to the inhabitants of warm climates.

The edifice is an oblong with several towers; the two principal faces have between six and seven hundred feet front, and upwards of fifty in height; each angle is flanked by a tower of two hundred feet elevation, and within side is a magnificent church. At the distance I viewed it from the stile of architecture appeared to me to be heavy.

When at Madrid, I had much satisfaction in being told by many Spanish ladies, that they fled to the Escurial for protection during its occupation by the English, under the command of Sir John Hope; and although I believe the British force was four thousand men. it gave me still greater pleasure to hear them remark. that the discipline and good conduct of the. soldiers were such, that it was scarcely possible to perceive there was one in the palace. On the summit of the mountain we observed a large square obelisk, erected by order of Charles the Third, to mark the limits of the two Castiles. As I am now about to quit New Castile, I shall beg leave to offer my readers a few observations on that kingdom, drawn from the authors I have read on the subject, as well as from the information of intelligent Spaniards with whom I have conversed,

New Castile occupies the central part of the peninsula, being surrounded by the kingdoms of Valencia, Arragon, Old Castile, Murcia, Estramadura, Cordova, Jaen, and La Mancha; it is about fifty-five leagues in length north and south, and fifty broad east and west, including the tract of country named Celliberia by the Romans.

The principal chain of mountains in this part of Spain are those anciently called Mons Orespadani; they commence with the Sierra d'Olla, and form the Sierras de Molina, de Cuença, and de Consuegra. This chain is also connected, by other ridges, with the Sierras d'Alcalas, Segura, and Cazorlo; thus forming a communication with the great chain of Grenadines already noticed, which extend in a south-west direction to Gibraltar and Tariffa, while the Sierras de Guadarama, from whose summits I am now supposed to write, connect them in a north-west direction with the Pyrenees.

If the British government was to reflect on the chains of mountains that run in all directions through Spain, I ain satisfied the mode of carrying on the war in this country would be immediately changed: for the many strong passes in these mountains are particularly calculated for *partisan* warfare; and if they had been properly occupied, the French would have found it totally impossible to have penetrated into the country as they have done.

Although this is not the only instance of negligence or mistake, on our parts or on that of the Spaniards, yet such is the present temper of the latter, that the minister who should give up their cause as hopeless or desperate, would deserve to lose his head; while the French must, in the end, be convinced of the absurdity of attempting the conquest of a country of such a nature and extent. New Castile possesses three considerable rivers, navigable from the sea for a considerable distance: they are the Tagus, the Jacar, and the Guadiana. The lesser rivers are extremely numerous, but the enumeration of them would afford little gratification to the reader; if, however, he wishes for more minute information, it will be found in Monsieur La Borde's *Itinéraire descriptif de l'Espagne*, a work chiefly consisting of topographical and statistical details.

The principal towns of New Castile are Madrid, Toledo, Cuenca, Talavera de la Reyna,[1] Villa Nueva de los Infantos, Illescas, Zunita, Consuegra, Guadalaxara, Tremblique, Alcala de Herrarez, and Alcolea.

Among the numerous revolutions of the peninsula, New Castile has been conspicuous for the struggles it has made in defence of its liberties, and which have been sung by its bards with a degree of enthusiasm, that cannot fail to inspire the present race with the same patriot zeal in the defence of their country against the French. The title of King of the Two Castiles became extinct in the year 1475, and by the marriage of Ferdinand and Isabella the whole of Spain was united into one monarchy: this period is the most glorious of the Spanish history.

---

1. This town has become celebrated by the battle fought near it in 1811, between the French and British troops, when the latter gained a glorious victory under the command of the Duke of Wellington.

Ever since the reign of Louis XIV. it has been the policy of the French cabinet to keep the Spaniards in a sort of childhood, which, added to the effects of the Inquisition on the acquirement of knowledge, seem to be the cause of Spain producing so few men of talent in recent times.

Having descended the ridge of Guadarama, we halted at a large *venta* [2] at its foot, called Fonda de St. Raphael, two leagues from Guadarama. Here we found a strong guard posted, composed chiefly of engineers, who had taken advantage of a stream of water to execute a whimsical and very ingenious piece of mechanism, consisting of a ludicrous figure with a huge cocked hat, a sawyer cutting timber, a group of merry dancers on a horizontal wheel, and a band of musicians; the dress and faces of all these figures were admirably ridiculous, and the whole was put in movement by the force of the stream, in such a manner that any man must have been sadly philosophic, who could refrain from laughing at them; moreover, the variety of costume and manner of the spectators added not a little to the singularity of the scene.

Monsieur Crochard having with him a caravan filled with eatables (amongst which I was surprised to find some uncommonly fine oysters and Jamaica rum, of which latter the French are extravagantly fond), invited me with several others to partake of his breakfast, and his invitation was the more acceptable, as I had neither eat nor drank the day before. I may here observe, with respect to Mr. Crochard's good things, that paymasters and commissaries general in all armies have more than their share of comforts.

In the evening we reached Antero de Herrares, after passing through a bleak country without trees, but retaining some traces of cultivation, though now entirely neglected; for so inveterate are the Spaniards against their invaders, that they say they would cheerfully starve themselves to cause the French to perish also. Antero de Herrares is the poor remains of what seems formerly to have been a tolerable town, and at present consists

---

2. An Inn

of wretched mud houses and dirty streets. Here the experience of the last evening induced me to procure a non-commissioned officer, to prevent the soldiers from forcing themselves into my quarters. The serjeant appointed for this purpose was retiring to France on leave, in expectation of procuring his discharge, and was a steady, decent man.

December 31. In the morning we quitted the village for Segovia. The frost was now very severe, and the cold greater than I ever experienced in England, owing to the great elevation of the country above the level of the sea. Indeed it is a very mistaken idea that the degree of heat or cold depends on the latitude, for though this has a certain effect, elevation and local circumstances have still greater. There are parts of Europe, several degrees south of England, where the winters are infinitely more severe than in the latter country. At Grand Cairo, though in thirty degrees north, I have experienced a heat much greater than between the tropics, which is doubtless caused by the winds blowing over large tracts of burning sands.

We reached Segovia, which is four leagues from Antero de Herrares, at two o'clock in the afternoon. The street we entered by was so narrow and so crowded with carriages, driving in every direction, that it took us a considerable time to reach the municipality, situated at the farther extremity of the town.

Here is an aqueduct, considered one of the greatest curiosities of Spain, and believed by the Spaniards to be so ancient that my landlord very seriously assured me it was the workmanship of the same architect who built the temple of Seraphis in Egypt; more moderate antiquarians however ascribe it to the reign of Trajan. By it the water is conducted across a ravine, and traverses the place and valley of Azoguego; it is from seventy to eighty feet long, and eighty to ninety high; and a great number of little canals or pipes branch off from it and convey the water to all parts of the city.

I was billeted in a magnificent house, of which I occupied a large apartment, covered with ancient gilding and looking glasses, but without fireplace or *brasier*, so that I was, starved with cold. I dined with our officers, who were quartered at the next door, and where a priest and several Spaniards of consideration paid us a visit in the evening, and indulged themselves in abusing the French; for having a perfect confidence in us they spoke their sentiments freely. My landlord and his family paid much attention to the Spanish officers, and made many anxious enquiries after their son who had been made prisoner at Ciudad Rodrigo. There were also two daughters of the, master of the house, of very superior manners, handsome, and obliging.

I here passed the last night of the year most wretchedly, almost frozen from want of bed covering or fire, and suffering greatly from the pain in my chest and spitting of blood. Nor did the morning of the new year (January 1,1811) bring with it any melioration. Cold and unrefreshed, when I arose, my reflections were melancholy in the extreme, from the contrast of my present situation with that of the preceding year,—when I received the congratulations and compliments usual at this season from those friends whose expressions and looks spoke the sincerity of their good wishes,—now a prisoner in a distant country, and separated for an undetermined period from those I loved most dearly. I attempted to drive away these sad thoughts by a walk in the town; but the streets were so covered with ice, that walking was disagreeable and dangerous, and I was obliged to return.

In the forenoon I however received the visit of a forward little Irish priest, whom I accompanied to the hospital, where I found several wounded English soldiers of the Guards, 61st and 78th regiments, most of whom had lost a limb, and some two. It seemed to me that the treatment of wounds by the French surgeon, was by no means what might have been expected, from their supposed excellence of this art. The priest, as chaplain, had considerable influence in the management of the hospital, and introduced me to the director, who was very civil.

From hence I paid a visit to General Filhie, commandant of the town, and an officer of the old school, which supposes a gentleman in manners and address, He invited me to dinner; but his hour being three o'clock, I was obliged to decline it, for as I was to continue my journey next morning, I wished to employ the afternoon in seeing the town. The general was lodged in the palace of the Alcazar, a very ancient and interesting building; the apartments richly ornamented with mosaic and gilding, but generally ill proportioned. It was inhabited by Alfonzo the Wise, celebrated for his astronomical tables.

In the chapel there still remained some pictures covered with dust, and in a gallery several statues of Spanish princes and great men, amongst whom I noticed that of Ferdinand Gonzalez, proclaimed first Count of Castile in 923, and of the famous warrior Roderigue Dias de Bivar, better known by the name of the Cid Campeadore.

From the Alcazar I visited the cathedral, with my guide the priest, who told me that though he had been twenty-eight years in Segovia, be now for the first time entered this church; and yet few in Europe are more worthy of observation, either as to architecture, situation or internal decoration. Though built only in the sixteenth century, it is chiefly Roman; among the ornaments which remain (for it had been plundered of the most valuable) are several marble statues well executed by an artist named Manuel Pachero. In the chapels are also some tolerable pictures and figures in bas relief, but a large silver figure of the Virgin has disappeared.

Having satisfied my curiosity here I accompanied the priest to the castle, a Moorish work situated on an elevated granite rock, with the river on the right and a perpendicular precipice some hundred feet deep on the left, at the foot of which runs another river, so that the rock is placed at the junction of the two rivers. Its shape has a considerable resemblance to that of a ship, the town being longer than it is broad, swelling out in the middle and narrowing towards the stern; and when looking down on it from the castle, you may fancy yourself in the foretop of a vessel. The castle was now filled with soldiers, who were committing all kinds of depredations on the floors and walls, which are covered with elegant mosaic.

On quitting the castle, I heard myself wished a happy new

year in English; and certainly Robinson Crusoe could not have been much more surprised at hearing his parrot cry "poor Robin!" than I was at being addressed in an English voice from so unexpected a place.

The compliment was several times repeated; but I for some time looked round in vain for the speaker, until at last I observed the unfortunate lad, Archibald Lindsey, looking through the grate of an upper apartment, and learnt from him that he was confined there in chains, without fire, or one earthly consolation. The miserable situation of this poor fellow made me feel most forcibly how little my own was to be complained of, when compared with his, which united captivity, cold and hunger, and brought to my recollection a passage in one of Sterne's sermons, admirably appropriate.

> *Heaven have pity upon the youth, for he is in hunger and in distress, strayed out of the reach of a parent, who counts every hour of his absence with anguish; cut off from all his tender offices by his folly, and from relief and charity from others, by the calamities of the times.*
>
> *Nothing so powerfully calls home the mind as distress: the tense fibre then relaxes, the soul retires to itself, sits pensive, and is susceptible of right impressions. If we have a friend, 'tis then we think of him; if a benefactor, at that moment all his kindnesses impress upon our mind.—Gracious and bountiful God, is it not for this that they who in their prosperity forget thee, do yet remember and return to thee in the hour of sorrow! When our heart is in heaviness, upon whom can we think but thee, who knowest our necessities afar off, puttest all our tears in thy bottle—seest every careful thought, hearest every sigh and melancholy groan we utter!*

Every effort, as I have before noticed, had been used to induce this poor lad to enter into the French service, but without effect; and as a punishment for his virtuous patriotism, he was now thus starving in chains. Indeed, I have observed many instances of heroic constancy in this respect, as well in Spaniards as in English, which proved the great strength of character of the former, and raised them infinitely above the Germans, who change sides with circumstances, and are indifferent into whose hands their country falls.

From the castle we proceeded to the Governor's residence, where the priest, who was entirely Irish as to the absence of *mauvaise honte*, called for wine and brandy, to which he did ample justice. From hence we went to the place of military execution, where the victim is placed on a marble slab, close to a wall, which I observed pierced with vast numbers of bullets, and the ground strewed with pieces of the skull of a Spanish lieutenant, who had been shot here the preceding day. From this fatal spot, well calculated to inspire the most melancholy reflections, I retired, oppressed and unwell, and visited the mint, where brass is now only coined, and but little of it; the building is insignificant, and by no means answers the descriptions I have read of it.

In returning to my lodging, I met Messrs. Cavallos and Hervot, who pressed me to dine with them, which I promised, if I could get rid of my priest; and in this I only succeeded by plying him with brandy. I did not feel without alarm in going to dinner, for the evening was very dark, and I knew that several French had been killed the same day in a scuffle with the Spaniards. I had not gone far when I heard the firing of muskets and a great outcry, and soon after heard that four Frenchmen and a woman had been massacred; one of the men, it seems, was a follower of the army, a description of fellows who commit infinitely more depredations than the soldiers.

In the act of spoliation, the female campaigners are worse than the men; for being lost to every feminine virtue, they plunder and murder with the greatest coolness and composure. The house we dined at had formerly been an extensive woollen manufactory, but was now much declined. The party was pleasant, and the dinner tolerable.

On my return to my quarters, I found my landlord and his amiable daughters assembled in the kitchen. They expressed the anxiety they had been under for my safety: and finding the old man in a conversable humour, I sat down with a *segar*, and gave him all the information I could respecting the state of affairs in the interior of Spain.

He soon became animated with the subject, and grasping the tongs, exclaimed with energy, "would I were young again! but old as I am, I hope before I die to assist in expelling these villains from Spain!"

Such, indeed, is the common sentiment of the Spaniards in general, and it is to be hoped and expected that they will be ultimately successful, for they are truly fighting *pro aris et focis*.

Chapter 22

From Segovia to Valladolid

On the morning of January 2, I quitted Segovia some time before the convoy, and accompanied only by my batman Pierre, who was charged with the care of the mules, and who was much terrified from the number of French killed the night before, expecting every moment to share the same fate. We rode along the bank of the river, having the walls of the town, which are very high, on our left, and the castle, situated on a rock, affording a romantic view. We soon came up with the convoy, whose march was much retarded by wagons loaded with bread, sent from Madrid, and intended for Massena's army in Portugal, of which two hundred out of the original five hundred were already lost from various accidents.

The country we passed through was rather hilly, and now covered with snow, so that I could not well distinguish the nature of the soil; but it appeared to have been formerly cultivated. At a late hour we reached Santa Maria de Neva, an uncomfortable town. Here I found the quarters assigned me occupied by a German colonel, whom I soon discovered to be my old acquaintance, Colonel Baron de Faustein, Chamberlain to the Emperor, and colonel of the regiment of Baden. With great politeness he offered me the choice of three tolerable apartments, besides which there was a good kitchen, and plenty of accommodation for the servants.

The baron soon putting himself at ease *en déshabille*, took post in the chimney corner with his pipe; and certainly was a most extraordinary figure, his thin body beings wrapped up in flannel. He wore immense *mustachios*, and had on a large curious night-cap; so that he extorted a laugh even from the solemn gravity of our Spanish host.

As we were dependent for our supper on what the baron's stock, afforded, we both began to prepare our repast, he undertaking to compose a soup of pork, rice and eggs, while I manufactured a hash, and fricasseed the fragments of a turkey. During my employment in this momentous business, we drank plentifully of snaps of brandy, and when I laughed at the grotesque figure of the baron, which there was no resisting, he thinking I was laughing at our employment, joined heartily in it, while sympathy acted upon his man Frederick, and by a kind of merry contagion, all the persons present, amounting to ten or twelve, resembled the picture of "all in good humour."

At our repast our solemn host joined us, and he felling fast asleep, I could not resist the pleasure of blacking his face with a burnt cork, which set the baron in so loud a roar of laughter, that it actually woke the Spaniard, who, in his turn, thinking there must be some good joke, but ignorant that it was at his own expense, laughed also; and thus these two caricatures amused each other, to the entertainment of us all.

Before I went to bed I visited the cattle, suspecting that they might be neglected, and found that they had neither been cleaned or fed, nor their toddles taken off, and that Monsieur Pierre had appropriated the sheet of my favourite mare to cover himself. On sending for him, I received a most insolent answer to my remonstrance, and knowing I could get no other redress, I revenged myself pugilistically; a kind of art the French are totally unacquainted with, and very averse to. He decamped next morning, and left me to take care of the cattle myself; for though I had another servant, be had an antipathy to horses and dogs, neither of which he would approach.

January 3. On quitting Santa Maria de Neva, the country we passed through was very romantic, the soil rich, and retaining the marks of cultivation; but now a waste. The villages we saw were composed of wretched mud hovels, and the peasants universally drest in coarse brown frieze, and both themselves and their habitations seemed equally miserable. In several of these villages all the, doors and windows were closed, nor did we see a single soul in them.

The convoys had been often attacked in this part of the country, and we were therefore now ordered to keep in close order. At last we reached the. Moorish palace of Las Navas de Colla, most beautifully situated on the banks of a river, and commanding an extensive view of a very rich country. Accompanied by M. Crochard, I went forward to view this building. We observed that it had been fortified, and, from its position, must have been impregnable before the use of cannon. It is surrounded by a ditch, crossed by a drawbridge, so crazy, that we passed it with some difficulty. The palace is of considerable extent, and retains all its Moorish, ornaments, the floors being. of fine mosaic, and the ceilings richly gilt and grotesquely painted. Indeed, it seemed that neither expense nor art had been spared to render it magnificent according to the Moorish taste, which was so different to ours, that their mode of life, as described by historians, resembles romance.

While examining the palace, a heavy firing announced the convoy's being attacked by the *brigands*, who, it appeared, were composed of the inhabitants of the village, of which we had seen the windows and doors closed, and who had concealed themselves until the convoy had arrived at a bridge, crossing, the river, which was very winding, and bounded on each side by steep hills. In this spot they attacked the rear of the convoy, and I had a complete view of the affair from the summit of the hill. A detachment of the 10th Hussars charged the *brigands*, and troops were sent in various directions.

This skirmish cost the French eight hussars and two wagoners killed; some soldiers, twelve horses and four loaded carts taken, on one of which was the paymaster's military chest. These brigands were commanded by a German captain, who had deserted with his company from Santa Maria de Neva, of which he had been commandant Their number did not exceed two hundred, while the convoy was upwards of twelve hundred; a proof of the daring spirit of the Spanish peasantry! Every individual Frenchman, however, according to his own word, would not have hesitated to attack the whole party; indeed, nothing could be more disgusting than these fellows' continual gasconade.

After this affair, we passed through a very hilly and sandy track, and as our horses were in wretched condition for want of forage, we proceeded very slowly, added to which the breaking down of several bread wagons, retarded us still more. One of the officers requested me to ride forward and inform an officer of the 10th Chasseurs of this accident, and to tell him, that as it was necessary to break up the case, his people might have as much bread as they pleased. This message I delivered in pure kindness, and without any signs of satisfaction in my manner; nevertheless it put the officer in a violent passion, which he expressed both in his language and gestures. He was a German, and, as I have already observed, the inferior German officers in the French service are anything but gentlemen.

Late at night we reached Olmeda, an insignificant town, and next morning proceeded, through a very sandy country, by very deep roads, to Val de Stillas, where I was billeted at the house of a poor old man, whose habitation consisted only, of two apartments, one of which was occupied by himself and son, and the other, was half unroofed. There was neither chair, stool, nor table, and but one earthen pot, in which I boiled a few onions and some mutton I had brought with me, and which made a mess sufficient for myself and servants, as well as the old man and his son; a treat indeed to them, for they had not tasted flesh for a twelvemonth!

We washed down this homely repast with *agua ardiente*. Our table, at which we all set indiscriminately, was a board I had procured in the village, and our seat a bank of earth. My bed was the uneven mud floor, wet from the rain, which poured in through the roof; and I had no other covering than my clothes on my back, which were likewise very wet from the day's rain.

Notwithstanding my situation, I slept as soundly as if on a bed of down; nor was this the first time that I enjoyed a sweeter repose, thus exposed to the inclemency of the weather, than in a splendid apartment, surrounded by luxury, but at the same time annoyed by sameness and want of occupation.

During the night, a wretched old man sought refuge in the house, and informed us that his son had just been murdered, and himself desperately wounded by the soldiers, who had torn the roof off his hovel to make a fire. It is impossible, without having witnessed it, to form an adequate idea of the horrors inflicted on the; Spanish peasantry by the French soldiers; over whom, in consequence of their being generally in long arrears of pay, and often in total want of provisions, their officers have scarce any control.

In the morning we found that the peasants had, during the night, gone off with the bullocks which were to draw the bread-wagons, and the bread was in consequence heaped up on the outside of the village, without covering; and a heavy rain coming on, it must have been soon totally destroyed. Thus Marshal Massena, for whose army it was intended, was disappointed of this expected and greatly wanted relief.

January 4. The day being wet, the march of the convoy became very irregular, for as there are two roads leading to Valladolid, the first division took one, and the second the other; so that when the bugle sounded a halt, one party, not hearing it, pushed on, and arrived at Valladolid long before the division that remained with the commanding officer. From the irregularity of the march, many of the English prisoners effected their escape; indeed, latterly, no great pains were taken to prevent them, and seldom any inquiry was made on their disappearing. Close to the town, at the meeting of two roads, we were greeted with the spectacle of a man's head stuck on a pole.

CHAPTER 23

The Cid

At Valladolid I was billeted in comfortable quarters, at a merchant's house, which was some compensation for the various privations I had lately suffered. As soon as I had made myself fit to appear I waited on General Keller man, who received me most politely, and whose mild and gentlemanly manners could not fail to make a strong impression in his favour, when compared with the ferocious and vulgar brutes I had encountered. He speaks English tolerably well, and seems to admire the English character; though, from the illiberality of his master, it is not very prudent to express this sentiment openly. He invited me to dinner with Monsieur and Madame Crochard and M. Diniez; the repast was good and the wines excellent In the evening, the General advised me and M. Diniez to proceed with a convoy of dismounted dragoons going to France to be remounted, by which we should expedite our journey; and to this proposal we readily assented.

On my return to my quarters I found the family at cards, in which I joined, and at ten o'clock supper was brought in, consisting of a salad of beetroot and other vegetables, and some anchovies. Indeed the Spaniards are extremely frugal or rather abstemious in their diet, of which flesh meat forms a very small portion; nor have they the least idea of those enormous joints under which our English tables groan.

January 5. In the morning I strolled about the town, which appears to have been for some time on the decline; most of the magnificent gateways are in ruins, and many have never been finished, as though the proprietors had began on too great a scale, and wanted the means of completing them. The two principal squares are the Campo-Grande and Plaza Mayor; the buildings of the former are without regularity, and it is scarce possible to pass through it for heaps of ordure. The Plaza Mayor is surrounded by a colonnade, under which is a promenade, adorned with all the best shops. It is probable that this colonnade was intended to be very magnificent, and it may look well on paper, but the execution is below mediocrity.

The Ochavo is an octagon place, the buildings of which are in ruins, and the centre occupied by heaps of mire, into one of which I plunged up to my middle, in returning home from dining with our officers, who had their quarters in this *Plaza*.

Valladolid is built on a low swampy soil, which, added to the national want of cleanliness, renders it filthy in the extreme. Its promenades are celebrated, but neither the weather (which was very wet) nor my time would permit me to visit them; the latter being occupied in purchasing provisions, which we were always obliged to do in every large town to last us to the next, generally a journey of three or four days. I saw however the Prado de la Magdelaine, on the Esquiva, which has some large trees, and is probably a pleasant walk in summer, but at this time all was dreary and gloomy from the cold, wet and uncomfortable weather.

The churches of Valladolid seem not to equal those of many other inferior towns of Spain. The cathedral is but half finished, and I observed nothing in the others worthy of particular notice; except some good paintings in that of the Augustins, particularly a Descent from the Cross, by Hernandez.

January 7. We quitted Valladolid an hour before day, but halted a considerable time at the gate, which I believe was intentional; for I found on reaching it an officer waiting for me, who informed me that he had instructions to apprehend and convey me *vi et armis* into a *posada*, where Messrs. Cavallos and Hervot had prepared a sumptuous breakfast of cold ham, hot mutton, salt fish, and many other substantial things which I was obliged to wash down with several parting glasses of liqueur and brandy; and, on taking leave, Monsieur Hervot presented me with a small silver cup, as a *souvenir de l'amilié éternelle*. Embracing these gentlemen, who were here to quit the convoy on their way to Portugal to join the French army in that country, we bade each other an affectionate farewell; not without sensations of regret, on my part at least.

Monsieur de Billi, another gentleman, and myself, who had partaken of the repast, were obliged to gallop on to overtake the light convoy. We found the road covered with carts and wagons loaded with wool, which had been levied by the French as part of; the contributions, and was on its way to France. Our convoy was now composed of the 20th and 21st Light Dragoons returning from Portugal, and proceeding to Pau to be remounted. These regiments, it was said, neglected their horses very much, and consequently were no favourites.

One of the officers, as is usual with Frenchmen, entered familiarly into conversation with me, recounting the miseries of the campaign in Portugal; but which were scarcely worth mentioning in comparison with their sufferings since, particularly in Massena's retreat. We halted at a village where Monsieur Diniez and some gentlemen had ordered a repast to be prepared; after partaking of which, we continued our march and arrived in the evening at Turcomania, eight Spanish leagues from Valladolid. This place we quitted early in the morning of January 8, being anxious to get before the other convoy.

The road was good, and we advanced rapidly. I was amused by the conversation of a Monsieur Vilmansen, who introduced himself by telling me, that he should soon be happy, eating oysters at Bourdeaux; and related the enormous quantity he had eat when last there, with such an expressive manner, as if he was swallowing them at the moment. Our conversation was not however confined to *gourmandism*, for the appearance of the country leading us to the subject of botany, I found he was tolerably acquainted with this branch of natural history, and as

I knew a little of it myself, we kept up the conversation with mutual satisfaction, In the evening we arrived at Alada, a small insignificant village.

January 9. Next morning, though the escort was much fatigued, we left Alada at an early hour, and proceeded by a narrow and broken road along the banks of the Arlançon, which was now an insignificant stream, but sometimes swells so much as to overflow, and cause considerable damage. A little before dark we reached Burgos, on the outside of which we perceived the shocking spectacle of eighteen poor wretches hanging. These sights, so often presented to us in our march, are doubtless intended to intimidate the Spaniards, but have a directly opposite effect, inspiring them only with revenge.

After crossing a bridge over the Arlançon, we entered Burgos by a gate, and passed along a handsome promenade on the banks of the river, planted with trees and in good order. I found some difficulty in procuring a billet, but at last was quartered at a priest's house, who with his sister, a handsome girl, and maid servant; composed the family.

The females at first received me in a most uncourteous manner, but when they were informed that, instead of being a German or other follower of the French, I was an English prisoner, they entirely changed their tone, and everything the house afforded was brought forward, and the mules accommodated in the hall, for want of any other place. In short, I experienced the utmost hospitality, which was the more agreeable from the first forbidding reception. Nor was this the first time by many that I had the satisfaction of experiencing, that the name of Englishman is a passport to hospitality and kindness in all parts of the world: even among the Arabs of the desert I have found it so, when entirely in their power.

January 10. In the morning I called to pay my respects to General Count Dorsenne, the governor, but not finding him at home, I strolled through the town, which is one of the best built that I have seen in Spain. The gates, of which there are several, are handsome; and a large square, surrounded by a colonnade supported by marble pillars, and under it rows of well filled shops, has the appearance of industry and prosperity. At one side of the square is a magnificent arch, also supported by marble columns of the Corinthian order, which leads to the promenade on the banks of the river. Opposite to this gate is the tomb of the Cid, to whom Burgos has the honour of giving birth, as well as of possessing his remains.

The exploits of this renowned warrior (the relation of which is supposed by Cervantes to have principally caused the derangement of the worthy knight of La Mancha), are collected from the old Spanish chronicles and ballads, and admirably put into English by Mr. Southey. As all my readers may not have seen this extraordinary and almost romantic narrative, I trust I shall be excused for transcribing a sketch of it from the review of Mr. Southey's work.

> Roderigo of Bivar, a youth strong in arms, and of good customs, destined to protect his country from the Moors, was born at Burgos in the reign of King Fernando of Castile; and in the year 1026 his father Diego Laynez, chief of the noble house, had received a blow from the Count Don Gomez, the Lord of Gormay. Now," says Mr. Southey, Diego was a man in years, and his strength had passed from him, so that he could not take vengeance, and he retired to his home, to dwell there in solitude and lament over his dishonour; he took no pleasure in his food, neither could he deep by night, nor would he lift up his eyes from the ground, nor stir out of his house, nor commune with his friends, but turned from them in silence, as if the breath of his shame would taint them. Roderigo was yet but a youth, and the Count was a mighty man in arms, one who gave his voice first in the Cortes, and was held to be the best in the war, and so powerful that he had a thousand friends among the mountains.
>
> Howbeit all these things appeared as nothing to Roderigo, when he thought of the wrong done to his father, the first

which had ever been offered to the blood of Layn Calvo. He asked nothing but justice of Heaven, and of man he only asked a fair field; and his father, seeing of how good heart he was, gave him his sword and his blessing. The sword had been the sword of Mudarra in former times, and when Roderigo held its cross in his hand, he thought within himself that his arm was not weaker than Mudarra's. And he went out and defied the Count, and slew him, and smote off his head and carried it home to his father. The old man was sitting at table, the food lying before him untasted, when Roderigo returned, and pointing to the head which hung from the horse's collar dropping blood, he bade him look up, for there was the herb which should restore to him his appetite; the tongue, quoth he, which insulted you, is no longer a tongue, and the head which wronged you is no longer a head. And the old man rose and embraced his son, and placed him above him at the table, saying, that he who had brought home that head should be the head of the house of Layn Calvo.

The Castilian monarch for some offence afterwards banished the Cid from his dominions. On his going the Cid then assembled his relations, *vassals*, and retainers, whom his influence and high military reputation had attached to his person, and resolved at their head to have Castile, and subsist by a predatory war among the Moors.

"And as he was about to depart he looked back upon his own house: and when he saw his hall deserted, the household of chests unfastened, the doors open, no cloaks hanging up, no seats in the porch, no hawks upon the perches, the tears came into his eyes, and he said, 'my enemies have done this! God be praised for all things.' And he turned towards the east, and knelt and said, 'Holy Mary, Mother, and all Saints, pray to God for me, that he may give me strength to destroy all the Pagans, and to win enough from them to requite my friends therewith, and all those who follow and help me, &c. &c.'

CHAPTER 24

From Burgos to Mendragon

We quitted Burgos at five o'clock in the morning of January 11, in an extremely hard frost, and passed through a fertile and well cultivated country, with numerous villages, in all of which were parties of the French imperial guards, who had fortified themselves against the brigands, and seldom stirred out of the works. In the evening we reached the village of Bribiesca, eight Spanish leagues from Burgos; where I had the good fortune to be billeted at the house of a worthy priest, who the moment he found I was English, studied in every possible manner to make me comfortable, even to the offering me money, which, however, not being in want of, I declined accepting. Indeed, the enthusiasm of the Spaniards of all classes, in favour of the English, was now at the highest; and it is to this general attachment, as well as to their hatred of the French name, that we are to look for the final triumph of Spain. The assistance of the English is however not the less necessary, in expediting this result, for the Spanish regular armies scarce deserve the name.

January 12. At a very early hour, we recommenced our march; and about noon reached the village of Pancorvo, so strongly situated that a thousand men might easily defend it against a great army. On the summit of a hill is a regular fortification, but from the inequality of the ground I should think it of little use; neither does it command the village, which is placed between two high rocks, and approached by a winding road with very short turns. After quitting this village I had much conversation with

Colonel Natalis, of the engineers, a very diffident but well informed officer, who expressed his conviction that the conquest of Spain was at this time more difficult than ever.

After a tiresome march of seven leagues we reached Miranda, a tolerable village; and here I was once more quartered on a good priest, who was no less rejoiced than myself; for had he been saddled with a French officer, he must not only have furnished him with everything he required *gratis*, but most probably would have been insulted into the bargain.

January 13. In the morning we pursued our march along the banks of a small river, which flows through a very rich valley, to the village of Mont Alban, where we breakfasted, and at three o'clock entered Vittoria, by a very handsome promenade, on which, the day being fine, a great crowd of persons had assembled to view us. After dressing I waited on Count Caffarelli, the commandant, but he not being at home, I amused myself viewing the *chasseurs légers* of the Imperial Guard, who were on the parade and made a good appearance, their band was extremely strong, there being thirty-nine performers on the parade.

The superior pay, and high consideration in which this corps of the army is held, creates a general jealousy among the rest. I observed that the officers inspected their soldiers nearly in the same manner as in our service. In returning from the parade I met General Caffarelli, who received me politely; and while we were walking to his residence he informed me with rapture of the capture of Tortosa and nine thousand two hundred Spanish troops; at the same time giving me the French official account to read, seeming to forget that such news could not be very agreeable to an English officer.

He was however very civil, and regretted his being prevented from asking me to dinner by an engagement abroad. We walked together to the bishop's palace, situated in a new square, the buildings of which, though small, are very handsome, and kept in great order. Indeed, in every respect, Vittoria is one of the best looking towns I have seen in Spain, having in general the appearance of industry and comfort It is the chief town of Alava, formerly one of the provinces of Biscay, but now united to Old Castile; and has considerable iron works, the produce of which is sent to various parts of Spain.

It was formerly also an *entrepôt* of colonial produce, but this advantage it has almost totally lost by Napoleon's prohibitory decrees, Its manufactories of woollens, silk, and cotton, however, still exist, and it has a great number of straw, chair, and tin workshops; Its population is about six thousand. The most conspicuous public building is the hospital, which is well distributed and regulated; it has two hundred beds, and though intended for the use of the people of the town alone, it was now full of French soldiers.

I dined late and alone at my quarters, and in the evening enjoyed the pleasing society of my landlord, a physician, and his family, who with some neighbours, among whom were some pretty girls, were assembled in the kitchen. We played at *Bouillotte*, and the young ladies, I suppose from my being a stranger, took a great interest in my game. The evening closed with a supper, and some delightfully wild and simple Spanish airs, accompanied by the guitar.

Having now quitted Old Castile, and entered into a totally different country, I trust my readers will not be displeased with a few observations I was enabled to make on the former. The soil of Old Castile, though inferior to that of several other parts of Spain, is, generally speaking, superior to France, and most other parts of Europe; and industry is alone wanting to bring it to a high state of forwardness. Some districts afford good wine, and the finest wool of the kingdom.

Two considerable rivers, the Douro and the Ebro, rise in Old Castile; the former in the Sierra d'Urbino, from whence it runs in a western direction across Spain, and after a course of three hundred and twenty miles empties itself into the Atlantic Ocean, at Oporto. The Ebro has its source in the mountains of Santillane, near the Asturias, and runs easterly to the Mediterranean. Besides these principal rivers Old Castile has a number of inferior ones, amongst which ire the Arlançon, Arlanca, Nazarilla,

Valtayo Buryo, and the Paz, which runs through the fertile valley of the same name, and of whose waters the inhabitants have taken advantage to carry irrigation to a high state of perfection. The peasants of this valley, known by the name of Paziegos, are celebrated for their bodily strength and personal courage.

Old Castile has several considerable towns, but the present state of uncertainty (as to who shall eventually remain master of the country, as well as the natural indolence of the Spaniards,) paralyses all industry; and hence the towns in general present the appearance of lifeless stupor.

As it is impossible to repeat too often how effectually the Spaniards might resist their invaders by a proper occupation of the mountain passes, I shall just notice those of Old Castile, not only from my own observations, and an attention to the maps, but also from various authors who have written on Spain. The mountains of St. Andero extend from Old Castile to the Bay of Biscay, and have several passes of such a nature that a regular army could never force them, if properly defended by the mountaineers.

The Sierra d'Atujio covers almost the entire of Castile, to the frontiers of Arragon; and the Sierra d'Occa, the Mons Idubeda of the Romans, extends to the kingdom of Leon and the borders of Biscay, separating Old Castile from the Asturias. Besides these principal ridges there are several ramifications, rendering this country one of the most defensible of Europe.

Having quitted Vittoria at five o'clock in the morning, the 14th of January, the arrival of daylight presented us with the view of a country very different from that which we had hitherto traversed. The mountains of Biscay appeared wooded to their summits, and the fertile valleys, even at this dreary season, presented the most romantic scenery, which the appearance of industry rendered doubly pleasing.

The soil appeared to be in general a stiff clay, requiring many drains, and where a plough can seldom be used; instead of which, the ground is turned up with long three pronged forks. Four men, with one of these implements in each hand, place themselves at the side of the drain, and sticking the fork in the ground spring up on them, keeping exact time, while a woman clears the drain. Here I observed extensive fields of various kinds of vetches, and of turnips, not so large, but more solid than our Norfolk turnips. This is the first time I have seen this root cultivated in fields in Spain.

We frequently met mules with a strong basket slung on each side of them, something resembling those in which oysters are carried in England; on inquiry I found they contained horse-shoes, which are manufactured to a great extent in this part of Biscay, and sent to all parts of Spain. It is here customary to shoe the oxen, which is thus performed. The animal is placed in a frame resembling that in which our farriers cut horses' tails: in the centre is a pulley, by which, and by the power of a windlass, the ox is raised off the ground, the fore knees are bent and kept so by iron clasps near each knee, the hind feet sure extended on a board, so as to present the flat of the hoof to receive the shoe, and the tail is made fast to the top of the frame, so that altogether the animal makes a strange ludicrous appearance as if going to fly.

From the summit of a hill we got the first view of the village of Salinas, where we were to breakfast; it appeared to be perpendicularly beneath us, and no visible road to descend by; we however found a zig-zag, which reminded me of Ladder Hill, in the island of St. Helena; but with this difference, that there nothing but barren black rocky precipices present themselves to the eye, commanding a boundless view of the Ocean; while here you wind down the hill through a thick wood, and hear the fall of a cascade concealed among the trees.

As we entered Salinas, a discharged French soldier solicited charity, telling me a lamentable story of his sufferings, and wounds; I gave him a *picette*,[1] and while sitting at breakfast at a *fonda*, I was surprised to see him enter the robot, draw a chair and seat himself at the table, with all the nonchalance possible, while with a part of my small donation he procured a hearty

---

1. A silver coin worth about fourteen pence.

breakfast, and during the repast conversed with me with perfect familiarity.

Here I may observe, that certainly I gained more knowledge of the manners of foreigners during this *bon gré mal gré* journey through Spain, than I should probably have done in travelling my whole life in the usual manner; for I was now obliged to mix with all descriptions of persons, from the general to the private soldier, and with Spaniards, French, Poles, and that motley and debased species of Germans that forms the contingents of the Confederation of the Rhine. From Salinas, the distance to Mendragon is only four leagues, by a rapid descent, so that we reached this latter place early, and I had the good fortune to be again billeted on a priest.

I found however much difficulty in procuring rations for myself or provender for the mules, from not having a *feuille de route* (my name being only included in the general list of prisoners) which was left with the officer commanding the preceding convoy; but at last succeeded, and after dinner spent the evening in the kitchen, where were assembled several girls, who while they spun, amused the time chanting Spanish ditties, which derived an increased agreeableness from the innocence and simplicity of the singers, I was told that a girl could earn by spinning at her leisure hours only, and merely as a pastime, three *reals* a week, or about twenty-one pence English.

The appearance of the French *chasseur* who took care of the mules, immediately checked the gaiety of the Spanish girls, and a gloomy silence succeeded, of which I immediately perceived the cause, and taking an opportunity of getting rid of the *chasseur*, good humour was immediately restored.

Mendragon contains about three thousand inhabitants; is built between two lofty hills, and intersected by a large river and several rivulets; and was formerly much frequented for its mineral waters. A few days before our arrival, the Cabildo and his son had been executed, for (as we were told) the assassination at various times of upwards of two hundred French. When led to execution, instead of feeling any compunction for their murders, they gloried in them, and reminded their countrymen, "that, if every Spaniard had, like them, performed his duty! the French would long before this have been exterminated and, the country freed."

CHAPTER 25

From Mendragon to St. Jean de Luz

January 15. We resumed our march at an early, hour, and passed through a mountainous country, of which some parts were highly cultivated, while others were covered with hanging woods of oak and ash. The oaks were in general small and crooked, nor was the common ash luxuriant; but the mountain ash, intermixed and covered with its red berries, had an agreeable effect.

About noon we reached the town of Tolosa, the ancient Iturissa, on the rivers Arexes and Orio, over each of which is a handsome bridge. It being market-day, we had an opportunity of seeing a number of Biscayners assembled, who had the appearance of prosperity in their dress, and of affability in their manners. The women of this province are celebrated for their beauty, and those we saw justified this character. The market seemed to be well supplied with all kinds of provisions.

Here we found an excellent inn, a very uncommon thing in the small towns of Spain. Monsieur de Billi, who was ordered to quit as to join General Mont Marie, as his *aide-de-camp*, at Valencia, gave a sumptuous breakfast; after which we proceeded, and de Billi accompanied me out of the town, being obliged to wait at Tolosa for an escort. I hoped that, as I was on horseback, I should have escaped departing embrace, *à la Françoise*; but was disappointed, for when about to return, he stopped his horse in the middle of the convoy, and kissed me very cordially on each cheek. He was, however, a good fellow; and I was afterwards very sorry to learn, that he lost one of his arms in an affair at Valencia.

During the day's march we passed through several narrow and winding passes in the Pyrenees, excavated in the solid rook at vast labour; and had an opportunity of observing the singular mode of travelling of the Biscay women, two being usually conveyed by a mule, one on each side, balancing each other, while the strange caparison of the animal, and the still stranger costume of the women, afforded a subject worthy the pencil of a Hogarth.

In the evening we reached Villa Reale, a middling town, and the following morning (January 16) continued our journey in a heavy rain, that had prevailed throughout the preceding night, and produced a great number of cascades, some of considerable size, which tumbling perpendicularly from great heights, gave an additional interest to the romantic scenery around. A commissary invited me to take shelter in a *caisson*, and I was somewhat surprised to find so much good sense and candour in a Frenchman of that class, but was soon undeceived, by him telling me that he had the honour and happiness to be a Swiss.

Adverting to the number of dismounted dragoons returning to France, and who principally formed our escort, I inquired the cause of so great a destruction of horses in the French army, and learnt that it was owing to the neglect in the management of them. The commissary, who was in a situation to ascertain the fact, assured me that the French armies in Spain had lost sixty thousand horses, valued each at sixteen *louis*; which makes the total loss in this article of military expenditure alone, amount to near one million sterling. From this person I also received some account of the French army in Portugal, which he said was at times so short of provisions, that the soldiers were frequently upon one-sixth allowance; hence he concluded that they would soon be obliged to evacuate that country, and that the evacuation of Andalusia would probably soon follow.

He also spoke of Napoleon's popularity among the superior officers in a very different manner from what I had heard from others; and if he was correct, the control and obedience in which he keeps them, shews great ability, as well as firmness of character.

We reached Urnietia before dark, and I was quartered at the extremity of the town, where, my reception from my landlady was so uncouth, that I was obliged to threaten her with applying for other quarters, in which case she would have a French officer billeted on her; a threat she did not at all seem to relish. On my return front procuring provisions and forage, I was quite surprised at the change in this lady's manner, for she was now civil in the extreme. After dinner she entered the room, and first fastening the door, asked me if it was really true that I was an English officer, as somebody had told her; and when I answered in the affirmative, and related the manner of my being made prisoner, her sensibility got the better of her; her eyes gradually filled, and at last she burst into a flood of tears.

When I asked her to sell and dress me a fowl for next day's march, the offer of payment made her think I was still offended; and to convince her of the contrary, I was obliged to accept some fowls and ham "of her own curing." She also begged permission to introduce her brother, who, she said, had been quite melancholy since the entrance of the French, and that the sight of an English officer would be highly gratifying and reviving to him; he accordingly made his appearance, and his deportment was such as to command respect and create confidence.

He regretted that while England was so generously shedding her blood and expending her treasures for the support of Spanish liberty, she had neglected sending officers and arms to Biscay, for that, to his knowledge, there were sixty thousand stout, determined fellows registered, and ready for organization at the first favourable moment.

He also mentioned the ports where arms might be landed with safety, as well as those which should be avoided, as being strictly watched by the enemy. At the same time he drew a topographical sketch of the country, pointing out the passes most capable of defence; adding that, though the Biscayners wanted no other stimulus than their patriotism, they would be sure to find ample pecuniary reward, by the capture of the treasure every day passing from France into Spain. Before we parted,. I concerted some arrangements, in case a future chance should cause me to land on that coast.

January 17. I was waked early in the morning by the sound of the *tocsin*, announcing a fire, and on inquiry, learned that the town-house had been set on fire by the French soldiers. As my host told me that it was very unsafe to walk alone in the streets, even in the day, from the inveteracy of the inhabitants towards the French, for one of whom I might be taken, he offered to accompany me through the town; and I found, that his caution was not unnecessary, as we met several scattered groups of sullen and apparently irritated people in the streets.

About a league from the town we fell in with a convoy of sick and wounded, belonging to the army of Portugal, going into France. Here, from an elevation, we caught a fine view of the Bay of Biscay, the port of Saint Sebastian (abort half a league distant), and those of St, Andero, Santona, Guetaria, and Bilbao, all in sight, being situated on a curve of the coast

We reached Irun to breakfast; and as we were to separate here, I invited sixteen of my *compagnons de voyage* to partake of as good a breakfast as could be procured in this miserable place; the last town of Spain: on quitting which, there being no longer any necessity for an escort, each individual of the convoy was free to push on as he thought fit for the place of his destination.

After crossing a wooden bridge over the Bidassoa, which separates Spain from France, I at length arrived on the territory of *la grande nation*. Here my baggage was examined, at a kind of custom-house, where the duties are paid on merchandize passing from Spain into France. This ceremony over, I was about, to pursue my route, but was stopped by a *gend'arme*, who demanded, my *feuille de route*; and on my saying I had none, refused to let me proceed. A Polish major just then coming up, offered to pass me on: but this I declined, fearing he might esteem it a great favour, and be inclined to honour we with more of his company than would be agreeable; I therefore, returned back to Irun, and applied to the commandant for the necessary paper, which he did not think himself authorized to grant, although the corporal of a guard might have gone farther without straining his responsibility.

I however met the lieutenant commanding the convoy, who accompanied me to the barrier; and shewing my name in the *feuille de route*, I was allowed to proceed to St. Jean de Luz, about eight miles distant, and over a heavy road. Here I was billeted at the house of two ancient maiden ladies, who every moment expressed their dread of a visit from the Spaniards; but as I assured them that their virtue and property were equally safe in that respect, I succeeded in tranquillizing their fears.

According to agreement made at Irun, I met Monsieur Pole and the Swiss commissary at dinner at the Porte Impériale, an inn of considerable repute, but which fell far short of the idea that had been given me of it. Our dinner was made up of scraps, consisting of the legs of a salt goose, and the legs and neck of a fowl, with some vegetables. The wine was little better than vinegar: added to which, the whole was thrown on the table as if it fell from Heaven by chance. My companions praised everything, exclaiming, "*quel bonheur! nous voilà en France!*" but for my own part I could not help observing, that if such was the fare I had to expect in France, I should prefer returning into Spain. I however at last succeeded in procuring a little good Claret, which in some degree compensated for the other deficiencies.

Before continuing my journey through France, I shall offer a few observations on the province of Biscay, and the road through the Pyrenees, to cross which it took us three days most fatiguing march.

Biscay is formed of three subdivisions, *viz*. Guipuscoa, Beisorio, and La Montana. The only carriage road through the Pyrenees, on this side, is between St Jean de Luz, through Irun to Vittoria, and was at this time almost impassable, from the continual passage of vehicles and the total want of repairs. Between

Vittoria and Irun the road is skirted by numerous villages, wearing the appearance of industry and comfort.

Biscay has twenty-one considerable towns, of which the principal is Bilboa, possessing a good port and considerable trade,—with an air so pure that it may be called the Montpelier of Spain; patients, therefore, particularly with chronicle complaints, ace ordered here by the faculty, The extent of the territory of Alava, which formerly was included in the province of Biscay, but is now united to Old Castile, is fourteen leagues east and west, and ten north, and south. Guipuscoa, which is considerably the largest of the divisions of Biscay, is eighteen leagues east and west, and twelve north and south; its surface is composed of lofty mountains with narrow passes, and inhabited by a brave and warlike people, who should, above all the inhabitants of the Peninsula, call the attention of the British government in the present contest.

This division has ten leagues of coast, in which there are several good ports, *viz.* St. Sebastian, Passages, &c. Those of Guetaria, Orio, Zaraus, Zumaya, Deva, and Motrico, though of less consideration, are accessible to vessels of a certain size; and indeed it seems astonishing that England neglected occupying these ports at the commencement of her alliance with Spain, for their possession would have been of inestimable value at different periods of the war.

Besides the three divisions already noticed, there is a territory included in Biscay called the Four Towns; each of these divisions is of; a triangular shape, and they all join each other. When Caesar invaded Spain, in the century before the Christian era, the whole of Biscay formed one province under the name of Cantabria, and its inhabitants in the fastnesses of their mountains defied the armies of the Romans; and aided by their neighbours the Asturians, and by the Gallicians, carried desolation into the subdued provinces.

Although Augustus entered Avala and Guipuscoa with a formidable army, and defeated the Cantabrians and their allies in the plains; they still held out in their mountains, and were never entirely subdued. The Asturians, after sustaining a long and bloody siege in Oviedo, surrendered; but the Gallicians, surrounded on all sides, preferred death to subjection, and were exterminated in the most desperate and unequal conflicts.

The Cantabrians, in want of provisions, determined to die by each others' hands, and a great number put this desperate design into execution; those who remained harassed the Romans by a predatory warfare, and although Fabricius erected forts in the mountains, and adopted every other means to subdue them, after a century of glorious struggle, they succeeded in expelling their invaders, and continued to enjoy undisturbed liberty until a century after the establishment of the Moors in Spain. From what I saw of them the modern Biscayners have not degenerated from their Cantabrian ancestors in firmness and courage.

Chapter 26

Route to Bourdeaux

On the 18th of January I quitted St Jean de Luz for Bayonne. The Bay of Biscay presented its vast expanse of waters on the left, and called up the reflection that these waters alone separated me from all I held dear in life, and that with a favourable breeze I could reach the coasts of England in four days. Two British cruisers which appeared in the offing, did not fail to add to my regret at the impossibility of realizing my visions.

After a long and wishful look and many a heavy sigh, I pursued my journey, but could not recover my spirits for the rest of the day. The road between St. Jean de Luz and Bayonne is very hilly, and was now much broken up by numbers of wheel carriages, passing to and from Spain. On my arrival at the latter town, I found all the inns so crowded, that no accommodation was to be had in them; I therefore presented my letters of introduction to Messrs. Dehne and Bourdehus, extensive merchants, who were extremely civil, and not only procured me lodgings, but insisted on my dining with them. I spent the evening, also, agreeably in their society.

January 19. I waited on General Sols, the commandant, who received me with the politeness of the old French school. After some conversation he shewed me a letter from General Beliard, who it seems wished to follow up his persecution, by recommending the strictest surveillance over me, being, according to his expression, "a dangerous character." Fortunately however General Sols had made inquiries, respecting foe of some of the officers of the escort, whose answers did away all the unfavourable impressions that might have been made by General Beliard's letter. I also waited on General Quesnel, commanding the staff, for whom I had a letter from General Sebastiani, and met with a frigidly polite reception.

January 20. Having received intimation from Marshal Bessières, Duc d'Istrie, that he desired to see me, I accordingly waited on him, and was received with great *fierté*; but after some conversation his manners altered, and became most gentlemanlike. He mentioned the desertion of Captain A—— who had been made prisoner, with me, and who had escaped from an escort in the North of Spain, in a manner that gave me reason to fear that myself and another officer might in consequence be deprived of our parole. I therefore avoided entering into the merits of the case, and only replied, "*c'est un malheur, mais il faut attendre à ces choses.*"

My subsequent conversation with the duke however removed all my fears, for having introduced subjects with which I happened to be well acquainted, he took an interest in me, and invited me to dinner the following day. On my return to my lodgings, I received a visit from Colonel F—— and the commander of the convoy, who behaved in the most handsome manner, and we made out a satisfactory statement of Captain A——'s escape.

January 21. According to invitation, I proceeded to dine with the Duc d'Istrie, in full uniform. He was very attentive, gave me an excellent dinner and wines, particularly Madeira, of which he had opened a case purposely for me. Our conversation turned principally on the events in Spain, in which he appeared, as might be expected, much interested.

On retiring he begged me to call on him, before I quitted Bayonne next day, and he would give me some letters to his friends at Bourdeaux, which would at least ensure me a good dinner and excellent wine; this of course I did not fail to do, when he not only presented me several letters but also an hundred *louis-d'or*, offering to furnish me with more if I wished; but I declined his obliging offer, and we parted with mutual regret.

During the few days I remained at Bayonne, I visited the environs, and particularly that part in which were several American vessels, lately confiscated, in consequence of the Berlin decree, and re-purchased by the Americans.

There were also in the river seven American built schooners, under the French Imperial flag, ready for sailing, and which had been equipped to make a run to the isle of France with troops, and to bring home the produce of the island. The crews of these vessels were mostly composed of boys, raised by a recent maritime conscription,. and of whom it was doubtless intended to make seamen in this voyage *de longue course*. I felt no small satisfaction, while viewing these schooners, in knowing that the isle of France was already in our possession, and that the intention of this expedition was therefore entirely frustrated.

The town of Bayonne is about three miles from the sea, at the junction of the little rivers Adour and Neve, which divide it into three parts; the entrance of the port is narrow, and a very dangerous bar crosses it, on which, in westerly winds, there is a most furious surf; but which is not without its advantage, for it shelters the port towards the sea. The commerce of this town was formerly very considerable, but the war and the anti-commercial decrees of Buonaparte, have left it only an insignificant coasting trade.

I must not forget to observe, for the benefit *des gourmands*, that Bayonne is celebrated for its hams; and I could not quit it without satisfying myself whether it deserved this celebrity. I accordingly had one drest under my own inspection, and as a considerable degree of science is required in dressing a ham, I am sure the lovers of good eating will not be sorry to have my receipt. Boil it in hock, a quarter of an hour to each pound; then put it in an oven and bake it another quarter of an hour to; the same weight; and I will venture to say, the epicures will acknowledge that nothing can be more delicious. While I am on the subject of cookery, I may be pardoned for mentioning an anecdote which comes *à propos*. In a passage to South America, a confident epicure who was continually giving us receipts for dressing the *albicore, bonettas* and sharks; we occasionally took, and as continually expatiating on the excellence of the dolphin (of which we had not yet caught one) when properly drest, I begged him to give me his receipt, which he did at full length, and when he had finished his tedious detail, I told him my receipt began in a very different manner. After his expressing much anxiety to know my plan, and keeping him long in suspense, I told him I always followed Mrs. Glass's receipt, which begins with, *First take*[1]

While at Bayonne, and happening to be in company with Colonel Natalis of the Engineers, I observed an officer regarding me steadily, and who at last asked me if I had ever been in Egypt? On my answering in the affirmative he recalled to my recollection my having been sent in advance, with a detachment of British troops and some Arnauts, by order of Colonel Stewart, when we surprised and captured a convoy of twenty-two boats, near Ramaniah, which were conveying stores to the French army. It was a most fortunate capture for our officers, who were almost barefooted, for we found in the prize, boots and shoes, with which we immediately fitted ourselves. This officer, who was in one of the boats, expressed his gratitude for the protection the English afforded him against the savage ferocity of our Turkish allies.

Having received a *feuille de route*, on the 27th I commenced my journey to Bourdeaux on horseback. The road to St. Vincent, the first stage, is a deep sand, and was now almost impassable, being so much broken up by the passage of wagons, &c. St. Vincent contains nothing worthy of notice, and St. Juan, the second stage, consists only of a few straggling houses. At the lat-

---

1. On the following day we actually did take a dolphin, and the dressing of it was left to me. I ordered it to be simply boiled in salt and water, and to be shewed up with abundance of melted butter in a sauceboat, with plenty of Cayenne pepper to mix with it; and though this was so simple a process, I found it was more universally relished than that of the officer's, which was very complicated, and attended with great trouble.

ter I put up for the night, and found the landlord of the inn civil, and more particularly attentive when he learned my country. He provided me with a tolerable supper, and I had nothing to complain of except a legion of rats, that amused themselves dancing about my room all night.

January 28. As I found the high road crowded with soldiers and carts, whose rencontre every moment was far from agreeable, I inquired of my landlord if I could not avoid it, and learned that by crossing the country about two leagues, I should get into the old road, which would shorten the distance to Bourdeaux, and that, though deep, I should be able to get on very well on horseback. He also offered to send his son to shew me the way, and having taken a glass of brandy with the obliging old gentleman, and received his *bon voyage,* I proceeded across a heath, and through a little wood, till I reached the road, where my guide left me, and I entered into an immense forest of firs. Most of the trees; I observed, had large slices of the bark stripped off from top to bottom for the purpose of procuring the turpentine.

I soon arrived at a beautifully romantic village, called Castels situated in a ravine, near a cascade. The houses were of wood, and the whole had a neat and cheerful appearance, which, as well as the civility of the *aubergiste,* induced me, though it was only noon, to rest here the remainder of the day. It was the fête of the patron saint of the village, and groups of peasants were collected, dancing and running for small prizes. The neat and simple costume of the *paysannes* in particular struck me.

My landlord, however, assured me with a sigh, that this appearance of cheerfulness covered a great degree of misery, from the total stagnation of trade, leaving them no means of exporting the produce of the pine forests, in which consisted their sole riches. At the same time, the price of corn had nearly doubled, and sugar and coffee, which in this part of the country long habit had almost rendered necessaries of life, from twenty to twenty-four sols the pound, were now five and six *francs.*

Here I could not help reflecting, that sugar and coffee, being luxuries, might at all events be dispensed with, and therefore their high price could only be felt by the superior elate; but the dearness of grain, on the contrary, falls entirely on the lower order, for grain is an article of absolute necessity, that cannot be dispensed with. I may here also observe, that the exorbitant price of sugar and coffee reducing the consumption, reduced the revenues and prosperity of the country, in a proportion that the framers of the decrees of Berlin and Milan seem not to have been aware of.

With respect to the produce of the pine forests in this department, I received some information here, which I trust will not be found uninteresting.

The species of pine which composes the forests of this and the neighbouring department, is that named in France the Pin Maritime, which thrives in the most sandy soils. When the tree has attained from three to five feet circumference, a hole is bored at the bottom of the trunk, an inch deep and three inches in diameter; below which a small excavation is made in the ground to receive the resinous sap of the free, which distils from it.

The wound is made at the commencement of spring, and is enlarged upwards several times during the summer, and in successive years. The substance received into the reservoir is boiled to a certain consistence, to form what is called in commerce *brac sac*; and it converted into resin, by the following simple process. While boiling, it is suffered to run from the boiler into a wooden trough, filled with water, from whence it is again returned into the boiler, and this continual transversement gradually combines the water and the *brac*, until by their intimate union they become resin.

Tar is the producer of the sap of the pine, combined with resin by the action of fire

Besides resin and tar, the pine affords turpentine, and lampblack, which is produced by the combustion of the resin.

On the 29th I resumed my journey through a very deep sand, which doubtless was the reason for changing the great road, and reached a place, called Harrie, consisting of a few houses, where I baited the horses, and again proceeding, arrived in the evening at La Bohat, the whole day's journey being through pine forests. Though my fare at the *auberge* was far from sumptuous, the civility of my landlord and his wife, who produced the best their humble but romantic mansion afforded, reconciled me to remain here the night.

They expressed their surprise at seeing a person of my appearance travelling in so wretched a country, and I found next morning that as they seldom had such visitors; they were determined to make the most of me, and to be well paid for their compliments to myself and my country. I at first thought of remonstrating on the exorbitance of their charges, but when I recollected that the honour of England was concerned, I determined to pay as they charged, *comme un Milord Anglois*; a title which the innkeepers in France not seeming to understand properly, generally act as if they supposed lord to mean *l'or*, and consequently that an Englishman, being a heap of gold, ought not to be let to pass without a handsome contribution.

January 30. This day's journey lay through a more open country, but very swampy; with numbers of small sheep scattered over it, jumping from hillock to hillock to graze. The boys who herded them at first greatly surprised me, by the apparent length and slenderness of their legs; but on approaching, I found they were mounted on stilts, fastened with a strap to each thigh, by which means they were elevated three or four feet from the ground, and were enabled to walk dry over the little pools of water.

As the stilts do not sink deep in the sandy soil, they manage them with great dexterity, running and jumping with vast activity; and have also a greater command in the superintendence of their little flocks, While thus occupied, they are also employed in knitting stockings. I this night slept at a place called Bard, and in the morning commenced my last day's journey to Bourdeaux.

Chapter 27

Bourdeaux

The road on approaching Bourdeaux became excessively bad, but the country was highly cultivated; nevertheless there was a general appearance of declining prosperity. The merchants' country houses, which in a state of flourishing commerce are usually conspicuous for their neatness, seemed now generally neglected, and the *châteaux* presented a still more desolate appearance.

On my arrival at Bourdeaux I proceeded to the Hôtel de Funal, on the Chartrons, which commands a fine and extensive view up the Garonne. I had formerly visited this city, when "commerce proudly flourished in the State;" the river was then covered with a forest of masts the whole length of the Chartrons, which extends four miles in the form of a crescent, and its quays presented a scene of bustle and activity never to be forgotten. What a contrast did it now offer! The few ships in the river were unrigged and their hulls rotting; and a miserably dirty sloop of war displayed the imperial colours as a guard ship, on board which, however, all the ceremonial and etiquette of a man of war seemed to be enforced. Not a boat in activity, except those that ply on the Dordogne and Garonne for passengers; in short, the port and the quays evinced a total stagnation of business.

Hearing that M. Crochard was in the hotel, I paid him a visit, and received from him instructions as to the most agreeable way of living at Bourdeaux. I ordered my dinner according to his advice, commencing with a dish of oysters, which are here of a very fine quality, and found the Sauterne, which by prescription is the only wine drank with these fish, deserving of its celebrity. It may be useful to some of my readers, whose appetites are feeble, to know that oysters are an excellent whetter, taking them immediately before dinner, and not exceeding a dozen at the most, with a small proportion of lemon juice squeezed into each.

In the evening I accompanied Monsieur and Madame Crochard to the theatre, to see the *Médecin malgré lui* of Molière, which was followed by a ballet; but it being Saturday, which is the worst day in the week for the receipts of the theatre, the house was very thinly attended. February 1. In the morning I strolled about the town, and as Bourdeaux is one of the best places in France to get equipped *à l'Anglaise*, I called at a tailor's to order some clothes, of which I stood much in need. I also visited a coachmaker's repository, having some idea of purchasing a carriage, but the assortment was chiefly confined to *cabriolets*, which did not suit me.

Like all his countrymen, the coach-maker neglected his business, *pour causer*, and instead of an eulogium on his carriages, entertained me with a violent philippic against the commercial measures of the moment; and certainly the daily bankruptcies of the first houses in the country, in consequence of the decrees of Buonaparte, are sufficient causes for the complaints of the mercantile class.

In the evening I again went to the theatre, which was now brilliantly attended, the Sabbath being the day of amusement as well as of rest from labour in France. The piece was *Cendrillon*, taken from the story so well known to children of the Little Glass Slipper. The music was in general tight and cheerful, and among the airs was the "*bon voyage of Monsieur du Molet*," at this moment a favourite popular tune throughout France, and of the same stamp as those airs which in England get possession of all classes for a few months, until some fresh nonsense supersedes them; such are Nancy Dawson, the Grinder, Yankee Doodle, &c. to which airs many add verses of their own composition.

The carriage which conveyed Cindrellon to the ball was drawn by real ponies, and the fat coachman and lackeys came out of a hole on one side of the. stage, intended to denote their metamorphosis from rats; the machinery was indeed superlative, and the whole had an admirable effect The concluding piece was *Montano et Stephana*. Bourdeaux at this time possessed Mesdames Clairville and Folleville, with Mortelli, all superior performers in the *grand opera*.

In the *petit opera* it had Mesdames Begran and Lorraine, as first dancers. Of the men Ferdinand was considered the firsthand Chou Chou the second; the former was engaged for the opera at Vienna. It is said there is much more difficulty in finding good performers for the comedy and *petit opera* than for the *grand*, for which there are always abundance of candidates. The salary of the first men dancers, in the *petit opera*, is ten thousand *francs* a year.

In the course of the following day (Feb. 2) I visited several parts of the town, and engaged an English party to dine at the Hôtel du Prince, *ci-devant* Hôtel d'Angleterre, a name which the proprietor found it advisable to change in the present government mania against whatever bears any relation to our country, but which he means to restore when this frenzy ceases. Our dinner was uncommonly good, and the wine so delicious, that several of the party who had long been obliged to put up with the wretched.

Spanish trash, did such credit to the Bourdeaux, that its effects soon began to appear in their merry pranks, which astonished the people of the house, who were not at all accustomed to the freaks of an English drinking party. Indeed a Frenchman, who is ten times more volatile when sober than an Englishman, becomes stupidly, serious as the liquor mounts. This trait of national character is doubtless owing to the independent ideas instilled into us from the cradle, and which gives to every individual a peculiarity of manner and of mind.

All Frenchmen, on the contrary, resemble each other; being unused to think for themselves, their conversation is made up of quaint sayings and hackneyed *bons mots*, stupid beyond conception. The sayings of a great man, who has the reputation of possessing *de l'esprit*, are repeated to satiety. In short, the manners, dress, and address of a Frenchman are equally disgusting, with the exception of the few remains of the old *noblesse*, who retain the polished manners of their order, so totally opposite to those of the parvenus of the present day.

February 3. In the morning I waited in uniform on General Boisvin, the *commandant de place*, and was shewn into a room by a servant; here I waited some time, and no general appearing, I again sent the servant to announce me, and to inquire if it was convenient for the general to receive at, adding, that my visit was merely of ceremony, and that I had nothing particular to say.

On his appearance he seemed surprised, not having been informed by the servant who I was, and the uniform of a British general officer seemed to have an imposing effect; besides, I assumed a distant and dignified air, which made him perceive that I was displeased at being kept waiting, for which he blundered out an apology as well as his abilities would admit. On retiring he had, however, the civility to attend me to the carriage.

Having disencumbered myself of my uniform, I called on some of my acquaintances; and also on Monsieur Lynch, the mayor of the city, descended from an Irish family, and of most gentlemanly manners. From him I went to visit Monsieur Pierre Pierre, the commissary of police, a personage of no small consequence in a French town, and whose good will it is necessary for all strangers, like myself on sufferance only, to conciliate.

He immediately told me the number of bottles we had drank the evening before, with the whole particulars of our conversation, and appeared extremely proud of his *espionnage*; for he seemed to have the vanity to think, that because, he received information of whatever passed in all companies, public or private, he, thence derived as much consequence as if he had been admitted to them.

To humour him, I expressed my astonishment at the correctness of his information, although I was very sure that he received it from an American doctor, who by making himself useful to all the English passing through Bourdeaux, was always invited to their parties; and although it was well known that he was employed by the police, it was advisable to keep on good terms with him, as a denunciation, however false, would probably have been productive of a lodging in a *cachot*, without any investigation; besides, he was capable of being extremely useful to a stranger, knowing everything and everybody in Bourdeaux.

After paying several other visits, I dined off a boiled leg of mutton and turnips, a dish I had not seen for so long a time, that I almost fancied myself in England. At dinner I met with Captain Geils of the 3rd Guards, Captain Reynolds of the 83rd, and a quarter-master of the 4th, all taken in Spain, and the two former severely wounded. As they were very inquisitive about affairs in. Spain, and the wine being excellent, we made a late sitting.

February 4. Strolling through the streets in the forenoon, I observed a very pretty girl standing at a shop door, whom, *pour passer le temps*, I accosted with a compliment on her beauty, which she received as most pretty girls do, and more particularly French *grisettes*, as if it was only her due. Soon perceiving that I was an Englishman, she launched into an eulogium on the nation, but at the same time observing that we had faults, of which not the least was our neglect of the *beau sexe*; then changing the subject with abrupt vivacity, she observed that my coat was rather tarnished, and recommended its being scowered, which her father, whose trade it was, would speedily perform. I allowed her to shew me into a back apartment, where the old gentleman was at work, to whom I promised to send the coat as soon as I got another from the taylor, this being the only one I at present possessed.

"*Tenez*" replied he, "*en voici un qui vous ira à merveilles*" and though the cut was rather *outré*, I put it on and left him mine, "to come out;" as he expressed it, "entirely new!"

From the repeated assurances of the father and daughter that the coat fitted me *à merveille*, I thought I might pass without notice; but I had scarcely quitted the shop when I met with three English gentlemen, who burst into a horse-laugh at my costume; and, it being carnival time, observed, "that I was already drest for the masquerade."

Although I joined in the laugh, I did not choose to expose myself to a repetition of it, and on reaching the hotel immediately sent for my coat, but was told that it was in the tub: and the taylor not having finished either of those I had ordered, I was under the necessity of confining myself to the house for the rest of the day. As our officers had taken up their quarters at a hotel opposite, and were in the article of dress even worse off than myself (having only the old torn regimentals on their backs), I invited them to keep me in countenance, and we passed the day together in playing at piquet and laughing at each other's dress.

In the evening I sent to desire the company of my friend the scowerer, who immediately arrived, and afforded me much amusement. Knowing the character of this description of Frenchmen, I proposed to send an excellent supper to his house, in order to have the pleasure of passing the evening with him and his lovely daughter, with which proposition he immediately complied, and retired to make the necessary preparations. I shortly followed him to his apartments, which were very neatly furnished.

The young lady was very entertaining, and the old gentleman so *complaisant* as soon to retire, and leave me to enjoy her fascinating conversation till late in the evening. I afterwards learnt that this man had acted a conspicuous part in the revolutionary committees, and during a part of that blood-stained period was the terror of Bourdeaux.

February 5. The next morning, according to appointment, I went, accompanied by the American doctor as Cicerone, to inspect the curiosities of Bourdeaux.

We first visited the military hospital, in which were several English officers, particularly a Mr. Grant, of the 24th regiment, who had been badly wounded at the battle of Talavera. He was in the same ward with several French officers; for in the French service an officer who reports himself sick is obliged to go immediately to the hospital, which effectually prevents their attempting to evade their duty by pretending illness: and it would be well if some strong regulation was adopted in our service, to prevent the numberless abuses which take place in this respect

In the course of our walk we passed a very fine Roman triumphal arch, disfigured by modern ornaments; and on inquiring of my companion, (who in whatever regarded the things or people of Bourdeaux was a perfect Asmodeus) he informed me that the arch had been erected to Trajan, but that the modern decorations were attached to it when Buonaparte was at Bourdeaux, it being expected that he would pass under it, which he however declined; whether from a modest diffidence with respect to his equality with the Roman Emperor, or as some people said, from the conviction of his own superiority, which caused him to despise this kind of half homage, I cannot undertake to decide.[1]

Bourdeaux formerly the capital of Guienne and at present the chief town of the department of the Gironde, is considered in the first class of French cities, and contains upwards of one hundred thousand inhabitants. It had formerly an university and an academy, of arts and sciences, a court of admiralty, &c. In 1642, it was granted a parliament, by Louis XI. Its public establishments at present are, a lyceum, the most magnificent theatre in France, and a mint. It is the residence of a prefect, and has a criminal tribunal and a tribunal of appeal, for the departments of Charente, Dordogne, and Gironde.

I this morning accompanied Monsieur Cabanis to his country seat, about two leagues from Bourdeaux, which is pleasantly situated, commanding a fine and extensive view, but greatly neglected. He informed me, that the want of a market for the produce, reduced the value of the vineyards to less than the expenses of their cultivation, and that he would gladly let his house and domain rent free, on condition of keeping the vineyards in

---

1. I afterwards understood the real cause was its not having been erected from the foundation expressly for himself.

order. In many of the walks I observed snares for taking woodcocks, and one got entangled while I was there.

It being Sunday the theatre was crowded as usual, and I must confess I am not so rigid as to see anything contrary either to religion or good morals, in attending this amusement on the Sabbath. In our protestant countries Sunday is a day of moping tiresomeness, yet surely we may observe with Sterne,

> That the Great Father of all does not expect us to vex and shorten a life, short and vexatious enough already; that he who is infinitely happy cannot envy us our enjoyments, or that a Being, so infinitely kind, would grudge a mournful traveller the short rest and refreshments, necessary to support his spirits through the stages of a weary pilgrimage; or that he would call him to a severe reckoning, because in his way he had hastily snatched at some little fugacious pleasure, merely to sweeten this uneasy journey of life, and reconcile him to the ruggedness of the road, and the many hard jostlings he is sure to meet with.

The entertainment this evening at the theatre, was, however, analogous to the day, for it was the story of Susannah and the Elders, metamorphosed into a pantomime. The two ancient sinners attempt to accomplish their purpose on the chaste damsel, while she is in the bath, but being foiled, they denounce her guilty of a *faux-pas*, and wickedly swear that they found her under a tree in an awkward situation.

On this evidence she is condemned, and about to be executed, when the angel Gabriel descends and advises the judges to examine each old man separately, when their stories not agreeing, the damsel is released, and her accusers are sentenced to be stoned to death. The music of this entertainment was exquisite, the scenery superb, and the descent and ascent of the Archangel very well managed. Indeed it was impossible not to admire the ingenuity with which so serious a subject was brought on the stage in the shape of a pantomime.

A Mademoiselle Byrom acted Susannah, who appeared a chaste actress, at least on the stage. A melodrama succeeded the pantomime. This is a new species of theatrical entertainment, composed of a mixture of comedy, opera and pantomime, and is at present quite the rage in France.

CHAPTER 28

Masquerade

From the theatre I went to sup with the American doctor, who had invited a party to meet me; the formality and ceremony with which I was treated, did away all idea of comfort, and I was glad to be relieved by pleading an engagement to the *bal masqué*, where I was fully recompensed. The price of admission was very trifling, and the hire of a dress only thirty *sols*. I first chose the character of a Benedictine Monk, which I thought so easy to support, that there was no fear of my being discovered; but I enjoyed myself so much, and the scene was altogether so novel, that I forgot the gravity of my character, and was soon discovered to be an *Anglois*!

My fellow officers, who were also present, were soon known, and we were obliged to accept numberless invitations to drink Champagne-punch from our French acquaintances, who paid many liberal compliments to the British character. I now changed my dress for that of a miller, and got on very well for some time, until I met by chance one of our officers, whose mask was off, and who was tormented by a tall priest following him all over the room.

When I came up to him my friend was in close conversation with a pretty orange girl, and the priest looking at him fixedly, uttered a deep groan; " d—n the priest," said the Englishman, forgetting himself, "he persecutes me everywhere:" at which I could not help laughing aloud, and my laugh again discovered me. Round the lobby were coffee rooms with all kinds of refreshments, besides several convenient private apartments elegantly fitted up, I accompanied my countrymen through all the rooms, and it seemed as if the pleasure we expressed gratified the whole assembly.

Among the most entertaining groups were thirteen boys, who exhibited a singular dance on stilts four feet from the ground, on which they kept time and performed the most difficult figures with the exactness of opera dancers. A boy of eight years old was the leader of this amusing group, and when any mistake was committed, he would frown on the defaulters, and put his finger to his nose, so as to intimate forcibly, "beware how you make a second blunder!" At five o'clock I retired, with a sufficiency of pleasing reflections to last me a twelve-month;—nor shall I ever forget the *bal masqué* at Bourdeaux!

February 7. The following morning I accompanied M. Crochard to a milliner's to purchase some cravats; but being no great judge of muslin, I requested a pretty shop girl to select some for me, and bring them to my hotel, where shortly after my return she made her appearance. There was an interesting seriousness in her manner that induced me to inquire into the cause of so uncommon an appearance in a French milliner of nineteen; and I learnt that she had lost both her father and mother (who were of the lesser *noblesse*) by the guillotine, in the revolution; that about a year back she had formed an attachment to a young man, who returned her love, and with whom she hoped to be happy the remainder of her days, and to be in some measure recompensed for the loss of her parents at so early an age; but that her lover was drawn for the conscription a few months since, and sent to Spain, where he added one to the numberless victims of Buonaparte's ambition, having been killed in battle.

She told her tale with a degree of melancholy sweetness and sensibility, whilst the tears forced their way in spite of her, that not a little affected me. While she was recounting her story the American doctor entered, and when she withdrew he bore testimony to its truth, being well acquainted with her misfortunes.

On my arrival at Bourdeaux, the doctor had recommended me a *laquais de place*, who, according to his own account, was unequalled by any of the tribe. Amongst his other qualifications was that of dressing horses; and though his appearance bespoke very little of the groom, I took him at his word, and entrusted him with the care of mine. He was a grey-headed old fellow, with a pigtail; two curls at each side; silk stockings much soiled; black velvet breeches, and a peagreen coat, with standing collar, and slack sleeves; in short, he answered completely to the description of the squires that attended the ladies in the days of chivalry.

After a day or two I recollected that it was possible this piece of antiquity might not be so *au fait* in the management of horses as he pretended, and on visiting the stable I found my doubts changed into certainty, for although there were fifty-nine empty stalls, the stupid fellow had put my horse and mare into the sixtieth; nor had they been rubbed down since my arrival, he conceiving it quite enough if they had *assez à boire et à manger*. I immediately turned the sorry groom off and could not resist abusing him, when my landlord called me aside and advised me to beware and say little, as he was a spy of the police, and might do me mischief. This information induced me to make further inquiries, when I found by a female of the house that I was surrounded by spies who doubtless reported all my actions and words.

I this day dined with one of our officers and the quartermaster, who towards the evening, as the wine began to operate, became so laughably amusing that I persuaded him to accompany me to a French party. Though he had risen from the ranks, he had a perfect confidence in his good breeding, and to shew it off made such strange gestures, kissed the ladies hands, and scraped and bowed till he became quite ridiculous.

As his compliments were paid in English they remained unanswered; and the silence of an old lady, to whom he particularly addressed himself, I persuaded him was owing to deafness, when he bawled so, loudly in her ear, that the poor woman was near going into a fit. At last dancing commenced, and, in spite of all my entreaties, he resolved upon taking out a partner; but being unused to waxed floors, his heels were soon tripped up, nor was he able to get again on his legs, for as often .as he attempted to rise the slippery floor again brought him down, and thus he remained, to the great amusement of the company, who exclaimed, "*Dieu, qu'il est drôle!*"

I proposed dancing round this fallen hero, which was immediately agreed to, and I never saw people enjoy anything more: one of the young ladies observing that, "certainly *Messieurs les Anglois* were, from their singularities, always the life and spirit of the company."

I had now become quite the lion[1] of Bourdeaux, and not a day passed without a party being given on my account. These pleasurable days were however approaching towards their termination, for General Boivin began to look on me with an evil eye, probably from not being invited to these entertainments; for although his pretensions to *esprit* were very high, he was in reality so silly that people did not choose to be annoyed by his company.

One morning I was not very agreeably surprised with a visit from the *adjutant de place*, a Pole, to inform me that I must immediately depart from Bourdeaux. I begged this officer to accompany me to the general, to which he consented, and we stepped into a hackney coach. The general, who was followed by a large greyhound, which seemed a great favourite, received me with an air of displeasure, and demanded the cause of my remaining so long at Bourdeaux? Instead of answering his question I exclaimed, "*Dieu, quel jeli chien!*" and begged permission to inquire if it belonged to him?

Upon this his countenance immediately brightened, and he anwered, "*oui, monsieur, et j'en ai trois autres.*" I then told him I was fond of dogs *à la folie*, and should esteem it a particular favour if he would allow me to see them.

---

1. Lion, according to the English fashionable imagination, is a person who all are curious to see.

"*Volontiers*" was the reply, and he conducted me to the yard, where they were passed in review, and I of course did not fail to praise their beauty and points, although neither was very conspicuous. The general next shewed me his stud, which I also pretended to admire, and begged to be gratified by his permitting me to mount one of his chargers, that I might judge better of his movements. A horse was accordingly got ready with a demi-peak, and I made him shew off to the best advantage, with which the general was so satisfied, and pleased with my compliments, that he forgot, or at least made no farther mention of my quitting Bourdeaux, and we parted with mutual compliments.

The two succeeding days passed without hearing anything from, the general; but on the third he sent for me, and informed me that he had received a letter from the Minister of War, mentioning me "as a dangerous character," and directing him to send me off immediately with an escort; he therefore recommended my departure immediately, to avoid the disagreeable attendance of a *gend'arme*. I told him that I should certainly set out next day, being obliged to wait for my linen from the wash.

"*Monsieur*," said he, "a warrior should always be ready to put his foot in the stirrup."

As I saw that he wished to inspire me with a high idea of his military character, I replied, "certainly, *Monsieur le Général*, that must always be the case with an officer who has seen so much service as you, and who has also such horses at command."

"Do you know, *Monsieur*," said he, "that I travelled from Germany hither in the depth of winter, and never thought anything of it!"

"I have no doubt of it, *Monsieur le Général,* but your situation and mine are very different: you travelled in a good warm carriage, with all the comforts attached to the rank of a French general; while I have made a long journey through Spain as a prisoner, suffering many privations, and extremely unwell with a spitting of blood, owing to the bruises I received when taken; therefore you surely cannot deem me unreasonable in asking to remain until tomorrow;" to which he consented, and we parted.

In the evening, accompanied by the American doctor, I went privately to see some Portuguese, who had been arrested at the commencement of the war with Portugal, and detained as hostages. Our visit was obliged to be secret, for if the police had had knowledge of it, it might have produced disagreeable consequences, both to the Portuguese and to myself. One of them, the Marquis de P——, had been chamberlain to the Queen of Portugal; and certainly her majesty did not shew much taste in her choice, for he had much more of the baboon than of the human being in his appearance.

His son, a *chevalier*, was also a strange looking animal; with his hair in curls and plastered with powder and pomatum, his feet resting on the railings of his chair, and his elbows on his thighs, he grinned so strongly, that he reminded me of jacko just about to make a spring, and I could scarcely keep my countenance. His father, however, seemed to entertain a high opinion of him: most certainly if he possessed abilities Lavater knew nothing of physiognomy.

The brother, of the marquis, the grand prior, was however a rational man. But the person who pleased me most was *le Sénateur*; he was turned of fifty, with a noble deportment and general information; he spoke French. and English, and formerly executed the English business at Lisbon, where he recollected having seen me with the Duke of Sussex. Cards were introduced, and I played with such success, that winning two rubbers I found myself a gainer of twelve *sols*.

Afterwards tea was served as a compliment to me, and it was certainly of an excellent quality; but M. le Marquis unluckily taking it into his head that I must be fond of sweet things, to which however I have a mortal aversion, obliged me to swallow a great piece of cake, that had nearly made me sick, which was only prevented by the introduction of some excellent old Port, in the praise of which I launched forth, in hopes of inducing them to produce a few bottles more, but we were obliged to be content with two.

We talked with warmth of the affairs of Spain and Portugal,

and I related the various successes of our armies in the former country, particularly Busaco, which led the Portuguese rather too far; for I had little doubt but that the doctor would repeat every word of our conversation to the police.

Recollecting that Madame le Tapis had promised me a good supper, and also to invite Mademoiselle Byrom and some of the opera performers, I quitted my Portuguese friends; and returning home found an excellent table set out, to which I had invited the Polish Major Sitowiski and one of our officers. The party was so agreeable, that with conversation, music, and champagne punch, the night passed away imperceptibly, and it was five o'clock before we broke up, when I retired with the melancholy reflection that the following morning I was to quit this charming scene of dissipation. It has often been remained, that we can no more endure intense pleasure than intense pain; but at this time I should liked to have tried how much of the former I could bear. The privations I had suffered in my journey through Spain, were excellent preparations for the full enjoyment of the pleasures of Bourdeaux.

Early the following morning the cook informed me that some fine sea fish and other good things had just arrived; and while he was enumerating them my landlady made her appearance, and expressed her sorrow at my departure, adding that her house was never so gay; and promising., if I could only remain that day, she would prepare a dinner that would do her credit, and induce me to recommend her to my compatriots. Having agreed to this moderate request, I ordered dinner for six; the first coarse to be entirely of sea fish, and the dishes were suited to display the talents of the loquacious cook, to whom I regularly paid a visit every morning before breakfast.

I had scarcely finished giving him my orders, when the Polish *major de place*, accompanied by two police officer, paid me an unwished for visit, and demanded what detained me at Bourdeaux? I answered that I had intended setting off that day, but that the persuasion of my hostess and the abilities of her cook had prevailed on me to remain; that I was sure Monsieur Pierre

Pierre would not be so unkind as to deprive the good lady of the profits of her dinner; and still more, that he would not wish me to quit Bourdeaux without the favourable impression that this dinner could not fail to make.

I moreover promised solemnly to depart the next morning; on which stipulation he unwillingly consented to my remaining. I soon after received a visit from Mr. Johnston, who apologized for not having invited me to dine; for which however there was no necessity, knowing as I did, that had the English merchants shewn any expensive attentions to their countrymen, they would most, probably have attracted the notice of the government, and might have been doubly taxed, upon the principle that if they could afford to give their countrymen entertainments, they could no doubt also afford to contribute largely to the state.

I however concluded, that though it might be dangerous for Mr. Johnston to give me a dinner, there could be none in his dining with me, and therefore invited him, as well as Mr. Nero, who called himself a Swede, but who spoke English and several other languages so well that it would have been difficult to tell to what country he really belonged: for my own part, I was convinced of his being an Englishman.

He had just returned from Paris with a licence to freight a vessel for London, which was to sail in a few days; and he was so kind as to offer to take charge of a very beautiful Spanish pointer, which I had procured at Burgos, and for which, for fear of losing him, I had taken an apartment in the hotel at nine *francs* per day, to the great surprise of my landlady. I have since heard that he arrived safe in England, and was much admired.

The evening passed very pleasantly over some of Mr. Johnston's wine, which he had brought with him, and which I found so excellent, that I would recommend him to all who import their own wines. When we broke up I went to a small but pleasant society, where I supped, and did not get home till four o'clock.

CHAPTER 29

Conscription

February 20. This being the day of my departure, became indeed a day of reckoning, for Madame le Tapis's bill was enormous. At three o'clock I took leave of my Bourdeaux friends, and whether their regret was real or fictitious, I will not presume. to say, but all the females of the house were in tears; nor did I depart without a painful sentiment on my side.

Having crossed the Garonne by a ferry, I mounted my horse on the opposite bank, and had not proceeded more than a league beyond Carbonblanc, the first post between Bourdeaux and Paris, when I overtook three of our officers on foot. It was raining hard, and neither them nor myself had a change of clothes, for I had brought only a few shirts, a second waistcoat and pantaloons, in a small portmanteau behind my servant. The officers were still worse off than myself, as they had spent all their money at Bourdeaux, and had only their travelling French pay of fifty *sols* an *étape* (a day's marching allowance) to support them on their journey to Verdun, a distance of about four hundred and forty miles, during which they were liable to all the disagreeable circumstances that usually assail foot travellers.

They were however cheerful, and laughed at the prospect before them; such are the advantages of good health and spirits, which in every situation in life, are infinitely superior to riches. On inquiring into the strength of their purses, they produced a *petit écu*[1] and some *sols*, which was to last them to Angoulême, a

---

1. *About half-a-crown.*

distance of about twenty leagues. In order to make their marching money last out, they proposed walking two or even three *étapes* in a day, and by this means doubling or trebling their daily receipt.

Although my purse was very low, I spared them a part of its contents, which set them up, and we parted, our *feuilles de route* being in different directions. As mine directed me to pass through Perigueux, I turned off the great Paris road to the right, and soon reached the village of St. Ubes, where I made myself as comfortable for the night as the small *auberge* would permit. In the morning, finding my horse's back so sore that it would have been cruel to ride him, I determined on pacing the day at this village.

After breakfast I walked to a café, the landlord of which, surrounded by a numerous audience, was reading the *Moniteur*, for which I learned that the whole village united to subscribe, on the express stipulation that the host should read it aloud. This was just the time when the Regency bill was passed in England, and which the French politicians expected would immediately produce a change of ministers and measures favourable to a negotiation for peace.

The *Moniteur* of this day however informed them, that no change either of men or measures would take place, at which my host of the café seemed rejoiced, exclaiming, "*Bravo! voilà un nation! voilà des gens qui ont du caractère!*"

As these exclamations surprised me, I asked the old gentleman, "why he wished so well to England?"

"Because," replied he, "the English *sont des braves gens*. I have had many dealings with them, and always found them most correct and honourable; but," continued he "since this cursed silly decree of Berlin, all is misery in this country, and as was formerly said of the Non-Importation bill of the Americans, it may be justly called an act of political suicide."

I now told the old gentleman I was an English officer taken in Spain, on which he immediately produced some cakes and wine, made many, bows, and requested with, much earnestness to be informed of the real state of affairs in that country, for that he knew the papers never told a word of truth; "and indeed," added he, "they are now become so notorious that their falsity is become a proverb, and *il ment comme le gazette*, is the common expression to denote a first rate liar."

He thanked me for the information I gave him concerning Spain, concluding with a "*parbleu, quelle sottise de prétendre faire la guerre contre tout un peuple.*"

Having drank the health of this politician and his audience in excellent wine, I departed, receiving from them a hearty *bon voyage*. In returning to the *auberge* I met a party of musicians playing before an uncommonly fine ox, adorned with ribbons and garlands; on inquiring the meaning of which, I learned that this was one of the amusements of the carnival which had now commenced, and that they were leading the ox thus adorned to the slaughter-house; a custom, which reminded me of the victims in the Pagan festivals: and indeed the carnival has, in every respect, more of a Pagan than of a Christian festival, and may well be compared to the Roman Saturnalia. It commences the Sunday before Lent, and lasts till the eve of Ash-Wednesday; during which period, all the lower kind of people of the town parade the streets in masquerade habits, and plague the quiet passenger with impunity.

At night masked balls are given at the theatres, to which all persons are admitted for one or two *francs*, and here the worshippers of Venus may pay their devotions at her shrine without fear of detection; here the wife, repays her infidel husband in his own coin; the widow consoles herself for the ungallant restrictions of the Code Napoleon, by which she cannot take a second, until ten months after the decease of her dear first husband, and the pale maiden here finds a never failing remedy against the strange propensities to feeding on brick and mortar.

While paying a visit to the stable, I heard an extraordinary noise, and on inquiry learnt that it was produced by skinning the ox, I had just before seen so finely ornamented. On looking into the place I found that they were literally beating the animal out of his skin; for while one woman was blowing with a great pair of bellows between the flesh and the hide, three others were threshing it with sticks, which loosens the skin and makes it come off more easily. When this operation was finished, the carcase was hang up and covered with artificial flowers, ribbons, &c.

In the morning, though it rained heavily, I resumed my journey, and passed through a continued vineyard to the river l'Isle, which falls into the Dordogne. I crossed the latter (which is here of considerable breadth) in a good boat: but before my arrival at the river I had stopped under a handsome gateway for shelter from a heavy shower. I had not been here long when a respectable looking old gentleman came out, and begged me to alight and put my horse in the stable till the shower was over; his countenance bespeaking benevolence,, prevented a refusal, and I accompanied him into the house, through a spacious hall, over the chimney of which hung a large *escutcheon* with the arms of a nobleman.

This hall led into a saloon, with large, windows opening on vineyards that sloped frown to the river; pointing to them, the old gentleman said with a sigh, "*Ah Monsieur, voilà ce qui faisoient autrefois ma richesse; aujourd'hui ils me sont une perte.*"

He then observed that apparently I was an Englishman, and on my answering in the affirmative, he invited me to partake of his soup with his wife and daughter. This kind offer at first declined on account of the darkness of the evening and the badness of the road; but he would not be refused.

"You will get on the better for it," said he, "and I will immediately order your horse a feed of corn that both may proceed more on the road."

The lady and her charming daughter now entered, and insisted so kindly on my partaking their repast, that I could not resist. We proceeded to the dining room, where the old gentleman placed me next his daughter, who was as blooming as Hebe, and attired in a very neat morning dress. Some superior wine made me feel myself entirely at ease, so that I, conversed on several topics that pleased the old gentleman. Another bottle succeeded, which as it was emptied raised his spirits and increased his civility.

He swore that if a French marshal had stopped at his door, he might have got wet to the skin before he would have, invited him to enter his house; but that the favour an English officer of my distinction had conferred on him and his family he could never forget. He then spoke of the misery to which France was reduced by the ambition and mistaken policy of its ruler.

"For what," said he, "do we make war? for what end do we exhaust the population and the resources of the empire?"

"Doubtless, *Monsieur*," replied I, "you must have read Montesquieu's *Esprit des Loix*, and you may recollect the passage where, he observes, that a country governed despotically only makes war to augment the power and increase the dominions of its ruler. The French nation I believe now began to see this truth, and instead of exulting, as formerly, at the victories of your armies, it reflects that these brilliant successes serve only to rivet its chains and perpetuate its distress; while they cover with misery and desolation the countries of which they have gained Napoleon the possession.

"How different is it, Sir, with the conquests of England, which not only enrich herself, but also the countries she subdues, by the reciprocal advantage of free markets for the manufactures of the one and the produce of the other. But, Sir," I continued, "it has been the unvarying system of France, since the revolution, to undermine and level every ancient government; while it has been the principle of England to support them as far as possible. Unfortunately for the cause of humanity, the imbecility of monarch, and the corruption of their counts, have assisted the views of France, in a greater degree than the energies and the disinterestedness of England have been able to counteract them.

"Such, Sir, are the causes of the calamities under which

Europe is now groaning; and strange it is to observe, that Spain, (which is of all countries of Europe the least advanced in manufactures, commerce and civilization,) should be the first to see its own interest, and to resist the torrent. Hitherto the French arms have been generally successful, but the war in Spain is of a very different nature from those you have hitherto been engaged in. In Spain, you have to contend against a people in whom revenge is the riding passion, and every act of despotism exercised by the French in that country, instead of tending to bend the people to your yoke, only augments their hatred and animates their exertions.

"Really, Sir, as a British subject, and still more, as a friend to humanity, I should not wish to see the French too rapidly driven out of Spain; for the continuation of the war for two or three years longer, must so exhaust the resources of France, both in men and money, as to oblige your Emperor to listen to reason; for, surely, he will not be so infatuated as to go on towards his destruction, when he finds that God no longer gives him the power to accomplish what he wills."

"On these grounds, Sir," I concluded, "as a patriotic Frenchman, you ought to rejoice at the defeats of your armies, for though by their victories Napoleon may increase his dominion, I believe his subjects have always found, that the only effect of such additions have been the increasing their burthens."

To this discourse the family paid much attention, and the old lady often remarked, "*c est bien vrai*"

Turning to the daughter I observed, that

she ought also to rejoice at the defeat of the French armies, for that was the only means of bringing about a peace on reasonable, terms, and peace could. alone ensure young ladies husbands, which were now so scarce that the amiable sex were really to be pitied.

I rose to depart, but the whole family with one voice insisted I should not quit them so soon, for that it was not every day they had the honour of entertaining an English officer; at the same time the old gentleman sprung up, and hurried off to the cellar for another bottle, which I agreed to see out provided the ladies would stay and partake of it; "*volontiers, Monsieur*" replied the old lady, "for I admire the English;"

"*Et pour moi,*" cried the young one, "*je les adore!*"

"*C'est un peu fort, Mademoiselle,*" said I.

"*Non, en verité, Monsieur!*" and this she said in so kind a manner that proved it to come directly from her heart. Indeed, had I been inclined to vanity on a certain point, I might have supposed that I was not indifferent to this young lady; particularly when she continued, "go where you will, Monsieur, this family can never forget you."—She seemed inclined to say more, but the return of the old gentleman interrupted her.

While emptying this bottle I related my adventures at Bourdeaux, and impressed both the ladies with an anxious desire to visit that city, and partake of its amusements, I now recollected that my servant would be quite at a loss to know what had become of me, for as I cannot bear a servant riding behind or near me, I always send him on before. The one I now had, not speaking a word of French, often committed blunders, and at one time I lost him for two days; but in the present case, as the road was direct, and he must be stopped by the ferry, I was not afraid of his going astray.

Having taken an affectionate leave of this .worthy family, I proceeded, and soon met my servant returning at full gallop, and in the utmost consternation. He informed me that he had waited some time at the ferry, but at last, conceiving some accident had happened to me, he was induced to return, and on reaching a river had observed a dead horse on the bank, which he fancied resembled mine, and thence concluded that I had been drowned in giving the horse a drink, and that someone had carried off the bridle and saddle.

On this conviction he determined to return to Bourdeaux,

and tell the news. At the same time that I wished him at the devil for his precipitation. I congratulated myself on not having delayed longer at the hospitable old gentleman's, which alone prevented the report of my death being carried to Bourdeaux, from whence it would have been immediately forwarded to England.

Having crossed the Dordogne, I proceeded through a flat and fertile country to the village of St. Suzanne, where I determined to halt for the night at a little *auberge*, the people of which were very civil; but on inquiry into the state of the larder, I found it afforded nothing better than modest bacon and eggs, of which I partook with the family before the kitchen fire. The wine was so truly execrable, that I was obliged to ask for some spirits, and they produced a kind of brandy distilled from the husk of the grapes after being pressed.

As, however, it is a fixed principle with me to take things as they come, I swallowed my humble repast cheerfully, and amused myself with the children, who crowded round me to admire my watch chain and seals. The eldest daughter, a fine girl, sung some pretty airs, and the father recounted his campaign in Italy under Massena, of whom he spoke with enthusiasm. I inquired, of the old man if the carnival was yet over, and he answered with rapture, "*Dieu soit béni*, we have yet three days to come!"

Happy people, thought I, who laugh at all the cares and evils of this life, and, while they are not prohibited from dancing and singing, consider with indifference the tearing away of their sons by a conscription, and the impoverishing themselves by arbitrary taxes!

Next morning, February 23rd, after passing through a flat and swampy country, I reached a rather considerable town called Mussidan, where I put up at the post-house,. which was also an *auberge*; and though it had no very promising appearance, the windows being broke, and the ascent to the bedroom by a ladder, I found the larder better supplied than at my last night's sojourn, and in the morning was for the first time surprised by the reasonableness of the charge, for my supper, consisting of some roast beef, a fowl and bacon, and two bottles of wine, besides breakfast for myself and servant, came to only four *francs* ten *sols*; and including the horses the whole charge was but ten *francs*:

While breakfast was preparing I inquired of a decent looking man if there was a coffeehouse in the town? he answered there were several, and offered to conduct me to one of the best. We entered a large apartment, in which was a billiard table, and a great number of chess and trick-track boards. The former game is particularly a favourite among the French) and the public tables are seldom vacant, day or night. I expected to hear some of the persons call for coffee, but on inquiry I learnt that no such thing was to be procured here, for that this article, which was formerly as great a necessary to the middling class in France as tea is to the English, was now only within the reach of the wealthy.

Sugar also, of which the French are immoderately fond, they are obliged to forego; for though they have been amused with the idea of extracting this article from raisins, beetroot, &c the produce is only yet to be found in the *Moniteur*, not a grain having appeared in the market It is true, indeed, a sirup of grapes has been introduced into commerce, but those who have once made use of it will never be taken in a second time; for, independent of its possessing a very small proportion of the sweetening principle, which renders its use as dear as sugar, it contains a powerful acid, that acts most disagreeably on the bowels.

The idea of ruining England, and rendering colonies unnecessary to France, by the perfecting of indigenous substitutes for colonial productions, is indeed ridiculed by all classes to a degree very uncommon in France, of making it the subject of caricatures; some of which have more humour than is to be found in the generality of those seen in the Paris print-shops.

One represents George the Third and Napoleon at opposite sides of a table, with a cup of coffee before each; our king is dissolving the point of a great loaf of sugar into his, while Nap is grinning horribly in trying to squeeze a drop of sweetening from a large beetroot.

A second caricature cm the same subject, shews how deeply the French are interested in it; it represents the King of Rome sucking a beetroot, making wry faces, and exclaiming "*voilà un joli morceau de sucre que mon papa m'a donné!*"

Feb. 24. This day's route was through a clayey and swampy country, by very deep roads, on which I was obliged to walk twenty-five miles, my mare being unable to bear the saddle; at length I reached a single house, called La Marsolia, and which, there being no other *auberge* on the road, is much frequented. Here heavy rains and the consequent floods kept me three days, during which I saw .numerous parties of Spanish prisoners and refractory conscripts pass; the latter were always tied together, often forty or fifty in a string, like negro slaves going to the market, and only escorted by two or three *gendarmes à cheval.*

Though their guards are seldom more numerous, there is scarce an instance of their resisting them, or attempting to escape; which, however, is made a capital offence. The *gendarmerie*, indeed, forms the most efficient military police in Europe, and is so well distributed, that not only the roads are safe, but the people are also kept in complete political subjection. The tame and submissive disposition of the French is the great cause of the perfection of this police; and in nothing can this disposition be more strongly shewn, than the conscripts being thus led like flocks of sheep to slaughter; for if any of them desert, the *chefs de complot* (the leaders) are sure to be punished with death, and the others have only to expect the galleys. When several conscripts desert in company, and no *chef de complot* can be discovered, then the oldest is considered as such, and suffers death.[1]

The Spanish prisoners that passed through the village were in a most miserable condition, and treated with the utmost brutality by their escort. Their shoes, which had been originally only a leather sandal, fastened to the foot with a thong, were worn out, and their feet dreadfully lacerated. In this condition, half starved and half dead with fatigue, they were goaded on by the *gendarmes*, who had orders to shoot those who should lag be-

---
1. See later pages in this chapter relative to the conscription.

hind, and vast numbers of them were actually thus murdered in cold blood!!!

While France! exists as a nation, the barbarous treatment of the Spanish prisoners must remain a stain on its character. Formerly the French soldier would have refused to be the instrument of the sanguinary orders of his superiors; but the revolution has entirely changed the French character, and more particularly that of the army.

Before that event, the officers were chiefly nobles, who, however proud and licentious they might be, at least possessed the elegance of manners and liberality of sentiment which usually distinguish that order. At present, the great majority even of the superior officers are sprung from the dregs of the people, without education or principles; their manners are brutal, and their courage is ferocious. The revolution, in fact, swept away whatever was estimable, and left only the dregs of a corrupt society. It began by destroying a generous and brave nobility, and annihilating the clergy. Wealth then became the object of persecution, and, finally, the miscreants who composed the ephemeral governments, ignorant and wicked themselves, proscribed all talent and virtue.

If we formed our opinions hastily, we might suppose that the revolution, like the torrent which washes down the soil from the mountains to fertilize the valleys, had distributed the spoils of the rich among the poor, and that consequently the peasantry had derived inestimable advantages from the new order of things. A slight observation and inquiry will, however, convince us that their situation is very little, if at all, mended. The division of property which the revolution and the system of assignats produced, has, indeed, enabled every peasant to become a proprietor, and the estate which formerly scarce supplied the luxury of a single noble, or a few pampered clergy, is now divided amongst a thousand families.

This acquisition of real property by the lower class, which in theory seems to add to the sum of human happiness and national prosperity, in practice has been found to produce the very contrary effects. Instead of improving agriculture, cultivation has gone considerably backwards, for the small proprietors are too miserably poor to meliorate their lands; they are often even obliged to borrow money at usurious interest, to defray the charges of common cultivation, and the crop is thus mortgaged before the seed is sown.

Commons were complained of before the revolution, as injurious to cultivation, and all the commons of France were divided among the peasantry, as nearly as possible, in equal portions of good and bad land. The evils of this hasty measure are now very severely felt, for the good patches of common, thus made property, are alone cultivated, while the bad are entirely useless, because divided among individuals, whereas when in common they served to pasture the cattle of the peasants. But to return from this digression to the poor Spanish prisoners. I did what little was in my power to relieve them, by remonstrating with their guards, and by bargaining with the landlord to furnish them with a substantial soup of meat and vegetables, for which they were extremely grateful.

On the 28th the floods permitted me to quit La Marsolia, and I pursued my journey towards Perigueux, accompanied by my landlord. The country was low, and many parts overflowed, so that I had often to ride in water up to my saddle skirts. About a league from the town my companion pointed out a well, celebrated throughout France for a phenomenon which has occupied the attention of many naturalists, without its being yet satisfactorily accounted for. Its water rises every morning so precisely at nine o'clock, that watches and clocks are set by it; it overflows with great force, and covers the country for some extent until eleven o'clock, when it again begins to fall; and though the ground is very flat, the water is all gone off in the course of an hour.

The reader will not perhaps be displeased at learning in what manner the conscription, which may without impropriety be stiled the palladium of French slavery, is effected. The first compulsory enrolment, termed a levy by requisition, took place in

February 1793, and the army continued to be recruited in that manner till 1798, when the first conscription was decreed, by which every French subject, of whatever class, is when he arrives at the age of nineteen, obliged to take his chance to become a soldier.

When a conscription is decreed, notice is given to all those whose age is completed within the year, to assemble at the town house, or other public place of the chief town of the department, where they are examined by surgeons, in the presence of the officers of Government, and those who have any bodily defects are passed over, while the rest draw lots for the chance of becoming heroes. Those who fall (the French expression is *tomber*), if they cannot procure a substitute, are immediately marched off to a depôt, where they are exercised, and from thence sent to join their regiments.

During the drawing of a conscription, the town hall is surrounded by the relations of the youths, and an ignorant spectator would rather suppose they were waiting the sentence of a criminal court, about to award life or death to their friends, than the decision of chance, whether they are to be citizens or soldiers. The only son of a widow above sixty years of age, whose subsistence depends on the cultivation of the ground by this son, is exempt from the conscription. If twins fell in the same conscription, one only is taken; and the youth who has a brother killed in battle; if he falls, is not obliged to march, unless a supplementary conscription is decreed for that year.

Since this was written, the waste of the French armies has been so enormous, that the conscription of the current year has not been able to replace it, and hence the conscriptions of the succeeding years were at first anticipated; but latterly, this method being found still inadequate, recourse has been had to the back years, and those who had drawn and escaped, have been obliged to draw over again. The price of a substitute, which at the beginning of the war did not exceed one hundred *louis*, in 1812 had risen to five hundred; and in 1813, a substitute was, to make use of a colloquial but strong expression, *not to be had for love or money.*

CHAPTER 30

Execution of Four Gentlemen

1811.

I found Perigueux extremely crowded, and inquiring the cause of my landlady, she informed me that four gentlemen of the *ci-devant* first and richest families in the country had just been tried and condemned to suffer death, for robbing a carriage conveying specie to Spain. After seeing the horses taken care of, I walked into the town to pick up more information; and going into a tobacconist's shop, to purchase some *segars*, I entered into conversation with the owner respecting these unhappy men.

He informed me they had emigrated to England in the revolution, and had returned after the peace of Amiens, in hopes of recovering a part of their property, and finishing their days in peace in their native country; but found that the whole of their property had been confiscated and sold in such a manner, as to render it impossible for them to recover the smallest portion. Their names were Calvimont, Pourcheri, Brion, and la Roque: a fifth who had been concerned in the robbery, had saved himself by flight. On their trial they did not attempt to deny the fact; but Calvimont, in the name of the whole, addressing the tribunal, said:

> as descended from the noblest families in the province, we scorn even to save our lives by a falsehood. We formerly possessed large fortunes, of which we have been unjustly deprived; and thus, being without any means of support,

our necessities obliged us to commit the act for which we are about to be judged. We solicit not mercy, we know we have none to expect; nor would we accept of life, if offered us—for what is life without the means of existence? That death, intended as a punishment, we therefore welcome as a relief from misery; and we are prepared to meet it, not only with resignation but with joy."

This short speech, my informer added, was delivered with such modest firmness, that, added to the great age of the speaker, it made the deepest impression on the court; they were however condemned, and as justice is very summary in France, the next day was appointed for their execution.

February 29. A desire to see the too celebrated machine, by which the noblest and purest blood of France had been shed, induced me to be present at this awful catastrophe; and I begged the tobacconist to secure me a place from whence I could view it. The guillotine was erected on a large platform, in a little place opposite the Hôtel de Ville. The executioner wore a grey frieze waistcoat and pantaloons, a white nightcap covered his head, and his shirt sleeves were tucked up, like those of a butcher going to slaughter an animal.

The victims were attended by two priests, and after a short time spent in prayer they were brought towards the fatal instrument. La Roque, who suffered first, went through the terrible preparation without shewing the smallest emotion; and his head being severed from his body, the executioner held it up, streaming with blood, and said something which I could not distinctly hear, but which I suppose designated the crime. The guillotine did not perform its office so well with the second victim, for the head remained attached by the skin, and the executioner separated it, with a long knife prepared for the purpose.

The two others saw their comrades suffer without their countenances betraying any signs of fear; and, I doubt not, only envied them the privilege of going before them. For my own part, I was heartily sorry that my curiosity had led me to witness this sight: I could not for a long time get rid of the recollection, and in the. night guillotines and headless trunks flitted before my eyes.

Nor were these sensations weakened by the stories my friend the tobacconist and others related to me, of the horrors they had seen perpetrated in this same spot during the revolution, when more than once the daughter had been sprinkled with the blood of the mother, and the father forced to witness the execution, or even to become the executioner of his son, or the son that of his father. It was by such scenes that the revolutionary monsters accustomed the people to sights of blood, and prepared the mind for the perpetration of those horrid acts, at the bare recital of which humanity shudders, and man almost despises his own nature!

Perigueux is a very ancient town, with little but its antiquity to recommend it; the streets being, like those of all old places, narrow and irregular, and the greatest number of the houses mean. Some fragments of the wall that anciently surrounded it, and of the fortifications erected before the invention of cannon, still remain. On the outside of the town is a very handsome walk, planted with trees, and kept in good order. Perigueux was formerly the chief town of the Perigord, and is now of the department of the Dordogne, It is thirty-two leagues distant from Bourdeaux, and one hundred and sixteen from Paris; its population is five thousand seven hundred; and it has criminal tribunals, of the first class, and of commerce.

Its chief trade consists of *pâtés* of partridges and truffles, which it exports to all parts of France; but it does not seem to be much enriched by this traffic, though the number of *traiteurs'* shops equal all the others taken together; the general appearance, indeed, is mean, and denotes poverty. It has, however, the advantage of being situated in a cheap country, for which reason several English families of small fortunes, who liked to live well, chose it for their residence before the revolution.

As this town is celebrated for its truffles, I would not quit it without enabling myself to judge how far it merited its celebrity, and accordingly ordered a turkey stuffed with these vegetables, which certainly is one of the choicest dishes in the *catalogue des gourmands*; but I regretted that I had no one to partake of it with me, and of a bottle of excellent old Madeira, which my landlady found remaining of a stock she had laid in when the English frequented her house. In order to. keep off the blue devils, I was obliged to invite the tobacconist in the evening, to partake of a bottle of la Fite, and, as he was a good-humoured fellow, I got over the time pretty well.

The floods having rendered the line of road I was pursuing almost impracticable, and also learning that the inns were wretched, I determined to cross the country to Angoulême, and get into the great Paris road. I had not proceeded far, through a wild and hilly country, when I was caught in a violent shower, and found that the preceding rains had swelled every stream into a river, so that I was in considerable danger in crossing them; and should actually at one time have been swept away at a mill stream, had it not been for the miller's assistance.

On entering Beautoin, I wandered in the street for some time, looking for an *auberge*; at length a decent looking man addressed me, and invited me to enter his house, the sign of Notre Dame, which, he assured me, though small, afforded excellent accommodation. The first part of his statement I found to be true, but with respect to the second he exaggerated a little, for I could only get half a salt goose for my dinner; but a good fire, and two bottles of Madeira which I brought from Perigueux, made up for other wants: and as my landlord seemed to be a companionable old fellow, fond of news and society, I invited him to drink some of his own wine, of which, though little better than vinegar, he finished two bottles, praising it to the skies.

He informed me that the ruins of a celebrated Benedictine convent, in the neighbourhood, were worth seeing; and the following morning I accompanied him to them. The external wall and the roof only remained, the inside having been entirely destroyed in the revolution. Its situation on the banks of the Adela is most romantic; and close to it is a stupendous rock, with a cavern, on the sides of which Charles the Fifth of France, the founder of the convent, caused to be cut various statues and representations of the battles of the age. In general the figures had been mutilated by the revolutionary Goths, nor had they even spared those of Du Guesclin and the Chevalier Breton, the most successful and renowned warriors of that period. Under that of Du Guesclin was an inscription, so much defaced as to be now illegible, but which a priest, who had collected the whole of them, informed me was the celebrated speech of that warrior to his army before the battle of Cocherel:

> "*Pour Dieu, mes amis, souvenez-vous que nous avons un nouveau Roi de France, que sa couronne soit aujourd'hui étrennée par vous!*"

The representations of the battles of Cocherel, where du Guesclin defeated the army of Charles the Bad, and that of Aurai, fought between Charles de Blois and the Count of Montfort, are the least injured.

Du Guesclin, after a long series of successes, was at length made prisoner, being covered with wounds, by Chandos, one, of the most celebrated English warriors of his time. At the conclusion of the war France was so infested by the brigands, known by the name of the Grand Companies, and which were composed of the disbanded soldiers, that Charles found it necessary to stop their depredations by taking them into his pay, and employing them against Peter the Cruel, with whom he had declared war.

In order to take the command of these companies, du Guesclin was ransomed for one hundred thousand crowns, and after assisting in dethroning Peter, and placing Henry of Transtimere on the throne of Portugal, was made Constable of France. He died in 1380, and was followed in a few months by his master, Charles the Fifth, whose reign was one of the most eventful in the history of Europe: in it, the English were driven out of France, artillery was first used in sieges, earthen ware and glasses were first manufactured in Italy, Gallileo invented the telescope, and the Bastile was erected. But though the *belles lettres* now began to be cultivated, and the arts that tend to increase the comforts of life, to be improved and extended, they were still only in their infancy; glass windows, the wearing of linen, and the use of spoons and forks of silver, were considered as great luxuries.

My imagination had often carried me back to this age, when the long night of darkness that succeeded the fall of the Roman empire began to clear away, and the dawn of civilization again appeared in the west; but I could never form a satisfactory idea of the state of society at that time, until I visited Grand. Cairo in Egypt with a detachment of the English army.

Here I observed magnificent edifices with their porticos and columns, their floors covered with the richest carpets, but the windows composed of lattices of open cane-work grotesquely stained of different colours, and the whole furniture confined to sofas and cushions. The pride, pomp and ignorance, of the Beys and Turkish chiefs, and the Dervishes reciting their exploits, recalled the chivalric Barons of ancient times, whose sole occupation was war, and who while they could neither read nor write themselves, maintained hosts of bards and minstrels to chant their valorous deeds.

In this capital of Egypt the scenes that continually passed almost made me believe myself in a dream: long files of loaded camels conducted by Arabs, and bending on their knees to be relieved are freed from their burthens; a haughty Bey, magnificently clothed, mounted on a superb Arabian charger, caparisoned with gold and silver cloth, and preceded by guards on dromedaries armed only with staves, whose business is to proclaim his name, his titles, and his victories; the procession closed by Dervishes, covered with their white *albarques* thrown loosely round them, and their green turbans, denoting them as the ministers of the prophet, and who, instead of walking like rational beings, move onwards, continually spinning round like a top; the bazaars crowded with groups of the strangest figures; conjurors in every corner shewing off. their *legerdemain*, and exposing extraordinary animals, particularly the *ichneumon*, which they instruct in all kinds of tricks;—these, and a thousand other novel sights, almost realize the descriptions of the Arabian Nights.

March 2. In the morning I quitted Beautoin and proceeded by a very bad road, and in still worse weather. At about three leagues distance my horse dropped a shoe, and I stopped at a small village to replace it; where the landlady of the *auberge*, discovering me to be an Englishman, informed me that there was a country woman of mine residing in the village, and married to a Frenchman; I accordingly paid her a visit, but from her conversation formed no high opinion of her rank in life.

Although settled by choice amongst the French, French, she abused them as most odious animals, and told me, that notwithstanding tea was unknown to any other person in the department, and enormously dear, she had not been able to bring herself to forego it, and that she should certainly die if deprived of it. Such are the effects of national prejudice and habit. This woman added another to the many instances I have observed of the little credit the generality of English settled in France do their country, which they pretend, to prize above every other, despising whatever is not English, or does not come from Old England;—for the credit of which, such persons should always remain at home.

After quitting this village the country became exceedingly wild, neither cultivated nor inhabited, and the road impassable for a wheel carriage. There were however considerable tracts of wood, but the trees appeared to be stunted. At a late hour I reached Rochebeaucour, a town of tolerable size, but very irregular, and the streets badly paved and dirty. The only meat the *auberge* afforded was veal, and that little superior to what is known in Ireland by the name of "staggering bob;" the calf not being more than a week old, which is the usual time it is kept in France, in order to give the meat a little solidity. Veal is indeed generally the only meat to be met with in small *auberges* and cabarets, at this season, while in those of a higher rank, you are always sure to find, according to the language of the hosts, either *un superbe gigot*, or *un magnifique dindon*.

March 3. Next morning being Sunday, the peasants flocked into the town to mass. The costume of both sexes was singular. That of the women consisted of broad brimmed white hats, a frill round their necks and breasts, like Queen Elizabeth's ruff, their waists of unconscionable lengthy and kept in by a girdle, fastened with an enormous brass buckle, the petticoat very short, and so thick on the hips as to resemble hoops, and large brass buckles in the shoes. The men had immense cocked hats, coats with standing collars, and buttons according to the different fashions of the time the coats were made, and between some of them there could not be less than half a century; for among these good people the holiday suit descends from father to son for several generations, and they prize them as much for their antiquity, as a British peer does his robes.

My route this day lay through a romantic country along a rocky bank, with extensive woods on each side, but the road miserably bad. After riding four leagues I reached a. few poor houses, and as I was passing the door of one which hung out a bush, I was called to by the landlady, who it seems had learned something of me from my servant, who had been making rather too free with the brandy bottle, and was half-seas over in the kitchen. I accordingly alighted and found a neat little table prepared, on which was immediately served the eternal dish of stewed veal; which reminded me of an anecdote on the subject of one constant dish, when I first entered the army.

We were once in a situation where we had for a long time no other meat but salt pork; one of the officers, one day, rubbing his back for a long time against a window shutter, somebody asked him, what was the matter, when he replied, "why d—n it, I have eat so much pork that I feel the bristles growing out of my back."

In fact, several of us experienced the same sensation; but whether it proceeded from the cause assigned, or not, I must leave the Faculty to determine. After quitting the hamlet, which is situated on an elevation, I passed through a wood into a fine valley of meadow ground, through which the Charente winds its course, and arrived at Angoulême. I did not think it prudent to stop at this town; for having deviated from the route laid down in my *feuille de route,* I might have been noticed by, and have received annoyance from the *gend'armes:*.

I therefore left my horse at a bye place, and, accompanied by an old man, walked through the town, whose size I found not unimportant, it containing thirteen thousand inhabitants. It is finely situated on the banks of the Charente, which, forming a bend, nearly encircles the rocky eminence on which it is built. The streets are in general wide, and many of the houses built of hewn stone, which the rock affords. It has the appearance of some trade, there, being considerable bustle, which however is no criterion to form a judgment upon in France, where the people always make much ado about nothing.

Angoulême was conspicuous in the civil wars of the Ligue, and was taken in 1508, by Admiral Coligny; it was also the birth place of the famous Ravaillac. It is now a prefecture; has criminal and commercial tribunals of the first class; and possesses considerable paper manufactories, which employ a good number of hands.

On leaving Angoulême I proceeded by the great Paris road, which was crowded with carts .and wagons. The construction of the latter attracted my notice from their being very heavily laden, and only drawn by three horses an end: they are very long, have but two wheels, and are loaded in such a manner that the horizontal line is preserved, so that the axletree is in a line with the horse's body, and by this means there is neither an updraft nor one that presses too much downwards. By this preservation of the equilibrium the wagon follows with the utmost ease, and the animals are not distressed, though the weight is above three tons. Finding all the cabarets filled with wagoners, I pursued my journey till near night, when I was at last obliged to put up at one with wretched accommodation;—but I made myself as comfortable as circumstances would admit, and by the assistance of a *segar* passed the evening without much yawning.

March 4. The following day the roads became very bad. The

soft free-stone of which they are composed, must prevent their being ever very good; but at this time, the heavy rains and the constant passage of wheeled carriages, had rendered them almost impassable, from the deep ruts and the dissolution of the stone into mud resembling mortar.

In the evening I reached a middling town, named Ruffec, where the landlady of the inn spoke so fairly that I did not think it necessary to make any previous bargain; but in the morning had reason to repent of not taking that precaution, for the charge was so enormous that I refused paying it, and had recourse to the mayor, who without hesitation reduced it one half.

Here I must strongly recommend to all persons travelling in France to agree for every item of their accommodation before hand: with this precaution, in no country is comfortable travelling more cheap; but neglect it, and you are sure to meet nothing but extortion and vexation. A dinner rather a supper, with a bottle of common wine, a fire and a bed, ought not to cost more than four *francs* a head. The charge of the *tables d'hôte,* where the diligences stop, is from two to three *francs*; and for this sum you have two courses and a desert, with a bottle of table wine.

March 5. The road this day was even worse than yesterday, and on coming up with my servant, who preceded me as usual, I found his horse had thrown and much hurt him, which caused some delay: I did not therefore arrive at the village of les Minieres, till late in the evening, from whence next day's stage brought me to Poictiers.

CHAPTER 31

Field of Battle

The first view of Poictiers is fine: situated in a valley, through which the river Clain serpentizes in the most agreeable manner, it at once bursts on the view from an eminence by which it is approached. The town is however dull, gloomy, and very dirty; and the inn of. the Trois Piliers, to which I was recommended, I found so abominable, that I determined to proceed on my journey after the horses had rested; during which time I took a rapid glance at the town.

The public walk runs along a steep cliff overhanging the river, on which are several mills, and the opposite bank presents an ascent of corn fields, in form of an amphitheatre, interspersed with patches of romantic rock; but though there are many situations eminently fine, not a single house of any appearance is seen throughout the whole landscape.

The cathedral is a grand edifice; and what is most extraordinary respecting it is, that though it served as a barrack during a part of the revolution, no part of it received the least injury, except that all the aristocratical emblems and titles were carefully erased from the gravestones, and republican ones substituted. The bishop's mitre was metamorphosed into the *bonnet rouge*; and instead of *"ci-gît Monseigneur,"* was read *"ci-gît le citoyen évêque de — ."* The mitre has however again resumed its place; and the noble shades can no longer be offended by their names being prefaced with the republican epithet *citoyen*.

Poictiers is the chief town of the department of Vienne, and contains about eighteen thousand inhabitants. It had formerly some flourishing silk manufactures, but they are now almost abandoned, and there is little appearance of industry or business in the streets. It has a special school for the study of the law; and a lyceum, in which two hundred and fifty students receive board, lodging, and instruction, for about £30 a year. This city was the residence of Charles the Seventh, who removed hither the parliament of Paris during the wars with England.

Near Poictiers are the ruins of a Roman amphitheatre, in sufficient preservation to shew its shape and extent; also an aqueduct, and other antiquities.

March 6. Quitting Poictiers, I passed through a very beautiful country, highly cultivated, and enlivened by many respectable houses. The soil here changes from the loamy sand I had hitherto noticed, and which is. chiefly preferable for vines, to a stiff clay. About a mile and a half from the city was fought the famous battle in 1356, and a countryman, of whom I inquired, pointed out a meadow as the field of battle; but in its rear is a rising ground in the shape of a crescent, on which I suppose the French army, was placed, as it would then have had the city behind it.

I did not pass this spot without an interesting recollection of the renown gained here by our ancestors, more than four centuries ago, and consoled myself for the loss of our dominions in France, with the reflection that, had that dominion continued, instead of unadulterated Britons we should now perhaps be half French.

Pursuing my route, I crossed the river Vienne by a handsome stone bridge, at the little village of Barres de Nintré, and arrived at Chatelleraut, on that river, which is here two hundred yards wide, and is navigated by sailing barges, which bring all bulky merchandise from Nantes by the Loire, entering the Vienne, where it falls into that river near the town of Chouze.

Chatelleraut is the Birmingham of France; but the hardware and cutlery fabricated here, though well polished, is wretchedly finished; and the steel of very bad quality. The iron with which the manufactories are supplied is procured from mines in the neighbourhood, as well as the coals for working it. I visited one of the most extensive manufactories, in which there was much bustle, but little work; nor did the labour seem to be divided to advantage, for one person performs two. or three operations, which must not only diminish the product, but also reduce the specific profit. Adam Smith, in his *Wealth of Nations*, admirably explains the advantages of the division of labour, in the instance of the seemingly trivial operation of making a pin.

> "A workman," says he, "not educated to this business, which the division of labour has rendered a distinct trade, nor acquainted with the use of the machinery employed in it, to the invention of which the same division of labour has probably given occasion, could perhaps with his utmost industry scarce make one pin in a day, and certainly could not make twenty; but, in the way in which the business is now carried on, not only the whole work is a peculiar trade, but it is divided into a number of branches, of which the greater part are likewise peculiar trades. One man draws out the wire, another straightens it, a third cuts it, a fourth points it, a fifth grinds it at the top for receiving the head; to make the head requires two or three distinct operations; to put it on is a peculiar business, to whiten the pin is another; it is even a trade by itself to put them into paper; and the important business of making a pin is in this manner divided into about eighteen distinct operations, which are all performed by distinct hands."

Chatelleraut was formerly the property of the Comte de Clermont, and was purchased from him by Louis XV. in 1736, who established here some manufactories of fine woollens and ratteens, which, while assist, by government, were in a flourishing state; but since that assistance has been withdrawn they have rapidly declined, and are now almost totally inactive, from the want of capital and of confidence, which at this moment throughout France prevents any considerable mercantile speculation, either among individuals or associations. Nothing, indeed, can prove the commercial stagnation more forcibly than the short credit given to country dealers by the wholesale merchants, which never exceeds three months.

On quitting Chatelleraut, I was happy to find the road clear of carriages, which had hitherto considerably annoyed me from the bad management of the horses, by which they formed a kind of *echelon*, that occupied the whole road, and obliged me often to perform the figure of a country dance, to extricate myself from them. At Chatelleraut, as I have before observed, the goods brought by land are embarked on the Vienne; and the road follows the course of this, river, the banks of which are fertile, and well cultivated.

In the evening I reached the little village of Agron, two leagues from Chatelleraut, where I put up at a very indifferent *auberge*. In the morning (March 7) I observed several droves of very fine bullocks passing through the village, and, on inquiry, found some of them had been driven from considerable distances, and were going to Paris, which is seventy-eight leagues from this village. The expense of each bullock in this long journey is valued at twenty-five *francs*; but as the capital always offers a sure market at a fixed price, it is found more profitable to send them there than to dispose of them in the country.

On the morning of the 8th, I passed through the; village of Ormes, near which is the magnificent *château* of the *ci-devant* Marquis de Voyé d'Argenson, whose family has been famous in the political annals of France. The present representative of the family was long confined in the revolutionary dungeons, and all his property confiscated. Enough, however, was saved by his friends from the general wreck, to repurchase this *château* and its domain, and its proprietor has deigned to accept the title of Count from Napoleon, and to fill the office of prefect of Antwerp.

After quitting Ormes, I crossed the river Creuse; which unites with the Vienne near the village of Beauvais. Here I baited the horses, and dined off a pig's ear in the kitchen of a cabaret, which was crowded with strange figures, with whom I amused myself so long, that it was night before I arrived at my destination, and a most violent rain and storm, with a pitchy darkness, rendered it difficult to keep the road.

At length I reached a single house, called St. Catharine's, the landlady of which was a perfect monster in appearance, and her manners did justice to her figure. While making me a fire, an old female servant let me into her mistress's, history; who, she acquainted me, had amassed considerable property in her business, and being now grown purse-proud, instead of being civil to travellers, to whom she owed everything, she did not even thank them for the money they spent in her house; "but," continued my informant, with the air of having made a notable discovery, "ingratitude is too common in the world."

This old woman's language was so far above her condition, that I could not forbear inquiring into her history, and learned that before the revolution she had possessed a considerable property in the town and neighbourhood of Chatelleraut, left her by her husband; that she had an only son, whom she bred up with the fondest care, but who, when all law had ceased, unnaturally seized on the property, and turned her out a wanderer on the world.

She wrote to her husband's brother, who came from Normandy, to endeavour to procure her justice; but the son being one of the *sans culottes*, denounced him to his fellow miscreants as a royalist: when he was seized, and without being permitted to vindicate himself, was cut off by the guillotine. The son still enjoys the property, and revels in luxury, while his aged mother has for twelve years been obliged to labour for a miserable subsistence. "Thus, *Monsieur*," she concluded, "God knows I have experienced my share of ingratitude!"

A call from without, obliged her to quit the room, and left me to ponder on the vicissitudes of human affairs, and on the effects of revolutions. The recollection of this being the anniversary of the landing of the British army in Egypt, roused me from these melancholy thoughts; but I had still to regret the want of society to celebrate that memorable day, and render palatable the very bad wine I was obliged to put up with.

March 9. Pursuing my journey the following day, through a flat and marshy country and over a paved road, I arrived at Tours, by a very fine avenue of trees; extending to the gates of the town. I had hardly got safely housed in the Hôtel de l'Impératrice, when I received a visit from Mr. Cane, a domiciliated Irishman, usually known by the appellation of Claret Cane, from his superior judgment in and excellent cellar of this wine. He was accompanied by Captain Gerrard, of the East-India Company's service.

With these gentlemen I spent a pleasant evening, and the next morning (March 10) was visited by several other English gentlemen, particularly Mr Holland, a person of considerable property. I dined this day with Captain Gerrard, and found his wife an agreeable woman, surrounded by a delightful little family. At dinner was Mr. Wilkes, who, I believe, had been a priest, and who to his other knowledge, by his long residence in France, added that of all the distinguished families in the neighbourhood, and of their sufferings during the revolution.

He entertained us with a lively and interesting sketch of the civil wars, which so long desolated this part of France during the contest between the Guises and the Condês. As I was well acquainted with the principal families of Tours, by having studied at the academy of Angers, I was gratified in hearing their histories; but I found that very few remained, and that Tours and its environs, from having been one of the most sociable parts of France, had become one of the dullest, every person being suspicious of his neighbour. All social intercourse was at an end, while the jealousy of the Government and the system of *espionnage* destroyed confidence even in the nearest relatives.

March 11. In the forenoon Mr. Gerrard accompanied me to visit the commandant of Tours, General Bonnard, whom we found writing in his office, and who had not even the civility to notice us, but continued to write on, or at least seemed to do so; for from his vulgar appearance one might doubt whether he could write or not Captain Gerrard had with him a little terrier dog, of which the general took more notice than of his master, for he ordered one of his staff to turn him out of the room; but the latter being sufficient of a gentle, man to know that an injury to a dog is considered as an. insult to its master, replied, that it belonged to that gentleman, pointing to Captain Gerrard. "*C'est égal,*" said the general, "*faites le sortir.*"

While examining the countenance and appearance, and observing the manners of this general officer, I could not help wondering how. the French Emperor, who has the character of great penetration, in the selection of his officers, could have made choice of such a fellow, whose manners , scarcely fitted him for a shoeblack. It is indeed such upstarts that have brought discredit on the French military service since the revolution. By a haughty contemptuous, manner, they doubtless think to inspire a high idea, of their courage, but which, to those who have a knowledge of character, has a directly opposite effect.

In the proud days of chivalry, courage and politeness were inseparable, and incivility and cowardice were almost synonymous terms. Disgusted with the rudeness of the general, I rose, and was departing without having spoken a word , when he followed me to the door, and inquired if I had anything particular to say? I replied, that I had merely called to pay him a visit of attention; on which he muttered something I did not understand, and making a most formal bow, I retired, without uttering another word. I then mounted my horse, and rode along the south bank of the river, which was low, and, in several places, covered with water. The northern bank was covered with chalky and stony hills, rising like an amphitheatre from the river, and which are highly cultivated, and thickly dotted with villages. On this bank was situated the celebrated monastery of Marmoutiers, of which scarce a vestige remains.

March 11. This day I dined with Mr. Holland, in company with several Englishmen, and among the rest Mr. Latter, a grave and sensible gentleman, but rather eccentric in his appearance and dress, the latter being far behind the fashion. His manners, which were quite gentlemanlike, however, covered this singularity; and, besides, he possessed the character of benevolence and kindness.

March 12. In the morning I strolled through the town, which is the chief place of the department of the Indre and Loire. It is situated at the confluence of the Cher and Loire; the latter river is here very broad, and is navigated by sailing barges of sixty to seventy tons, which ascend from Nantes to Orleans, where they enter a canal that conveys them to Paris. The Loire is crossed at Tours by a handsome bridge of sixteen elliptical arches. The manufactures of this city are confined to a few of silk, which are in a languid state; and its principal trade at present consists in the quantities of prunes it sends to all parts of France.

The principal street of Tours is uniform and elegant, the fronts of the houses with cut stone, having been built by government; several are however still unfinished. The cathedral is a beautiful gothic structure. During the revolution it was converted into a Temple of Reason, for which use it was fitted up like a Roman theatre; and from a rostrum, in the place of the grand altar, the republican demagogues fulminated their anti-social and anti-Christian doctrines. It is now restored to its original appearance and use.

Tours was anciently well fortified, and the ramparts which still remain afford a pleasant promenade, though the trees which formerly shaded them have been all cut down.

The tower from which the Duke of Guise made his escape, in the wars of the League 1591, still remains, and retains the marks of the artillery that played on it from the opposite, side of the river. The manner of the duke's escape is thus related:

Having made his guards, who were ordered never to lose sight of him, partly drunk, he proposed to wager, that if they would give him so much distance, he would hop to the top of the tower by a winding staircase, faster than they could run it; the wager being accepted, and the distance given, the duke set out, and reached the top before his staggering followers; he there found a rope, prepared for him secretly by some of his friends, by which he descended, and swimming across the rivets joined his army, and revived the hopes of the league.

The ruins of the ancient bridge are still seen opposite the town, where so many bloody battles were fought between the English and French.

On the right bank of the river, opposite the town, are several neat villages, and handsome: country houses. On. this side is also a perpendicular rock, against which houses are built in parallel rows above each other, so that some can only be reached by descending from the summit of the rock, and others only by ascending from its foot, these houses form a kind of suburb, extending a considerable way along the river, and are said to possess the advantage of being extremely cool in summer.

While I was getting my hair cut in a hairdresser's shop, the master of which entertained me with violent complaints of the hardness of the times, and of the many bankruptcies, in consequence of, what he termed, *le maudit décret de Berlin*, a poor woman, who had lost her senses from being ruined by one of these bankruptcies, ran wildly into the street, and throwing herself under the wheels of a loaded wagon, was instantly crushed to death!

As I was returning home, I recollected wanting some cord to secure my trunks, and observing a kind of tent or booth with some hanging out, I entered it. The master was not above four feet and a half high, with his arms short in proportion to his height; and I found that he took advantage of his want of stature to increase his profits; for instead of using a regular measure he sold his goods by arm's length, which he calculated, as is usual in, a middle sized man, at six feet, although his did not extend tend more than four feet and a half. As he, however, sold his goods nominally cheaper, and was a most ridiculous and humorous fellow, people flocked to his booth to purchase his goods and laugh at his repartees.

Thus Nature, ever bountiful, where she leaves a part of her work defective, compensates in another, and thus the world goes on, each contented with himself and with others.

I had a party to dinner this day, but all my rhetoric was insufficient to prevail on my landlady to serve it *à l'Anglaise*; that is, to give the fish and vegetables as part of the first course. Her obstinacy so put me out of temper that, to her great astonishment and mortification, I threw the whole of her first course, consisting entirely of French dishes, out of the window, dishes included; and, ordering up the second, we made a tolerable dinner off it.

March 13. This morning I found my host's family in the greatest despair and consternation; and on inquiring of the daughter, a beautiful girl, into the cause, she informed me that her only brother had just been drawn for the conscription; and, weeping bitterly, added, that she loved him like herself, and that they had never yet been, separated. The father and mother could not have expressed more sorrow, if they had just received the news of their son's having been drowned in the Loire; and I learnt that this sorrow was not without reason, for on this only son, in whose education they had spared no expense, rested all their hopes and wishes, I was induced to visit the Hôtel de Ville, where the conscription was drawing, and witnessed the different feelings of mothers, sisters, and mistresses, in the countenances of the females on this melancholy occasion.

The conscription is indeed considered by all ranks with the most profound horror: parents grasp with avidity at every means of saving their children from it, and hence arises impositions and roguery to a great extent; for swindlers, pretending to have influence, and the means of shielding youths, levy enormous contributions on their families; and though there is a severe fine and imprisonment attached to this violation of the law, yet it is too profitable not to be universally practised. Many instances are known of young men going a surer way to work, to escape the conscription, by previously cutting off one or two of their fingers.

CHAPTER 32

Amboise

On the morning of the 14th of March I quitted Tours and proceeded towards Amboise, accompanied by Messrs. Holland and M'Clure. Our road lay along the left bank of the Loire, and through a most beautiful country, well deserving the name it had received of the garden of Touraine. Amboise is eight leagues from Tours. Here we put up at the Lion d'Or, and got a tolerable dinner, particularly some fine eels; but with the usual obstinacy of the French, they were served up without sauce, and before we could prevail on the cook to melt some butter they were cold: indeed, plain melted butter is the only sauce difficult to be procured from a French cook, who considers it an abomination. It is a common expression in France, that "the English have fifty-two religions, and but one sauce," and we may very fairly retort on them, by replying, that they have fifty-two sauces and no religion.

March 15. I breakfasted this morning in company with my Tours friends at Mr. Cramer's, an English gentleman, married to a French lady, whose brother and sister also formed a part of the family; the former had just returned from the army in Spain, and seemed to find such an essential difference between the comforts of his brother's house and the miseries of a Spanish campaign, that he proposed spending a considerable time with him, Mr. Cramer, I should however suppose is little calculated to be comfortable in French society; for his serious and studious disposition could not well assimilate with the frivolity of French manners and conversation.

After breakfast we visited the castle of Amboise, situated on the rocky height overhanging the town. Its antiquity is dated to the first of the Roman emperors. In it were born Francis the First, Hugh Capet and Charles the Seventh: the latter prince as well as Louis the XI. also died in it. After passing through many hands, it became the property of the late Duke de Penthievre, and when wrested from him at the revolution, was converted into a state prison; at present it belongs to a senator.

At one angle of the castle is a round tower, within which a carriage with six horses may ascend from the town to the courtyard of the castle; in the centre of the tower is shewn the remains of an *Oubliette,* destined for the punishment of state criminals, in the reign of Charles XI; during which upwards of four thousand persons of rank, suffered death in public or private. Amongst those of the first consequence, were, the Constable de St. Paul and his brother-in-law the Count d'Armagnac. The Duke de Nemours was shut up in an iron cage, by order of this sanguinary monster, and as a refinement in cruelty, when brought to execution at Paris, the king ordered his children to be held under the scaffold to be sprinkled with the blood of their father.

But to return to the *Oubliette*: it is a wall forty feet in diameter, and about one hundred feet deep; wooden rollers were placed across it at certain distances, turned round by machinery, and to which were fixed several two edged knives. The victim being precipitated into the abyss, and falling from one roller to another, was minced to pieces before he reached the bottom. As this punishment was always inflicted secretly, and the victim never more heard of, it received the appropriate name of *les Oubliettes.*

In this castle the sanguinary Louis XI. instituted the order of St. Michel, in 1649, In the chapel are preserved the horns of a deer, (killed in remote times in a hunt,) which between the points are twelve feet eight inches French; the ribs of the same animal were six feet four inches long. We were shewn the apartments occupied by the unfortunate Princess de Lamballe, and those of the amiable and virtuous daughter of the Duc de Penthievre, the wife of the abominable Egalité. Voltaire was once governor of this castle. It is now fitting up for the residence o the Senator, to whom it has been granted; but the modern stile of the furniture does not at all harmonize with the antique appearance of the apartments. From a balcony enclosed by an iron railing and entered from one of the windows, is a noble view of the river. This balcony was formerly the place of execution of state criminals, and the blood of one victim was seldom dry on it before it was again wet with that of another, during the civil wars of the Guises and the Condés, in the reign of Charles IX. and during the administration of Catharine de Medicis.

The garden of the castle are curiously laid out, and contain a number of scarce plants. An *Acacia tricanthus* particularly struck me from its enormous size, having the dimensions of a timber tree. Of the branches of this species of thorn was formed the crown placed on the head of our Saviour at his crucifixion. There is also a pleasant walk formed and shaded by evergreens, and a Cesar's camp in view.

Leaving the castle of Amboise we visited the *château*, of Chanteloup, about half a league distant, situated on an eminence, a little way from the banks of the Loire, of which it commands a fine view. It belonged to the celebrated Duc de Choiseul, and hither he retired when exiled from court. Lord Bolingbroke, when banished from England, also resided in this *château*. It is at present the property of M. Chaptal, *ci-devant* apothecary and chemist, and now Secretary to the Senate and Comte de l'Empire.

The gardens are laid out in the ancient stile of formal walks and regular *parterres*; and there is an artificial piece of water on the domain on which was a boat intended for sailing, but rigged in such an uncouth manner as certainly to be unmanageable. The dullness that reigned throughout could not fail to affect us, when we reflected on the scenes of gaiety and pleasure which formerly made the walls resound. The old concierge, who shewed the *château* told us that he had often seen fifty different bedchambers occupied by visitors, add thirty to forty carriages, with four and six horses each, parade before the gate every morning. The company were not only accommodated with horses and carriages, but dogs and guns were at the command of those who chose to shoot, while a pack of hounds afforded those fond of nobler sport the pleasure of hunting the wild boar and deer.

The present possessor seems to neglect this mansion, as if he was still uncertain whether he might not be again called on to restore it to its rightful owner. Two or three rooms only are simply furnished, to serve for a day or two's visit, and all the rest present the naked walls; even the tapestry hangings having been torn down and the glasses removed. The stables and out-offices were equally empty, with the exception of some appreciated to Merino sheep, of which M. Chaptal has here a flock of sixteen hundred.

These animals have furnished a considerable object of speculation since the invasion of Spain; all the generals serving in that country, and possessed of lands in France, having taken the opportunity of sending vast numbers to their estates. When I past through Bourdeaux there were six thousand head for sale, on account of General Beliard, which, allowing them to bring the low price of three *louis* a head, makes no small addition to the other trifles the general could not have failed to pick up in Spain: for nothing in the way of plunder comes amiss to a Frenchman; and we may safely wager, that if France was to wage war in Circassia, the Grand Seignior's harem would be replenished by the French generals.

The person charged with the care of M. Chaptal's Merinos, informed me that the increase of lambs enabled him to dispose of sheep to the amount of eighty thousand *francs* a year. The wool sells for three *francs* the pounds, and the average weight of a fleece is ten pounds.

March 16. Pursuing my journey from Amboise, I crossed the Loire by two bridges; one of stone, extending from the left bank of the river to an island, and the second of wood, joining the island to the right bank. The country still continued extremely fertile and well cultivated, and I observed that vetches were more attended to here than in any part of the country I had yet passed through. The river Loire it navigated by barges of considerable size, but of the clumsiest construction, with an immense rudder and a long tiller, the traversing end of which is above the head of the man that steers.

Two leagues from Amboise is the *château* of Chenonceau, built by Bohier, a general under Francis the First, and the residence of the beautiful Diana de Poitiers, mistress to Henry the Second. It afterwards was successively occupied by Catherine de Medicis, by the Princes of Vendome and Condé, and by Monsieur du Pin, *fermier-général*. At present it belongs to Monsieur Villeneuve, Chamberlain to the King of Holland.

On the opposite bank of the Loire to the village of Eu, where we fed our horses, is another *château*, of an ancient and respectable appearance, with many towers, and commanding an extensive view of the river. It belongs to Monsieur Ré, an ancient noble. On my arrival at Blois, I put up at the Boule d'Or, and was put into a good looking apartment, in which was a glass through the chimney, that afforded a. beautiful view down, the lower end of its handsome bridge. My dinner here was very bad, and rendered. still more disagreeable, by the intrusion and impertinence of the cook, who every moment entered the room to demand, "*Eh bien, Monsieur l'Anglois, comment trouvez-vous votre diner?*" adding, "*On dit que les cuisiniers de votre pays ne sont pas trop habiles.*"

I replied, "if that is the case, you may be assured they won't come to you to learn, for of all attempts at cookery I ever met with, yours is the very worst."

This, fellow now entered on a defence, of his cookery, which I put a stop to, by inquiring if there was nothing else dressed in the house? He disappeared, and; soon after returned with a roast duck, a bird to which of all others I have the most mortal aversion; I therefore, to the astonishment of the cook, threw it deliberately into the fire, and sent the other dishes after it; at the same time desiring *Monsieur le Cuisinier* to take himself off; if he did not wish to follow them. Soon after his quitting the room, a great, stout, impudent looking girl entered, and, with a sort of officious raillery, asked me, "if I wanted a *bonne amie*, for if so she was at my service?"

I retorted in her own manner, by saying, "indeed, *Mademoiselle*, your manners are so engaging, that there is no resisting you; but at present I shall not trouble you farther than to desire you will clear the table, and bring me some wood."

When she returned, the cook accompanied her, and both began a species of banter, which not approving, I desired them to call the landlord; on whose appearance I asked him, "if the revolution was not yet over?" and on his answering "yes," continued, "then, *Monsieur* you ought to inform these *bêtes,* that there again exists in France a distinction of rank and persons;—therefore, either make them immediately quit the room, or order my horses, and I shall depart from your house."

This remonstrance had the desired effect and I passed the rest of the evening without further molestation.

March 17. The following morning I walked out early, and ascended a steep hill, on which is the castle famous on account of the assassination of the Duke de Guise. Its elevated situation gives it the complete command of the town, and of a fine and extensive view. It has a considerable square, with two fronts, formerly very grand, but now going fast to decay, and used as a barrack; the avenues to it are also in a shamefully dirty and degraded state. Below the castle, on the side of the hill, is the prefecture, beautifully situated, with some handsome gardens and walks, in good order.

The prefect of a department in France is the highest civil officer, and may be assimilated, as to his functions, to our lord lieutenant of a county; all the civil offices of the department, such as roads, civil buildings, bridges, &c. being within his resort, as well as the embodying of the national guard and the levying of conscripts. He is attended by a guard of *gend'armes*, when he visits any part of the department; has a house found by Government, and receives a very good salary. He always resides in the chief town of the department; and in one of the secondary towns is usually a *sous-préfet*, subordinate to the prefect, whose house is also found by Government, with a good salary.

The *maires* of towns are the next civil officers to the *sous-préfets*; they are elected annually, and receive no salary or other emoluments, except what they can abstract from the money belonging to the town, which passes through their hands.

This was the day, although Sunday, for drawing the conscription; and in order to drown sorrow, those who were to ballot had recourse to the wine bottle, and were playing at a variety of games. This appears to be greatly encouraged by the magistrates, in order to prevent the discontent that results from this abhorred measure. Indeed in every respect, it seems to be the chief principle of the French Government to suppress the murmurs of the people, by pompous declamations on the glory of *la grande nation,* by occasionally giving them representations at the theatre *gratis,* and by the idea of being conquered by the English, whom their Emperor decorates with the title of "tigers of the sea."

Blois is the chief town of the department of the Loire and Cher, and the seat of the various courts of law. It is built on the side of a hill, and contains about five thousand inhabitants, but the streets are so narrow and steep, that in some places they are formed by flights of steps. The bridge across the Loire is very handsome, being of cut stone, with several elliptical arches, an iron railing and lamps on the battlement, and a flagged pathway on each side, kept clean, which is a very unusual thing in France.

After breakfast I continued my journey over the bridge, in order to visit the *château* of Chambor, at which I arrived, after crossing a most intricate country, the roads consisting of mere pathways. The approach to the castle (an immense pile, with many large towers, and some lesser ones, crowned with spires), is by a very long avenue, through an extensive wood of fine full grown trees. The entrance is through a square, the sides of which form the offices, and are of great extent. The hall is extremely grand, and the ceiling forms a superb dome; the staircase is double, and winds round a pillar in such a manner, that persons may ascend and descend at the same moment, without the knowledge of each other. The whole is of massive stone.

This *château* was, I think, built by Francis the First, of whose reign there are many magnificent vestiges in France. It was possessed by Marshal Saxe, who died here; and the marble table was shewn me on which this great man had been embalmed, previous to his being sent to Strasburg to be interred.

The ceilings of the apartments, though much decayed, still shew proofs of the, ancient elegance. The *salle de spectacle*, in the centre of the building, is spacious, and was lined with very large pier glasses; the spaces they occupied are risible, but the glasses were destroyed in the revolution. The panes of glass in the windows exceeded four feet square. The park was more than fifteen miles round. In short, everything evinces that Chambor was formerly one of the finest palaces of France.

It being already evening when I quitted the *château*, I was at a loss where to put up for the night; but on inquiry, learnt that the village of St. Diey was only a league distant, I therefore proceeded thither, and found it a poor place. On stopping at the house to which I had been recommended, I found the landlord so very drunk and the house so uncomfortable, that I left my servants and horses there, and proceeded to another, where, although the fare was but middling, I was more comfortable. I had scarcely finished my dinner, when the *adjoint*, or deputy to the mayor, entered with the first landlord in the uniform of a *gend'arme*. The *adjoint*, interrogated me in an overbearing manner, and concluded by informing me that "I must go to prison, my account of myself being very unsatisfactory; and that persons of my description going through the country might be attended with imminent danger to the state."

Rotten state, thought I; if such is the case, your foundation cannot be more solid than this block-head's understanding! As however, I was in the fellow's power, policy directed, me to be civil, and asking him to sit down, and take a glass of wine, I observed to him that, "my *feuille de route* being in every respect regular, pointing out a certain day for my arrival, at the depôt, and ordering that I was not to be molested, but that I was to receive every assistance, and facility from the authorities, to pursue my journey, he could scarcely answer for detaining me on the suggestion of a drunken landlord, who was jealous because I preferred another house to his."

I concluded by informing him, that, "if he persisted in sending me to prison, I should state the business to the Minister of War, and he might expect the most serious consequences." This remonstrance had some effect, and he contented himself with informing me, that I must return to Blois the following morning with a *gend'arme*, where they could act more decisively.

March 18. I accordingly returned to Blois, escorted by a *gend'arme* and my first landlord, and the distance being only a league and half, over a beautiful turf, I enjoyed an excellent gallop, which repaid me for the detention. I was first escorted to the residence of the mayor, and thence to the commune; but not meeting with this magistrate, I was taken to the senior officer of the troops, who remanded me back to the mayor. This gentleman was now at home, and received me with true French politeness, telling me, with many bows, that my "*air distingué, ought to have been a sufficient passport;*" adding, that "I must excuse the ignorance of village magistrates; but that when I entered a town, I should be sure to meet with *les hommes d'esprit et raisonnables.*"

"Certainly, *M. le Maire,*" replied I, "this observation is proved in the present instance;" and having thus returned his compliment with an equal sincerity, after much scraping, we parted.

My quondam landlord and the *gend'arme* looked as if they expected to be paid for their trouble; but instead of giving them any money, I begged they would "present my compliments to *Monsieur l'Adjoint,* and tell him that I hoped he would recompense them for the unnecessary trouble he had given them."

I now pursued my journey through a beautiful and highly cultivated country, and by a very broad road, but much in want of repair. About two leagues from Blois I stopped to look at the *demesne* of Menaro, once the residence of the celebrated Madame de Polignac, and now a magnificent ruin. The gardens are cut into terraces, and must have been very grand; but are now totally neglected, and the alleys strewed with fragments of statues, broken to pieces by the revolutionists. The apartments appear to have been fitted up in a light and cheerful stile, and those of the grand front command a fine view of the Loire. The extensive deer park, which is surrounded by a wall, is now turned up and cultivated. I inquired of the people in the home to whom the *demesne* at present belonged, but they could not tell me. Doubtless, it is the property of some *parvenu,* who resides at Paris, where he can conceal the meanness of his origin in the crowd, or, at least, where he may find a host of fellow upstarts to keep him in countenance.

I had intended remaining the night at a village near this mansion, but the people of the *auberge* were so uncivil, that I determined to proceed. French and English innkeepers are perhaps equally extortionate; but by the latter you are, at least, civilly cheated, while the former fleece you, and at the same time treat you with neglect, if not impertinence. You may alight from your carriage or horse without attendance, and it is often some time before you can find any one that will take the trouble of shewing you a room; besides, as there are no bells in one house out of ten, you must go to the kitchen yourself for whatever you want.

Another nuisance in French inns, is the coarse strapping wenches who usually attend, and whose loquacity and impudent familiarity there is no checking. About three leagues from the village I met with a small house and a more civil reception, and here I put up for the night. The succeeding morning (March 19) I pursued my journey, through a flat country, along the banks of the Loire, to the middling sized town of Meung, where I experienced scarcely a more civil reception from the host and hostess of the Turk's Head than if they had been Turks themselves. I therefore quitted them in the morning without breakfast, and reached Orleans at two o'clock.

CHAPTER 33

Birth of the King of Rome

I was scarcely housed at the Dolphin, at Orleans, when I was waited on by an English shoemaker named Chalmers, who appeared to be a complete *quidnunc* in French politics. He however met with a very cool reception, as I generally conclude that these kind of gentry have either quitted their country to escape the gallows, or Botany Bay, for treasonable practices; or what almost deserves the same punishment, to introduce or improve manufactures at the expense of their own country.—I had a more agreeable visitor in Mr. Thompson, an old companion in scenes of gaiety in London, and with whom I dined, in company with Major Popham, another old acquaintance, with whom I had been encamped at Marmorice Bay, in Asia Minor. Here I spent a most agreeable evening with Mrs. Thompson, her amiable daughter, and promising son, who seemed to burn with military ardour, and whom I find has since entered the service, to which I have no doubt, he will be an ornament.

March 21 In the morning I visited the town, which contains upwards of forty thousand inhabitants; it was the capital of the ancient Orleanois, and is at present of the department of Loiret. Its situation on the Loire, and nearly in the centre of ancient France, as well as the fertility of the surrounding country, renders it one of the most flourishing inland towns of France. It was formerly a considerable depôt of colonial produce, which it received by the Loire from Nantes; and in despite of the present general stagnation of commerce, still retains a considerable share of business, its chief manufactures for export being brandy, vinegar, leather, wax candles, earthenware, and woollen bonnets, with which latter it supplies all the adjacent departments.[1]

The sieges which Orleans sustained by Attala in 450, and by the English in 1418, render it celebrated in history. A new statue of its heroine, Joan of Arc, has been erected in the principal place; the old one of this extraordinary Amazon having shared the general fate of great characters during the revolution, though it might be, supposed that the memory of her services would have saved her head from the general proscription.

I paid Mrs. Thompson a visit in the afternoon, and was amused by some curious anecdotes of our countrymen, whom she had occasion to see passing through Orleans. She had at this time an English sailor in the house, whom she desired might be called in; but Jack was searched for in vain, until the cook demanded if the well had been looked into, for that its bottom was his usual place of retreat? We therefore accompanied her to it, and on her callings "*allons*, Jack! she was immediately answered with a "*holla*, here am I!"

"Come along Jack," said I in a slang sailor's voice, and up came a fine manly looking tar, hand over head, by the iron chain from a depth of sixty feet.

Seizing me by the hand, and shaking it with Herculean power, "why, then, d— n me," cried he, "but I am glad to see a real countryman, for as for these here French people they talk so fast, and plague me so, that I can find no place of rest but the bottom of the well, and there I am sure none of them will dare venture to follow me."

He then related his story, as how he had been wounded and taken in a gun boat; and as how, in passing through Orleans in a most miserable plight, Mrs. Thompson had kindly taken him into the house; "but," continued he, "through these people

---

1. The forest of Orleans is fifty miles in length, and sixteen in breadth.

are too civil to me by half, I would prefer a piece of salt junk and a biscuit with a countryman, to the finest dinner with your French people; for, somehow or other, I, don't over and above like their ways."

The cosmopolite philanthropist will here doubtless pity that ignorance, which thus creates national partiality and perpetuates national jealousy. But though we may desire to see this narrow prejudice swept from the minds of persons in the higher classes, God forbid that ever the genuine John Bull should be so far enlightened. While every English soldier and sailor is intimately convinced that he is equal to two Frenchman in any kind of fight, there is little danger of his not supporting that superiority; but let him once begin to doubt if a Frenchman is as good as an Englishman, and the odds are entirely done away. With respect to national hatred, however, there is, to use the old adage, very little love lost between the French and ourselves, but the causes are very different: they envy us, but we despise them.

"I hate a Frenchman," says Goldsmith's old soldier, "because he's a slave, and wears wooden shoes!"

This being the anniversary of the much lamented death of General Sir Ralph Abercrombie, under whom Major Popham and myself had served, we dined together, and did not fail to drink to the memory of that good and gallant officer.

March 22. The following day I dined with Mr. Thompson, at whose house the mayor and a polite party met in the evening. In the morning I had a very early and unexpected visit from the commissary of police, who desired to see my passport, and after reading it observed, "that my servant's name was not inserted in it;" then putting it in his pocket departed, saying " he would return in a few minutes."

In fact, he very soon reappeared, accompanied by a corporal, four soldiers, and three *gend'armes*, one of whom held a piece of rope in his hand. I was at a loss to divine what their intention was; but the commissary soon let me know, that my servant's name not being in my *feuille de route*, he must go to prison till the Emperor's pleasure could be known.

"A very interesting subject indeed to the Emperor!" said I; "but pray, *Monsieur*, why all this formidable preparation? a single *gendarme* might, I should suppose, have been sufficient to secure an unarmed man, and you would have besides avoided drawing a mob round the house."

To this he made no reply, except by a look of official consequence, and a *gend'arme* proceeded to pinion the poor fellow with the rope, and then putting a noose over his thumb, twisted it tight with a bit of stick.

Thus secured he was driven into the street, where a great crowd was assembled. Lest the people might believe that he was taken up for a robbery, or some other heinous crime, I told them it was entirely owing to the stupidity of a clerk, who had omitted inserting his name, as my servant, in the passport; then turning to the commissary, "now, Sir," said I with a sneer, "have but the kindness to draw your sword, and the scene will be complete."

He grumbled something in rage, which making me laugh, the whole mob also set up a roar, which almost put him into a convulsive passion. He however marched off the man, and confined him in a subterraneous dungeon.

I immediately waited on the mayor, in whose company I had spent the preceding evening, and in whose liberal manners I was not mistaken, for he immediately ordered the man to be released, and reprimanded the commissary, who he informed me had only been in office a few days, and he imagined, wished to give a brilliant proof of his zeal. This fellow called on me afterwards, I suppose to make an apology, but I desired him to go about his business.

March 23. The following day, the birth of the King of Rome was known by an express from Paris, and announced by *les affiches* in the streets, directing a general illumination, and pompously declaiming on the joyful events which fixed the destinies of the French nation, and which every true Frenchman must hail as the greatest blessing from Heaven! I remained a considerable time pretending to read one of these *affiches*, to observe the people collected for the same purpose; and although none made any verbal comments, it was easy to read the expression of their sentiments in their countenances. A few seemed to read it with indifference, but not one shewed the slightest movement of approbation. Among the crowd a barber particularly amused me; for though he was as silent as the rest, his sharp nose, whimsical countenance, and comic shrugs, were supereminently characteristic of a Frenchman bursting with the desire, but afraid to speak. The illumination was most miserable, and reminded me of Milton's *darkness visible*.

March 24. In passing through the street the next morning, a fellow blowing a French horn, and surrounded by a great crowds attracted my attention. I found he was one of the numerous corps of itinerant sleight of hand performers, who infest every part of France, and who certainly would not be allowed to vagabondize about the country, if they were not of some utility. The fact is, that they are all spies of the police; and therefore not only tolerated, but paid, in order to discover and report the opinions of the people. In the course of their tricks these fellows make some humorous allusion to the government and its measures, and their companions, who are dispersed amongst the crowds watch for the remarks and even the gestures that it occasions.

Should anyone be indiscreet enough to speak his opinion too openly, though no immediate notice is taken of him, he is almost to a certainty arrested some days after and thrown into a dungeon; from which if he ever comes out, it is only to be placed under the *surveillance de la haute police*, a punishment nearly as bad as imprisonment; for he cannot absent himself twenty-four hours from his residence without the permission of the officers of police, before whom he is obliged to appear once a week; and who have also the right of paying him a domiciliary visit by night or day, to examine his papers, and, if they choose, to arrest him, without any form of law or assigning any reason. It short, to make him suffer all the vexations that the subaltern agents of a despotic and suspicious government are always so willing to inflict when they have the power.

How may Old England bless the memory of those barons bold, who, in the field of Runnimede, forced a tyrant to accord the palladium of liberty! how may Britons pride themselves in that constitution and those laws, which establish and preserve the true rights of man, in the protection of property, personal liberty, and the equal distribution of justice!

The forced rejoicings for the birth of an heir to the. empire were the following day succeeded by real sorrow and consternation at the failure of the house of Tassien, supposed to be the richest in the country. Its deficit was three millions of *francs*; a sum which, even in England, would be considered as of consequence, but which in France, where there is so little capital, is enormous. This house carried on an extensive woollen manufacture, the ramifications of which were spread all over the neighbouring departments, and gave employment to a great quantity of persons, who, as well as a vast number of retail dealers, were entirely ruined by its failure.

This event supplied the whole conversation of the coffee-rooms; for being debarred talking politics, the frequenters of these plates catch with avidity at anything that affords them an opportunity of setting their tongues in movement. I visited several of these rooms, and found that instead of coffee the decrees of Buonaparte had forced the substitution of sugar or sirup land water, a small glass of which costs two *sous*, while a cup of coffee costs twelve, and is consequently far above the pocket of the generality of the coffee-house loungers, whose chief inducement in frequenting these places is to kill time or save firing.

For the former purpose, the rooms are furnished with chess and backgammon boards; and two persons will sit down to a party at *trictrac* for four hours, for a stake of two *sous*, or perhaps a bottle of four *sous*, which nobody but Frenchmen could swallow; and which, being little better than vinegar, is probably the predominating cause of the *maigreur* of the. men, as the women, who drink only water, have in general quite sufficient *embonpoint*. A billiard table is also an invariable appendage to a French coffee.; room, and during the day is never, unemployed; but at night it is seldom occupied, from the expense of lighting it up.

On the first of April I quitted Orleans, and travelled on a very wide and well kept road, which evinced, as I proceeded, the approach to the capital, in the frequent towns, villages and *châteaux*. Few of the latter are however now occupied by their owners, who, as I have before observed, generally prefer residing in Paris, and leave these noble seats in the charge of agents or farmers; while the still existing fear of their being reclaimed, prevents their spending any money in their repairs or embellishments.

Such indeed is the general idea of the insecurity of the titles to confiscated property, that it sells for thirty *per cent* less than patrimonial or church property. Many of the *châteaux* of the ancient *noblesse* have also become the property of their servants, who, by the plunder of their masters, and the means of assignats, were enabled to purchase these mansions, which they have not funds to keep in repair.

I slept this night at the town of Etampes, and next morning (April 2) after passing through a highly cultivated country, arrived at Arpajon, near which are several deserted *châteaux*, particularly one formerly belonging to the Marshal de Castries. In this little town, as well as in every other between it and Paris, the traveller finds *tables d'hôte* at all hours, for the accommodation of passengers in the stages.

On entering the capital I preferred passing round by the Boulevards, to parading through the streets, and arrived opposite the palace of the *Corps Législatif*, formerly the Palais Bourbon, but which has been so altered and improved since my last visit to Paris, that I did not know it again. The front towards the bridge is now decorated with a rich and regular colonnade, with statues of Sully, Colbert, l'Hôpital and d'Aguesseau. The two grand doors are of solid mahogany with gilt stars, and the peristyles of white marble richly carved.

Having gratified myself with a general view of the exterior of this edifice, I crossed the Pont Louis XVI. and entered the Place Louis XV. now Pont and Place de la Concorde. This bridge is the last in Paris towards Versailles, and though the river is not here wide enough to render it magnificent, is deserving of notice, for its simplicity and good taste. Passing along the Quai de la Conférence, I entered the Place de la Concorde, one of the finest in Paris, being a parallelogram of one hundred and twenty *toises* by eighty. On the. side fronting the river are the magnificent, edifices of the Hôtels de la Marine and de Courlande; on the right the gardens of the Thuilleries, and on the left the Champs-Elisées, of which the gardens command a view.

The reflections that forced themselves on me in passing this place were not of the most cheerful kind, when I recollected that since I visited it before the revolution, the weak, but well meaning and unfortunate Louis had brought his head to the block, and here shed his own blood, because he would not permit the shedding of that of some of his subjects', while crowds of his most faithful adherents had here also shared the same fate.

Being now arrived almost at the end of my long journey, over nearly the whole breadth of France, my readers will permit me to sum up the. few general observations my mode of travelling permitted me to make, and which, though necessarily superficial, I trust will afford some information respecting the actual state of the country.

The very few equipages met with on the roads that could possibly be mistaken for gentlemen's, is the first great difference that strikes an Englishman between this country and his own. Except in the vicinity of the very large towns, a few single horse *chaises*, or covered carts, and an occasional creeping diligence, alone shew any symptom of communication between the different parts of the empire. The peasantry whom I have had occasion to converse with universally complain of the conscription; of the requisition of their horses and carts, without payment, for the use of the army; of the billeting of soldiers, and of the heaviness of their taxes, in general; but particularly of those on wine, salt and tobacco. As a general proof of the poverty of the towns, may be adduced the very few houses building, or that have been built since the revolution.

In moist of the towns I observed that the streets and places which underwent republican baptism, have resumed their ancient names, except where they recall the remembrance of the unfortunate Bourbon family. Even the names derived from the religious orders have been restored, and the Rue des Augustins, des Capucins, &c. have again superseded those of Jean Jacques Rousseau and Voltaire. The ancient names of streets are indeed a kind of historical records, and therefore should never be changed; for though no longer appropriate they carry us back to the time when they were, and afford a field of entertaining and instructive inquiry, both to the native and the foreigner. Such are in London, the White Friars, the Old Jewry, Lombard Street, and many others.

In the national character, the revolution seems to have made no perceptible alteration. The French are still what Voltaire describes them, a compound of the tiger and the monkey: under the monarchy, the sanguinary disposition was concealed by the mark, of external politeness, and the monkey then predominated; the revolution opened an unbounded field to the exercise of natural cruelty, and the incessant: wars in which their rulers have ever since kept them, have nourished and perfected that disposition. Their wars, indeed, instead of being conducted on those principles of generosity, which the French in particular formerly prided themselves on, are wars of brigandage and extermination. That of Spain, in particular, presents a tissue of atrocities and wanton cruelties, that must render the name of a French soldier execrable to the latest posterity.

The scarcity of men forcibly strikes a stranger travelling in France. In villages of one hundred houses, I have never been able to count above half a dozen old men, and scarce a youth is to be seen in the country. The greatest share of field labour falls on the women, who, when they have infants, bandage them up like Egyptian mummies, and set them down in the corner of the field to squall their lungs away, while they follow the plough or turn up the ground with a spade.

At the post houses the duty of the ostler is usually performed by females; and, as I have before observed, the attendants at the *auberges* are invariably strapping wenches, whose loquacity and familiarity are equally tiresome and obtrusive. That this scarcity of men is entirely owing to the waste of war, there cannot be the smallest doubt, when it is known for fact, that since the year 1793, thirty thousand conscripts have been raised for a single regiment.

CHAPTER 34

Palace of Luxembourg

From the Place de la Concorde I proceeded to the Hôtel de Helder, Rue de Helder, where I had directed my baggage; but finding the accommodations extremely bad, I again quitted it in search of better, and at last got comfortably suited at the Hôtel de Richelieu, in the same street.

Opposite the Rue de Helder are the Bains Chinoises, or the Boulevard Italien, where, when before at Paris, I usually breakfasted; the cutlets and coffee being excellent, and served with the greatest attention by a very pretty barmaid. I had now the curiosity to look in, and to my surprise found the identical damsel officiating exactly as I had seen her nine years before, and with much fewer marks of the all corroding power of time than I could have expected. She also immediately recognized me, and engaged me to pursue my former routine of tepid baths and breakfasts.

On my return to the hotel, I found several English gentlemen had called on me; by whose advice I proceeded to announce myself at the Etat Major of the Minister of War, and was introduced to Monsieur Plantin, the minister's secretary, who received me politely, and gave me no reason, to suppose I should meet with any *désagrémens* in remaining at Paris, though I had no permission for that purpose. Thus thinking myself secure, I looked out for a good house where I could dine, and recollecting the Salon des Etrangers, Rue de Richelieu, where I had formerly been member of a dinner club, I went thither: but soon discovered that it had much: fallen off, the cookery being now entirely French. It had also become a regular gaming house, to which a certain number of members, all French, subscribed three *louis* a year; foreigners not being allowed to subscribe, though they might be introduced by one of the members.

Every Saturday evening the proprietor. Monsieur Perrin, gives a splendid dinner to the subscribers and strangers, and there is besides a public supper every night. Two commissaries do the honours of the table, and superintend the establishment. Amongst the constant frequenters pointed but to me was the Chevalier de Reul, a *bon vivant et bel esprit* of the old regime. Mons, Perrin is the farmer general of the gambling houses in France; and besides numerous establishments in Paris, there is no, watering place or public situation of great resort in which he has not a *salon de jeu*. For this monopoly he pays government six millions of *francs* a year, and, is said to be rapidly making a fortune.

April 4. This morning I visited the Thuilleries, and found no alteration in the, gardens, but the front, towards the Louvre has been greatly improved. The celebrated bronze horses, which formerly ornamented the Place St. Marc at Venice, each on a separate pedestal, are here seen drawing a car of victory at the entrance of a triumphal arch, erected. to the, grand. army. The car being empty has given rise to a pun, for, supposing it to be waiting for Napoleon, the wits say, "*le char l'attend!*"[1]

The Thuilleries, which derives its name from occupying a spot where tiles were formerly made, was founded by Catherine de Medicis in 1564, for her own residency the King then occupying the Louvre. The Thuilleries was finished by Louis XIV. in 1634. Though a very magnificent edifice, and worthy of any capital, it is not without its faults, of which the most prominent Is its complete exposure on every side. The terrace, in particular, has the appearance of a stage, intended to shew the persons on it to public view.

From the Thuilleries I visited the Louvre, the name of which

---

1. *Le charlatan!*—the mountebank.

has given rise to many etymological conjectures; among Others, that it is derived from *Lupara*, as being a spot formerly celebrated for wolf hunting. This it appears was its name under Philip Augustus, who added several towers, surrounded it by a wide ditch, and converted it into a fortress. Charles the Ninth began the grand gallery leading to the Thuilleries, and Henry the Fourth completed it.

The external appearance is heavy and inelegant, but the alteration and additions that have been recently made evince taste and judgment, and have considerably improved it. The grand front is between eighty and ninety *toises* in length; along it is a range of columns of the Corinthian order, with a picture of Victory in a triumphal car, in *bas relief*; and another *bas relief*, representing Minerva placing the bust of Napoleon on a pedestal, on which the muse has just written, *Napoleon le Grand a achevé, le Louvre*.

Emblems of victory ornament other parts of the pedestal, and the Muses fill up the Vacant spaces. The grand entrance is superb, and well worthy of the building. Along the gallery which leads to the Thuilleries are alternately placed an N and an eagle, as if Napoleon thought his subjects have not quite sufficient reasons to recollect him, without thus obtruding his initial on them in every corner.

I had only time to take a cursory view of the interior; but as far I could judge, the pictures and statues are extremely well arranged. To study them properly required at least a month; and, had I remained at Paris, I should certainly have given a great portion of my time to them, and particularly to the historical subjects, as one of the surest ways of impressing the facts they represent on the mind. The busts of La Fontaine, d'Aguesseau, Rollin, Sully, Molière; Corneille, Descartes, Montesquieu, Fénélon, and Racine, placed in this great national repository, prove at least that the age of reason has again given way to the age of taste and good sense.

Having several letters for the friends of officers whom I had met in Spain, I employed this morning in delivering them, and first waited on Madame de Coignée, mother-in-law of General Sebastiani, for whom I had one from her son, the general's *aide-de-camp*. Formerly a stranger in Paris was obliged to hire a job carriage by the day, week, or month, with a *valet de place* to go behind it; for to be seen walking in the streets was considered as superlatively shocking.

On the contrary, at present, it is the mode to walk to, stand, and call a *fiacre* or *cabriolet*. These vehicles are far superior to the London hackney coaches, being always clean, and the drivers never thinking of extorting more than their regulated fare. Splendid private equipages are now, indeed, very scarce in Paris, for the foreigners are few, and the chief officers with the army; and as to the resident Parisians, they do not now ran into this line of extravagance. A fashionable female was formerly seen in a *curricle* in the morning, and in a diligence in the evening; she went to the country in a *tap-cul,* to the theatre in a *berlin*, to a route in a chariot, to her creditors in a demi-fortune, and to her husband in a *dormeuse*, while the *élégante* of the present day is content on all occasions with an humble *fiacre*.

Understanding that Madame de Coignée was at her sister's, Madame de Conflans, *faubourg* St. Germain, I proceeded thither; but on my arrival, finding she had just quitted it, I drove back, and passing by the palace of the Luxembourg, observed little alteration in it, except that the magnificent buildings, which had formerly encroached on and disfigured it, had been removed. This palace was commenced by Mary de Medicis, widow of Henry the Fourth, in 1615; at present it is destined to the meeting of the Senate. The Salle des Savans and the staircase leading to it are admirable. On the latter are the statues of Generals Kleber, Hoche, and Dessaix, and of the legislators Beauharnois, Mirabeau, Thouret, Condorcet, &c. The gardens still preserve their ancient strait alleys, *jets d'eau*, statues, &c.

On my second arrival at Madame de Coignée's, my inquiry if she was at home was avowed in the negative by the servant in English. On asking him why he answered me in that language, he replied, "Lord, Sir, I knew you directly to be an Englishman;

for let the French do what they will, they can never look like us! and though they try to ape us in everything, they can never succeed."

The repetition of, and emphasis he laid on, the word us, induced me to examine him a little closer, and I observed he was a good jolly English coachman, whose present service had not divested him of his national contempt for the French. He shewed me General Sebastiani's hotel, where I found Madame de Coignée, and to whom I was introduced in the garden, where she was amusing herself with the general's amiable little daughter, about eight years old.

Nothing could be more polite than Madame de Coignée's reception of me. She said her son had mentioned me so kindly in his letters, that she had longed to see me; "in short," said she, "I was quite angry with him, for instead of informing me about himself and his proceedings in Spain, his last letter of four pages is taken up with you. I must, therefore, expect that you will compensate his neglect by giving me a faithful account of him."

She heard of his losses at play, and questioned me on the subject; but. my answers were such as to quiet her fears, without committing myself or my friend. The house and gardens of General Sebastiani are amongst the most splendid in Paris; they have a fine view of the Champs Elisées, and, a good deal of shade. On taking leave, I found the English coachman waiting to request me to visit the stables, with which I complied. Among the stud were four stallions, English, Arab, Spanish and Norman, each possessing the strongly marked character, of his country. The groom was also English, and the appearance of the horses proved their superiority over the French. Indeed, they were the only ones I had seen in real good order since my arrival in France.

I dined this day with an English party at Verres in the Thuilleries, where I unexpectedly met Mr. Patterson, an old acquaintance, and an American, with whom I had visited Cadiz, Seville, and other parts of Spain, during the peace of Amiens.

After dinner we went to the opera; the piece was *Trajan*,

which was now in the height of its run. L'Ainé, was first singer, and Vestris the first dancer: Mesdames Branchard and Gredall were also excellent. Paris reckons four regular theatres, besides a vast number of places of entertainment. The regular theatres have each their separate line of performances, and collection of stock pieces, which are said to amount to two thousand one hundred and forty-two in the whole.[2]

The following morning I received an invitation from Messrs, Dennis, Pool, and others, to meet them at the Café Tortoni to breakfast. This coffee-house is the fashionable lounge of Paris, and is well situated for this purpose, being on the Boulevards, half-way between the Rue de Helder and Rue de Richelieu, which is a much frequented promenade, where a good deal, of amusement may be derived from observing the different characters walking there. Though, doubtless, no plains are ever spared with their *toilettes*, yet there is very seldom a well dressed man among these loungers. One is seen with an enormous gold buckle in the front of his hat; another, with white topped boots and black breeches: nor among the whole did I observe more than one figure who might have passed for an English blood, had it not been for an enormous embroidered neck handkerchief, which did not at all coincide with his boots.

After breakfast I returned to my hotel, having promised to meet M. de Harcourt, whom I had formerly known in Holland, where he had been *aide de camp* to his uncle the general, when commanding the English army in the absence of the Duke of York. On entering I was informed that the myrmidons of the police had been inquiring after me, owing, as it appeared, to the landlord not having properly given in my name, rank, condition, &c.

Accompanied by Monsieur de Harcourt I visited the Jardin des Plantes, founded by Louis XIII. at the suggestion of Guy de la Bronze, his physician. It received considerable additions from

---

2. The regular theatres may be thus classed: the Grand Opéra (Académie Royale de Musique); Théâtre François; Opéra Comique; Odéon. The minor theatres are the Vaudeville; the Variétés; the Théâtre de la Gaiété; the Ambigu Comique; &c. &c. besides a variety of other exhibitions in almost every quarter of Paris.

the ministers Richelieu, Mazarine, and Colbert; but it is to the celebrated Buffon that it owes its present perfection. It contains also a *ménagerie*, where every animal has a separate court to range in, and a house to retire to. We next visited the Cabinet d'Histoire Naturelle, the front of which looks into the Jardin des Plantes.

The principal object that presents itself on entering is a marble statue of Buffon, to whom this collection, as well as the garden, is greatly indebted. The first range of apartments is occupied by the vegetable reign, and by the weapons, dresses, and utensils of the South Sea Islanders, Caraibs, and other savages. To these succeed the mineral reign, composed of ores of all kinds, &c. Then shells, corals, sponges, and other marine substances, and animals, amongst which is a fish, brought from Chandernagore, called *rechardet*, and esteemed a rarity. Foreign birds, with their eggs and nests, and insects, occupy other apartments.

In a room, containing various animal monstrosities, is a child with two heads, four arms, four legs and thighs, which is said to have lived a week. The most interesting objects in this collection are the skeletons of every species of animal described by Buffon, arranged in a gallery. To the cabinet is attached an extensive library, open to the public on Tuesdays and Fridays.

CHAPTER 35

Column of the Grand Army

This morning I visited the Palais Royal, to make some purchases and lounge away an hour, for there is no place in Paris more proper for killing time. The circular row of buildings which constitute the Palace, was built by Cardinal Richelieu for his own residence in 1636, and was bequeathed by him to Louis XIII. Anne of Austria, wife of Louis XIV. inhabited it, and changed its name from Palais Cardinal to Palais Royal. On the death of Louis XIV. it devolved to the house of Orleans, in whose possession it remained until the infamous Egalité, lost it and his head in the revolution. During the reign of terror it received the name of Palais d'Egalité, but its ancient denomination has been again restored to it.

At the extreme end of the palace are two elegant statues of Cicero and Demosthenes, The whole of this fine building is surrounded by a Corinthian colonnade, with shops of all kinds, coffee-houses, *traiteurs* and *restaurateurs*, on the ground floor. The first story is composed of gambling rooms, and other places of dissipation. In the centre of the circle are tents or booths, with fanciful little gardens, where ices, lemonade, and other refreshments, according to the season, are sold.

From the Palais Royal I visited the Place Vendôme, in which is the Column of the Grand Array, erected in memory of the Austrian campaign of 1805. It is in imitation of Trajan's Pillar, one hundred and thirty-three feet high, including the pedestal and the statue of Napoleon which crowns it: the latter is ten feet high, and weighs five thousand one hundred and twelve pounds. This monument is of cut stone, entirely covered with plates of bronze, representing in bas relief and in chronological order, the principal events of the campaign, from the departure of the troops from Boulogne to the battle of Austerlitz. The bronze is entirely the produce of the cannon taken from the Austrians. A staircase within the column leads up to a gallery, from which rises a little dome, surmounted by the statue of the Emperor. On one side of the pedestal is the following inscription:

Napolio Imp. Aug. Monumentum belli Germanici, anno M.DCCC.V. trimestri spatio, ducto, suo, profligate, ex aere, capto, glorie exercitus, maximi dicavit.[3]

It is not difficult to perceive in the inscription, that the monument has been rather erected to the ostentation of the general than to the course of the army.

I dined this day at a restaurateur's, and had an excellent dinner. The plan of these houses is certainly far preferable to those of the generality of English eating-houses. On entering, a card is presented to you, on which are marked the various dishes with their prices, as well as those of the wines; so that every person may suit his own convenience, and know to a fraction what the expense of his dinner will be. The dinner hour is six o'clock, and though the room was crowded with parties, before seven it was again completely empty; so short is the time that the French usually remain at table.

As I had no appointment for the evening, I passed away a couple of hours at a puppetshew, and must do the French justice in avowing, that in this branch of the dramatic art they far excel us. The subject of the piece brought on this small theatre was the intrigues of a married couple, in the class of citizens; and from the pleasure the audience seemed to receive, I could have no doubt of the scenes being taken from real life. The general frailty

---

3. Napoleon, the August Emperor, had consecrated to the glory of the grand army, this column, composed of the cannon taken from the enemy, during the war in Germany, in 1805. A war, which, under his command, was terminated in three months.

of French women, indeed, justifies the satire of Pope,

That every woman is at heart a rake.

Chastity, though it may be considered a desirable marriage portion among the higher orders in France, is by no means deemed indispensable to the happiness of wedlock; thus, the husband is generally pretty well satisfied that he is the father of his wife's first child, but has often too much reason to doubt his share in the rest; and even when he can have no doubt on the subject, he makes no complaint, but seems to reflect, that.

La plainte est pour le fat; le bruit pour le sot;
L'honnête homme trompé s'éloigne et ne dit mot.

A recent French writer, who acknowledges that the conduct of many wives is very mysterious, apologizes for them, by laying the blame on their husbands, who confide too implicitly in the male friends they permit to escort them to the promenade and to public places; the contradiction which the wife sometimes meets from her husband in the article of toilet expenses, he also considers as a sufficient excuse for her aberrations.

> "Nevertheless," continues he, "to persecute a wife is always odious, and whatever may be the private conduct of either party, they should never forget that they owe each other a mutual forbearance. It often happens that a couple, after having each led a most libertine life, reform and renew their first ties towards the end of the career, mutually forgetting and forgiving their past errors. A sweet friendship then forms the charm of their declining age, and they enjoy (though rather late) that domestic happiness, the want of which nothing can compensate. Such persons would have loved each other all their lives, had they not sworn to do so at the altar."

One may safely presume this is a kind of domestic happiness, which few British husbands will envy, notwithstanding its sweet friendship!

It must not however be supposed that French women, above

the common class, give themselves up to that degrading libertinism that confers favours on a multiplicity of lovers. Gallantry is in France a word of very different import from prostitution, signifying the tender preference of one amiable being at a time, besides the husband, and whatever lengths this attachment leads to, they are excused as the amiable weaknesses of sentiment and sensibility:—

> "thus," according to an eloquent and moral writer, "shame is mutually communicated, and mutually pardoned, and levity joined to excess, forms a corruption at the same time deep and frivolous, which laughs at everything that it may blush at nothing."[4]

Indeed the mere absence of chastity does not in France, even among the middle classy carry with it that stigma which attaches to the want of it in England. A husband, for instance, of the respectable class of citizens (*bourgeois*) feels no repugnance at lodging in the same house with a notoriously kept mistress, nor does his wife see any indecorum in conversing with her familiarly when they happen to meet. The same disregard to the virtue of their female servant is observed in the *bourgeois* mistresses.

If a maid shews by outward and visible signs that she has no longer a right to that honourable title, her mistress, instead of turning her out of doors for a "strumpet as she is," consoles, encourages, and instructs her in making the necessary preparations for the event. A few days before she expects its arrival, she procures a substitute to do her work, retires to the house of a *sage femme*, and in thirty-six hours after the delivery of her burden returns to her place, and is as well received as if she were as chaste as Diana. The child is either put into the asylum of *les Enfans trouvés*, or sent out to nurse with a peasant.

Next morning I rode in the Champs-Elisées, Bois de Boulogne, and the Place d'Etoile. In the latter a triumphal arch has been lately erected on the marriage of the Emperor. Indeed these kind of temporary monuments strike the eye in every

---

4. *Essai sur les Caractères des Femmes.*

quarter of Paris and its environs; and though in general they are very trifling things, yet they are supposed to prove *la bonne volonté de la bonne ville de Paris*, and at least gratify the vanity of Napoleon.

Having accepted an invitation to dine at the Salon des Etrangers, I met there several of the ministers of state, and a number of members of the higher classes of the Legion of Honour. The dinner was in the first stile, and among the luxuries were *pâtés de foie gras*, a dish fit for Heliogabalus himself. It is composed of the livers of geese, and truffles. In order to prepare the liver, the poor goose is crammed for a certain time until it becomes immensely fat; its feet are then fastened to the ground, close to a very hot stove, which produces a violent thirst, and it is supplied with as much water as it will drink; the effect of this cruel treatment is, that the whole fat of the body concentrates in the liver, which swells to an enormous size, while the body is emaciated to a skeleton.

Lest the bird should die before the completion of the business, it is said that a physician is employed, and allowed a handsome salary to attend these operations. Although I must acknowledge that these *ptés* are exquisite, I should have no objection to see the inventors and manufacturers of them brought under the lash of those worthy members of society whose study is the prevention of cruelty to animals.

After dinner the company retired up stairs to coffee and liqueur, from which I went into the Salon de Jeu, where in a very short time I lost three hundred *louis* at Rouge et Noir. The Chevalier de Reul, whom I have before mentioned as one of the constant frequenters of the house, then called me aside, and advised me to risk no more, but to accompany him to the Comédie Françoise, where he promised to introduce me to the first performers; with all of whom he was intimate, and particularly the females, among whom it is a kind of prescriptive necessity to pay the *chevalier* a visit previous to their *début*, in order to secure his powerful aid towards their success, as well as to get into society.

I gladly accepted the gallant *chevalier's* offer; but in passing through the hazard room I could not resist temptation, particularly as the manner of playing was novel to me. The bank covers, any sum the caster lays down, and mostly in silver, while the players usually stake gold, being less cumbersome. The difference, which is seven *sous* in the single, and sixteen in the double *louis*, forms no small portion of the gain of the bank. I was here more fortunate than at Rouge et Noir, winning, two hundred *louis* in a few minutes, with which I contented myself, and accompanied the *chevalier* in his carriage to the theatre, where, according to his promise, he introduced me behind the scenes to several of the performers.

One of the females, conspicuous for her beauty, and well known in the annals of gallantry, accompanied me into the stage box, on which she drew the eyes of the whole audience. After the performance, the *chevalier* conducted me to a *restaurateur's*, where he had invited this actress and two others to partake of an elegant supper, with I, accompanied by delightful singing end sprightly conversation, the night insensibly glided away, and we did not separate till three o'clock.

The pleasures of the day were of a nature, to make me wish for their repetition, and I promised myself to dine every day at the Salon de, Etrangers; to go to the Comédie Françoise every evening; and to sup with agreeable actresses every night. But all these charming prospects vanished in a moment, "like the baseless fabric of a vision." I had not even time to dream of them, when a violent knocking at my door announced a most unwelcome visitor from the *adjutant de place*, with a guard to arrest and conduct me before the general commanding in Paris. The adjutant entered my room with two of his myrmidons, and demanded, with all the insolent airs of office, what brought me to, and, what detained me at Paris?" adding, "that if I could not give a good account, of myself to the general I must expect the most serious consequences."

While I was huddling on my clothes, he exclaimed every moment, "*Allons, f— , ce n'est pas le temps de faire la toilette!*" I was therefore obliged to march off with my coat and waistcoat on my arm, and to tie my neck-cloth in the street, through which I was hurried by these ruffians as if I had been a criminal.

They first conducted me to the hotel of Comte Hulin, the Governor of Paris, who ordered me to be transferred to the office of his Etat Major, there to be strictly examined, and a report made to him. The questions put to me were of such a nature, that it might have appeared they suspected me of some heinous plot against the State. At first their language was most menacing and imperious; but finding I would confess nothing, having indeed nothing to confess, their tone softened; particularly when I told them that, though a stranger, I was not without friends of the first respectability at Paris, and mentioned among others Madame de Coignée.

These names caused the *adjutant de place*, who was my principal examiner, to reflect how he treated me; and as he gave me the materials for writing, with permission to address whom I chose, I sent a note to Madame de Coignée, and some other friends. I soon after received a visit from Sir John Coghill, who immediately went to speak to the Duke de Rovigo, Minister of Police. While I was in momentary expectation of being ordered to occupy an apartment in the Temple, I was visited by Lieutenant Owen, of the Royal Navy, who had also called on me twice the preceding day.

This gentleman had been arrested at one of the depots of prisoners; on a charge of having been engaged in a plot with some Swiss officers, to corrupt the Swiss garrison of Belle-Isle, to give up that island to the English; a plot certainly as ridiculous in all its parts as ever entered into the head of Don Quixote. Mr. Owen was now under the close inspection of the Police, being permitted to absent himself from his lodgings only a couple of hours in the day.

His visits to me were to ask my advice how he was to act in these circumstances, but I declined entering at all into the subject, and moreover begged him to discontinue his visits, which, without being of any utility to him, might have very unpleasant consequences to me. On his retiring, I asked the adjutant if he knew him, to which he answered, "*Oh qu'oui! et vous le connoissez aussi, pa bleu!*"

It now struck me that his visits were the cause of my being arrested, and I observed to the Adjutant that surely it could not for a moment be supposed that I had anything to do with the absurd plot of which Mr. Owen was suspected; adding; that the French government lowered itself in paying attention to so ridiculous a story. "Perhaps, Sir," I added, "you do not recollect, that in 1761 the capture of Belle-Isle by the English was only effected by a large fleet and army, commanded by three admirals and several generals; and you fear that it may now be taken by such a detachment as is usually commanded by a lieutenant; for, if I have been correctly informed, it appears that Mr. Owen proposed himself to command the expedition."

These observations seemed to make some impression, and the adjutant became more civil, informing me that I ought not to consider him as the cause of my arrest, for that my name had been some time in the books of the police, and that I had left Spain with a recommendation to be well looked after. I immediately recollected General Beliard's letter to General Sols at Bayonne, and had no doubt but he had sent a similar one to Paris.

But though the Adjutant became more civil in his manner, he could not help expressing his fears of my attempting to escape even from this place; and when I once, in walking up and down the room, approached the door, he cried out, "*gardez bien ce Monsieur-là;*" and I was prevented from again going near the door. While I remained in this state of suspense, I was not long without finding something to amuse and interest me, in the various persons who, like myself, were brought hither *malgré eux*. Among them was a refractory conscript, accompanied by his disconsolate parents, who threw themselves at the feet of the adjutant, imploring for their son.

The unfeeling brute first grossly abused them, as the instigators of their son's crime, and assured them that he would either be shot, or inevitably sent to the galleys for life, and that he had only to thank their evil councils for his fate. It appeared that this lad was an only son, who had learned a trade, and having escaped the first drawing of the conscription, had set up in business, and with the produce of his industry supported his aged parents.

A supplementary conscription being called for the same year, he hoped to escape the drawing by concealing himself till it was over; but he was discovered in his place of refuge, and now brought before the military authority, for having endeavoured to evade the conscription laws. The adjutant, however, seemed to be softened by the tears of the parents, and concluded by ordering the lad out with one of his myrmidons, most to receive all to receive all the money the poor people could raise, as the price of not bringing him to punishment, while the lad himself was as certainly sent off instantly to join a regiment.

To these poor people succeeded a decent looking woman, inquiring after her husband, who, according to her story, belonged to the national guard, and had gone out the evening before, and had not been heard of since. The only answer she received was desiring her to go to the Place de Grêve, where she would probably find him; and with this consolatory advice she retired in tears. The Place de Grêve, the place of public execution, is near la Morgue, where all the dead bodies, picked up in the streets during the night, or taken out of the river, are exposed to be recognized by their friends. The number of violent deaths in Paris is very great, and increases daily, from the increased frequency of suicides and murders.

Although I assumed an air of indifference, I could not help being disturbed at my situation; nor was I quite at ease with respect to the result, having no sort of wish to occupy poor Captain Wright's apartment in the Temple. Madame de Coignée, and some other friends, having interested themselves for me, the affair terminated with ordering me to be escorted to Verdun by a *gend'arme*. One being immediately appointed for this service, he first conducted the to the Temple, whose gates I did not enter without a kind of chill, from reflecting on the horrors that had been committed within them.

The purpose of bringing me here was, however, only to arrange with the colonel of *gend'armerie* the sum I was to pay to my guard, which he fixed at twelve *francs* a day, with the obligation that he was to dine and sleep in the same room with me.

The corps of *gend'armerie*, composing the civil and military police of France, is nearly on the footing of the ancient *maréchaussée*. It consists chiefly of cavalry, though, a small number are infantry; and the men are all picked from different regiments of the line, being such as can read and write, as that is required. Their duty is to *patrole* the country, either on horseback or on foot; to arrest deserters from the army, refractory conscripts, and all persons not having regular passports; and to assist the civil magistrates in the execution of their warrants, in all cases of correctional or criminal police.

From the idea I had received of the police of Paris, I expected to have found it crowded with *gend'armes*; and was, therefore, not a little surprised to learn that there were only fifteen cavalry and twenty-five infantry constantly stationed there. In all the surrounding villages are brigades of five, who keep up a daily correspondence with the colonel in chief in the capital. In the same manner detachments are stationed in every town of any consideration throughout the empire.

CHAPTER 36

Arrival at Verdun

Early on the morning of the 8th of April I quitted Paris on horseback, with my *gend'arme;* and as I had long found that no situation was so desperate as to be without some advantage, I endeavoured to render him useful, by questioning him respecting the country.

We passed through the Porte St. Martin, one of the finest entrances to Paris, built by Louis XIV. in 1674. It is composed of three arches, ornamented with four *bas reliefs*, representing the talking of Besançon, the rupture of the Triple Alliance, the surrender of Limburg, and the defeat of the Austrian army by Louis XIV, under the figure of Hercules, with his club, repulsing an eagle.

Immediately outside of the gate we came to the fine canal of l'Ourcq; the country was enchanting, and the weather superb. After refreshing the horses at the village of Claye, we arrived in the evening at the handsome town of Meaux on the Marne, the capital of the *ci-devant* Brie, celebrated for the elegant spire of its principal churchy for being the first town that opened its gates to Henry IV., and for its excellent cheeses. The road from Paris hither was lined with seemingly deserted *châteaux*.

April 9. After some hours ride through a country, finely diversified with hills and levels, and with abundance of wood and water, we reached La Ferté sous Jouarre, a small town, in the vicinity of which are immense quarries, on the side of a hill, which supply a great part of France with millstones, and are of so superior a quality, that they formerly found their way to Germany, Holland, and even England. We slept this night at the village of Vieux Maisons, where I began to reconcile myself to the company of my *gend'arme* at supper, and to his sleeping in a bed in the same room, as all remonstrance I knew would be useless. Indeed he was superior to the generality of his brethren, and by no means deficient in education or intelligence; so that his company, which was intended as a punishment, became rather a pleasure.

April 10. We pursued our journey this day through a dreary country, and by a very bad bye road, having quitted the highway way for some reason which I could not learn, and arrived at the miserable village of Etage, close to which we visited a very fine *château*, lately the property of Marshal Lasnes, but now of a Monsieur Genova. It formerly belonged to Monsieur Charmilly, first *valet de chambre* to Louis XVI., and who fell a victim to his attachment for his master. It has handsome gardens, beautifully situated woods, and some waterfalls. In one of the apartments are the pictures of its successive possessors; amongst whom was the Comte Langlum, who sold the demesne, with ninety-nine villages attached to it, to raise a sum for his ransom, when made prisoner by the Turks.

April 11. Our journey this day lay through Champagne, part of which province is called *Pouilleuse*, on account of the quantity of barren land it contains. In the evening we arrived at Chalons, and found comfortable accommodation at the little inn called the Ville de Metz. Chalons is an ancient and considerable town on the banks of the Marne, which bathes a part of its walls. It is mostly ill built, many of its houses being of wood, and the streets in general narrow. It has, nevertheless, some buildings worthy of notice; amongst which are the cathedral, constructed in the thirteenth century, in the Arab-Gothic stile of architecture.

The hotel of the prefecture is a handsome modern stone edifice. The Hôtel de Ville is also modern, and its grand *façade* and hail of audience are of the Corinthian order. The promenade, called the Jard, is considered one of the finest in France, The population of the town is about twelve thousand. It is celebrated for two great battles fought near it; the first in which Aurelian defeated Tacitus, his competitor for the empire, and the second in which Attila and his allies were defeated and dispersed by the Romans, the French, and Goths, in 451. Chalons has a public library of thirty thousand volumes, and an imperial school of arts and trades, in which are four hundred and fifty scholars, nominated by the Emperor, educated at the expense of the state, and chosen chiefly from the sons of the military.

It must be acknowledged, that France excels every country in the world in the institutions for public and gratuitous education. Primary and secondary schools are established in every commune, under the inspection of the civil magistrates, and partly supported by government. In the first, children learn reading, writing, and arithmetic; and in the second, they are taught the learned languages, and the elements of the sciences.

To these first seminaries succeed the lyceums (also partly endowed by government, and which supply the place of the ancient colleges), one of which is established in every two or three departments; and to each is attached a library, a botanic garden, and a cabinet of natural history. The two latter cannot fail of being of infinite utility to the students, who have thus before their eyes all the productions of nature, the reading of which subjects, even when assisted by plates, can give but an imperfect idea.

From the lyceums those who are des tined for the public service, or the learned professions, enter into the special schools, of which there are several in different parts of the empire, and in which the range of instruction is much more extensive than in our universities, embracing every branch both of the useful and elegant arts and sciences, natural history, painting, sculpture, architecture in all its branches, music, medicine, law, the veterinary science, &c. all have their respective places.

Besides these are numerous military and marine establishments, for the education of young men destined for those professions. Even the art of swimming has become a branch of public education. Corporal chastisement is strictly prohibited in the schools; and all the scholars are obliged to wear an uniform, accompanied with a cocked hat, and to learn the manual exercise; by which means it is doubtless intended to familiarize them to the idea of becoming soldiers, and to blunt their feelings when they fall into the conscription.

But though public instruction seems to be so well organized in France, yet by no means must it be inferred that the diffusion of general knowledge is prevalent even amongst the upper class; in fact, though many Frenchmen have reached the highest point of science and literature, the number of those who may with propriety be called well informed is extremely small, while the truly ignorant are very numerous.

The cause seems to be in the multifarious sciences which form the routine of the schools, and of which it is impossible to acquire more than a very superficial knowledge during the period of education; and after leaving school, not one Frenchman in a thousand ever thinks of reading for any other instruction than that necessary to his profession or business. In geography and general history in particular, the ignorance of Frenchmen in the respectable class of society often forces a smile. I was once in company with several, from whose rank in life might have been expected, at least, that general knowledge which is attendant on a liberal education; an English officer, who had sailed round the world, was also of the party.

After a thousand questions respecting the countries be had seen, one gentleman asked him, if New Holland was not a port of North America? while another desired to know what he thought of the naval arsenal at Toulon? On his replying that he had never been in the Mediterranean, the Frenchman, with a look of sagacity, exclaimed, *"Mais, Monsieur, vous n'avez pas done fait le tour du monde!"*

Something similar was the idea of a midshipman, who insisted that the Bible was all a romance, for that had there been a Red Sea, so often spoken of in it, he must have seen it in his voyage round the world with Lord Anson. Besides the seminaries of education I have mentioned, there is in every bishopric a school for the education of youth for the church; church; but as theology has since the revolution been a study that promises neither much reputation nor profit, these seminaries were almost entirely abandoned; and if government had not lately taken measures to provide a succession of priests, the next generation would have presented the appearance of the patriarchal ages, when every father acted as priest in his own family.

The paltry salaries of the clergy prevent the middling or higher classes from destining their children for the profession. The government has lately formed establishments for the education of the sons of inferior citizens and others for the church. At the expiration of the term of their studies, if they find they have not employment, they have no alternative but to become soldiers; government determining not to be at the expense of their education, without being remunerated one way or other.

The annual salary of the archbishops in but fifteen thousand *francs*; of bishops ten thousand; of *cures*, or beneficed clergymen, from fifteen hundred to a thousand, and of the other priest, but five hundred. The heads of the church have, however, in general, sinecure places in the court of Napoleon, and the inferior clergy augment their revenue by the fees on burials, marriages, and baptisms.

Three great sources of the former revenues of the clergy are, however, nearly annihilated: confession has almost entirely fallen into disuse, or at the utmost, a general annual confession is deemed sufficient. Purgatory, that bugbear of the Catholic world for so many ages, has almost totally lost its influence on the minds of the people of France I and thus a second fertile source of riches to the clergy, in the celebration of masses for the dead, is almost most entirely dried up. Lastly, the great majority of the enlightened French pay very little attention to the rules of their religion respecting fast days, and hence the sale of indulgences is much reduced.

With respect to the seminaries of female education in the provinces, they have been in general extremely bad since the revolution, the suppression of the convents having created a long void in this object. At present boarding schools are becoming more numerous, and there are likewise many establishments for the education of girls, formed under the direction of several orders of *religieuses*, authorized by the government: particularly the "*Dames de la Congrégation de Notre Dame*," and the "*Dames de la Congrégation des Nouvelles Catholiques*."

April 12. Pursuing our journey from Chalons, we were obliged to stop at a miserable village, the *gend'arme* declaring his horse unable to proceed; but, in fact, his object was to get another day's pay, by retarding our arrival at Verdun.

The following day (April 13) I halted awhile at St. Menehould, a small town of three thousand inhabitants, situated in a marsh, between two rocks. Here the Prussians were defeated by the Carmagnoles in 1792, which may be said to have sealed the destinies of France and of Europe, at least for a time; for the defeat of a regular army, which, according to the Duke of Brunswick's manifesto, was to march to Paris, inspired such confidence into the armed mob of France, that nothing could afterwards resist them.

St. Menehould is also famous for the sieges it stood in 1048, 1089, 1436, 1560, and 1614. Hither retreated the Prince de Condé, the Duke de Bouillon, and Prince de Nevers. In 1616, it was taken by the Marquis de Praslin; in 1652, by the Spaniards, and the next year retaken by Louis XIV. in person. The walls which surrounded it have been levelled, and it is now; entirely open.

The country from St. Menehould to Clermont is diversified by romantic hills and valleys well wooded, watered and cultivated, and with extensive cherry and plum, orchards. Near Clermont, my *gend'arme* pointed out the position, on a commanding eminence, occupied by Arthur Dillon's army. Clermont is most romantically situated at the foot of a rocky eminence, rising from an extensive plain. The remains of fortifications are seen on the summit, and as three sides present a perpendicular face of 60 to 80 feet high, it must have been an extremely strong post. At one of the extremities of this hill is an artificial mound, where the republicans used to repair, to celebrate their civic marriages and take the civic oath.

April 14. I quitted Clermont for Verdun, with something like the apprehensions of a boy, on his first going to school, being unacquainted with the nature of a depôt, and having heard no favourable account of the treatment of the prisoners. On entering the town I was conducted to the citadel, and before the commandant, a Colonel Courcelle, whose appearance was not calculated to do away the unfavourable account I had heard of him. A red woollen cap, and a grey frieze jacket and pantaloons, constituted his dress, and he filled the room with a cloud of smoke from a great pipe. He was however civil, and when the clerks had, according to the Verdun expression, "drawn my picture," that is, taken down my description, size, the place of my birth, and my father and mother's names, and having signed, a parole not to quit the town without permission, I was allowed to retire at perfect liberty.

CHAPTER 37

Sketch of its History

My readers will not expect a minute history of Verdun, which, were I to compile it from the archives, would make a large volume, and after all be neither amusing nor instructive. As however it will long be remembered by many an Englishman who has languished for years within its walls, suffering that worst of misery, "hope deferred," a rapid glance over its annals may not be uninteresting. Before the incursion of Attila, Verdun was one of the principal towns of Belgic Gaul; but in the universal devastation that accompanied the progress of that scourge of God and his followers, it was so reduced, that in the middle of the fifth century, it was only an insignificant castle.

Again gradually risings in 502 it was taken by Clovis, and soon after became part of the kingdom of Austrasia; but was governed by its own Counts, till 977, when the reigning chief granted it to the Bishop of Verdun and his successors, which grant was confirmed by the Emperor Otho.

The bishops governed the city and its territory by their viscounts, but the latter often usurped the supreme power, and several times in the eleventh and twelfth centuries besieged the bishops in the town and burnt it. From the middle of the thirteenth to the end of the sixteenth century, it was governed by its own magistrates independent of any other authority, and generally enjoyed tranquillity.

By the treaty of Vienna, in 1745, the Duchy of Lorraine being annexed to the crown of France, Verdun and its territory received the same form of government as the rest of the kingdom.

The town is situated nearly in the centre of an oblong valley surrounded on every side by hills, which taking a direction between north west and south west, afford a bed to the Meuse, whose course is here extremely tortuous. The citadel and part of the town stand on the summit and declivity of a rocky eminence on the west bank of the river, and the rest of the town on several islands in it; so that it is divided into the upper and lower town.

When France was circumscribed within more narrow bounds, Verdun, as a frontier town, was of considerable importance, but since the fortune of Buonaparte has extended the empire to the banks of the Rhine, and reduced the princes beyond it to a state of vassalage, it is no longer deemed of any consequence; the works are allowed to go to ruin and are dismantled of artillery. The ramparts which surround the town are about three miles in circuit, with regular outworks, and being planted with trees afford a pleasant promenade.

The citadel on the summit of a rock was finished under the direction of Marshal Vauban, but is commanded by the neighbouring hills, from one of which the Prussians bombarded it, in 1792, and in a few days obliged it to surrender. The governor put an end to himself, well knowing that the guillotine would otherwise have done so, and his death has afforded a subject for one of the best modern French tragedies.

At the revolution Verdun contained eighteen religious communities, whose revenues amounted to two millions and a half of *livres*. The whole of the conventional buildings have been either pulled down for the materials, or converted into magazines, hospitals, &c. The Episcopal palace, situated on the margin of the rocky elevation before mentioned, is an extensive but plain edifice, now granted to a senator.

The cathedral is a very handsome gothic pile, and had formerly four square towers, but two of them have been destroyed by lightning. With respect to commerce, Verdun is celebrated for its *dragées*, comfits and liqueurs; the former even constituted one of the luxuries of the *seraglio* of Constantinople, and of the Imperial palace of Petersburg. The decrees of Buonaparte, which have raised the price of sugar to six *francs* the pound, have decreased the manufacture of these objects three-fourths. A few manufactories of coarse felt hats, and some tanneries, are the other trading speculations of the town.

Having now reached the place of my final destination, I shall quit the journal form, and present the reader with such observations as occur to me, without regard to the order of time. The first that naturally presents itself relates to the situation of the prisoners. As the depôt is solely appropriated to those on parole, each has a passport which permits him to walk or ride in every direction, two leagues from the town, between the opening of the gates at daylight and their shutting at dark.

Field officers and naval captains sign a public register once a month; all other commissioned officers every fifth day, and every other prisoner (except by particular indulgence) every day. All general convivial meetings of the prisoners must be sanctioned by the commandant; and as this has never been refused, the anniversary of His Majesty's birth, and of St. Patrick, have been always celebrated at Verdun, with as much loyalty and devotion as in the capital of the British kingdom.

Sometime after my arrival Monsieur Courcelles was superseded in the command of the depôt, in consequence of the complaints of the prisoners, particularly the midshipmen, who (without the slightest cause, except his villainous caprice,) he confined in the citadel, where they were subject to every kind of ill treatment and extortion. As a new system commenced with the arrival of the new commandant, my readers will not be displeased at an endeavour to paint the old system, as it was described to me by persons resident in the depôt since its first establishment.

The first commandant was a General Roussel, who treated the prisoners in the best manner; but in a few months he was replaced by General Wirion, as great a rogue as the revolution has produced. Under him everything was venal, and the prisoners of all ranks were plundered, both by himself and his underlings, in every possible manner.

From those whom he knew possessed fortunes, he extorted immense sums, as the price of the indulgences he granted them, or of refraining from sending them to Bitche, which he had the power to do without assigning any cause; and more than once a number of the most quiet persons in the depôt have been dragged from their beds and marched off to that infernal cavern, without having the slightest knowledge of the reason; and many of them, after suffering two years of the most complicated misery in its dungeons, when they returned to Verdun were still quite ignorant of the motives of their arrest. One instance will be sufficient to give an idea of General Wirion's character:—

A number of the English of good fortune frequently invited him to dinner, and allowed him to win their money, as a certain way of keeping on good terms with him; one of these gentlemen however had offended unknowingly, and Wirion destined him to Bitche; but receiving an invitation to dine with him, he accepted it, and appeared to be on the very best terms with his host. He was not a little astonished to find, when the general retired towards the morning, two *gend'armes* enter, and tell him that he had only till daylight to prepare himself to march for that place.

The system of extortion of the lieutenant of *gend'armes*, who was second in command, and of the non-commissioned officers of that corps, was regularly organized. At this time every prisoner without distinction was obliged to sign twice a day; and by another regulation of the general's, if they neglected to do so, they were obliged to pay three *francs* to the *gendarme* who went to visit them. It was soon found that this measure brought in but little, as none but persons of fortune could afford to pay a crown a day for the liberty of sleeping in the morning and riding out in the afternoon. Hence the system was changed, and for six or twelve *francs* a month, a tacit permission was granted to forget these frequent signatures.

The masters of merchantmen, by far the greater number of whom were in a state of the greatest distress, did not escape the grasp of these harpies; by the regulations they were obliged to live ten in a house, to be mutually responsible for each other, body for body, and besides were mustered twice a day.

In order to be freed from the effects of these regulations, which deprived them of all comfort, they were forced to pay the *gend'armes* whatever they could scrape together. Besides this open and general system, the *gend'armes* had another efficient method of raising contributions, by lotteries for horses, watches, trinkets, &c. that often had no existence; of if they had, it made no difference, the winner being well assured that the consequence of insisting on receiving the object would be a visit to Bitche, as was experienced by a gentleman who won a horse in this manner from the lieutenant of *gend'armerie*, and did not choose to say, as half a dozen others did, who had won the same animal at different times: "*Monsieur, je vous prie de le garder, comme un souvenir de l'amitié!*"

During the administration of Berthier, as minister of war, the complaints made by the prisoners of the conduct of Wirion, were not paid the smallest attention to, Wirion being one of his *protégés*, and not taking an active part in forwarding these complaints. Sir T. Lavie, the senior naval officer, was dragged out of his bed, and hurried off to the fortress of Montmedy, where he was kept close confined, as a state prisoner, for some months, and not allowed the use of paper, pen or ink.

On General Clerke's being appointed to the head of the war department, the prisoners renewed their complaints against Wirion, who was now called on to explain his conduct; for which purpose he went from the depôt to Paris, but his explanation not exculpating him, it is supposed that a public inquiry was ordered, to avoid which he became his own executioner by blowing his brains out in the Bois de Boulogne; while the lieutenant of *gend'armerie*, who so well seconded him in his system of extortion, was reduced to the ranks.

Wirion was succeeded in the command of the depôt by

Monsieur Courcelles, a colonel, who before held the situation of *commandant de place*; as great a villain as Wirion, but taught by his example to avoid the rock on which he split. The open system of extortion now ceased, and he contented himself with what could be picked up by underhanded means.

The first of which was in the monthly payment of the prisoners, in which an abuse had existed from the commencement of the depôt, without having been noticed, or at least complained of. Instead of paying in *francs*, the prisoners were paid in *livres tournois*, by which the persons who paid the money put one and a quarter, or more, *per cent*, into their own pocket; eighty *francs* being equal to eighty-one *livres*, which amounted to above fifteen *louis* a month.

Besides the old perquisite, which Courcelles continued, he struck out a new source of extortion, which fell almost entirely on the midshipmen. On pretence of some desertions among this class, he caused the whole of them to be arrested and closely confined in an old convent of the citadel; here they were obliged to pay thirty *sous* a month each, for the lights kept burning by their guards, besides being charged most enormously for every dilapidation: and the whole produce of both these taxes went into the pocket of Courcelles and his *affidés*; for the lights were allowed by the government, and the dilapidations were never made good.

Upon a moderate average, these two objects produced twenty *louis* a month. But the third and grand speculation was the wine. Courcelles having a vineyard near Verdun which produced a *vin de pays*, worth about six *sous* the bottle, he obliged the persons confined in the citadel to purchase the wine at fifteen *sous*, from his natural son, whom he had appointed turnkey at one of the dungeons.

From an accurate calculation, the profits arising from this monopoly amounted to forty-five *louis* a month, making in the whole eighty *louis*. But independent of these extortions, the midshipmen were treated with the most brutal inhumanity, and on the slightest murmur were thrown into a dungeon called the

"Tour d'Angoulême," being a round tower, with but two apartments, in which the Duc d'Angoulême had been confined.

At length the midshipmen seeing no prospect of any remission of their sufferings, detailed them in a letter to the minister of war, which produced an inquiry into the conduct of Courcelles, and though he had been too cautious to allow any proof of his sharing in the plunder to be brought home to him, and threw, the whole burthen on the shoulders of the lieutenant of *gend'armerie,* his conduct was evidently disapproved of by his being immediately removed, both from the command of the depôt, and from the situation of *commandant de place.* With respect to his catspaw, the lieutenant of *gend'armerie*, he followed Wirion's example, giving himself a *quietus* with a pistol on the glacis.

The prisoners who formed the depôt were, at the commencement, distinguished into two classes, *viz. détenus* or hostages and prisoners of war. Among the former were many respectable families, who were travelling peaceably on the supposed sacredness of the laws of nations, when they were suddenly arrested and rigorously confined; but there were also some among this class, who having given the King's-Bench the slip, came to the continent to live by their wits, in which many of them admirably succeeded.

Among the lower class of *détenus* were also many tradesmen, who fled from their country to avoid the punishment due to their seditious principles, and several of them, particularly tailors, bootmakers and *traiteurs,* have succeeded better at Verdun than they would probably have done at home, being employed by most of their countrymen. The *traiteurs* in particular, during the first years of the depôt, made fortunes by the epicurism of the *détenus*. In their shops were to be found the most delicate and expensive *viands* from the most distant provinces of the empire: the celebrated *pâtés de foie gras*; the *poularde aux trufles* of Paris; the oysters of Concale; the turbot and cod of the North Sea, and the tunny-fish of the Mediterranean.

The prices of these delicacies were enormous, a *poularde* costing two *louis*, and turbot and cod four *francs* the pound; but were never considered, for as Verdun was then full of accommodating Jews, who lent money on personal security at a hundred *per cent*, interest, it was by no means difficult to raise the wind; and hence, in many instances, there was but little difference in the stile of living of the *détenus* of the first fortune, the midshipman of the navy, and the bankrupt blacklegs.

At this period Verdun had a Pharo bank and a Rouge et Noir table, to which every description of persons were admitted, where perfect equality reigned, and where our countrymen of the first rank might be seen seated alongside a ragged Jew, a mud covered peasant, or a *fille publique*. This bank was a ray from the grand gambling luminary of Paris, which I have already noticed; and here a great number of young men were completely ruined, it being supposed that while it continued, £50,000 were lost by the prisoners every year. It was at last shut up, in consequence of general regulations limiting the number of the licensed gambling houses. We need scarce remark, that a nation must be very far gone in corruption, whose government openly sanctions one of the most destructive of vices, in order to increase its revenue. A recent French writer, in describing the gambling societies of Paris, says,

> that the intention of government, in authorizing public gaming houses, is to hinder the national gamblers from transporting themselves and money to foreign countries, as well as to attract foreign gamblers into their own.

The same reasons may, with equal justice, be adduced in favour of licensing brothels, and houses to receive stolen goods, from both of which considerable revenues might be raised.

It is not surprising that .amongst the variety of characters brought into contact at Verdun, there should be frequent disputes, and that many duels should be the consequence, by which several young men have lost their lives, who, had they been spared, might have been ornaments to their professions.

CHAPTER 38

Arrest and confinement

As soon as I had got fixed at Verdun, and had time to look round me, my first object was to inquire into the situation of the soldiers confined in the depôts, which I found extremely distressing, both from want of clothing and from scanty nourishment. As senior officer, I felt it my duty to represent their sufferings to the government, which immediately empowered me to draw for and pay them the moiety of their pay, besides an allowance for clothing; the result of which was, that these poor fellows have since enjoyed comforts they never knew before.

The inducements to desertions have been entirely done away, and many valuable lives have been saved, by the comforts of warm clothing and good food during the inclemency of winter. The corresponding with the several depôts, and the necessary regulations I was obliged to form for supplying the prisoners, were sufficient fully to occupy me; but from the situation I was placed in, I was every day addressed by foreigners, who, though not actually in the British service, had been made prisoners, fighting in the general cause; all of whom were relieved as far as propriety would admit.

The general measures I adopted in every instance, I feel happy in being able to say, have been approved by the government; and though captivity is incalculably injurious to my own interest, I feel the counterbalancing satisfaction of knowing that I have left nothing undone to render it supportable to my fellow prisoners; and the still greater pleasure of observing, that I have succeeded farther than I could have hoped, from the situation of the depôts on my first arrival.

I was not, however, long allowed to enjoy the tranquillity I hoped for; jealousy and suspicion, the constant companions of weak governments as well as of little minds, soon became fixed on me, and at seven o'clock one morning my house was surrounded by guards, and every avenue of escape secured. A general officer, commanding the department, then entered my bedroom, in which I was dressing, and addressing me very politely, informed me, "His Majesty had received certain information of my being in possession of papers of consequence, which he was ordered to seize, and. forward to Paris."

In consequence, my writing-desk, &c. were soon emptied, and the whole of the private letters and manuscripts they found, were carried off to be examined. Among other papers of equally little importance, were some drawings of the country, and a few rough sketches of imaginary, fortifications. At sight of these the general thought he had caught me; but being unable to make anything of them, he said, "certainly you have taken plans of the neighbouring country;"

To which. I replied, "surely, *Monsieur le Général*, you cannot think I would throw, away my time in secretly taking plans, which I can buy in any bookseller's shop for a few *francs*, and infinitely more accurate than it would be possible for me to make them."

He then said, "but you have written disrespectfully of His Majesty the Emperor!"

In answer to which I observed that, "he was in possession of my papers, and would most probably find on perusing them, that I never gave myself a thought about his Emperor; but that if he should happen to find him mentioned, he would be pleased to consider that I was a British officer, by whom His Majesty could not in reason expect to be paid compliments."

My papers, after being six weeks at Paris, were returned to me, with a polite note from the Duc de Feltre, Minister of War, to the commandant of the depôt, expressing his sorrow for the trouble occasioned me on this subject.

Not long after this, I was visited one morning by the lieutenant of *gend'armerie*, who notified the commandant's desire to see me immediately. On my arrival, this officer expressed his concern at the very unpleasant duty imposed on him, in being obliged to inform me that I was a close prisoner, by order of the Emperor, and then read a letter from the Minister of War, explaining the cause.[1] From the general I was conducted to the convent of St. Vannes, in the citadel, where a small room, about fourteen feet square, was allotted me, the window of which was strongly barred. Two *gend'armes* were placed in a little passage leading to the room, each of whom I was obliged to pay for guarding me.

The commandant was, however, so kind as to permit me to take the air within the citadel during the day, at which times a *gend'arme* always kept a few paces behind me; but during the night I was grievously tormented by these myrmidons, for as they kept watch alternately for an hour, each, when it was his turn to mount, opened my door, and politely inquired if I wanted anything? So strict were their orders to take care of me, that not content with this hourly intrusion, they would often repeat the same kind inquiry in the interval; so that during the whole time I remained here, I scarcely got one hour's continued rest. I could not help comparing my situation to that of the unfortunate Dauphin, in the Temple, when Simon the monster of a shoemaker, who had charge of him, and who, no doubt, was directed to torment him to death, would cry out every hour, "*comment tu portes toi, Capet?*"

In this close confinement I remained for seven weeks, as an hostage, to deter the English government from punishing a French general officer, who had not only broken his parole, but had also laid plans for arming and raising of the French prisoners in England; which, according to the laws of war, subjected him to the punishment of a spy. When I was at length set at liberty, it was without the slightest expression of concern that such harsh

---
1. Appendix.

measures had been necessary; a species of apology I had a right to expect at least.

During my confinement I feared nothing so much as being removed to Bitche, of which place I had received such accounts; as left scarce a doubt of death being preferable. One of these narratives, which I received from a gentleman who had inhabited its subterraneous dungeons, I shall beg leave to present to my readers.

We quitted Quesnoi with a detachment of Spanish and Swedish prisoners; and refractory conscripts. Among them was the wife of a Swedish captain of a ship, who had died of his wounds at Mezieres. He had fought his ship with great gallantry, and his wife had received two musket-balls in the thigh, from which she had not recovered when she was dismissed from the hospital, for the depôt at Roquelon, and was every night shut up in the common prison with the rest of the prisoners; though her youth, not being above twenty-two; her sex; and above all her beauty, it might be supposed, would have procured her other treatment.

The prisoners were thirty-nine in number, all chained together and handcuffed, except the two English, who, though also handcuffed, were indulged with being only tied to the tails of two of the horses of the escort, which was composed of Portuguese *chasseurs à cheval*, and who treated the prisoners in the most inhuman manner, preventing their receiving any succours from the inhabitants of the towns we passed through; so that many of the Spaniards died of hunger and fatigue. The prisoners were drummed into the towns in ranks, and if any one ventured to look round he was sure to receive a *coup de sabre*.

At last we arrived at Bitche, and were marched to the Petite Tête, where we were searched for concealed instruments with which we might attempt our escape. From hence we were conducted to the subterraneous dungeons, and, to our great surprise, were better received than we

View of the Castle of Bitche

expected. The first night we were put into the great dungeon, in which were three or four hundred midshipmen, soldiers, sailors, and others, jumbled together. The descent to it was by about fifty or sixty steps; and on reaching the bottom we were received with three cheers, immediately hoisted on the shoulders of four men, and marched round the place with hallowing and shouting.

A blanket was then produced, into which we were forced to enter, and received a hearty tossing. These ceremonies we thought would make us free of these gloomy abodes, but in addition we were obliged to give two bottles of *snick*, an ardent spirit made from potatoes, which, when mixed with water, turns quite blue; it is not, however, considered more unwholesome than other spirits.

In two or three days we were shifted from the grand to the little dungeon, called by the seamen Saint Giles's. The descent was by nearly the same number of steps as to the great one, and we were made free by going through the same ceremonies as before, with a double allowance of *snick,* which being drank, and some of the party being half-seas over, I was asked 'if I could shew?'

To which, not knowing the meaning, I answered, 'yes.' A ring was immediately formed; I was stripped to the buff, and a champion, nearly of my height, but much stouter, stood forward, and in self-defence I was obliged to commence a boxing match, which was regulated by all the rules of pugilism, each having his bottle-holder and second. At the end of every third round we each got a glass of *snick* , and in this manner I was forced to fight for an hour and a half: but being inferior to my antagonist, I received a drubbing that prevented my moving for six days.

The dungeon, which resembles a large wine vault, is sunk twenty-five to thirty feet underground, and excavated in a saltpetre rock. In many places the water drips continually from the vaults, and in winter the cold and damp are beyond description; nor had the prisoners in general clothing sufficient to prevent the baneful effects on their health; the blanket allowed to each being usually one condemned from the soldiers' barracks. In these shocking dungeons the prisoners were locked up from eight o'clock at night till the same hour in the morning, when they were mustered out, and permitted to remain in the yard, which is about one hundred and twenty paces in length and thirty in breadth, until noon; they were then again mustered into the subterraneous receptacle, and remained there till two, when they were again let out into the yard until six in the evening.

From such horrid abodes it is natural to conclude that many attempts would be made to escape. In many instances they have been successful, neither bars nor walls being capable of resisting the perseverance and determination of despair. Four midshipmen in particular escaped, by excavating a depth of seventy feet, until they arrived at a subterraneous passage, which leads from the fort to the neighbouring woods, and is three leagues in length.

This successful attempt some time after induced the whole of the prisoners to make a similar one, and each was sworn to secrecy and perseverance. In a few days they arrived at the subterraneous passage, but there were still three wooden doors and an iron one to be forced, before they could gain the outside of the fort.

These obstacles were also overcome, and the moment of accomplishment had just arrived, when one of the prisoners, a Jersey man named Williams, waited on the commandant, to whom he discovered the whole plot. The commandant, with a degree of ferocity without excuse, because without necessity, ordered a guard of veteran soldiers to be placed at the spot where the prisoners were to emerge from their gloomy abode, with orders not to fire till a dozen at least were on the outside. These orders were exactly obeyed: the whole were shot dead, and their bodies exposed in the yard of the fort.

This indeed was not, by many, the only instance of prisoners being killed in a cruel and wanton manner. Among the most lamented was Mr. Thomas Thomson, of His Majesty's cutter the *Dove*, who was run through the body with a bayonet by a sentinel, who quitted his post sixty yards for the purpose.

Another circumstance of cool atrocity also deserves to be mentioned; Lieutenant Essel, of the navy, and fourteen others, had prepared a rope, to descend the formidable wall of the fort, which was well secured and sufficiently strong, but as descending one at a time would have caused too much delay, the whole fifteen determined to descend at once. This plan, however, was discovered to a veteran officer, who waited patiently until all these unfortunate young men were on the rope, when, to the shame of humanity, he cut it: several were dashed to pieces, and their mutilated bodies exposed, while none escaped without a broken limb.

Such is the melancholy picture of what the English prisoners had to expect from French generosity.

Chapter 39

Excursion to Clermont

During my residence at Verdun, I received permission from the commandant to make several excursions in the departments the first of which was to Clermont, the environs of which are extremely picturesque, being extensively wooded, with openings that afford the finest views. Here we dined at the Saint Nicholas, a good inn, and the next morning set out for Beaulieu; and after travelling through woods for some miles, arrived at an open spot, with a rock at one extremity, in some measure resembling the bow of a ship in shape.

On the left, and on a very deep declivity, with a south-east aspect, was a fine vineyard; remarkable for the good quality and abundance of its produce. The scenery around was romantic, being diversified with wood and well cultivated and fruitful lands. After taking some refreshment at a cabaret in a little hamlet, we returned by a different route, entirely through woods, until within half a league of Clermont, where we stopped a moment to examine the position taken up by Arthur Dillon, when the Prussian army was advancing into the heart of France, at the commencement of the revolution. The neglect of not occupying this position has been considered as a great fault on the part of the King of Prussia, instead of allowing his army to waste itself in idleness and sickness in the town of Verdun.

The following morning we proceeded towards Varennes, the name of which will descend through the annals of history, from the arrest of the weak, and therefore unfortunate Louis XVI.

While we sent the carriage by the direct road, we made a circuit to the left, but lost our way in the wood, though guided by a gentleman who had resided some time at Clermont. At length we reached an open spot, with some beautiful meadows, watered by a small river, which in one spot formed a circular basin. At the foot of a hill was a manufactory of table earthenware, established by some respectable individuals, who had formerly belonged to the order of *noblesse*, but who, having lost everything by the revolution, sought here a retreat, and the means of existence by their industry.

The manufactory, however, is said to be on the decline; and indeed it has no appearance of prosperity. We met several of the persons interested in this speculation, and observed a striking contrast between them and the other inhabitants of the country, not only in their language, which was pure Parisian, but in that civility and politeness, for which Frenchmen were much more conspicuous under the ancient than the modern regime.

We next reached a small but romantic village called La Chalade, where we refreshed ourselves and horses. Here 'we were struck with the beauty and manners of a *couturière*, which were particularly conspicuous, as the lower class of Lorrainese females are remarkable for their ugliness and coarse manners, and a handsome female peasant is quite a *lusus naturæ*. This coarseness of feature doubtless proceeds from the hard and continual labour in the open air, to which they are exposed from their earliest infancy, which while it gives them a masculine air and robust health, totally destroys those delicate traits of feature and form, so commonly observed among English country girls. Amidst such a scarcity of beauty, it is no wonder that our handsome *couturière* made an impression on us, and afforded subject for conversation for several days.

In the evening we arrived at Varennes, and put up at an inn, the landlord of which enjoys the infamous celebrity of having arrested Louis XVI.: an act which, beyond doubt, entitles him to, be considered, as one of the conspicuous characters of the revolution; for had the Monarch escaped, it is more than probable that all the horrors, of that terrible convulsion would have been spared; but when once the blood of the King had been shed, the cutting off all those who were suspected of adhering to him was the necessary consequence; until at length, habituated to slaughter, the very existence of the miscreants who were successively in power depended on a continuance of the horrid system.

There seems to have been a fatality attending every action of the unfortunate Louis, who, had it not been for his paternal wish to spare the blood of his subjects, might have saved both his crown and life. Had he put himself at the head of a few of the most popular nobles, his standard would have been flocked to by all classes of his subjects, and he might have marched to Paris and annihilated the revolutionists, whose principles at that time were not yet successfully disseminated throughout the country. The infatuated monarch, however, like a bird upon the spray, contemplated the venomous reptiles beneath him, until every energy became paralysed, and he suffered himself to fall into their grasp.

But to return to our innkeeper: his countenance denoted all that I had conceived of a sanguinary revolutionist, to which his dress considerably added; for he held a knife in his hand with which he had been just cutting up meat, and his shirt sleeves were tucked up, like those of an executioner. Curiosity led us to visit the house to which the King was conducted, after being arrested; it is, however, totally unworthy of notice on any other account.

On our return from Varennes to Verdun we struck off the road to visit Montfaucon, a very small village, situated on the highest elevation of the country, and commanding a most extensive view, with considerable woods, although since the revolution they have been constantly cutting down.

CHAPTER 40

Excursion from Verdun to Metz and Nancy

My second tour from Verdun was to Metz and Nancy. At the former we stopped at the Hôtel de Pont à Mousson, where we had an excellent dinner, of which salmon and crayfish sauce formed a conspicuous part; the Moselle being celebrated for the abundance and excellence of this fish, with which Metz supplies Verdun and all the neighbouring towns; for though the Meuse is a river of much greater magnitude, it has neither salmon nor trout, both of which abound in the Moselle.

Near the bridge which crosses the Moselle, and close to the inn, are public hot and cold baths, which from their external appearance, and from the report I received of them, led me to flatter myself with the hope of enjoying the luxury of a comfortable warm bath; but the following morning I found myself completely disappointed, for instead of a comfortable apartment to dress in, and a quiet bath, I found public room, the length of the building, appropriated to the men, with small, inconvenient and uncomfortable pigeon holes, the heat of which, as well as the filthy appearance of the persons in waiting, removed all inclination to bathing. I therefore retired, disappointed and disgusted

In the forenoon I waited on the Préfet Monsieur Vaublanc, to whom I had letters, and who received me with the frankness and ease of a polished gentleman, He is of an ancient family, and possesses those polite and affable manners for which the *noblesse* of France were formerly so justly praised. Monsieur Vaublanc speaks a little English, and is a great admirer of the English character. Our conversation turned on the merits of the celebrated British authors, particularly Gibbon, of whose work on the Roman Empire a new French translation had just appeared, which was considered much superior to any of the former ones.

During the revolution Monsieur Vaublanc had been obliged to emigrate into Germany, through which country he travelled as a performer on the violin, his musical talents being , very considerable. He pressed me to dine with him, but having fixed on our plan of proceeding to Nancy the following day, I declined his kindness for the present, promising to avail myself of it on my return.

The remainder of the day we devoted to visiting the objects most worthy of notice; and first made the circuit of the ramparts, until we came opposite the arsenal and citadel, into which no stranger is admitted, but of which we could form a correct idea from the rampart. Their situation is low, and they appear to be completely commanded from a height of considerable extent on the left entering the town. The *préfet* assured me that nothing was to be apprehended from this position, but its appearance would not permit me to give credit to the assertion.

The citadel is celebrated for its vigorous defence in 1552, when commanded by the Duc de Guise. It was besieged by the Austrians, under Charles the Fifth: but the perfection to which. engineering and artillery has been since brought is such, that I should suppose it could not long hold out, if besieged in form. At this time the workmen, in the arsenal were busily employed in preparing and forwarding guns and ordnance stores to the army.

Metz possesses several handsome public walks, and a fine gothic cathedral, but which has lost all its former internal splendour. Here is also an academy for the education of officers for the engineers, on a large and liberal footing, extensive barracks and military magazines, and one of the finest military hospitals of France; a handsome theatre, and a public library, containing sixty thousand volumes, and many valuable manuscripts. It has also a lyceum, in which, it is said, the sciences and *belles lettres* are taught with success.

The streets of Metz are in general narrow, badly paved, and worse lighted, the funds for these, as well as all other municipal purposes, having been seized on by Buonaparte for his military chest. A few days previous to our being here, the Emperor passed through, and inquired in a careless manner of the mayor, what was the strength of the city chest? The latter not expecting the result, and wishing to shew the prosperous state of the town, gave it in as considerably greater than it really was; upon which Napoleon very coolly ordered one of the commissaries of his suite to receive the amount for the *caisse militaire*: and the mayor, of course, not daring to contradict his first assertion, was obliged to make up the deficiency.

Metz is considered a very ancient town, having been the capital of the Mediomatrici at the period of the conquest of Gaul by Julius Cesar. It was then called Diodurum, Having fallen under the dominion of the Francs, it became the capital of the kingdom of Austrasia. After. the decline of the dynasty of Carlovingians, it declared itself free, under the protection of the Emperors of Germany. In 1552, it was ceded by way of guarantee to France, and was finally united to it by the treaty of Westphalia in 1646.

Metz contains a great number of Jews, who before the revolution enjoyed a kind of separate political existence, under the special protection of royal letters patent. Their progressive multiplication affords a curious fact in the history of human propagation. In 1562, there were but four families; in 1589, eight; in 1603, twenty-four; in 1614, fifty-eight; in 1624, seventy-six; in 1657, ninety-six; in 1674, one hundred and nineteen; in 1681, one hundred and seventy-four; in 1698, two hundred and sixty-four; in 1789, five hundred and fifty. This increase will appear more extraordinary, when it is considered that they were long subject to all the humiliation, that could be inflicted on them, by a people who held them in detestation. According to an ordinance of 1567, they were forced to hear mass in the churches every Sunday, under a penalty of forty *sous*.

By another, in 1635, they were forbid to quit their houses on the Sabbath; and by a third, in 1703, they were obliged to wear yellow hats. They were also subjected to the same toll duties as cloven-footed beasts. It might have been hoped that the revolution, by which the Jews were admitted to a community of rights with the other classes of citizens, would have tended to inspire them with sentiments of justice and honesty. This, however, seems as yet to be far from the case, and they universally give themselves up, as formerly, to cheating and usury.

Since the assembling of the Grand Sanhedrim at Paris in 1806, political and religious regulations have been established, which they are bound to obey, and which the chief Jews are legally authorized to enforce.

CHAPTER 41

Spanish *Renegadoes*

Quitting Metz early in the morning, for Nancy, we reached Pont à Mousson to breakfast. This is a considerable town of from six to seven thousand inhabitants, situated on both sides of the Moselle, which is here crossed by a stone bridge, and divides the town into nearly two equal parts. Many of the houses appear to be very ancient, but there is a handsome palace, and the streets we passed through were broad and strait. Near the town is a mineral springs celebrated for its efficacy in the cure of several disorders. Pont à Mousson possessed an university, founded, by Charles the Third, Duke of Lorraine, in 1572, but which, by order of Louis XV. was removed to Nancy, in 1768.

Previous to reaching this town, and about two leagues from Metz, we passed a Roman aqueduct, noticed by Gibbon in his *History of the Roman Empire*, together with that of *Segovia in Spain*, as being the two most perfect Roman constructions to be found in Europe. By this canal, which extends near one thousand two hundred yards across an extensive valley, forming a communication between two hills, the water was formerly conveyed to the public of Metz. Though several of the arches are broken, the pillars all remain entire, and the whole forms an imposing and fine ruin.

From Pont à Mousson to Nancy the country is extremely picturesque, being finely diversified by hills and valleys, well wooded and watered. The extreme heat of the day induced us to halt and refresh ourselves at a little village about two miles from Nancy, where we met with a neat public house, which reminded us of those of our own country. The landlord soon discovering we were English, entered freely into conversation on the passing events, and told us that he considered England as the greatest nation in the world, from the immense exertions she made since the French revolution, to preserve the balance of power in Europe.

The mention of the revolution led him to enter into the sufferings of the neighbourhood during that period. From the door of his house, he pointed out six magnificent country seats, formerly inhabited, during a great part of the year, by their noble owners, who disseminated throughout the country the cheerfulness of opulence, content and prosperity; now, on the contrary, a gloomy melancholy is remarked in every countenance, and it is easy to perceive that sullen discontent, which dares not vent itself in words; "in short," said our landlord, "one would suppose that the natural disposition of the people was entirely changed Instead of the splendid equipages which formerly rolled in every direction, no other carriage is how to be seen, but a creeping diligence, or a miserable one horse *cabriolet*, while the *châteaux* have become the property of the revolutionary *parvenus*, who entirely neglect them, or of *scélérats*, who have acquired possession of them by the most infamous means."

Near our inn, a handsome bridge of cut stone crossed the Moselle, which river, after serpentizing for some distance, disappears from the view, in a picturesque wooded valley. The landscape in general was extremely pleasing, and recalled to mind many passages in Goldsmith's *Deserted Village*, which though not always entirely applicable to the scene before us, had a sufficient resemblance to make us dwell on it with pleasure.

We entered Nancy through a very handsome arched gate, which terminated a promenade planted with trees, and having a row of buildings on the left. Several Spanish officers, prisoners of war, (for whom Nancy is a depôt) were on this walk; and amongst them, I easily recognized the Duke of Grenada, by the description I had heard of him. Though it is probable the greatest part of this nobleman's estates in Valencia, are in the hands of the French, he still draws large sums from Spain, of which unfortunately he does not make the best use; for being an Extreme bigot, instead of relieving his unfortunate countrymen in captivity, his wealth is chiefly squandered in donations to the priests who surround him, and who have still sufficient influence to persuade him, that giving to the church is lending to God, and that he is thereby laying up for himself a treasure in heaven.

We put up at the Aigle Impérial, an extensive, convenient, and well conducted hotel, where we got an excellent dinner and good wines. In the evening we received a visit from Monsieur Duchard and another gentleman; with the former I had formed some acquaintance at Verdun, where he paid several, visits during our races, which took place once a fortnight. I had several horses on the turf there myself, and ran them for large sums with various success, winning considerably at first, but leaving off a loser.

The following morning we waited on the general officer commanding at Nancy, to shew our permission from Baron de Beauchene, for making this tour. As the general had been an officer in the ancient *régime*, I expected to find in him the manners of a gentleman, but was disappointed; nor did I wonder at it when I learnt that he had deserted the cause of his sovereign, and received his promotion from the revolutionists. It would appear that this class of rogues, being apprehensive that they might be suspected and sacrificed for not going far enough, generally exceed all others in atrocious and inhuman acts.

The room into which we were introduced to this wretch was filled with officers, conscripts, and peasants, with whom he was occupied, When our passports were presented to him, he fell into a rage not to be described; struck the table violently with his hand, stamped and made frightful grimaces, and gave vent to his passion in low and unbecoming invectives against the English, whose insolence he knew how to curb, and that if the Emperor was of his mind, he would exterminate the whole race from the face of the earth. Such observations I of course thought unworthy of notice; and looking at the little deformed wretch who talked of exterminating us, with an expression of contemptuous pity rather than of resentment, I disdainfully walked out of the room, like a king in a tragedy. The *aide-de-camp* followed and begged me to return; to which I replied, that, "he could not suppose I would enter again into the company of a madman, for whose conduct nothing but absolute insanity could be pleaded in excuse."

This fellow, for he is unworthy the title of officer, is named La Coste; he positively ordered us to quit Nancy that moment, writing on the back of our passport, that he acknowledged no permissions but the minister's for prisoners to quit the department of their depôt. This order we however did not think proper to obey, but remained till next morning. A moment's consideration might have shewn him, that if there was any impropriety in allowing us as prisoners to visit Nancy, it was the Baron de Beauchene he should have addressed and not us, and that his conduct could not tend to injure anyone but himself, in thus shamefully disgracing the situation and rank in which he was placed.

On my return to Verdun I wrote to the Baron de Beauchene on the subject, and took care that the contents of my letter should be made known to M. La Coste.[1]

In the course of the day we visited whatever was worthy of notice in Nancy, which is one of the handsomest towns in France, the chief place of the department of the Meurthe, and has a population of thirty thousand inhabitants. It is divided into the old and new town; the former has little to recommend it except a circus, round which were placed in niches the statues and tombs of the princes of Lorraine, but which were mutilated and demolished by the barbarous revolutionary fanaticism of a regiment of Marseillois which passed through the town in 1793.

In the new town, the houses are fronted with hewn stone, and are very elegant and regular, and the public buildings magnificent: amongst the latter is the cathedral, a superb gothic edi-

---

1. 1. *Vide* Appendix,

fice; the Place Impériale, formerly Place Royale, in which is a triumphal arch; the Hôtel de Ville; the Palais de Justice, and the Exchange. The public walks in the centre of the town are also extremely grand. Most of these beauties it owes to Stanislaus, who, when a second time deprived of the crown of Poland, received from France the Duchies of Lorraine and Bar.

The memory of this prince, whose benevolence acquired him the merited title of le Bienfaisant, is still revered by the Lorrainese; and his monument, which had been preserved during the revolution by its removal to the lyceum, has since been replaced in the cathedral. Stanislaus owed his elevation to the throne of Poland, to his happy countenance and air of grandeur, which gained him the esteem and friendship of Charles XII., who obliged the Poles to elect him for their king.

The Battle of Pultawa, in 1709, having overturned the power of Charles, Stanislaus was obliged to quit Poland, and cede the crown to his rival Augustus, supported by Russia. Stanislaus lived retired in Alsace. until 1725, when Louis XV, married his daughter; and on the death of Augustus in 1733, hoping to remount the throne, he repaired into Poland, but his competitor, the electoral prince of Saxony, prevailed over him, and by the treaty of 1736 Stanislaus was to preserve the empty title of King of Poland, and retain the duchies of Lorraine and Bar, during his life; which was terminated, by the unhappy accident of his *robe de chambre* taking fire, in 1766.

Before the revolution Nancy was one of the gayest and most flourishing towns of France. It was the winter resort of the English families from Spa, and the chief nobility of Lorraine resided during the summer at their *châteaux* in the vicinity. Having lost both these sources of opulence and gaiety, it is now equally poor and dull. Its manufactures, consisting chiefly of coarse woollen, paper, candles, and earthenware, are insignificant, and do not find their way out of the department.

The handsome buildings of the ancient university are now occupied by a lyceum, in which is a good gallery of pictures. Here is also a public library of fifty thousand volumes, a cabinet of natural history, and a botanic garden, with above four thousand indigenous and exotic plants. All these establishments are open to the public as well as to the students of the lyceum, and render Nancy one of the most literary and instructive towns of France.

Having seen everything worthy of notice in the town, we proceeded to dine, by invitation, with M. Duchard, where a select and well bred company was assembled; which, with the comforts of an excellent dinner, finished the day in the most agreeable manner.

The following morning we set out, and arrived at Metz, where we found an invitation to dine the following day with the prefect. At this dinner were collected above eighty persons, consisting of the chief authorities of Metz, and the heads of the academies of Metz and Nancy, who had been called hither on some subject of public discussion. The dinner was sumptuous, and we received all possible attention from the company; which was indeed carried so far, as to remain at table after the ladies had withdrawn, in compliance to our English custom; for which reason, also, Port and Madeira were set before us.

Many of the party had emigrated to England during the revolution, and hence the conversation turned upon the history of English families, and their connexions in France. This subject afforded me an opportunity of noticing the number of English families, descended from or connected by alliance with those of Holland, Germany, Prussia, &c. which led to the idea of one grand connexion throughout the continent; and I could not refrain, from observing, "how much it was to be lamented that, instead of being cultivated, this connexion was every day, declining, from the regulations enacted by the French Emperor, which prevented all commercial intercourse between the nations."

On joining the ladies we passed through a superb suite of apartments, the centre one, in particular, being lofty, well proportioned, and magnificently furnished. This I learnt was the *Salle de Réception*, in which the Emperor received the public authorities, in his occasional visits to Metz. A full length picture of him, inimitably painted by David, and several well executed representations of battles, covered the walls.

Among the ladies was the prefect's daughter, Madame Seconde, the death of whose husband, an officer of engineers, killed in the memorable siege of Saragossa, had thrown her into a state of melancholy, which seemed to gain ground by time; and a delicate charming boy, her son, was now her only consolation. Her manners were gentle and engaging, and we conversed together for some time, when she suddenly rose, and apologized for abruptly quitting me by saying, that my having come so lately from Spain brought her misfortunes to her recollection, and unfitted her for society.

The prefect was extremely fond of riding, and being seldom able to get anyone at Metz to accompany him, as few Frenchmen ride either for pleasure or exercise alone, gladly accepted my offer of accompanying him, and we set off on a gravelled circular road, outside of the town, about half a mile in circumference. He was followed by what he called a *joquet Anglais*, who was however more like anything than an English jockey, his dress being a huge cocked hat with a gold loop and button, a pair of stiff hessian boots coming half way up his thighs, yellow breeches richly ornamented, and a silver laced jacket

The horse he rode shewing some blood, I observed to the prefect that from his appearance he ought to have speed, of which I said I should be able to judge, as I had a stop watch, if he would order him to be galloped with dispatch round the circle. The jockey on receiving this order stuck his spurs violently into him, and soon quitting the course, performed a zig zag between the trees at full speed, so that I was apprehensive of his fate; but at length he reached the main road, which he pursued at full gallop until both horse and jockey disappeared from our sight.

The prefect was now *au déséspoir*, I therefore rode on to gain tidings of them, in which not being successful, it was concluded they had fallen into the canal, and that both horse and man were drowned. On our return, however, we found they had reached home in safety, with no other damage than the loss of the cocked hat and a stirrup, both of which were recovered in the course of the day.

The following morning we returned towards Verdun, and on the road met many Spaniards who had entered the French service. On inquiring of some of them their inducement for joining the enemy of their country, they told us that nothing but the last necessity had forced them to it; that they had suffered for two years every species of persecution and hardship, being obliged to work, both winter and summer, on the canals up to their middles in water, with an insufficient allowance of the very worst provisions, and no clothing but the tattered rags in which they were taken; that a great number of their comrades had died; and that some of their officers setting the example, they had entered in despair. Their woeful appearance, indeed, was sufficient to convince us of the truth of the story: for, as Shakespeare observes of the apothecary in Romeo and Juliet,

Sharp Misery had worn them to the bone.

I therefore condoled with them; commiserating and pitying, rather than condemning them, and sharing with them the small sum which remained in my pocket.

CHAPTER 42

Death of the Commandant

On my return to Verdun, in order to enliven the sameness and *ennui* which pervaded the depôt, I had some horses on the turf, and our races were established. They were attended by the first families of the department; and wishing to return the attentions of the prefect of Metz, I invited him and his family to a dinner, at which one hundred and ten of my countrymen, with several French, were entertained to their entire satisfaction. Among the latter was the Chevalier de la Lance, an excellent musician and composer, as well as poet.

On this occasion he invoked his muse, and produced some verses suited to the subject. The old observation, that people are generally poets before they are philosophers, is particularly true with respect to France, where you may find a poet in every village, but very rarely a philosopher even in a city.

Where so many persons are collected, without occupation or internal resources for passing the time, it is not strange if scandal should predominate; the destruction of each others' characters, indeed, formed the chief occupation of many of our countrymen, and no story, however improbable, but was well received, provided it tended to the prejudice of another. We had amongst us also a number of people, who might with great propriety be called mischief-makers, who, in pure friendship, retailed and aggravated everything they heard in society.

The latter, from these causes, became confined to a few, who could hurt each other, and a distinction was formed between the mischief-makers and the safe persons.

Being tired with the monotonous life I was obliged to lead, I took a small cottage for the summer, in a village about six miles from Verdun, which served to vary the scene, at the same time that it afforded me an opportunity of making myself acquainted with the rural regulations, and manners of the villagers.

In one of my excursions I visited Varennes a second time, and stopped at an *auberge*, with the sign of the Bras d'Or, which afforded no little occasion for reflection on the vicissitude of human opinions, within the last twenty years. The sign had formerly been the Arms of France, surmounted by a crown. In the revolution the crown had been effaced, but not so completely as to prevent its being still perceptible, and the *fleur de lis* had been converted into a basket of eggs.

Over the arms had been painted "*le noble jeu de billiards;*" the word noble had been also daubed over, but plainly appeared, and, as well as the crown, seemed to intimate to the people, "you may attempt to extinguish monarchy, ancient order and establishments, but sufficient will still appear, in spite of you, to put you to the blush."

On this same sign the words *Caffé, des gardes nationals*, and *Caffeé des amis de la Constitution*, were also but partly defaced, and over them written, *Bon vin de Champagne et Bourgogne, et liqueurs*! The total repainting of the sign would certainly not have cost above twelve *francs*; and this parsimony, though it may seem a trivial fact, affords a strong picture of the character of the French, and proves with what little difficulty they change their opinions their government, or their religion, yet cannot so easily bear to have their pockets affected.

Monsieur Drouet, the *sous-préfet* of Varennes, was the chief person in the arrest of Louis XVI.; he was then *maître de poste*. Sauce, a cooper and tallow chandler, and *adjoint* to the mayor, with the innkeeper already described, and ten or twelve others, stopped the carriage, and conducted the King to Sauce's house, which we had the curiosity to visit, but found it worthy of notice only from that circumstance. Varennes throughout seems to be greatly declining, the best houses being uninhabited and falling to ruin; and its whole appearance is gloomy and desponding, as if the vengeance of Providence had visited the people for their conduct to their King.

Nor does it seem that Napoleon shews them any favour, their anti-monarchical principles not being to his present taste. The landlord of the Bras d'Or is, indeed, an example of the vengeance I have mentioned. He was one of those concerned in the King's arrest; and he informed me that, before the revolution, having the reputation of being an excellent cook, he received a handsome salary from a convent of Benedictines, which, together with his inn, and other fruits of his industry, enabled him to amass a handsome competency, but which had been dissipated by the revolution.

His eldest daughter, whom he described as all perfection, had been carried off by a decline at eighteen; his eldest son and second daughter at the same age followed her; and his remaining son and daughter, who were now approaching this fatal time, evinced every symptom of the same malady!

On my return to Verdun from this excursion, I found the commandant, the Baron de Beauchesne, had received a letter from the Minister of War, stating that it was understood I acted as agent for the British governments, without any authority from that of the French, and desiring me to explain myself on the subject, which I accordingly did in a letter to the minister; and though couched in strong language, it seemed satisfactory, as I heard no more of the business.[1] It is probable that someone had denounced me to the minister; and in France, as formerly at Venice by the mouth of stone, the government receive every kind of denunciation, and none, however absurd, but is often acted upon, and the person denounced apprehended, without being able even to conjecture the cause.

The news published from the grand army, under the immediate command of Napoleon, began to be very contradictory, about the month of February 1813, and though the articles in

---

1. See Appendix.

the *Moniteur* boasted of wonderful successes and prodigious advantages, it was easy to perceive their falsehood, not; only from the contradictions from day to day, but from the impossibility of the armies making the rapid movements imputed to them. At length we received accounts of the death of Colonel Desiré, commanding the 11th Chasseurs, and of Captain Buffon, and several other officers of the same corps; and, finally, that this regiment was entirely cut to pieces.

At the same time, the French inhabitants were informed of the fate of many of their friends through circuitous channels; all direct communication being prohibited, which still more increased suspicion. At length the papers began to let out the real state of things, by accusing the Russians of treachery, in leading their army into such difficulties, when their cavalry had suffered prodigiously at first from the want of forage and water, and afterwards from the latter dement being in too great a profusion, a considerable proportion of their horse having been drowned.

By degrees the disasters of the army were announced in a semi-official manner in the papers; bat in such a way that, contradicting the private accounts of their losses, they met with no credit; and it was at last found necessary to state the whole truth, and the famous twenty-ninth bulletin appeared, which, as being worthy of preservation in every work that has France for its subject, I shall insert in the Appendix.

In the spring of the year the commandant of the depôt died, generally lamented, and particularly by the prisoners. His disease was an indigestion, and consequent inflammatory fever, produced by the too great use of rich and luxurious food, without taking sufficient exercise; and being of a full corpulent habit of body, together with the ignorance of the French physician as to the proper treatment of this disease, soon carried him off. Instead of copious bleedings &c. they loaded his stomach with ptisan and milk whey, which, on a stomach already overcharged, is supposed to have decided his fate.

The practice of the French physicians may, indeed,, be compared to that of Dr. Sangrado, in having only two remedies, ptisan and lavements. The latter indeed is the universal panacea, and the instrument for administering it is a part of the furniture of even the poorest cottage, as well as of the most splendid hotel; and I have seen a bet won more than once, when laid at a venture, that this instrument would be sure to be found in the possession of any peasant, for instance; into whose head it might be supposed such an idea could never enter, and which to an Englishman is equally strange and disgusting.

In passing through Ireland I have often observed, that in no peasant's house did I ever see a warming pan, while in England it is generally the first object that strikes you on entering a cottage. It is also universally seen in France, and thus they are here doubly armed. But to return to our deceased commandant: his funeral was attended by every Englishman in the depôt, whose good will he had generally gained, by the marked contrast between his treatment of them and what they had experienced from the tyrannical and cheating Wirion and Courcelles.

Among other institutions formed for the benefit of the prisoners, there had formerly been a seminary for the junior midshipmen of the navy, established by Captains Brenton and Woodriff; but which General Wirion had suppressed, and this class of young men were again permitted to become their own masters, and consequently ran into every species of excess. Captain Oller now again procured the permission of the commandant to re-establish a school, which was superintended by Captain Hoffman, of the navy; and a number of lieutenants and the young midshipmen were again drawn from the vicious and idle course they were running.

I cannot quit the subject I am now on, without also paying a tribute of deserved praise to the Reverend Mr. Jorden, for his proper and impartial distribution of the funds committed to his charge for the relief of the prisoners. His attention to his clerical duties was also highly praiseworthy, and his sermons being composed and delivered in a superior manner, his church was always regularly and fully attended. This notice I owe in justice to Mr. Jorden, who, from being placed in a high public situation, was exposed to the jealousy and envy of the evil disposed and malicious.

The commandant also knowing, that the surest means of preventing the desertion of the prisoners was granting them all the indulgencies that the nature . of their situation would permit, adopted this plan in its utmost latitude, by permitting them to reside, in the villages, not only within the established limits of two leagues round Verdun, but also at Bar, Clermont, St. Mihiel, and other places in the department, considerably beyond these limits; nor was there an instance of this liberty being abused, or taken advantage of to escape.

I frequently visited St. Mihiel, a town of three thousand four hundred inhabitants about seven leagues from Verdun, and on the banks of the Meuse. It is the seat of the criminal, and other superior courts of the department, which are held in an ancient convent of Benedictines, nearly in the middle of the town; the buildings of which are very extensive, containing, besides the courts, the common jail of the department, and a barrack for *gend'armes*.

The library still remains tolerably perfect, and is contained in an apartment near two hundred and fifty feet long by eighty wide; the books are numerous, and among them I observed a *History of England*, in four volumes folio, by Lanet, considered a work of merit, and a history, with engravings, of Greek and Roman antiquities, by Grævius; tolerable editions of *Herodotus Dionysius of Haltcarnassus*, and *Xenophon*; an antique and valuable history of Greece, by Georgius Palchymenes and others. *Byzantium Angliæ, sacra*, by Henry Wharton; *Monasticum Anglicanum*, in which are good engravings, particularly of Christ Church College, Oxford, and the ruins of Asney Abbey, near Oxford. It has besides some valuable manuscripts. The dome of the library is handsome and perfect. I am sorry to remark, that if it were not for the care of Mr. Perrin, the librarian, the books would soon be destroyed by damp; the town allowance for their preservation being quite insufficient.

In the insignificant church of St. Etienne, in an obscure part of St. Mihiel, is a piece of sculpture worthy of the first cathedral and the best artist in Europe. It consists of a group of thirteen figures, all as large as life. In the centre is our Saviour, supported by Nicodemus and Joseph of Arimathea; the Virgin; an angel bearing the cross; St. Veronica carrying the crown of thorns; Mary Magdalen kissing Christ's feet; the two Marys; the two Jews playing at dice for our Saviour's garments; a herald, and St. John.

Our Saviour is extended dead, after his crucifixion. The whole has inimitable expression, and is cut out of a single block of stone which has the polish of marble, and was dug from a quarry in the neighbourhood. It is the performance of an artist named Michin or Lygin Richier, a native of the little village of Dagonville, between Ligny and St. Mihiel, whose parents were originally Calvinists. Richier had so extraordinary a genius for painting and sculpture; that at fifteen he was quite a prodigy, and the celebrated Michael Angelo (who died in 1564) passing through St. Mihiel, on his way to Nancy, was so pleased with his performances, that he prevailed on his father to permit his accompanying him to Rome, Richiet, on his return to St. Mihiel, painted a crucifix for the chapel of the Benedictines, which was much admired and also executed a skeleton in white marble for the church of St. Etienne, at Bar, which is excellent.

The grand piece of sculpture at St. Mihiel occupied him twenty years. It evaded the exterminating process of this revolution by the care of the good people of St. Mihiel; for being placed in a large niche cut out of the rock, with an iron gate before it, they contrived to wall it up; so that when a deputation was sent down from Paris. by Robespierre, to seek for and destroy all religious monuments, this escaped their fury. Everything else that was capable of devastation within the church had been destroyed, except the stained glass in some elevated windows, which was beyond the immediate reach of the vandals. This church was used as a cow-house; and indeed all the religious buildings throughout France, in that calamitous period, were put to the most degrading uses.

St. Mihiel has some manufactures of lace and table linen, and in the centre of the town is a handsome barrack for one thousand cavalry.

From St Mihiel we pursued our tour towards Commercy, on the right: not far from the former is a Roman camp, occupying the entire circular summit of a hill, and which, even in the present advanced state of the art of war, would be considered a strong position. About a fifth of the camp is. protected by the Meuse, and there remains sufficient of the works on the other sides to render the whole plan very intelligible.

From hence we proceeded over a barren country, naked and ill cultivated, and again reached a rich valley on the banks of the Meuse, where we visited the government establishment of Sampigny, for the construction of *caissons, fourgons* and gun carriages. It is extremely well situated for this purpose, having the advantage of water carriage, and being in the vicinity of extensive woods and large iron works.

At this time there were sufficient carriages ready here for a considerable portion of the army, and the loss of which articles had been so enormous in the late campaign, that the depôt was now going to be cleared.[2] The building of this establishment has the appearance of an ancient castle: it is surrounded by a moat, cut from the Meuse and entered by a drawbridge. The vaults under it are very extensive, and some of them serve as dungeons, where the workmen guilty of any faults or negligence are confined.

The extensiveness of the building admits the residence of many families, who receive their lodging gratis from the court; so that it in some measure resembles our Kensington. The gardens are also very extensive, and furnish abundance of fruit and vegetables to the residents.

The nominal governor is a black man, of the name of Garting, who is in fact a state prisoner; never being permitted to quit the *château* or gardens. He is married to a cousin of the Empress

---

2. I have since had the satisfaction of knowing, that almost the whole of these carriages fell into the hands of the Allies at the disastrous retreat from Dresden.

Josephine; and in order to be united, both of them procured divorces from their former partners.

The manners of both are those of the higher class. The daughter of Madame Garting is married to a M. de la Valette, and holds a confidential place in Josephine's household. Mr. Garting. has also a son quite black, married to *bourgeoise* of Sampigny; they have three children, in whom there is this singularity, that the two boys are the colour of the father, a jet black, and the girl white. The father is employed in the payment of the workmen.

On our return to Verdun, the horseracing again commenced, and the schemes practised to discover the speed of the various horses, by trial, without being discovered, were curious. I once saw a friend of mine up to his middle in the river, with a Frenchman's coat and cocked hat on, and a fishing rod in one hand; while in the other he held a stop watch, to ascertain the fleetness of the horse going round the course. It is probable that these *ruses de guerre* would not be deemed admissible at Newmarket: but at Verdun, the humour rendered them merely laughable; and as they were practised by each side, they were treated as very fair, and none had a right to complain.

Every day, indeed, at Verdun produced some new anecdote, either to feed scandal, or to create a laugh. Among others, not the least ridiculous was the *quiproquo* of a good English lady, into whose education the speaking of French had not entered; she conceived however that by application after her arrival in France, she had acquired a competent knowledge of the language, though she mangled it in a most miserable manner, and often confounded the masculine and feminine gender, so as to make very serious *contre-sens*.

One day she had occasion to purchase some lace, and looking in her dictionary and grammar she found the phrase, *il me faut de dentelle*, which she repeated to herself in her way to the shop, until somebody accosting her, it escaped her memory, and she was long puzzled to recall it; at length the exclamation from a soldier passing, of *"je m'enfou,"* caught her ear, and the analogy of sound immediately striking her, she cried out to her husband, "that's the very word I have been thinking of," and the husband, who knew less French than his wife, exclaimed, "how fortunate!"

On entering the milliner's shop, the good lady, as if proud of her French, addressed the mistress with, "*Madame, il m'en fou de votre dentelle.*" The woman and her apprentices were of course astonished at such an apostrophe, they stared with wondering eyes, and mouths wide open; but soon recollecting the mistakes of language so frequently made by the English, the mystery was cleared up, and the woman spread out her patterns, doubtless not forgetting to make *Madame l'Angloise* pay for her ignorance of the French language and customs.

An anecdote of the same kind occurs to my recollection, and may not be unworthy of being preserved. Two naval officers being made prisoners, and carried into Havre de Grace, with their schooners, after the usual forms were gone through, the French officer commanding, invited the English officers to *déjeuner à la fourchette*. The lieutenant, who knew not a sentence of French, inquired of his companion (who from his nautical abilities he concluded, must know everything), "what the Frenchman said?" to which the other without hesitation replied, "that he said he had made her fast by the fore-sheet."

"Oh, d— n my eyes," says the lieutenant, "that's a good one, they will not ride her long, I'll warrant!"

During this period of my residence at Verdun, several detachments of Austrian and Russian prisoners passed through on their route to the depôt at Soissons, and I invited several of the officers to dinner, with whose observations I was much amused. On inquiry of one of them, from what part of the Russian dominions he was, he described a place near Kamschatka, from whence be had been nine months on his journey, travelling day and night, to go to school.

On demanding further, what kind of travelling there was? he replied, "that he found the dogs very good," alluding to the mode of travelling in Kamschatka and some parts of Siberia, in sledges drawn by dogs. Another came from Astracan on the Caspian Sea, The third said he was from Archangel; he was evidently of Lapland origin. It was not a little singular to unite three of the subjects of the vast Russian Empire, from its most opposite points, at an English table.

CHAPTER 43

Russian and Cossack Officers

In another of our tours from Verdun, we visited Bar sur Ornain, the chief town of the department of the Meuse, though less populous than Verdun, containing only seven thousand inhabitants. It is said to have been founded by Frederick I. Duke of Lorraine, in 951. It is built at the foot and on the side of a steep hill, being divided into the upper and lower town, the streets of communication being so steep, that they are almost impassable by a carriage, which is obliged to make a circuit of some distance out of the town.

The streets of the lower town are in general wide, many of them with rows of trees, and walks for the foot passengers between them and the houses. There are also some good squares in the lower town. The Ornain, though small, is of considerable utility, by the mills it turns. It passes close to the lower town, and is celebrated for its excellent trout, but which the French spoil by serving them up cold, with oil and vinegar for sauce. The side of the hill is covered with vines, the wine from which is considered the best of the department, and is peculiarly fit for summer, being light and wholesome.

The Paris road from Bar ascends a long hill, and is very broad; on each side is a long extent of vineyards, and the summit of the hill presents a forest of fine old oaks, intersected in various directions by carriage roads and bridle paths, affording pleasant rides in summer; of which I took advantage in the heat of the day, and in these promenades frequently met with Spanish officers, this being the depôt for the prisoners of war on parole of that nation. I often entered into conversation with them, but was generally disappointed in my hopes of deriving information from them.

On my first visit to Bar, the *préfet* was M. le Clerc, brother to the general who commanded at and lost St. Domingo. Although he was nearly connected with Buonaparte, by the marriage of his brother the general, with Napoleon's sister, and though Le Clerc's sister was married to Marshal Davoust, Prince d'Eckmuhl, yet these connections were insufficient to prevent his being dismissed from his office of *préfet*; for, as it was understood, not keeping up the appearance thought necessary to his elevated situation.

Here I must observe, in justice to Buonaparte, that he does not unnecessarily squander the public money; nor are there in France any of those sinecure places, which in England afford the Opposition a never-failing topic of violent censure. In all professions in France, whether the army, the law, the church, or any other; every situation has its active duties, and the persons occupying it have constant employment; the salaries are not more than barely sufficient to support the respective ranks. The uniforms of the civil magistrates are extremely splendid, and consequently calculated to create respect in the lower orders.

On public days, the *préfet, sous-préfet, maire*, and all the authorities, civil and military, appear in their dresses, covered with lace and embroidery, and attended by a guard of honour, proceed in procession to church to bear high mass, or possibly a *Te Deum* (by order) for a pretended victory, but which they themselves and all the world know to be a complete defeat. A procession is, however, to a Frenchman a business of joy, whatever may be its cause; and the pleasure he receives from it precludes all possibility of reflection.

Thus the intentions of Government are carried into execution without a murmur. In this respect, as well as in many others, the appearance stands for the reality, and, according to the trite saying, *fine feathers make fine birds*,—for these authorities have generally plumes of various coloured feathers in their hats.

I have often wondered at our Government not obliging persons holding high and lucrative employments, to maintain an appearance in proportion. A judge should go his circuit with the retinue adequate to his great office, which would create a respect for his person, and by a kind of reaction, a greater reverence for the laws which he comes to administer. A bishop should reflect that a portion of the considerable revenue of his diocese ought to be expended for its advantage, and in the support of his high dignity, and this, let it be remarked *en passant*, most particularly in Ireland; the contrary is however too often the case, the prelates in that country frequently neglecting their diocese, and considering it only, what they snugly term, a good thing, by which money may be amassed.

Monsieur Le Clerc was succeeded in the prefecture by the Comte St. Olaire, of an ancient noble family, near Périgueux. This gentleman was more hospitable than his predecessor, and I had the pleasure of dining with him several times. At one of these dinners, his father, the old Comte, was present, and greatly pleased me by the perfect accomplishment of his manners, and the high respectability of his appearance. At this repast I sat next to the Princess Dowager of Nassau, mother, to the prefect's beautiful wife, and who resided with the latter since the decline of her fortune by the conquests of the French.

During my stay at Bar I lodged at the Cygne, the host of which was a perfect picture of the landlord of an inn. His height about five feet, his breadth nearly the same, with a small head, short arms, and singularly good humoured countenance, happily qualified him to sit for the likeness of Boniface; besides, he possessed a vast fund of dry humour, and knew everything and everybody's history. His usual occupation was smoking on a stone bench at the inn door, and his answer to persons passing, who inquired, "*Comment se porte Monsieur Taffolo?*" was, "*Comme vous voyez!*"

Which certainly conveyed abundant information; for he was ruddy health and perfect contentment personified. He quickly discovered the dispositions of his guests, and would drink to the health of those whom he found liberal, vast quantities of his own wine at their expense. To myself and party he was peculiarly partial; for he sat with us, smoking, drinking, and telling entertaining stories, until six o'clock in the morning.

This *nonpareil* of a landlord accompanied us one day to visit Marshal Oudinot's (Duke of Reggio) domain, about one hundred and fifty yards from the town. The house, which seemed never to have been worthy of notice, was lately burnt down; but a large and interesting collection of ancient arms, consisting of antique implements of offence and defence, bows and arrows, darts, guns, and armour, collected from various parts of the world, were fortunately preserved. The domain which belongs to the house, though small, has been appropriated to the best advantage, and the gardens are laid out with taste.

The Duke of Reggio, in order to please his master and ruin Old England, almost ruined himself by speculations in the preparation of beetroot sugar. A large and handsome range of building was constructed for this manufacture; but when I saw it, the universal ill success of the undertaking had caused it to be entirely abandoned, and the marshal had converted the edifice to a more rational and profitable purpose, it being now filled with fine cattle of the Dutch and Flanders breed, fattening on the beetroot planted to make sugar, for which it seems to be much better calculated, and is besides said to give the meat a delicious flavour.

As this species of rural economy seems to hate much occupied the public attention of late, I shall beg leave to offer a statement as to its mode of cultivation in France for the purpose of fattening cattle, with this observation, that it is the *Beta vulgaris*, or red beet, that is used there.

Manner of cultivating the Beetroot

Deep, soft, and damp land ought to be preferred. Calcareous land is preferable to argillaceous; nevertheless the latter is good when it has been enriched during a long time, and softened by repeated turning, taking care that the last takes place before winter. Land that is dug is preferable to that which is ploughed, and that which will grow hops is always good for this purpose.

When the situation is well disposed, and the atmosphere is clear and warm, in the months of April and May, you will rake your land the depth of two inches, making trenches at the distance of eighteen or twenty inches from each other, in which you drop your seed three or four inches from each other, but nearer, if you doubt the quality of it. As each grain of seed gives generally many plants, you must transplant them the distance of eighteen inches from each other, when you conceive them sufficiently strong.

If it should happen that your land is not prepared so as to commence sowing the beginning of spring, you may sow two acres in any land well adapted for the purpose; and instead of separating the plants eighteen inches, place them at six inches, and be not sparing of the seed. When they are in some measure grown, you will take care to separate them, so as to preserve a sufficient quantity to transplant, taking care in digging them up to transplant them to another land in the beginning of May or June. The land destined to receive the plants should be prepared one or two days before you transplant. As soon as the plant has taken, or three weeks or a month after being transplanted, you must rake the land around them twice, particularly after a slight rain, or before.

Expense of Beetroot

	Francs.
One hectare, or nearly an acre of land, proper for the plantation of beet-root, will cost for its cultivation	40
Twenty loads of dung at four *francs* each	80
For plants or seeds	10
For the different cultivation of the plants	15
For digging plants and bringing home	15
Produce	160

An hectare, or, nearly an acre, will contain thirty thousand plants; each plant ought to weigh, at least, two or three pounds, which produces seventy thousand pounds, calculating each at two pounds and a half.

To fatten oxen or feed cows, eighteen or twenty pounds for each beast, it is possible to feed ten cows during the year; but supposing you commence feeding your cattle on beetroot in the month of November until the month of May, it will be necessary to have eighteen or twenty cows to consume the produce of the said acre or hectare. The leaf which the plant produces; will likewise feed pigs and cows. You may preserve them from the month of August until the frost commences; you will have sufficient for three months to feed ten cows and as many pigs. It is necessary when the cows feed on the leaves, to give then, four or five pounds of hay per day.

With this provender the cow will give one-third more milk per day than when fed on twenty pounds of hay, and the milk will preserve the same sweetness as in summer.

	Francs.
To feed twenty cows on hay seven months during winter, it will take eighty-four thousand pounds of hay, which is the produce of nine acres or hectares of meadow land, which you may esteem any common year at twenty *francs* the thousand pounds; which is a sum of	1680
Instead of which the acre or hectare sown with beetroot, for the rent of the land	180
Expenses attending the cultivation	160
Total	340
Difference	1340

The father of Marshal Oudinot was a *ci-devant* brewer at Bar, and the marshal was himself bred to that trade. The former still resides at Bar, and does not arrogate any consideration from his rise; and the latter, although a *parvenu* of the revolution, bears a most excellent character. His military services have been distinguished, and his liberality is such, that though he might have amassed great riches in his various commands, and particularly in the Low Countries, he is said to be considerably in debt.

He has received nineteen or twenty wounds, chiefly in the service of Buonaparte, yet has been latterly disgraced by him, for not doing *l'impossible*, when he commanded a, corps of the army in the late campaign; and being ordered to attack a much superior force, his whole division was nearly annihilated. The effect of this unmerited treatment was such as to deprive him of his senses, and he arrived at Bar from the army in a melancholy state, from which it is feared he will never entirely recover. Such are the recompenses to be expected from Napoleon for the most distinguished services.

At Bar is one of the establishments, latterly erected, called Depôts of Mendicity, on the principle of our poor-houses. It is said that the labour of the persons received into it pays two-thirds of the expenses, and the other third is provided for by contributions laid on the town and neighbourhood. In the places where these depôts have been established, no beggars are allowed. The regulations are such, that, if properly executed, the persons in them must be extremely comfortable.

During this tour we visited Dunmarsi, where there is an iron foundry and manufacture of pots, pans, and chimney tacks, belonging. to Monsieur Vivaux, who resides in a handsome house with elegant gardens. This gentleman and his wife received us with the greatest hospitality, and their son-in-law, who was lieutenant of the Louveterie, accompanied us on a *partie de chasse*, which afforded good sport, as we killed four foxes, and saw a wolf and a roebuck, but not within shot.

We met another wolf on our return, which stopped close to us on the road, and after regarding us for some time, trotted on. These animals are extremely numerous in this part of the country, and considerable premiums are given for their heads, as was formerly done in England and Wales. In the winter they become extremely ferocious, and daring instances have occurred of their committing depredations even in the town of Bar. In the summer they are not much less dangerous, from the great numbers of them that run mad.

Soon after my return from this town, I was called on at Verdun by Monsieur Crochard, whom I have had so often occasion to mention in the preceding pages. He invited me to spend a few days at his residence, not far from Verdun, and to partake of a *partie de chasse* on St. Hubert's day; the patron Saint of the Chase. This I accepted, but the day being very wet arid windy we had but little sport. The commandant and *sous-préfet* of Montmedy were invited to meet me, and I spent three very pleasant days in this society; some of whom were first-rate amateur musicians, so that we had evening concerts.

On the day of my departure, the commandant pressed me to stay dinner with him, and as an inducement, recapitulated all the good things he had prepared for me. On my assuring him that my being at Verdun that day was indispensable, he said that, at all events, they should not be lost, and that we should have them for breakfast: they were accordingly served up; and certainly such a breakfast for five people has seldom been put on a table. In the centre was a two-thirds grown pig, roasted whole; at one end a roasted turkey-cock of prodigious size, and at the other a roasted hare, while cutlets, pasties, and a variety of made dishes, garnished the sides and corners.

This was, however, only the first course, and the second was almost as substantial. The commandant seemed to think I could never eat enough, and was determined to fulfil the French expression, *il y avoit de quoi manger*. The outward appearance of the commandant was that of a hearty, open, good natured fellow; but such is the power of money over a Frenchman, that he was after my visit, accused and convicted of defrauding the miserable Spanish priests of a proportion of their wretched pittance, for which he was sentenced to be sent to the galleys for life.

Towards the end of October, the accounts of the military operations in the North and South were very satisfactory; and though the newspapers, as usual, pretended to make light of the disasters of the French, private accounts left us in no doubt of their extent, and at last the official document from Mayence appeared, which, as a companion to the 29th bulletin, I have preserved in the appendix. Shortly after, Napoleon again quitted his army, and went through Verdun *incognito* in the night.

Many detachments of the Russian and Austrian prisoners, taken in the battle of Dresden, passed through the town, and several of their officers dined with me. Among them was a Colonel of the Don Cossacks, who on being helped to one of the French dishes, made such grimaces, that perceiving he did not relish it, I made signs to him to send away his plate, and helped him to a solid wedge of fat bacon, at which he stroked down his stomach, and shewed all the marks of perfect satisfaction.

I helped him again and again to pieces of the same dimensions, and he devoured a quantity of solid fat, that the stomach of nothing but a Cossack could support. I recollect being at Leghorn once with a detachment of the Russian army, when the chandlers were obliged to shut their shops, to prevent all their soap and candles being devoured by the Russian soldiers; and afterwards I had occasion to observe the same partiality for grease when I was for some time at Suwaroff's head quarters at Augsbourg.

One of these officers speaking French, I asked his opinion of the French troops? To which he replied by a sign that shewed he did not think much of them; "but," said he, "the *cuirassiers* at first puzzled us, by the *cuirass* resisting our lances, which difficulty we soon learned to obviate, for when the *cuirassier* lifted his arm, we watched the moment, and struck him in the armpit."

This manoeuvre he described with such gestures and animation , that I fancied I beheld him in the very act. He had a servant of a most singularly striking appearance, whom I shall never forget; his penetrating and intelligent eye traversed in all directions, while, his countenance expressed an extraordinary mixture of ferocious courage and good nature, that no attempt) even of Guido himself, could delineate.

On the departure of these officers I hired a carriage to forward them on, and made each a present of a handsome pipe and a quantity of tobacco, besides supplying them with money on account of the government My friend the *cossack* pressed his pipe to his heart, saying he would keep it as an everlasting remembrance, and when dead, it should be buried in his grave. In this his gratitude exceeded the intrinsic value of the gift; and, however melancholy the acknowledgment, it must be confessed that gratitude is a virtue rather to be met with in a people emerging from barbarism, than among those who have arrived at a high state of civilization.

Shortly after the head quarters of the grand army were established at Metz, and the sick and wounded were removed from Mayence, &c. towards Verdun and the interior. For six weeks the roads Were crowded with wagons, and all the public buildings at Verdun were converted into hospitals. At the same time an hospital fever prevailed at Mayence, and was conveyed to Metz and Nancy, in which latter place Colonel de Bernière of the 9th regiment fell a victim to it, universally regretted. From thence the disease spread to Verdun and the surrounding villages. So that it appeared as though the Almighty had visited the country with a scourge, in punishment for the calamities which France had inflicted on Europe for the last twenty-four years.

CHAPTER 44

Evacuation of the Depôts of Metz

While at Verdun I was once awoke in the dead of the night by a violent ringing of the bell and knocking at the hall door; on opening which, a tall fierce looking man with large *mustachios*, wrapped in a great cloak, and armed with a sabre and helmet, stalked in. Such an object at such a time may be conceived alarming. He pointed to the door and made signs with great solemnity, as wishing to speak to me in private. On conducting him into a room, he looked round carefully and then secured the door; and my alarm naturally increasing, I secured the poker as if to win the field, but in fact as a weapon of defence.

With increased solemnity he drew forth a letter, which on openings I perceived to be in German, and informed him I could not read it. "Then (said he in French) I will unravel the whole mystery. I am a German officer in the French service, and it being in my turn of duty at Mayence to visit the prisoners, in one of the dungeons I found in chains the two officers who have written you this letter.

"Captain Doebel and Lieutenant Mosque, of the Duke of Brunswick Oels corps, being suspected of having acted as officers in Schill's insurrection in Westphalia, have for several months been treated with the most barbarous cruelty, being confined in separate dungeons, and with chains whose links are so heavy, that it is with difficulty they can move in their narrow cells, and which have worn their legs and arms to the bone; they are nearly naked, and have scarcely a sufficiency of bread and water to preserve their existence, as if the only intention was to prolong their misery. Having by some accident heard of your lordship as being senior officer of the British, and acting with the authority of your liberal government, they wrote to you, but concluded you never received their letter.

"As I am one of their fellow-countrymen, and compassionating their sufferings, I have, at the risk of my life, come hither from Mayence in their behalf. You will see the necessity of my thus visiting you secretly; for if it was known that I forwarded any communication between you and these officers, it would certainly be fatal to me, and might be very disagreeable to you."

On referring to the army list I found the names of these two officers in the Brunswick corps, in the pay of Great Britain. The stranger put me in the way of corresponding with Mayence, and I immediately sent them fifty *louis*, and from that time continued to pay them regularly their monthly subsistence. Money soon lightened their chains, and though still closely confined, they have been comparatively comfortable.

Nothing can equal their gratitude, as the reader will see by some of their letters, which he will find in the Appendix. I informed the Duke of Brunswick Oels of their situation, by letter, as well as that of some other officers of his corps, and received the most polite and friendly answer, inclosing the account of these officers with the agents, Messrs. Cox and Greenwood, by which it appeared that a considerable balance was due to them. Indeed, the interest His Serene Highness expressed for these and other officers of his corps, prisoners, did infinite honour to the goodness of his heart, and shews his zeal for the welfare of his soldiers.

In consequence of the defection of the Princes of the Confederation of the Rhine from their self-constituted protector, the whole of the German troops, in the service of France, were ordered to be disarmed. A corps of the Grand Duke of Berg, stationed at Montmedy, however, refusing to lay down their arms, General de Malard, the commandant of the department, marched from Verdun with some cavalry, to enforce the execution of the order, which he succeeded in doing without violence, by dividing the corps and marching them different ways in small detachments. A number of them were brought thus disarmed into Verdun; and there being among their officers several genteel looking men strolling on the parade before my house, I invited them in to take some wine and refreshment, for which they seemed extremely thankful.

They were all most violent in their invectives against Napoleon, whom many of them had served for eight or nine years in constant activity of service: for they, as well as all foreign corps in general, were always placed in the most dangerous find fatiguing situations, in order to spare the French troops; they were also, in other respects, treated with the greatest harshness, and had a long arrear of pay due to them, which they had no hopes of ever recovering. One of the officers was so exasperated with his treatment, that he tore the *croix d'honneur* from his breast and threw it into the fire. Such are the rewards to be expected by those who enter the service of such a government.

The advance of the allied armies produced scenes of a nature more extraordinary than we had yet witnessed at Verdun; for many days and nights there was a continual passage of families running away from Metz, Nancy, and other places, in the same direction; and their flight was so precipitate, that, added to the extraordinary inclemency of the season, the situation of many of them was truly distressing.

In one instance, I saw a mother and several children in a little cart drawn by a cow and a goat; and another, in which an ass and a large dog were yoked together. Shortly after, the town became the scene of the most complete confusion, in consequence of the sudden evacuation of the depôts of the army, formed at Metz. Day and night the streets were filled with pieces of artillery, *caissons*, wagons loaded with soldiers' clothing and other military furniture, followed by small detachments of cavalry of different corps, whose horses, as well as the men, were worn down with sickness, fatigue and famine. In short, the whole presented the appearance of the miserable remains of a totally defeated army;

and it seemed as if terror, famine, and all their concomitant associates, were now about to finish those who had escaped from the sword.

While contemplating this scene of confusion and misery, we received an order to quit Verdun immediately and prepare to march to Blois, which produced a confusion and distress little inferior to that of our enemies. Having been until the last moment assured that there was no necessity for the removal of the depôt, few were prepared for the event; it may therefore be easily conceived, what was the situation of families, many of whom had been fixed at Verdun for ten or eleven years, and who, by a long state of idleness had acquired indolent and sedentary habits, which rendered them as helpless as children; and, indeed, the appearance they made on the journey fully bespoke their imbecility, and their want of exertion and arrangement: besides, the scarcity of money was generally felt, and in many instances was the cause of the greatest distress. Those few who were more fortunate were therefore obliged to assist others; and my feelings so entirely overcame my prudence, that I left myself without sufficient funds to finish my journey, and was obliged to borrow on the road.

On the 12th of January 1814, the first division of our countrymen quitted Verdun; it was composed of midshipmen, masters of merchant vessels, and others of inferior classes. The midshipmen, above all, presented a singular add not unmeaning sight, from the *bizarrerie* of their costumes and equipage, which gave to the scene more the appearance of a masquerade than a march. These young gentlemen, to use one of their own phrases, "were up to everything;" and such seemed to be the partiality of the *beau sexe* for them that few were without a French female companion, many of whom had made a greater progress in plain English than I could have supposed; having perfectly at command the choicest selection of sailors, oaths and cant sayings, which they applied in the slang stile, and with a tone and manner as if they had received their education at the back of the Point at Portsmouth.

All the minor *bourgeois* of the town crowded together at the gate, to take leave of their English friends, and many of them to. make a last attempt at recovering the money due to them by the young prisoners. Few, however, if any, were the instances of success; for several of those who had any money contented themselves with letting their, creditors look at it, merely to tantalize them, and, returning it into their pockets, told them, "they would be paid by the Cossacks!" Indeed I am sorry to be obliged to observe, that the non-payment of the most just debts, so far from being considered as dishonourable, both to the individuals and the national character, was almost deemed meritorious, and the general expression for it was softened down to that of "distressing the enemy."

On the 13th, the second division, consisting of officers and families, left Verdun. My equipage consisted of a handsome dog-cart, drawn by two excellent Norman horses, which was much admired on the road, particularly by the French. Besides my clothes, this conveyance carried all my comforts, consisting of four dozen bottles of choice wine, and provisions for a week, so that I was entirely independent of inns, except for a bed. As I preferred riding, and having lent a spare horse to a friend to accompany me, I put my servants into the dog-cart, and we set off in a most intense frost.

On our arrival at Clermont, we found all the *auberges* so full, that it was impossible to obtain any kind of accommodation, and were obliged to have recourse to an old woman and her family, with whom I had got acquainted in my former excursions to this town. Though the mansion of these good people was of the most humble kind, being constructed of wood and twigs, and the crevices filled up with mud; or, in other words, that kind of cottage which is intolerably hot in summer, and intensely cold in winter; we prepared to make the best of it, and having with difficulty procured accommodation for the horses, and sent the servants to make them comfortable, my companion and myself set about preparing our supper.

On opening the provision cupboard, I was agreeably surprised by the sight of two unexpected good things: a piece of finely marbled beef, which had been kept fifteen days for steaks, and which I now cut up dexterously for that purpose, and a delicate *poularde aux truffles—videlicet,* a fine fat capon stuffed with truffles.

The want of a spit presented a difficulty, which was however soon removed, by means of a nail and string, which one of the old woman's daughters complaisantly offered to twits; so that having secured the *poularde* in a manner to prevent its bursting from the heat, and thus losing the truffles, my next care was to prepare a sauce for the steaks, and having no oysters, I was obliged to be content with onion sauce. Having succeeded, *à merveille*, in dressing the steaks and *poularde*, with the addition of part of a wild boar's head from our own store, and some toasted cheese, washed down by a bottle of Madeira and two bottles of good Claret, my friend and I braved our hard fate, and composed ourselves till morning, when we resumed our journey.

In the course of the day we passed many broken down carriages of our countrymen, whose equipages were in general wretched. The road was strewed with dead horses belonging to the fugitives from Metz, many of whom had themselves perished, from the inclemency of the weather, which the previous fatigues of the German campaign had rendered them incapable of supporting. About a league and a half beyond Clermont I stopped to take a more exact view of the position occupied by Arthur Dillon, which I have had occasion already to mention.

In a military point of view, this position is immensely strong, occupying nearly to the summit of a steep and winding hill, and flanked to a considerable distance on each side by thick woods, and ground so abrupt and irregularly broken, as to appear the effect of some violent convulsion of nature. As this is the only practicable road for an army to approach Paris on this side, and as it is impossible to turn this position, from the nature of the country, its occupation would have been of wonderful importance to the Prussians in 1793, for by it they might have checked the success of the revolutionary army, and thereby have given confidence to the Royalists, and probably have arrested the progress of that convulsion, which has since produced such unhappy changes and calamities to all Europe.[1]

Among the numerous groups of corps of fugitive cavalry I have already noticed, I observed several superior officers of hussars, who stopped their horses to admire my dog-cart; and one of them, an old colonel, seemed desirous to enter into conversation, by several times riding close up to me, and at last broke silence by praising the horse I was riding. I returned the compliment, at the same time adding, that the figure of the Arabian horse on which he was mounted was familiar to me. On farther inquiry, the old colonel and another officer perfectly recollected me at Madrid, and expressed their joy at our rencontre.

The former then gave me the history of his own and his horse's adventures since that time, informing me that the animal had carried him during the whole of the campaigns through Germany to Moscow, and was now the only survivor of his stud, from the fatigues and inclemency of weather to which they had been exposed in their disastrous retreat. We then spoke of the war in Spain, and I derived no small degree of internal satisfaction, from the handsome manner in which these officers spoke of the loyal, generous, and gallant conduct of the English troops in the Peninsula. Indeed I must observe, in justice to the French officers whom I have latterly met, that in this respect they are candid, and do ample justice to the merit and conduct of Lord Wellington and his army.

The old colonel observed, that he and one of the other officers in company now been in constant active service for twenty-four years, and that at present the successes or reverses of their arms were equally indifferent to them, as the former produced neither individual advantage nor national utility; "thus," concluded the veteran, "I am heartily tired of it, and am now going to a depôt for a remount, in which I shall endeavour to create as much delay as possible, in order to avoid the rest of the winter's

---

1. The Allies have seemed to be aware of the easy defence of this position, and have accordingly avoided it, and followed the route by Bar sur Ornain to Chalons.

campaign." Thus it appears a total change of sentiment has taken place in the French army, and those persons, who at the beginning of the campaign were enflamed by military ardour, and boasting of their exploits past and to come, now think there is equal merit in devising the means of escaping from "the pomp, pride, and circumstance of glorious war;" or more familiarly speaking, of evading their duty. How great, and how worthy of admiration, in the contrast between Old England and France during the course of this war! We may indeed say with perfect truth, what Napoleon has most falsely asserted: "we have never been too much elated by success, nor ever despondent in misfortune."

Having rode some distance at a very sharp rate, and stopping at an inn, I found my new acquaintance, like most Frenchmen, beginning to grow tiresome, by their fulsome compliments. I therefore took the opportunity of quitting them, and proceeded to Chalons, which I reached toward the close of the evening; and found it crowded with troops and carriages of all descriptions, and proceeding in every direction: an inconvenience to which Chalons was necessarily subject, from its central situation, and the many roads all leading to the same point.

CHAPTER 45

French Officers' Abuse of Napoleon

At Chalons I put up at the Ville de Metz, the same inn I was at in my journey to Verdun; but the house being now crowded, I found a great difference in the accommodation, though the landlord and his wife made every exertion to render me comfortable. Observing two fine capons on the spit, I bespoke one of them for my dinner; and while it was roasting, I entered into conversation with some genteel, and well informed officers of hussars, and some *gardes d'honneur*, who were in the kitchen.

They were all unreserved in their violent abuse of Napoleon, and it almost seemed as if they had ransacked the dictionary for abusive words, to select those most forcibly expressive of their detestation. Yet this is merely *vox et preterea nihil*, for no Frenchman has spirit to act alone; and any combination, however secret, is extremely difficult, from the rigorous laws imposed on society and the vigilance of the police, as well as from, the total want of confidence between members of the same family.

In the morning I accompanied an hussar, a very tall and bluntly honest officer, to the stables, in which there was the greatest confusion with the soldiers looking for their respective horses; for though it may seem strange, it is no less the fact, that the horses, instead of having been tied up, groomed, and fed, as is the usual manner with us, were indiscriminately turned loose into the stable.

On expressing my surprise at this neglect to the hussar officer, "bah," replied he, "the case is the same throughout the whole

French army." This in some measure accounts for the bad condition of the horses in the French cavalry.

"But, *diable,*" said the hussar in continuation, "it is time! should I look for one of mine;" which he at last found out; and, noticing his age and points, told me he had picked him up on the road, and mounted him without ceremony; adding that he intended to sell him to the first farmer who would give him a price, and then get another in the same manner: "*parceque,*" said he, "*notre solde est toujours enarrière; et cependant il faut vivre.*"

Quitting Chalons, we found it almost impossible to make our way through the streets for artillery, *caissons,* troops of all descriptions, and Spanish and Austrian prisoners changing depôts. At last We were under the necessity of falling into the line of a chain of guns and artillery furniture, all entirely new from the arsenal of Metz.

We crossed the Marne by a handsome stone bridge, near which we observed a magnificent triumphal arch, erected in honour of Napoleon two or three years since. This object could not fail calling up reflections on the change in his affairs, as well as in the destinies of France and of Europe in general, since its erection. Instead of destroying such trophies, they should be allowed to exist, as monuments of the folly, ambition, and vanity of the man, and to serve as useful lessons to princes, not wantonly or hastily to plunge their subjects into war.

In contemplating these memorials of the military successes of Napoleon, it is impossible not to reflect to what a height of power he might have arisen, had his ambition known where to stop; and to what a pre-eminence of greatness he might have raised France, had he known or consulted the real interests of his subjects. But, happily, there is a superintending Providence that governs and regulates all things, and exactly compensates good and evil.

The history of mankind seems to prove, that war is more congenial to the human race than peace; and doubtless this principle is implanted in us by Providence, in order to prevent the too great multiplication of the species; of the evil of which there is a sufficient proof in China, where the superabundant population not only produces frequent famines, but also in its consequences stifles the first affections of the heart; causing parents, without pity or remorse, to expose their infant offspring.

But supposing Europe to be now arrived at nearly the degree of population proper for its well being, it seems evident that wars, instead of decreasing will increase, in order to preserve stationary this degree of population, by counteracting the causes which now tend to the multiplication of the species more rapidly than in former times. Among these the two most powerful are the discovery of the vaccine, which saves the lives of millions, and the abolition or diminution of monastic orders throughout Europe.

In France, in particular, these two causes have operated most powerfully, and we have seen that the excess of her population has been only employed to disturb her neighbours. The person, however, at the head of the French Government, has left nothing undone towards preventing a redundancy of people, and in this respect his efforts have been eminently successful; for supposing, on a moderate estimate, that he has been the cause of the death of five millions of Frenchmen, and that, one with another, each of these men would have been destined to be the father of one child, it is evident that Napoleon has effected a diminution of ten millions of souls in France alone.

At Chalons I met Monsieur de Meulan, the commandant of the depôt, from whom I learnt that our route was changed, and that, instead of going by Chateau-Thierry and Meaux, we were, now to proceed by Arcis, Troves, and Sens, to Orleans. As I wished to avoid, the crowd, I determined on pursuing the first route, and accordingly turned off to the right for Epernay, where I soon arrived, the road being excellent and free from impediments.

The stables in the town were however so crowded, that I could not find a place for my horses, and was obliged to have recourse to Mr. Mowhil, the great Champagne merchant, whose family (he being absent) received me in the most flattering manner, and ordered a stable and remise to be appropriated to my horses and carriage. Mr. Mowhil soon appeared, and pressed me to dine with him, which I was obliged to decline, having invited some English acquaintance I had met on the road to partake of a dinner with me at the inn. Mr. Mowhil however insisted on my accepting some bottles of his Sillery Champagne, and accordingly sent half a dozen, with the ice necessary to do justice to this delicious wine, which differs from many other species of Champagne in not frothing; but on the contrary being perfectly still, with a slightly bitterish flavour, which makes it a fine stomachic, and very wholesome.

The estate which produces this wine is now the property of General Valence, a senator and general of division, who got it by his marriage with the celebrated Madame de Genlis, *ci-devant* wife to the Marquis de Sillery. General Valence is noted for having quitted the army at the same time with Dumourier and the Duke d'Orleans, the infamous *Égalité*. Madame de Genlis at present resides at Romanville, near Paris, and still makes a conspicuous figure in the literary world.

The estate of Sillery is rented by Mr. Mowhil, and its whole produce conveyed to his cellars, which are of surprising extent, forming a number of subterraneous apartments cut out of a chalky substance, and resembling a little world underground. The quantity of wine in wood and bottle is immense and from hence most of the inferior merchants of France are supplied, who however so generally adulterate it, that it is very difficult to procure the genuine Sillery except from Mr. Mowhil himself. This gentleman also supplies the Imperial table, and the fame of his cellars once roused the phlegmatic disposition of Napoleon himself so far, as to induce him to go from Paris expressly to visit them in 1810, an honour which is commemorated by an inscription, in large characters, in one of the vaults.

The engaging politeness of Mr. Mowhil and his amiable family led me to fear giving them offence, by having declined either dining or accepting a bed at their house. I therefore promised to breakfast with them the following morning, when I partook of an excellent repast, *à la fourchette*, at which the most delicious Champagne was introduced in perfection. When sufficiently iced, it was wheeled into the room on a little carriage constructed for the purpose. Mr. Mowhil assured me that the wine was so delicate, that the difference of five minutes more or less remaining in the ice would cause a sensible difference to the palate.

On my departure, my kind host insisted on putting a dozen bottles of the vintage of 1796 into the carriage; and though I resisted for some time, I found it impossible to refuse the favour. Taking leave of this engaging and worthy family, at four o'clock I set out for Château-Thierry, where I did not arrive until half past eight, the distance being twelve leagues over a hilly country, The town I found so full of troops, that I with difficulty procured very indifferent accommodation, and a bad supper, at an inn. In the morning, after an uncomfortable night, I strolled through the town, which is insignificant, with narrow streets, and irregularly built; but the Marne is here crossed by a handsome stone bridge, and on its bank is a good promenade.

The town has its name from an ancient *château* built I believe by Charles the Ninth. In recent times it has been possessed by the Princes of Bouillon, the last of whom dying without issue, bequeathed his estates and title to Philip d'Auvergne, an admiral in the British service, and commanding at Guernsey. This bequest was declared valid by the King of France, and Mr. d'Auvergne took the title of Prince de Bouillon with the sanction of the British Government; but the revolution deprived him both of the estates and title, and Château-Thierry now forms a part of the imperial domain, as well as Navarre, one of the finest estates in France, which also belonged to the House of Bouillon, but which is now the residence of the Empress Josephine.

From Château-Thierry I pursued my journey, over very hilly country, to Ferté sous Jouarre, wretched, dull and nasty town, situated in a hollow, with narrow streets, abominable inns, and, in short, nothing to recommend it. Here, however, I was prevailed on to pass the day, by my particular friend. Lord Boyle, eldest son of the Earl of Glasgow, and whose hospitality and kindness could alone have induced me to stop a single hour in this detestable place, where a five minutes' walk is sufficient to render one as dirty as a whole day's snipe-shooting in the bogs of Ireland.[1]

From La Ferté I proceeded by an excellent road to Meaux, a town I have already had had occasion to notice,[2] and from thence (it being forbidden to the English to enter Paris, and a strict look-out being kept by the police in this respect) by a very bad cross road, chiefly through a forest, to Melun. On the left we passed a most magnificent palace, formerly belonging to the Prince de Conti.

The woods of the domain are cut in numerous strait avenues, forming beautiful rides, as well as for the chase in former times, to which the last Prince was greatly attached, and particularly noticed for his uncommonly fine breed of wolf hounds. As I learnt here, the wolf is infinitely more swift than the fox, and as he runs directly ahead, the dogs would have little chance with him in a fair chase; hence the Prince had dexterous *chasseurs*, who wounded the animal so slightly as only to impede his running to a certain degree, and thus reduce him to an equality with the dogs. Under these circumstances, wolf-hunting is said to be excellent sport.

I could not but feel concern at the deserted and neglected state of this noble mansion and its domain. Nothing, indeed, can convey a stronger proof of the contrast between France before the revolution and at this day, than the sight of such numerous princely mansions mouldering into decay.

Late in the evening I arrived at Melun, which I found so crowded by the levy of the national guards and by troops passing to join the armies, that I with difficulty procured accommoda-

---

1. For my former visit to La Ferté, see Chapter 36.
2. Since writing this, Meaux and the other parts of the country I passed through, have been the theatre of war; and Epernay, in particular, has been alternately in the hands or friends and enemies, whence it is to be feared it has suffered, which would give me the greatest concern, as most probably the interesting and worthy family of Mr, Mowhil has not escaped the general disaster.

tion; yet, though my fare was not sumptuous, as the people were civil, I contented myself for the night.

In the morning I visited my old acquaintance, Sir Thomas Lavie, who had been made prisoner some years ago, by the wreck of the *Blanche*, near Cherbourg. His character as a naval officer had been established by the capture of *La Guerrière*, a frigate of much superior force to the *Blanche*, which he then commanded, and for which he was knighted, being the first naval action under Lord Grey's administration.

Sir Thomas Lavie's residence was adjoining that of the celebrated cavalry General, Latour Maubourg, Who lost a leg in the last campaign in Germany; in consequence of which he had retired to this small country seat, in which there is nothing very striking, but apparently a good deal of comfort. I was gratified by the sight of the general as he was taking the air on the steps before his door. His appearance was, as he had been represented, soldier-like, with the remains of a very fine person. He is of a *ci-devant* noble family of great consequence, but imbibed strong Jacobinical principles, which were still more inflamed by a personal dislike of the late Queen Marie Antoinette, who had given him some cause of offence.

From Melun I proceeded to Fontainbleau; I put up at the Dolphin, a very good hotel, where the people were civil, my dinner comfortable, and the wines good. The landlady and her daughters were in tears, from the son, the chief support of the house, having been just called out to march with the national guards, to join the army as a private soldier. The young man, while tossing the frying pan, observed to me, "*Monsieur, voilà mon métier*; this is the trade to which I have been bred, and now I am obliged to become a. soldier, for which I am not at all calculated, and of whose duties I am totally ignorant."

The next morning I was waited on by my old acquaintance Monsieur Larminat, who was in mourning for his father, the worthy old gentleman who acted with me as one of the stewards for the balls at Verdun. As M. Larminat held the respectable situation of inspector of the Imperial forest of Fontainbleau, he had the politeness to conduct me over the *demesne*, and pointed out, with much, satisfaction, some improvements of his own in the forest. The strait walks were still preserved, as they should be in so ancient a place, for they mark, the character of the age; and it would be as equally contrary to good taste to alter them, as it would be to add a wing of Grecian architecture to the body of a Gothic edifice.

By clearing away the wood on the summit of a sudden rise, M: Larminat has opened a magnificent and extensive view over a great part of the forest and neighbouring country, including the town and palace. Beyond the limits of the forest, the country is chiefly under vines, for which species of agriculture, its sandy soil is best calculated. The very small quantity of waste land must forcibly strike a traveller, in passing through most parts of France, and proceeds from the soils which are most ungrateful in other respects being proper for the production of the finest grapes, and accordingly covered with rich vineyards. Thus the lands of a nature to remain eternally waste in England from the climate, are in France a mine of wealth, owing to the extreme, munificence of the Almighty to a most ungrateful people.

The forest of Fontainbleau contains, according to the statistical description, twenty-six thousand four hundred and sixty-two *arpents*[3], chiefly of oak; which is however of a very inferior quality, owing, it is said, to the nature of the soil, and is therefore never used in ship-building.

After our promenade in the forest, I visited the palace, or, as it is called, the *château*, of which the external appearance is far from grand; nevertheless its antiquity and a certain melancholy semblance renders it respectable. We were shewed over it by an ancient Swiss, whose conduct and manners had imposed on the revolutionary barbarians, and caused them to respect the *château*, which only received some trifling damages, that have been in a great measure repaired by Napoleon.

The first apartment we entered is nearly a square, with a well-painted ceiling, executed, as well as the other ornaments, in the

---

3. An *arpent* is rather more than an English acre.

time of Henry II. One of the walls is almost entirely covered by a very fine representation of the Battle of the Pyramids, painted by Eukin. The second apartment shewn us is called that of St. Louis, from which we entered a *salle à manger*, richly but heavily ornamented, under the direction of Francis the First. The ceiling represents the history of Trajan and Cavillea. In another apartment is a modern clock, placed on a large marble table, which denotes the various changes of the moon.

We next entered a gallery, two hundred feet long by twenty wide, the windows of which look into a small but extremely neat garden, with very handsome *jets d'eau*, and fountains in marble, the whole laid out and constructed under the immediate direction of Napoleon. In the centre of the apartment, called *la Chambre de l'Empereur*, is a round table, about three feet and a half in diameter, entirely of a single piece of Seve porcelain, and some very large and valuable vases of the same manufacture. Adjoining this apartment is a bedchamber, so magnificently fitted up, that I should suppose a person unaccustomed to such splendour must sleep most uncomfortably in it. The tapestry and curtains are the *chef d'oeuvre* of silk and embroidery, from the Lyons manufactures.

The Salle de Trône is a large square apartment, handsomely ornamented, the ceiling painted in the time of Louis XIV. This was the favourite bedroom of Louis XVI. and not far from it is the *boudoir* of Marie Antoinette, now the dressing-room of Marie Louise, and which is only shewn by particular favour. The furniture is the same as used by the unfortunate Queen, and as much taste and expense has been bestowed on it as the dimensions of the room would admit. The Turkish sofa, in particular, is in the extreme of Eastern splendour. Near this was the council chamber of Louis XVI.

We were next shewn into a handsome gallery, ornamented in the time of Francis I. At the upper end is the bust of Henry IV. and along the sides, where it is probable were formerly placed those of the Kings and Queens of France, are now seen those of Napoleon's generals, who have fallen in the field or died in his service; such as Dessaix, Kleber, &c. The busts of Marlborough, Frederick the Great, and Washington, also occupy places in this gallery amongst the great captains of France. This seeming candour is, however, probably a more refined vanity, by which Napoleon thinks to impose on the world in making it believe that merit alone, to whatever nation it may belong, is worthy of a place in his gallery.

Here were also alternately placed representations of Napoleon's various battles, and views of Mount St. Bernard, and of all the spots in Italy marked by any military event, with explanations under them; and certainly, if we separate the character of Buonaparte from these representations and pictures, they have great merit, and are well worthy of observation.

The Pope at this time occupied apartments in the *château*, and I saw and saluted several cardinals who were attached to his Holiness. The servants who waited on him all wore the Emperor's livery. I was assured that he was regularly asked every day if he wished to ride out and take the air? but his invariable answer was, "No, I never desire to enter a carriage, except to depart for Rome."

Monsieur Larminat did me the favour to dine with me. In the evening I received several visits, and next day, rather late, resumed my journey, by a considerable portion of bad roads, to Pithiviers, where my accommodation was very uncomfortable, and the charges so exorbitant, that I told the landlord he must surely be out of his senses, and that I would neither enter into the details of his bill nor pay him anything; and at the same time I ordered the carriage to proceed. "But, *Monsieur*," said he, "what will you pay me?"

"Nothing," replied I

"But, *Monsieur*, that is very strange."

"Perhaps so; but had you been anything like reasonable, I should have examined your charges, and paid you what was just."

"Then will *Monsieur* think so and so too much?" reducing the sum at one blow to half its original amount.

"Reduce it one third more," said I, "and I may talk to you."

Finding he could make no better of it, he consented to receive one third; and I was about to depart, when I was accosted by a handsome and neatly dressed young woman, who told me, with, modest simplicity, that she had been but a very short time married to a captain in the Imperial Guard, when he received orders to join his corps in Russia, where she understood he had been wounded and made prisoner; "and, Sir,", continued she, "I have heard so much of the generosity of the English character, and of their extensive correspondence and communication with all parts of the worlds that I have presumed to solicit the favour of your forwarding a letter to Russia."

To such a modest request, made in so amiable a manner, and by so interesting an object, I replied, "that her appearance, language, and manners, were such as to ensure a favourable answer to any demand she could make, and that I would certainly most cheerfully forward her letter through England; that though there was a moral certainty of its reaching her husband, yet I could not promise her an answer, which, doubtless, must be the most anxious of her wishes; but at all events that her letter should be forwarded, and the answer must take its chance; therefore," continued I, "if, *Madame*, you will have the goodness to write your letter, I will wait for it."

"Oh, Sir," she replied, "that is already done, and I will bring it you in a moment;" which she accordingly did, and I pursued my journey.

Chapter 46

A French Acquaintance

At the moment of quitting Pithivers I was accosted by my name, in very good English, by a Russian officer, whose face was quite familiar to me, and I soon recollected having met him at the Duke of Sussex's in Lisbon, where he was secretary to the Russian Embassy. The road being slippery from the frost, this gentleman walked with me out of the town, and we mutually brought to our recollection several anecdotes which were talked of while we were at the Portuguese capital.

Our conversation then turned on the positions of the several armies, and the probable termination of the present important contest. His judgment was sound, and, like all his countrymen, he was warm in the cause, and sanguine as to its success. I observed to him;

> "that a favourable result entirely depended on the perfect unanimity of the Allies; but it was to be apprehended that discord and disunion might arise amongst so many powers, whose views and characters were so opposite."

> "Some time ago," replied the Russian, "this might have been feared; but twenty-four years experience must have taught them a lesson, and convinced them of the boundless ambition and deceit of the man at the head of the French government; therefore they must at this moment be united by one sole object; namely, the destruction of the tyrant and of the satellites who have been his instru-

ments in desolating Europe, and in reducing France to a state of ruin, from which she cannot recover for years to come."

Nevertheless," replied I (wishing to continue the argument in hopes of obtaining information), "I fear that the greater part of the people of France will still remain devoted to their destroyer, rather than risk the horrors of another revolution. Besides, all the leading persons throughout France, from the *bonne, ville de Paris* to the most insignificant village, are in the dependence of the government; such, for instance, are the *maires* and their *adjoints*, the *commissaires* and other, myrmidons of the police, the legions of custom-house officers, *gardes-forêts, gardes-champêtres*, &c., all of whom act in concert with the government, and at the same time form an organised system of espionage, which presents any combination of the lower orders, The Allies will therefore be greatly disappointed if they expect assistance from the people; and I sincerely hope they have entered France with a sufficient force to counterbalance the influence of the various authorities."

"*Soyez tranquille*," replied the Russian, "the French have so entirely lost their national character, that they will join the strongest party; and if we gain some decided advantages in the field, these authorities will be the first to abuse Napoleon and execrate his government; but if, on the contrary, he should be occasionally successful in attacking separate corps, or detachments, by large forces, these same wretches will regain their courage, and enthusiastically praise the same men and the same government that they the moment before abused as tyrannical and oppressive."

I agreed perfectly with these sentiments, the justice of which has been demonstrated by the fluctuation of opinion and language among the French of all classes, according to the turns of the war, since their country has been invaded, and their dearest interests threatened with the most imminent danger. The people of England, I most sincerely hope, will never be put to so severe a trial; if they were, their line of conduct would doubtless be very different

I learnt from my companion, that he had been, employed confidentially by this Russian Government at Paris, previous to the commencement of hostilities; but that some suspicion attaching to him, he had been arrested, his papers seized, and himself made a prisoner of state.

Having taken my leave of him, I proceeded by a very bad road and wretched country to Orleans; on entering which I met with Mr. Thompson, who procured me comfortable accommodation at a hotel, and also invited me to dinner, where I met a large party of English on their route for Blois. Mrs. Thompson and family being kindly attentive, we passed a pleasant evening in relating our various adventures on the road.

On returning to the hotel I found a fat good-natured French merchant, a Monsieur Consurge, whom I had formerly known. He had been waiting for me three hours, and politely told me, that understanding I was going to Blois, where possibly I might not be acquainted, he had written some letters of recommendation for me, which he trusted I would find useful. I thanked him for his kind attention , and we supped together, in the course of conversation he informed me, that since I had last seen him he had been very unfortunate in his affairs, and obliged to declare himself a bankrupt. I seized the occasion to comfort him, in return for his politeness, by remarking that, "though, Sir, you may have lost your money, which, as Shakespeare says,

is trash; 'tis something, nothing;
'Twas mine, 'tis his, and has been slave to thousands;

"yet you have preserved what is infinitely more valuable, an open, friendly-hearted, good disposition; and, Sir, a

good name, in man and woman
Is the immediate jewel of their souls."

I was afterwards very glad to learn, that he was still enabled to continue business.

The following day I remained at Orleans and was highly amused by the exhibition of the national guards and *levée en masse*, which were now organising, and one third of them ordered to be immediately armed. To comply with this order, fowling pieces that had hung for centuries over chimneys, Were now brought forward; some without locks, and others of which the locks were so rusty and out of repair, as to be totally unserviceable.

The number of these, arms not being sufficient, different articles were given to different persons; one having a musket, a second the bayonet, and a third the ramrod. The other two thirds of this motley group were armed with sticks, broken shovels or broken pitchforks, for their patriotism was not strong enough to induce them to bring forward any implement that was serviceable or useful in the farms. After being mustered by their names with great ceremony, an old drunken drummer, with a ragged coat, a cocked-hat, wooden shoes, and a broken drum, was placed at their head, and they were marched off.

What with their broad brimmed hats and *sabots*, their ragged clothing, and their own natural deformities, they presented so ludicrous a scene, that if Napoleon had studied to bring complete ridicule on. the great nation, he could not have chosen a more suitable expedients

While walking on the bridge, a carriage with six grey post-horses, and two others with four horses each, crossed it. On inquiry, I found, that it was the Pope, cardinals, and his suite, who had been hastily removed from Fontainbleau. A great crowd, followed the carriage; and as the postilions walked their horses slowly up the ascent of the bridge, I had the satisfaction of a perfect sight of his holiness.

His countenance is small, pale and mild; and the pictures of him that I have seen in France and England are sufficient resemblances to give an exact idea of him. He was drest in ermine, as he is also usually represented in prints. The crowd fell on their knees to receive his blessing, which he bestowed in so kind and benevolent a way, as made an impression on me I can never forget; and I have his countenance and manner at this moment before me. I was assured, that no provision having been made for his holiness's reception at Pithiviers, where he was to sleep the night before his arrival at Orleans, and the inns being crowded by French officers, he and his cardinals would have been without beds, had not some of the English passing through the town given up those they had engaged, which it was not without difficulty the Pope could he prevailed on to accept: such is the modesty of this worthy prelate and his cardinals.

The not giving proper orders for the accommodation of his holiness in his journey, was either a most scandalous neglect on the part of the French Government, or else an intended insult to fallen majesty; of which it is to be hoped, of all the nations, and all the monarchs of Europe, France and Napoleon could alone be guilty.

After enjoying an hospitable dinner with my friend Major Popham, at Orleans, I set out next day, and arrived at Blois early the following morning. On the road I passed several pieces of artillery, and wagons of military furniture, proceeding to Paris.

CHAPTER 47

Passage of Prisoners

The sudden influx of above a thousand persons, all of certain pretensions, into a town like Blois, containing only twelve thousand inhabitants, and where there had not been time sufficient to prepare for the reception of so many visitors, rendered, as may be supposed, the procuring lodgings extremely difficult; and besides those who had apartments to let, taking advantage of the moment, demanded such exorbitant prices, as could be afforded only by very few of the prisoners; such, for instance, as one hundred and fifty *francs* a month for two miserably furnished bedrooms on a second floor, to which the access was by an abominable filthy corkscrew staircase, without a ray of light.

Indeed, the general idea, of the French that the English are made of money, and that they squander it like prodigals without thought, was particularly exemplified at Blois. The price of all articles which were not strictly limited by a tariff, such as butcher's meat and bread, immediately rose fifty *per cent*: which, however, was little felt by the prisoners, who had already been used to pay dearer for them at Verdun. A large turkey, which at Verdun would have cost five or six *francs,* was sold at Blois for three, or three *livres* ten *sous*; salmon, fresh from the Loire, for thirty *sous* the pound; the established price of the best butchers' meat, was nine *sous* the pound. In short, the article of lodgings excepted, the English had no reason to complain of the change from Verdun.

During our stay at Blois, the town was constantly crowded by prisoners of war of all nations, changing depôts according to the movements of the Allied armies, Many of them were in the most miserable condition, from fatigue; from the intense inclemency of the weather, without clothing or shoes; and above all, from hunger, being often for many days together without receiving any victuals whatever from the French government.

Numbers sunk on the march under their complicated calamities, and perished miserably in the ditches, while others lost their fingers and toes by the frost, and were rendered cripples for life. The number of English soldiers were so great, that it was with much difficulty! could procure sufficient money to relieve them; and I am with much concern obliged to remark, that in too many instances that relief was badly bestowed.

The money instead of being expended for necessaries, being often squandered in drink, which, caused so many excesses, that the commandant of the town declared that a hundred English prisoners caused him more trouble than a thousand of any other nation. It is however but justice to observe, that this bad conduct was principally observed in the prisoners from Sarre Libre, the greater part of whom were vagabonds who had entered the French service, from which they had been sent back on account of their unruly and turbulent characters, and on finding that nothing advantageous could be made of them. In general, the prisoners from the other depôts conducted themselves well, and more particularly those from, Valenciennes.

Blois being at this time the thoroughfare for prisoners of war of all nations, I here received a visit from the Russian General Toutchacoff, with whom I had formerly some correspondence at Metz, and who now thanked me for the services and attentions I had paid to his countrymen in passing through Verdun. In answer to which, I observed, "that both my duty and inclination led me to render every service in my power to the officers of his nation; and that besides the self-satisfaction of being useful to them, I had the additional one of knowing that I anticipated the wishes of the British government, and gratified the general feeling of the English nation towards Russia, which had made such sacrifices, and stood forward so nobly in the general cause of Europe against Napoleon."

This compliment was received by a bow, and an air of pleasure; and the general continued to converse with a lively communicativeness, which as far as I have been able to observe, characterizes the Russians of any education; indeed, they seem in general to possess much animation, and to be enthusiastic in executing whatever they under take. Besides prisoners of war, several state prisoners passed through Blois; and amongst them I had the opportunity of conversing with a Spanish nobleman, who had formerly been ambassador at Rome and other courts.

The constant passage of English prisoners obliged me to pay frequent visits to the commandant of the department, and other authorities, from whom I experienced every civility; the commandant, in particular, was a polite gentlemanlike officer, who had been disabled for active service by a severe wound received in Spain. I had also occasion to become acquainted with Monsieur Le Fevre, the Receiver-General, whom I one day accompanied, at his request, and will several of the principal inhabitants, to visit the city hospital, in which their greatly prided themselves; it being superintended and partly supported by the voluntary exertions and contributions of the town's people.

The building had been formerly a Benedictine convent, consisting of a vast square, with a very extensive garden, well stocks with vegetables and medicinal plants. The monks' cells have been thrown open by an arch in each, so as to be at all times perfectly aired, and in each is a bed; the established number of which was one hundred, and eighty, but were now augmented to three hundred and sixty; the refectory, and other apartments, having also rows of beds placed in them.

The internal services of the hospital are performed by a superintending *sœur de la charité* and several subordinate ones. The neatness and cleanliness of these pious old ladies' dress; their orderly conduct, and the excellent arrangements and good management of the hospital in general, could not fail of affording me the greatest satisfaction; which was increased by observing many

English prisoners treated with the same tenderness and attention as their own sick and wounded countrymen, and who expressed their gratitude for the kindness of the respectable sisters.

At the moment that most of the English had formed as comfortable establishments as their circumstances would admit in Blois and the surrounding country, and were beginning to reconcile themselves to change of depôt; calculating that the superiority of the climate and, the beautiful scenery of the banks of the Loire would, in the spring and summer, compensate for the disadvantages of the town, they received orders for a precipitate removal, in consequence of the appearance of a body of the allied troops before Orleans, which for some time threw the authorities and inhabitants of Blois into the utmost consternation; the force of the Allies in that direction being much exaggerated, and it being even reported that they had entered Orleans; while in fact the business turned out to be, that a party of pillaging Cossacks had only presented themselves before the town, and finding no force sufficient to receive them, again retired, after a skirmish of little consequence.

At the same time Napoleon having gained some trifling advantage over the corps commanded by General Blucher, it was an object of consequence to make as much as possible of it, and accordingly it was proclaimed throughout the streets by sound of trumpet, trumpet, and afforded in large characters on the walls of all the public buildings, that the Emperor had gained a complete victory, and that the Russian army *étoit entèrement anéantie*.

The same evening I was at the theatre, and between the pieces one of the actors came on the stage, and read the bulletin, dispatch, or account of this grand victory, for it is difficult to give a name to the reports of the operations of the army at this time; indeed, the word, bulletin was now entirely dropped, from the ridicule in which it was held by all classes, on account of the gross and stupid falsehoods of which these reports were composed; in general the official accounts were given with this preface:"*Sa Majesté l'Impératrice, Reine et Régente, a reçue les nauv-*

elles suivantes des positions des armées." The *Moniteur*, as well as the minor papers, had also recourse to every possible means, such as supposed intercepted letters, private information, &c. &c. to blindfold and impose on the people.

The player, however, who, as I have said, came forward to announce this grand victory, unmindful of the advice of Hamlet, entirely overacted his part, and, by *out-stepping the modesty of Nature*, destroyed the impression he intended to make, and rendered the whole account absurd. After running on with a string of unpronounceable Russian names, and stating that the artillery, *caissons, fourgons,* baggage, and equipage, of the enemy had fallen into the power of the French, he concluded with,

"*Messieurs, l'armée Russe est entièrement détruite, et, je suis heureux d'avoir l'honneur de vous informer, sans nous, avoir coûté, un seul de tué.*"

All the persons under government having been ordered to attend at the theatre on this occasion more particularly on account of the English, the news was received with clapping of their hands, and acclamations of "*bravo! vive Napoleon!*" The eyes of the whole house were, as might be expectedly turned on the English; and they seemed to be not a little surprised, at observing John Bull louder in applauding than themselves, vociferating "*bravo! vive Napoleon! encore! encore!*" which brought the actor forward again to repeat the news, and he was even so stupid as to continue, until the French at last perceived that we were turning them into ridicule, and from several parts of the house was heard, "*bravo! ce n'est pas vraie! bravo! quelle mensonge!*"

So that the authorities would have done much better in not ordering the mention of this pretended victory on the stage. A few days proved the ridiculous exaggeration of the account; for this same totally annihilated Russian army resuscitated, as if by miracle, and gained some considerable advantages. Besides, the positions occupied by the French armies, as well as the falling of the funds, convinced the people of the successes of the Allies.

The orders for the removal of the depôt from Blois to Gueret, in the department of the Creuse, were forwarded through General Bonard, commanding the district, whose ungentlemanly manners I have already had occasion to notice. The execution of these orders resting with him, the directions he gave were such as might be expected from his character, and known animosity to the English.

He not only directed the order to be put into execution an hour after its being received, but also, to render the persecution more intolerable, marked out a line of cross roads, forming two-thirds of a circle, and entirely impracticable for carriages, and without any, or with only the most wretched accommodation. The littleness of mind of this wretch doubtless made him inwardly rejoice, at an opportunity of, as he conceived, annoying the English nation, by persecuting a few helpless families, and superannuated and distressed masters of ships; for though the orders were positive not to deviate from this route, those only obeyed them whose poverty obliged them to accompany the *gend'armes*, in, order to procure lodging *gratis* while on the march; the families who could afford it, and the officers of the army and navy paying no attention to them; and though the high road by Tours was particularly forbidden, and orders issued not to furnish post horses, many went by this road; which I also chose, determined to risk the consequences, being satisfied that these orders originated in General Bonard himself, without the knowledge of the Minister of War; and indeed this was clearly proved, by his taking no notice of the many persons who acted in direct violation of them.

February 21. Having sent my servants with the carriage and horses by the great road to Amboise, I proceeded along the opposite bank of the river, as well to see the country as to visit General O'Connel, at his seat named Madon, which I found to be a very respectable mansion, but the road and approaches to it abominable. Indeed, though the country was most romantic, and had some magnificent *châteaux*, I almost repented my curiosity, from the badness of the roads, where there were any; for in many parts there was no trace of a road, and my only direction was the course of the Loire.

These obstacles retarded my arrival at Amboise till late in the evening, where I put up at the comfortable little inn I have formerly noticed. I was soon called on by an old acquaintance, Captain Lutyens, of the 11th Dragoons, accompanied by a Swedish colonel, this being the depôt for Swedish officers prisoners of war. In the course of the next day I saw many these officers in the streets, and could not help admiring their decent and respectable dress and appearance, though they possessed no other resources than the pay from the French Government. In these respects they far surpassed the prisoners of other nations under similar circumstances.

It being Shrove Tuesday, I accepted the invitation of Captain, Lutyens to dinner on the express condition of having pancakes, for, such is my adherence to the respectable old customs of our country; that I should deem it almost a misfortune to omit a goose on Michaelmas Day, a plum-pudding at Christmas, or pancakes on Shrove Tuesday,

I passed the morning in a ride to the celebrated *château* of Chenonceau, built by, and the favourite country residence of Francis the First. It is above two leagues and a half from Amboise, but, as is very generally the case with the approaches to the best country seats in France, the road, or rather the no-road to it is execrable. The building consists of two parts, one on each bank of the Cher, the communication being by a bridge one hundred and eighty feet long, which crosses the river, and on which is built a gallery, so that one is ignorant of this remarkable situation, until, locking out of the window of the gallery, the rapid and handsome river is seen running beneath; and from the windows a person fond of fishing may amuse himself catching the finest salmon and trout

The gallery contains likewise a good collection of ancient pictures. An opposite door from that of entrance leads into the grounds and wood formerly appropriated to the royal chace. This *demesne* has been for some generations the property of the ancient and respectable family of Villeneuve; and the present proprietor is chamberlain to the Queen of Holland, a situation which it is to be presumed policy alone has caused him to accept. He possesses the manners and appearance of a gentleman, and politely invited Captain Lutyens, the Swedish colonel and myself into the drawing room, where we found some good company, several of whom were here on a visit, particularly Monsieur and Madame de Marcolle.

The latter surprised me by speaking English perfectly; but I soon learnt that she was an English lady, and married to Monsieur de Marcolle in England, to whom she brought a marriage portion of above £30,000. They reside near Chenonceau, at a small place called Chisay, which is, I believe, the family estate. Both were very pleasing in their manners, and pressed us to visit their house, and pass the day with them, which I regretted being obliged to decline, in consequence of my previous engagement at Amboise. Monsieur de Marcolle recounted to us the history of the *château* in ancient and modern days, and explained the historical pictures it contains.

Most of the events they enumerated I had already read of, and I was much gratified by, having them recalled to my memory by these representations. The *château* also contained the portraits off several princes, and great men conspicuous in history.—Among other curiosities, we were shewn a pair of black silk breeches of Francis the First, in which, however, there was nothing remarkable, except their having been worn by that monarch.

Among the pictures, as may be presumed, were several in which Francis the First figured; particularly one of the battle of Marignan, gained by that king in person over the Swiss, in 1575. Francis is represented in the act of succouring a cavalier, who has fallen nearly under his horse, in such a manner as to be unable to defend himself against two Swiss, by whom he is attacked; the prince alone attacks the Swiss with his sword, defeats them, and rejoices the fallen cavalier on his horse.

The Chevalier Bayard, celebrated in the martial annals of France by the name of "*Le Chevalier sans peur et sans reproche,*" and who contributed much to the gaining the battle of Marignan, is also complimented in this and several other pictures, and particularly in one where he is represented knighting the king, who had desired to receive a sword from this celebrated warrior. The speech addressed by the *chevalier* to his sword on this occasion is recorded in history

> *Glorieuse épée qui aujourd'hui a eu l'honneur de faire chevalier le plus grand roi du monde, tu seras comme relique gardée; je ne t'emploirai plus que contre les infidelles et ennemis du nom chrétien.*

In another picture the *chevalier* is represented as having received his mortal wound at the battle of Romagnano.

Much merit is due to Monsieur de Vilieneuve, for having preserved so many interesting pictures and remains of antiquity in this *château*.

From Chenonceau we returned to Amboise by a tolerable road, over some fields and through woods where the riding was good, until we reached the *château* of Chanteloup,[1] which I have before noticed as being the property of Monsieur de Chaptal, a senator. After dinner the commandant, a most respectable old gentleman, paid us a visit at Captain Lutyens; he strongly avowed his attachment to the ancient dynasty, under which he had served with distinction, and expressed his hopes of the campaign terminating in the destruction of the Usurper, and of . the satellites who are his accomplices, in subjugating, and degrading France.

---

1. Before the Revolution the princely residence of the Duke and Duchess de Choiseul, the patrons of the Abbé Barthelemy, author of *Les Voyages du jeune Anacharse en Grèce*, and who it is said wrote this celebrated work principally at Chanteloup. See Chapter 32 of this book.

CHAPTER 48

Russian prisoners

February 23. Quitting Amboise on the 23rd, in a very severe frost, I continued my journey for Tours, where I arrived early, and put up at the same hotel as when there before. Neither the house nor the people had undergone the slightest alteration, and the latter were employed exactly in the same manner, and in the same spot, where I had left them three years before. This unchangeable mode of life, so different from the rapid succession of variety to which I had been accustomed, made me reflect on the various habits and astonishing mobility of the human character, which enables us to accustom ourselves to manners of living totally opposite.

Though, like a horse in a mill, pursuing an eternal round of monotonous sameness, yet my hosts of Tours were content and happy. Their son, who had been drawn for the conscription when I was last at that place, had the good fortune to be placed and to remain as writer in the office of a depôt, and the daughter was on the eve of marriage with a person approved of by her parents.

Soon after my arrival I was visited by Captain Gerrard, to whom I had a few days before remitted some thousands of *francs* in cash, for the relief of the soldiers passing through Tours, and the distribution of which he had kindly undertaken.

The number of Russian prisoners I saw at Tours, exceeding ten or twelve thousand men, at first surprised me rather disagreeably; but I was soon relieved on this head, by a conversation with Mr. Wilkes, a remarkably intelligent and well informed English gentleman, whom I have already mentioned. He assured me that these prisoners were now only paraded to amuse and deceive the people, the greatest part of them having been taken near Smolensko, and in the course of the Russian campaign. This I found was now a common practice, for as even the most ignorant were so well aware of the hyperbole of the newspapers, that "*faux comme les journaux,*" has become a proverb, other stratagems were obliged to be resorted to, therefore, the same prisoners are kept continually marching, so as apparently to be in two or three places at once. This reminds me of the well known observation of Sir Boyle Roche in the Irish House of Commons:

and you know, Mr. Speaker, I could not be in two places at once, Mr. Speaker, unless I was a little; bird, Mr. Speaker.

Sir Boyle might however now observe, instead of the little bird, "unless I was a prisoner in France, Mr. Speaker."

Having dined and passed an agreeable evening with Captain Gerrard, I proceeded the next morning on my route, after delivering a letter to General Lynch, an Irish officer, long in the French service, and now inspector of reviews. The streets were so crowded with prisoners, that I could scarce make my way through them; but at length getting clear of them, I pursued my route by an excellent road, and through fine country, particularly in the vicinity of Tours, where are several magnificent *châteaux*, formerly belonging to the first families of France, but which by the effects of the Revolution have fallen into the hands of a very different class of persons. The former *évêché*, or bishop's palace, is on an eminence, about two miles from Tours, commanding a fine view of the Loire and Cher, and has the appearance of a respectable English country mansion.

Crossing the Cher by a handsome hewn stone bridge, I reached Loches late in the evening, the distance from Tours being ten leagues. Here I met some English acquaintance, with whom I proposed passing .the next day on a shooting party. We found the town's people extremely civil, and in the morning a French gentleman politely offered to accompany us to the ground, where we might find plenty of snipes, the only game now to be met with. In order to arrive at it, we had to cross a rapid stream in a punt, and one of our company being a naval officer, boldly undertook to manage it, at which the Frenchman expressed his apprehensions, from the rapidity of the current; but, on being told that *Monsieur* was *un marin Anglais*, he was perfectly satisfied of his skill and address, and embarked with entire confidence.

No sooner, however, was the boat cast off from the shore, than the current took her under the lee, and all the skill of *le marin Anglais* was of no effect, the boat being carried rapidly sideways towards a mill; when the Frenchman, seeing the danger, jumped up to his neck in the water, and having gained the shore cried out, "*vous êtes tous perdus!*" which was far from consoling. However, by doubling our exertions, we fortunately reached the bank without accident.

In conversation afterwards, the Frenchman observed that he had always entertained a high opinion of *la marine Anglaise* until now, but that he would never again enter into a boat of which, one of them undertook the direction. This I could not help thinking was something similar to the calling on Sir Joseph Banks to regulate the paper currency of England, because he was an excellent judge of coins; for certainly it is most impossible, to conceive a greater contrast, than between an English man of war and a river punt, managed with a single pole or a paddle: yet such were our French companion's ideas on the subject, that from this trivial circumstance he formed his opinion of the whole British navy, and doubtless in all societies will in future abuse them as lubbers.

The snipes being, wild we had little sport, and returned early to Loches, the castle of which I visited while dinner was preparing. It is celebrated for the long siege it sustained from the English, who were obliged to retire and leave it unconquered; as well as for containing the tomb of the beautiful Agnes Sorrel , the favourite mistress of the weak Charles the Seventh of France, and who governed this monarch until his death in 1450. This monument, which is in the prefecture, is only remarkable by the remain, of the celebrated person it covers, and by the four lines on it, supposed to be written by Francis the First, after her death, and which I copied:

> Gentille Agnes, plus d'honnear tu mérite,
> La cause étant de France recouvrer.
> Que ce que peut dedans un cloître ouvrer, .,
> Close nonnaire ou bien dévot hermitte.

Loches is said to contain between four and five thousand inhabitants, and was the residence of several English families during the last peace. Adjoining it is a little town, which having separate magistrates and separate customs, caused frequent disputes, until at last both towns referred themselves to the National Assembly, which, after mature deliberation, passed a decree that the town so close upon Loches should be considered as being distant ten leagues from it! Whether this curious revolutionary decree had the effect of terminating their disputes I could not learn.

In the morning I pursued my journey along the banks of the Indre, and through the town of Chastillon on that river. It is a miserable place with very narrow streets and an ill-looking race of inhabitants, who seemed to gaze with astonishment at my horse, the shortness of whose ears attracted their notice, as well as that of all the persons I had lately met on the road; nor was I aware of their ignorance of their being cropt, until overtaking two decent looking farmers, one of them, after expressing his surprise, requested to know where the breed of short-eared horses was to be procured? to which I answered "that it was extremely scarce, having been originally imported from the island of Ceylon into England by the late Duke of Queensbury, who specified particularly in his will that no more of the breed should be permitted to go out of the family; and that consequently it was now become impossible to procure one of them."

The former expressed his thankfulness for this information,

saying, "that he had always been curious in horse-flesh, and that he thought himself very fortunate in meeting so accidentally *un Monsieur Anglais, en route.*"

In the evening I reached the village of Buzançais, where I put up at the sign of la Tête Noir (the blackamoor's head), a small inn kept by a *mulatto* of St Domingo; who, from the little knowledge of the inhabitants of this part of the country of foreign parts, was as great a curiosity to them as my horse with short ears. Here, however, I got an excellent dinner, and comfortable accommodation, and from hence I sent an express to three Russian generals, to whom I had written from Loches, informing them I should meet them at Chateauroux, and from whom I received the answer in the Appendix.

Early in the morning I resumed my journey, and arrived at Chateauroux before noon, where I put up in a miserably uncomfortable inn, called le Petit St Jean, which I strongly recommend all travellers to avoid. Here I found General Poltoratski, who accosted me with the familiarity of an old friend, and introduced me to Lieutenant General Olsouffief and another officer. These gentlemen belonged to the corps commanded by the Prussian General Blucher, and had been made prisoners. General Poltoratski, asking me if I had seen the gazette, and on replying in the negative, proposed going to the café, which, being Sunday, we found crowded with a strange mixture of peasants, postilions, barbers, common soldiers, and officers with the *croix d'honneur*, jumbled indiscriminately, and playing, at domino, backgammon and billiards, for *sous*. The general was quite *au fait* in the proper reading of the French papers, giving to every line its true meaning, though dressed up in language to deceive the people, and shewing incontestably, from the local position of the armies, that what they announced as brilliant victories were in fact complete defeats.

On returning to the inn, where I had promised to dine with the Russian officers, we found in the apartment a factious and loquacious French gentleman, who made continual puns, and abused Napoleon and his government with the greatest freedom; at the same time expressing his attachment to Russia, and his admiration of the Russian character, which I could not help inwardly thinking was going rather too deep in the hyperbolic; for though a Russian may possess sterling good qualities, as to his amiability, according to the French acceptation of the word, it was too ridiculous.

On asking the general who this person was, he assured me that he knew nothing more of him, than from his self-introduction, with the profession of his attachment to Russia, and the offer of his services. To which I observed, "he certainly could not suppose that a Frenchman, in a miserable inland town, in a very remote part of France, could appreciate the Russian character, of whose country he had .probably never heard, until the events of the late campaign had so terribly forced the knowledge on him; and in this case his information could only be derived from the French newspapers, which it must be allowed did not place the Russians in the most amiable point of view."

Consequently I doubted much if this civil gentleman was not a spy, or at best had intruded himself into our society, knowing us to be foreign officers, with the intention of leading us to abuse Buonaparte, and of reporting our conversation to the authorities of the town, in order to ingratiate himself with them, or of denouncing us to the police.

> "But," I continued, "if this is his object, let us indulge him, by turning Napoleon and his government into ridicule, and shewing our contempt for the authorities; and, if he should attempt to espouse their cause, we can shew him the short way downstairs over the balusters, or the still more expeditious route, out of the window."

The Russian, who was a lively pleasant fellow, and detested a Frenchman from his heart, cordially agreed to this proposal, and we again resumed our conversation with him. We first discussed the character of the present French, expressing our surprise at their tamely suffering themselves to be trampled on by a tyrant, and to be made the tools of his wild ambition and vanity; adding, that, the authorities, who executed his atrocious designs, were, if possible, as worthy of universal detestation as himself.

"In fact, *Monsieur*," I concluded, "the word *canaille*, whose synonym is to be found in no language but your own, and which before the Revolution was only applied to a portion of the people, has since that period become applicable to the whole nation; for none but a *peuple canaille* could have so slavishly borne the various species of tyranny inflicted on them by their successive rulers, during the last twenty years,"

The Russian observed, it was not prudent to speak so freely before the servants, and the Frenchman agreeing with them, I replied;

that I had no fear in doing so; for the authorities must be aware of our sentiments, as prisoners, who asked no favours from them; who were constantly overlooked, and to whom the most they could do was to place us in closer confinement, by which we should be released from our *parole d'honneur*, and all obstacles be done away to our taking the first opportunity of escaping to our friends.

The Frenchman observed, with much complaisance, "*Monsieur a raison*," and then turned the subject by contrasting the national character before the Revolution with that of the present day; which was infinitely to the disadvantage of the latter.

Having finished our dinner, we were entering our carriages to proceed; when a crowd of people, who had assembled round them, cried out, "*Vive l'Empereur, Vive Napoleon*;" for which it is more than probable they were paid, in order to convince us of the *bons sentimens* of the people. The Russian general, instead of seeming annoyed, made a motion as if paying money from one hand to another; which clearly conveyed the idea of "poor devils, you are paid for this bawling!"

From Chateauroux (which is a wretched dirty town, though of eight thousand inhabitants, situated on the Indre, of which department it is the chief place) I pursued my route towards La

Chatre, while the Russian officers followed the post road; they being furnished with post horses at the expense of the French Government, a favour denied to the English in the same situation.

Soon after leaving Chateauroux I passed a very extensive iron forge, on a branch of the Indre; but which has been unemployed for the last ten years, the proprietors having become bankrupts from the destructive effects of Napoleon's continental system on every species of national industry. The iron mines are at a short distance in a forest, and their produce is remarked for its extreme softness. I slept at the village of Ardente, three leagues from Chateauroux; and the following day reached La Chatre, five leagues further; where I put up at the Grand St. Germain, an excellent house, with superior Bourdeaux and other wines.

At La Chatre was a corps of disarmed German soldiers, who had been hitherto allowed their rations and a certain daily sum of money, but which were now stopped, and they were ordered to be distributed in the villages and quartered on the inhabitants, for whom they were obliged to labour for their food. The want of money, indeed, began to be most seriously felt by the French government; and a total cessation of payment of their troops, as well as of those holding civil offices, and even of the clergy, was the consequence.

At the same time, all confidence being destroyed between the government and the people, no contracts could be established; those who had accepted such contracts, latterly, having been paid in government *bons*, which were now of no value. The bakers, therefore, refusing to furnish bread, were themselves put in requisition to bake the flour the millers were obliged to supply; and every other kind of provision for the army was procured in the same manner, until at length the people began to complain. In order to reconcile them to these requisitions, the most exaggerated reports of the atrocities committed by the allied troops, were industriously circulated in every village and hamlet, and the most forcible appeals made to the national spirit and energy, as well as to the personal fears of the people, to induce them to come forward with their last resources, as the only means of freeing their country and escaping, themselves from, the horrors of a visitation of Cossacks.

The more enlightened of the people, foreseeing that these appeals would soon be followed by forced contributions of every kind, hastened to sell their horses and cattle for any price they could get; and their suspicions were soon realized, by a general requisition of horses, cattle, sheep, flour, &c. Such was the discontent of all classes, that had the Allies adhered to the tenor of their proclamations in respecting the persons and property of the people, they would have been everywhere received as deliverers, with open hands; and the downfall of Napoleon would have been soon decided.

For six leagues from La Chatre, towards Gueret, the route is almost impracticable for carriages on springs; and had it not now been hardened by the frost we should never have got over it. In this direction a new road has been marked out and commenced at intervals, which if finished as it has been begun will equal in solidity even the Roman military ways; the foundation being laid of vast stones covered with flints, limestone, and in many places a species of marble. This road is intended to open a communication, by post, between Chateauroux and Gueret, and by that means with Tours and Orleans, with which the department of the Creuse has hitherto had no other public communication, except by Limoges and Moulins, causing a round of twenty and thirty leagues.

It is undoubtedly but doing justice to Napoleon to observe, that his plans for the internal improvement of France were vast and judicious; particularly in opening new communications between the different parts of the empire, by roads and canals; his wild ambition has however prevented the far greater number of these projected works from being finished, and many of them from being even commenced; and as there is no spirit of private enterprise or improvement among the French, such as we find in England, these projected designs will certainly lay dormant, until the government is sufficiently recovered from its present paralysed state to execute them.

The badness of the road between La Chatre and Genouillat (a poor village where I put up for the night), is in some measure compensated, by the appearance of the country, which is highly picturesque; presenting a succession of hills and valleys, almost entirely under pasture, and shaded by masses of enormous chestnut-tress. The habitations are here so thinly scattered, that the deserts of America can scarcely be more solitary; and the few human beings met with, are almost as savage in their appearance, and equally unintelligible in their language, as the most uncivilized of the Indian tribes.

From Genouillat the road is finished to Gueret, a distance of five leagues, and is excellent, winding round the bases of the hills in an endless succession of curves, so that the sun is alternately before and behind you. The country still grows more romantic, and about three leagues from Gueret the road is along the side of a glen, through which runs the Creuse, and which equals almost any spot of the same kind, even in Ireland.

The difficulty of procuring lodgings at Gueret was, as might be supposed, even greater than at Blois, the town containing only three thousand inhabitants; the prices asked were, therefore, not only exorbitant beyond conception, but there was not even room for one half the depôt; so that upwards of two hundred persons were obliged to sleep in stables or barns for several nights, and those who were lodged, were almost as uncomfortable, the houses being filthy In the extreme, and without even the most common and necessary furniture Added to which, the inhabitants appeared to be a most uncivil race, and soon proved that they merited the character we had heard of them, of being the most litigious and ill-disposed people of France.

A friend who had arrived before me. engaged me a lodging at three hundred *francs* a month, for which price I was to have a small dining room and anti-chamber, a bedroom closet for a servant, and the use of the kitchen. The landlord, his wife, and daughter, were all civility on my arrival; but after I had slept one night in the house, their conduct totally changed; doubtless, from the intention of making me so uncomfortable, that I should be obliged to quit the lodging, when they would force me to pay the three months' rent, and immediately let it to another. They began by informing me, at I could not dine in the dining room next, that my dinner could not be drest in the kitchen; and, finally, that my wine could not be put into the cellar, as it would interfere with their own.

Upon inquiring into the meaning of these strange restrictions, and why they had not mentioned them previous to my entering the house, they were all so civil, and made so many bows and grimaces, that I could not tell what to make of them, nor could I bring them to any direct conclusion; I was therefore obliged to tell them that their customs and habits seemed so directly contrary to mine, that it was quite impossible I could remain in the house, to put them so much out of their way; and I concluded, by asking, "what I should have to pay, if I immediately found a house to suit me?"

To which the landlord replied, shrugging up his shoulders, "*Rien de tout, mon Dieu, milord, on n'en pense pus;*" adding, that I might remain four or five days, until I could suit myself, and that he should be but too much flattered by the honour I did him."

The same evening I found a house in the country, two leagues distant, which I removed to the following morning, though the greater part of the road to it was totally impassable by a carriage, being across ravines and over huge masses of rock, morasses and deep fords.

On taking my leave of the lady and her daughter, I again asked if I had anything to pay for the two nights I had slept in the house? With abundance of compliments, she refused listening to anything of the kind, and we parted with mutual civilities, having made a handsome present to the maid, which I thought might be considered as a compliment to the mistress. Two days after, I was not a little surprised at learning, that the landlord had called on the gentleman who engaged the lodging for me, to demand the month's rent; I immediately caused the fellow to be informed, that if I was to pay for the lodgings not being able to occupy it myself, I, doubtless, had a right to dispose of it as I thought proper; and therefore should put two *tapageurs* of my acquaintance into it, who having hard heads and good lungs, generally sat up all night, smoking, drinking punch, and singing jovial songs; and whom I should request to accommodate three or four of my favourite dogs with the use of the dining room. In short, that I would occupy the lodging in what manner I pleased, until the expiration of the month.

This threat had such an effect on my extortionate landlord and his wife, that they came to an accommodation, and I agreed to pay them one hundred and fifty *francs*, rather than be involved in a litigious dispute, with such *canaille*. This is only one of a thousand cases I have had occasion to know and I mention it not only as giving an idea of French character, but as a caution to others to beware of complaisance and grimace, which generally only cover some design of imposition.

CHAPTER 49

Department of the Creuse

This department of the Creuse, comprising the ancient province of La Marche, is so much out of the track of English travellers in general, and so very different from the more frequented parts of France, that I trust my readers will not find a short descriptive sketch of it uninteresting, formed as well from my own observations as from the information of persons well acquainted with it, and from the printed statistical accounts.

With respect to the face of the country, this department is composed of chains and groups of mountains and hills, separated by very narrow valleys or glens; the summits, named in the country *puys*, have the form of rounded hummocks, and are evidently the remains of peaked mountains, whose conical heads have been worn away by the elements, and which there can be no doubt anciently contained volcanoes, from the strata of *scoriae* and basalts found in many of the valleys.

The composition of the mountains is granitic and schistose. Their greatest elevation in this department does not exceed eight hundred and fifty feet; but their ramifications, which extend into the neighbouring countries, rise to greater heights, the Golden Mountain, or Puy de Dome, in the next department, for instance, being six thousand feet above the level of the sea, and its summit retaining the snow nearly throughout the year.

La Creuse, as may be supposed from the nature of its surface, is most profusely watered; the rivulets, which have their sources in the mountains, descend with violent rapidity into the valleys, where their union forms numerous secondary rivers, whose waters in their turns are lost in the Loire. The springs which gush out from the surface are so innumerable, that it is difficult to find one hundred square feet of dry soil to build on; and hence, with the most trifling labour, every hamlet has a stream sufficient to turn its mill.

None of the rivers of this department are, however, considerable, either as to breadth or depth; their sources being very elevated and their courses short, they wind but little, running with great rapidity through narrow glens and ravines, and over a bottom of granite and schistose, which renders them useless for transport, even by floating, and present almost insurmountable obstacles to their being rendered navigable. The Creuse and the Cher, both of which have their rise in and traverse the department, are alone deserving of particular mention. The course of the former is almost internal, through ravines formed on each side by rocky precipices, whose bases are in many places so eaten into by the current, that they overhang add appear ready to fall into it. The Creuse, as well as the other rivers and rivulets of this department, generally abound in excellent trout, perch, carp, tench, pike, barbel, eels, and lampreys.

There are but few spots of, properly speaking, marshy land in the department, the rapid declivity of the soil not admitting the stagnation of the waters. It has, however, a great number of ponds, both natural and artificial, formed by the union of springs, and which serve as reservoirs of fish, from whence the market is regularly and certainly supplied. The water of these ponds being continually removed, is productive of no noxious effects on the atmosphere.

The temperature of the Creuse is subject to great variations; the air is in general very sharp and pure, but the sudden changes caused by, the thunder storms and rains, render the climate disagreeable and ungenial to foreigners; besides, the elevation of the soil, the mountains, and the superabundance of water, render the general temperature cold and humid. During the winter, rain is less frequent than snow, which covers the country for some months. In the summer, thunderstorms are frequent and violent, and in this season thick fogs also arise from the valleys. In short, according to the information of the inhabitants, the spring commences late, the summer is short, the autumn fair and pleasant, and the winter long and severe.

The diseases most prevalent seem to arise from the nature of the climate, and to be immediately caused by checked perspiration; besides, diseases not dangerous in themselves, are here often rendered mortal by the improper methods of treatment, the great mass of the inhabitants, and those of the country in particular, having recourse to the most absurd or most dangerous practices.

From what has been already said, it will be inferred that the department has no plain of any extent; nevertheless though the face of the country has in general a melancholy, and sometimes even a savage aspect, from the summits of many of the hills presenting only a black heath, fern, broom, furze, and other plants denoting sterility, the whole is far from being displeasing to the eye, and many of the valleys and glens having each its clear rivulet, shaded by antique oaks and chestnut trees, present a series of varied and picturesque sites of the first beauty.

With respect to the soil of the department, it is in general of little depths lights poor and infertile, covering a base of granite rocky which in many spots rises in naked masses above the surface. Both the nature of the soil and the superabundance of water, naturally point out this country as fit only for pasture and wood, and accordingly the portion of tillage is extremely trifling. The summits of the hills are generally barren wastes, the sides near the summits usually covered with coppice wood or chestnut, and towards their bases formed into meadows.

Though there are but few masses of wood deserving the name of forest in the department, the hedge enclosures, which are multiplied to a great degree, are thickly planted with oak, ash, beach, birch, poplar, chestnut, and other inferior trees, whose branches afford abundant fuel. The oak also affords , sufficiency of wood for buildings, as well as timber of the first size and quality for naval construction, but which the difficulty of transport to the naval arsenals renders so extremely dear, the quantity they receive from this part of the country is comparatively trifling.

The science of apiculture and rural economy seems to have made less progress, in the department of the Creuse than in any other I have had occasion to visit in France, and in these respects it is at least two hundred years behind the present state of improvement The minute subdivision of property, which precludes the employment of any considerable capital, and the general ignorance of the cultivators, and consequent inveterate adherence to old bad methods, are the principal causes of this want of improvement.

With respect to manure, the department possessing neither lime nor marle, the melioration of the soil is confined entirely to stable dung, or to the leaves of trees, collected and spread in the avenues to the farms to rot. The instruments of agriculture are extremely defective, the plough only turning up the soil at the very surface, and the use of the harrow and roller being almost unknown.

The grain cultivated are winter and spring rye, the former sewed in September and the latter in March. This is the only grain which does not degenerate, and its cultivation is therefore, the most extended. Sarrazin, or black wheat, is also cultivated in all parts of the department, and forms a considerable portion of the food of the inhabitants; it is also given to the hogs and poultry. The quantity of wheat produced is so trifling, that the department is obliged to import nineteen-twentieths for its consumption.

Oats are also in small quantity, and of a very poor and small kind. Potatoes are an object of considerable cultivation and form a portion of the constant food of the inhabitants, as well as of the domestic animals; either from the quality of the soil, or the imperfect cultivation, they are watery and insipid. The round turnip is also produced in quantity, and of good quality; and has of late years been employed in the fattening of cattle.

All the common fruit-trees succeed in this department, such

as the apple, pear, plum, cherry, &c. whose fruits form a small object of export to the neighbouring country. The chestnut tree covers a considerable portion of the department, but its fruit is small and insipid, no attention being paid to its cultivation, though in several districts it forms the chief food of the people for six months of the year. The climate is unfavourable to the finer stone-fruit; as the peach, apricot, or nectarine, as well as to the vine, which latter is only seen *en treillage* in gardens.

The principal riches of the department consist in its horned cattle; and the bullock is the only animal whose rearing and management is properly understood or attended to. It is also used in country labour, whether in the plough or in cross road conveyance; and when aged, is fattened up and sent to supply the markets of some of the great towns on the road to Paris. Cows are much more neglected, and being very badly fed during the winter give but little milk; and the butter, though it forms a trifling object of export to the chief towns of the adjoining departments, is neither cheap nor good.

The sheep are very small, their wool coarse, and their flesh indifferent, chiefly owing to the ignorant manner of keeping them, for the department affords abundant mountain pasture covered with aromatic herbs. The race of horses is also small and badly formed; and as bullocks are almost alone used in country labour, little attention is paid to their multiplication or improvement; and hence their numbers are only sufficient for the use of the department. The asses and mules are also small: the former are little used, but the latter form an article of export to the neighbourhood, and even to Spain. Hogs are a very material branch of rural economy; pork forming not only the greatest portion of the animal food of the people, but a considerable number of the live animals are exported to Bourdeaux, la Rochelle, and Rochefort, for provisioning the navy.

The department has abundance of game; such as hares, partridges, woodcocks, wild ducks, snipes, &c. Foxes and wolves are also numerous; but it has neither wild boars nor deer. With respect to market provisions, the beef and mutton are both very indifferent, the slaughter for the market being chiefly confined to old dried up cows; and the sheep being almost starved during the long winter, their flesh is uneatable until the month of June. The veal, on the contrary, is good, and with pork forms the chief provision of the flesh market. The price of all these meats vary from to seven *sous* the pound, according to the quality. The markets are poorly supplied with poultry, as well as with vegetables; a common sized onion costing a *sou*: in short, the delicate appetite will here find little to gratify it, and even the most indifferent soon grows disgusted with the eternal round of carp, veal, pork and hares.

The department possesses few minerals yet discovered; they are confined to antimony, iron and coals. The working of one or two mines of the first has been discontinued since the Revolution; those of iron have never been opened, and the want of convenient land or water carriage confines those of coal to a mere trifle. The department is known to possess only one warm springs which is sulphurous, and of the temperature of 47° of Reaumur. Ferruginous springs are found in several places.

The industry of the inhabitants of this department is almost entirely confined to rural economy; the only manufactures it possesses being a few of paper, carpeting and tapestry, and very coarse woollens, and common hats for the peasantry. The household linen is the produce of the female peasants, who while tending their sheep are also occupied in spinning. The exports are bullocks, sheep, hogs and mules, some butter; and of manufactured objects, paper and carpeting.

On the other hand, the department is obliged to import all its wine, nineteen-twentieths of its wheat, all its salt, iron, fine manufactures, and colonial produce: so that the balance of trade is entirely against it; and hence it would be one of the poorest departments of the empire, did it not receive an influx, of specie from another channel. It is calculated that forty thousand of its inhabitants emigrate every year, and visit all parts of France in search of employment: they are all workmen; chiefly masons, tilers, sawyers, house-painters, wool and flax-combers, &c.

They remain absent nine months, and return with their earnings to pass the other three with their wives and families in the department. It is said not to be uncommon for one of these work, men to bring back three thousand *francs*, and even so much as six thousand in specie, which produces a circulation far above what would result from the territorial products and balance of its commerce.

The inhabitants have a peculiarity of character, both physical and morale which distinguishes them, and by no means favourably, from the natives, of the other provinces. With respect to their persons; they are generally below rather than above the middle size, thick set, stout and robust; their features are far from giving a prepossessing idea of their dispositions, those of the men being morose and ferocious, and of the women coarse and ugly in the extreme. The contour of the face is almost a perfect circle, the chin being extremely short, the forehead low, and the cheeks elevated; which, together with their small round eyes, give them more the resemblance of certain Tartar tribes, than of natives of the interior of *la belle France*.

Their own countrymen accord them the praise of being naturally intelligent, sprightly and industrious; but we have almost universally found them to be uncivil even to insolence, litigious, cheats, and filthy both in their persons and dwellings, the latter being scarcely fit for the reception of hogs. In their favour, we must however observe, that the men are sober, which is sufficiently evinced by the very few cabarets in Gueret in comparison with towns of the same population in other parts of France; and that the women of the lower class, particularly in the villages, are chaste before marriage, and faithful after.

In short, the general corruption of manners, which we have had occasion to notice in other parts, seems as yet to have made but little progress in this obscure department, probably from the few communications it possesses with any large towns. The husbands are here the perfect lords and masters of their wives, the subordination and submission of the latter being extreme, and by far the greater portion of their laborious duties, both within and without doors, falling on them. In short, the good and bad qualities of these people, are those of the demi-savage, beyond which state of society they have scarcely arose.

The common language of the peasants is a coarse and harsh *patois*, a dialect of the ancient Languedoc, which differs in almost every commune. The men, however, also speak French, but the women, though they understand the language, always answer any question in *patois*. Education seems to be less attended to in this department than in any we have visited, few of the men being able to write, and none of the women. The town of Gueret, the principal of the department, has two booksellers' shops, of which about one hundred romances, and an assortment of church and children's books, form the whole stock; and it would be difficult to find a private collection of fifty volumes in the whole town.

We have noticed from our own experience the litigious disposition of the people of this department, and hence it is crowded with lawyers, bailiffs, and all the other myrmidons of litigation, with whom Gueret, in particular, is almost entirely peopled, and who find constant employment, and as constantly amass fortunes, to the total ruin of him who gains a cause, as well as of him who loses it.

We shall conclude this sketch with an extract from a published description of the department, which notices the gradual change in the manners of its inhabitants. By inference perhaps it may exhibit no unfaithful description of the general state of all the departments of France, since the present corruption of manners has borne sway in consequence of the Revolution.

> For some years past a great revolution has been going on in the manners and customs of the peasantry of this department. It is not above twenty years since they quitted their ancient costume, which consisted in their long hair flowing loosely on their shoulders, a very short coat of the coarsest grey frieze, a jacket of the same, almost as long as the coat, and a waistcoat under the jacket, pantaloons of

the same cloth descending to the ankle, and over them worsted stockings ascending and gartered above the knee, and *sabots*.

At present this dress is only used by some old men, the young ones universally adopting the long coat, short waistcoat, breeches, stockings and shoes on high days, *sabots* being still universally worn both in the town and country. Since the Revolution the peasant has also become less sober, and in his visits to the towns he spends a part of his money in the cabarets, in wine, beer, liqueurs, and even in coffee; of which, a few years ago, he had never heard the name.

The progress of luxury among the female peasants is equally remarkable: the girls accustomed to clean out the cow-house, and destined to do so all their lives, purchase for their weddings, silks, *cambrick* (which is passed on them for English[1]), silk stockings, and lace for their head dress, at forty *francs* an ounce. Twenty years ago the names of all these objects were unknown to this class of people.

The population of the department is estimated at two hundred and eighteen thousand souls. Its permanent contribution of taxes are.

	Francs.
Land tax	880,000
Personal and sumptuary tax	94,000
Doors and windows	27,800
Total	1,001,800

Which gives four *francs* seventy *centimes* (about four shillings sterling) *per annum* per cent, which is nearly doubled during war.

---

1. This parenthesis of the French author is worthy of notice, as it proves, that even in the most obscure parts of France, the superiority of English manufactures is known and appreciated.

CHAPTER 50

Departure of English Prisoners

The long and eventful contest, in which Europe and the world had been for such a period engaged, had now the appearance of drawing to a termination; each day conveyed intelligence, notwithstanding every artifice that could be imagined was practised by the Prefect and the authorities, to keep the English, and those of the French inhabitants of Gueret who were secretly attached to the Bourbon family, in ignorance. We read the French papers, all replete with accounts of the most brilliant victories obtained by Napoleon over the Allies, and at one time his advance looked rather despondent, judging from the date of his headquarters.

The plan however soon became evidently for the Allies to act on the defensive, either until their force was assembled, or with the intention of harassing the French troops, and increasing (if possible) their discontent. We heard of the surrender of Bourdeaux, as well as that of Lyons; and judging, from the small space of territory in Napoleon's possession, either for the advantage of conscription or for levying taxes, we had the secret consolation to know that his career, from such a diminution of resources, must very soon terminate. The people, moreover, refused paying taxes, and neither officer, soldier, or civil magistrate, received pay.

The prisoners, of which there were about seventy thousand in the neighbourhood, were billeted on the inhabitants of villages, who were forced to find them in everything, and they were of no farther expense to the state. At length the account arrived of the downfall of Paris, an event scarcely to be credited, were we to judge from the resolutions of its inhabitants, and their declaration so shortly before, on Napoleon's departure for the army, "that before the Allies should enter Paris a rampart should be made of the bodies of its citizens."

As to this wonderful rampart, and the change which so suddenly took place in the general sentiments of the French nation, it is so recent on the minds of every person, that there can be no necessity for mentioning further particulars. Paris was apparently, however, considered of no consequence by the Buonapartists, as the Emperor could retire and defend, the banks of the Loire.

The interruption of communication with Paris was of short duration, for Napoleon did not long survive the loss of his *ci-devant* capital; and most anxiously indeed did we all look for his downfall not only as the means of obtaining our personal liberty, but for the rescue of France and of Europe from the dominion of a tyrant, that at one time had contrived to rivet chains so firm as to secure the persons of the French inhabitants, and render them subservient to his tyrannical and frantic exploits; and by the means of artifice, treachery, and fraud, had so far got possession of men's minds, as to make them his accomplices, or the instruments by which he either executed, or attempted to carry into execution, deeds that Frenchmen, now that they have leisure sure or time for reflection, must shudder at the idea of, and be ashamed to consider that they had so long been the slaves and the dupes to the despotic will of such a ruffian,

I had a country house some miles distant from the town of Gueret, over a bad road, having ravines, rivers, woods, and morasses to pass previous to arriving there; and is such a place, it may be presumed I was removed from the source of intelligence or of news, unless I went into the town.

One Sunday evening, having invited some friends to pass two or three days in the country, a strange event took place. While drinking our wine after dinner, three of the wine glasses broke spontaneously in pieces, and the wine ran about the table and on the floor; the clock, which before had struck tolerably correct, now struck two hundred and sixteen; the screech-owls, of which there were abundance in the neighbourhood, made a hideous noise, and appearances were altogether so strange, that I observed there must either have been an earthquake, or some most extraordinary event had taken place. Our imaginations, from being wound up to the highest pitch of conjecture and anxiety, to devise a cause for such strange occurrences, were soon set at rest by a most violent rapping at the door, which proved to be an express, that brought us the agreeable and wonderful intelligence of Napoleon's abdicating the throne, and the extraordinary change such an event has since created on the civil and political system of the world.

My companions had no objection to a cheerful glass of wine, and I brought forth the best the cellar could produce, of which we drank copiously to "the success of 'Old England,'" with the cheering and delightful prospect of once more visiting our long absent native country and our friends.

On the following day I went into the town of Gueret; the English were elated to madness; white cockades were soon exhibited by them; but the prefect, who had been strongly attached to Napoleon, would make nothing known; and the event was altogether so sudden and so wonderful, that one half of the inhabitants could not believe it, and were afraid to shew symptoms of joy, however rejoiced they might inwardly feel.

Our midshipmen became riotous, and the Imperial eagles which were exhibited in various parts of the town, as signs and emblems of Napoleon's omnipotence, were soon destroyed. A confirmation of the good news was coming into the town continually, although the prefect was obstinate. On the following day we formed a party to go to the play. The players were Bourbonists, or assumed that character; and although the mayor and many of the authorities had not received intelligence regularly from the prefect, they mounted the white cockade; the players came forward also in white cockades.

One of them had obtained a very large *croix de St. Louis*, and appeared in the formerly much respected character of an old

French officer. He was loudly applauded; but the musicians, who unfortunately could not play the tune of "God save the King," which possibly they had never heard of, were saluted from all quarters with so sharp a fire of apples and other missiles for their ignorance, that they were forced to seek their safety in flight.

The playhouse now exhibited a scene of friendly riot, confusion, and noise; the French and English mutually crying out "*vivent les Anglois, vivent les François,*" and complementing each other, so that the parts of the play were totally changed, the spectators or audience assuming the character of actors, while, *vice versa*, the actors became spectators.

An old French general, with a large hooked nose, met with great attention, from his having a *croix de St. Louis* and a conspicuously large white cockade; his appearance was quite a caricature, yet he created additional interest in the English, by his crying out, "*vivent les Anglois! vivent nos libérateurs!*" An Irish officer next seemed to attract notice, and to supersede the old general by his sudden appearance in the house.

The first words he uttered were, "*nous sommes libres, b— e; arrah,* blood and wounds, boys, is there none of you who can sing God save the, King?"—and after a short pause; "then, by Jasus," says he, "since that is the case, I must sing it myself." He accordingly jumped on the stage from the upper row of boxes, and was getting forward tolerably well with his song, when poor Pat suddenly disappeared in the prompter's hole, to the vast entertainment of the audience; for, it may be presumed, he never calculated on the possibility of such a hole being placed nearly in the middle of the stage.

It had however a good stage effect, and as he received no very material damage from his fall, he reappeared and got through the song, supported by so many discordant voices and notes, as to leave the French musicians and actors much at a loss to know the real composition of English music.

A great many prisoners from the several depôts marched through Gueret, having been liberated on the restoration of the Bourbons. They had been in sad distress, for want of money to forward them on their way, as the mode adopted by the French Government was of a very economical nature; for they turned them loose without giving them any clothing, or paying any arrears that were due.

The poor fellows, after their long confinement, were naturally delighted, and never inquired or examined into consequences; so with a light heart and cheerful disposition they proceeded for the nearest harbour, which was Bourdeaux, without a farthing to support them. My duty was to supply them with money and shoes, as far as I could procure them; but, as persons of their description are not in general very provident, they mostly drank out the money and sold the shoes.

When elated with liquor they conceived all Frenchmen indiscriminately had been the authors of their long captivity and misfortune, the windows therefore of the inhabitants suffered severely; Scarcely a pane of glass remaining unbroken in the town of Gueret. The interference of *gend'armes*, or military, was useless, as they could not be brought to act; and indeed they would have had little chance: yet as it was necessary to have a battle of some kind, they were obliged to fight among themselves. My old landlord informed me he had seen thirty-seven regular pitched battles, and asked me if this was really the usual mode of deciding differences of opinion in England?

"But," says he, "what astonished me most was, their friends, instead of separating the combatants, encouraged them."

He also gave a half-finished description of a bottle-holder, but both the name and the character were so novel and extraordinary to him, that he was perfectly at a loss to know what to make of it.

A *gend'arme* whom I afterwards met, well known among the English by the name of Black George, informed me he imagined that he had acquired some knowledge of the English character, after nearly eleven years constant study and experience; but must now confess himself equally as ignorant as when he commenced his studies.

CHAPTER 51

English at Paris

Previous to leaving my .country house, near Gueret, my landlord (the baron) wished to take a parting farewell, so came there, accompanied by two other gentlemen, one of whom was his son-in-law. Immediately I heard of his design to pay me a visit, I went intentionally out of the way, and desired the servant to say, I should not return until the following morning. So having gone to Gueret, I returned about seven o'clock in the evening, under the impression that they could not, with any reason or propriety, remain in my absence; when, to my surprise, I found them comfortably seated in the kitchen, getting the servant to dress them dinner. I could not avoid, with the least degree of propriety, inviting them to dine with me, of which invitation they cheerfully accepted.

Dinner was scarcely over, when the baron proposed a game at cards; but committed himself so much by his anxiety on the occasion, that I began to suspect he had a strong desire to win my money; and therefore informed him it; was not my intention to play that night. He commenced, however, to play with Monsieur de V——, in whose favour I made some bets, and won them, I soon perceived the baron was greatly inferior as to skill or knowledge of the game, either to his son-in-law or to monsieur V——, and I shortly, after conceived I might venture to attack him myself; at the same time, however, high as my opinion might be as to those two gentlemen, I thought them too closely connected, both in relationship and friendship, for me as an Englishman to admit of their looking over my hand in a friendly manner, I therefore kept my cards very close; and by this precaution I was a very considerable winner, at which the baron and his friends appeared seriously disappointed.

The baron, however, determined on making a coup by some means, inquired how much I would have for all my furniture on my departure? And concluded by offering me considerably under its value, supposing, from the situation in which I was placed, I was incapable of removing it. To which I answered "*Monsieur le Baron*, you are apparently much attached to the cause of Louis, XVIII. therefore if you wish to see a handsome bonfire in honour of that Monarch's restoration, you shall see it, provided I cannot sell the furniture to some advantage; and those pretty things, *Monsieur le Baron*, which you so much admire, shall contribute to create a blaze in commemoration of the wonderful event."

The following day I advertised, by means of the town-crier, an auction at my house, and gave a grand account of everything that was to be sold, and which I observed the purchasers were individually to take home. I also prepared a sumptuous breakfast, and notwithstanding all the exertions of the baron to prevent attendance, there was an immense concourse of people from Gueret and various parts of the country, to visit me auction.

They bid one against the other with great acrimony, for there were but few of them who had not some private dispute and bore great animosity one towards another, which terminated the affair so much in my favour, that the furniture, and various articles of little or no value, sold to an amount greatly exceeding my expectations. Such articles as the baron contrived to prevent being sold, and which he calculated would fall to his share, I made a bonfire of, according to promise.

My landlord being now in despair, furnished me with a most exorbitant bill, in which, among other charges, he demanded forty *francs* for a pony I had turned out (from his being lame), three or four times on a goose common, where it is well known there is nothing for a horse to eat I thought it, however, advisable to pay the money, and we parted. I met the baron soon after at the curious old general's at dinner, where, in my life, I never passed a more extraordinary day.

On the following morning, being the first of May, and Sunday, (a day which I prefer for commencing a journey, because I conceive it lucky, and you have moreover the additional advantage of having the prayers of the church in your favour) I took my departure for Paris. The roads were so very bad by La Chatre, that I sent the servants and carriage by a more circuitous road, and rode myself across paths and bye-roads until I reached that place: I must here observe, that great part of this road was on the banks of the river Creuse, and the scenes were pleasing and fanciful in the extreme, and only to be equalled by some of the picturesque views in Switzerland.

The banks of the river were most formidable and steep, being composed of rocky precipices, covered in most places with hanging woods, at the bottom of which the Creuse rolls with great rapidity, and frequently down steep rocks and precipices, which creates romantic and beautiful waterfalls, accompanied by an awful and murmuring noise. The fields were in the richest *verdure*, and as there were no inhabitants near, the *tout ensemble* had a solemn and imposing effect.

After leaving the town of Genouillat, I had to pass the same road I have already described. I conceived that the season of the year might have made a difference, and the road be better than when I last passed; but it was, if anything, worse, being now of a sticky, glutinous nature, so that my horse found great difficulty in extricating his feet.

On my arrival at La Chatre the inhabitants were making great preparations to celebrate the Peace; and unfortunately for me there was a dance, which continued the whole night, next to my room. This town, however, was rather slow in bringing forward the festival indeed, the inhabitants the character of being more attached to Buonaparte than the Bourbons, and I have observed this to be the case in most small towns. They are, however, more than counterbalanced by Paris, Bourdeaux, Lyons, Marseilles,

&c. Being in their favour.

On leaving La Chatre I went to Chateauroux, and from thence in a direct line to Orleans, where the following day there was a pompous procession, an illumination, and, a great fête, in honour of the Pucelle, which, in this instance, embraced two objects, including that in honour of peace.

On my arrival at Paris I found it so crowded, that it was with much difficulty accommodation could be procured, but which I at last obtained at my old quarters, Hôtel du Rhin; Rue du Helder. Russians, Austrians, Prussians, and Cossacks, were in all quarters, of, the town; as well as about fourteen thousand English, all of whom had an opportunity of beholding these novel and extraordinary scenes; for who could have imagined to see guards mounted at Paris by Russians, Cossacks parading in triumph through the streets, and nothing to be seen but foreign costume and the most extraordinary dresses?

The playhouses were so crowded, there was no obtaining a place, and it was the same with respect to the coffee-houses; I therefore found Paris very disagreeable after the novelty was over. I chanced to make a dinner party one day with seven of my countrymen, not one of whom could muster French enough to call for a spoon, but came much under the description that Boniface describes his master;"he says little, thinks less, and does nothing at all; but then he's a gemman of large fortune, and cares for nobody."

Whenever I went to the Salon des Etrangers, or any place of public play, old Blucher was sure to be there. He had been fortunate in the commencement, but I cannot say how his luck terminated; for my own part, though I won at first, I left Paris a considerable loser. In the play-houses you, heard of nothing but the *bon Henri, vive Henri, quatre, vivent les Bourbons.*

Nothing can possibly be a stronger lesson to instruct us in the uncertainty of human events, than the character and the fate of the first (Henry IV.) and last of that family (Louis XVI.) previous to the revolution. Henry the Third having died without issue, the branch, of Valois became extinct in his person, and the succession to the Crown. was Henry de Bourbon, King of Navarre, and the first of the Bourbon race. This Prince was born at Pau, in Bearn, on the 13th of December, 1553, of Antoine de Bourbon, Duc de Vendome, and of Jean d'Albert, Queen of Navarre, which has since been the cause of the Kings of France being stiled "*Roi de France et de Navarre.*"

He was descended in a right line from Robert de France, Comte de Clermont, and the sixth son of St Louis. It was in the *château* of Coaroaze, situated in the middle of rocks, between Bijone and Bearn, that the young Henry received the first rudiments of his education, where he was sent by order of his grandfather, who died sixteen months after his birth. He was brought up in every hardship, fed on black bread and cheese, used to run across the Bearnois rocks bareheaded and barefooted, and from having acquired habits of regularity, moderation, and sobriety, added to this mode of education, became the ornament and the glory of France. He had a strength of mind likewise, and great foresight, which taught him to know that kings were mortal, and but men.

It was, Henry the Fourth that inspired France with that gallantry and sentiment, for which she was so conspicuous previous to the Revolution. Henry had to combat against a powerful enemy, in those times of fanaticism, for he was a protestant The Duc d'Epernon and many of the *noblesse* retired from the scene, under pretence that they could not serve under a heretic. Others remained faithful but the Duc de Mayenne was his bitterest enemy; he proclaimed the Cardinal de Bourbon, who was then a prisoner, under the title of Charles the Tenth; though Henry IV. was then besieging Paris.

At the commencement of the siege the army consisted of about thirty thousand men in number; they were reduced by sickness and other misfortunes to four or five thousand; so that Henry was forced to raise the siege and retire towards Dieppe, The duke, and the army of the Ligue under his command, pressed him so close, that they said "the Bearnois (for that was his nickname), had no chance but to throw himself into the sea;"

yet, after all their boasting, Henry at last gave them battle, which was called the battle of Arques, where he defeated an army eight times his force; and at the conclusion wrote to his friend the Duc de Crillon:

"pends-toi, brave Crillon; nous avons combattus à Arques et tu n'y étois pas!

After this victory, having received a reinforcement of four thousand English, he spread terror at the gates of Paris, where they had falsely reported his defeat.

The Duc de Mayenne again attacked Henry, and was defeated at Ivry, in the year 1590, which action of itself was enough to immortalize Henry.

Henry the Fourth possessed the means of obtaining every person's regard and respect. He was one of the most unassuming and pleasant companions in the world, full of wit, and fond of cheerful society; and although he might at times have given offence, he had the means of repairing that offence so as to convert it into friendship and esteem.

Schomberg, who commanded an auxiliary German force under Henry, desired to have the pay for his troops; the King, having no money, was vexed and irritated at this demand, and replied, *"jamais homme de cour m'a demandé l'argent la veille d'une bataille."* Henry however, at the commencement of the battle, feeling that he had offended General Schomberg, addressed him as follows:

Monsieur de Schomberg, je vous ai offensé cette journée sera peut-être la dernière de ma vie; je ne veux point emporter l'honneur d'une gentilhomme; je connois votre mérite et votre valeur; je vous prie de me pardonner, et embrassez-moi."

Schomberg replied;

il est vrai que votre Majesté, m'a blessé l'autre jour; aujourd'hui elle me tue, car l'honneur qu'elle m'a fait m'oblige de mourir en cette occasion pour son service.

The brave German on that day signalized himself, and proved

his attachment and his valour, for he was in two hours after killed close to the King. Such traits are those of chivalry, and such is the real character of Frenchmen. How different to that which they assumed during the Revolution! how awkward and unnatural was their *grossièreté* to minds possessed of such refined sentiments!

Henry was equally conspicuous for his gallantry and his amours, as for his courage and his conduct in the field. Among many other favourites, we may reckon the beautiful and accomplished Gabrielle d'Estrees, Duchess of Beaufort. Henry lived for a long time separate from Marguerite de Valois; and his object was to obtain a divorce, and make Gabrielle his wife, which could not be accomplished. Gabrielle soon after dying, he became desperately enamoured with Henrietta, a daughter of the mistress of Charles the Ninth. She perfectly enslaved him, yet would not gratify him in any other manner but by a promise of marriage, to which he consented. The contract of marriage being signed, Henry shewed it to the great Sully, and asked his advice; when this courageous minister took the paper and tore it by way of reply,

"What," said the King in a rage, "are you mad?"

"*Il est vrai, Sire, je suis fou; je voudrois l'être si fort que je fusse le seul en France.*" Sully had no expectation but of being immediately disgraced; the greatness of mind, however, of the King instantly promoted him to be grand master of the artillery. The Pope having, through Sully's intrigue, granted Henry a divorce, he shortly after contracted a match more worthy, and married, in the year 1600, Marie de Medicis, by whom he had issue Louis XIII This great, this generous, this accomplished character was, when arrived at the summit of his grandeur (and on the eve of an expedition against the House of Austria, being detained for the coronation of the Queen, in the year 1610), basely assassinated by a desperate fanatic named Ravaillac, who was instigated by the priests.

Thus perished, in the fifty-seventh year of his age, the greatest prince Europe produced; and this was the fiftieth conspiracy formed against his life—so little do we know how to estimate great qualities? To him France is indebted for the Louvre and Pont Neuf, with various ornaments at Paris; the canal of Briare, which joins the Loire and the Seine, by this means opening the communication through France with the English Channel and the Atlantic Ocean. As Sully observed,

> time, which is the grand estimator of the great qualities of this Prince, could only be the means of developing his grand projects and wonderful enterprises.

At the Louvre there are some fine pictures of this great monarch worthy the attention of travellers.

As to Louis the Sixteenth, his misfortunes are recent on our minds; though some particulars relative to his outset in life may have escaped notice. At the time of his coming into the world the court was at Choisy, and the Dauphin was almost alone at Versailles; no splendour marked his birth, and the courier, who was commissioned to bear the news to the courts fell from his horse and died on the spot, without being able to discharge his office. Louis was immediately created Duc de Berri. When his father died in 1765, his grief was extreme; and when, in crossing the apartment, he heard for the first time, "way for the Dauphin!" he burst into tears and fainted.

His marriage with Marie Antoinette of Austria, the daughter of Maria Theresa, was celebrated under fatal auspices; for in the festival which the city of Paris gave on the occasion, more than four thousand people perished in the Place de Louis XV, pressed to death and suffocated for want of precaution;—the same place on which the unfortunate Louis was so foully murdered!

The Dauphin, greatly afflicted at this circumstance, for seven months sent part of his revenue to the lieutenant of police, for the relief of the victims of this unhappy affair. In 1774, when called to the throne by the death of his grandfather, he exclaimed, "oh, my God, what a misfortune!"

I shall here beg leave to give an extract from the *journal* of Monsieur de Malesherbes, concerning the latter end of that good but unfortunate monarch.

"As soon," said he, "as I had permission to enter the King's apartment, I hastened thither; and no sooner did he perceive me than he rose from a little table, on which a Tacitus lay before him open; clasping me in his arms, while his eyes were moistened with tears, he exclaimed, 'your sacrifice is the more generous, as you expose your own life, and cannot save mine!' I represented there would be no danger, either for him or me, so easy was it to defend him successfully; to which he replied 'I am well convinced they will condemn me; they have both the power and the will; but be that as it may, let us busy ourselves with the cause as if I was to gain it; and in fact I shall, for I shall leave behind me an unspotted memory.'

"Every day he assisted in examining papers, explaining motives and refuting complaints, with a firmness of mind and a serenity which his defenders admired as much as I did. When Deseze had completed his defence, he read it to us, and never did I hear anything more pathetic than a particular part of it; it affected us to tears. The King said to him, 'this must be omitted, I will not work on their feelings.' When the time of trial drew near, he one morning said to me, 'my sister has told me of a good priest who has not taken the oaths, and whom his obscurity may eventually save from persecution; this is his address; I request of you to go and speak to him, and to prepare him to come when I shall have obtained permission to see him;' he added, 'it is a strange commission for a philosopher, and such I know you to be, but if you suffered as much as I do, and if you were going to die as I am, I should wish you the same religious sentiments, which would console you more than philosophy.'

"When I returned from the Assembly, where he had desired to appeal to the people, I informed him that on coming out I had been surrounded by a great number of persons, who had all assured me be should not perish, or at least not till after the m and their friends. He changed colour, and said to me, 'do you know them? return to the Assembly, endeavour to discover some of them, declare to them I should never forgive them if one single drop of blood was shed for me; I would not suffer it to be shed when it might perhaps have preserved my crown and my life; I do not repent it.'

"It was I who first acquainted him that he was sentenced to die; he was in the dark, his back was turned towards a lamp that stood in the chimney, his elbows rested on a table, and his face was concealed in his hands; the noise I, made awoke him, and, looking steadfastly at me, he rose and said, 'I have been for two hours endeavouring to find out whether I have in the course of my life merited the lightest reproof from my subjects; now Monsieur de Malesherbes, I swear to you in all the sincerity of my heart, as a man who is going to appear before God, that I have constantly desired the happiness of the people, and have never formed a wish contrary to it.'

"I saw this hapless monarch once more, and assured him the priest whom he desired to see was coming; he embraced me, and said, 'death does not terrify me; I have the most complete confidence in the mercy of God.'"

On the 20th January, 1793, Louis without murmuring heard his sentence read and imparted it to his family himself, that he might teach them resignation. At midnight he heard, mass, threw himself on his bed, where he slept peacefully till awakened in the morning by his *valet de chambre* Clery, who came to dress him for the last time. At eight o'clock those who were to conduct him to the scaffold entered the apartment, and with a firm step he descended the tower stairs, crossed the court, casting a last glance towards the prison that contained his family; he got into the carriage with the Abbé Edgeworth beside him, and in two hours arrived at the Place de Louis XV.

He ascended the scaffold, his hair was then cut off; he was

undressed; an attempt was made to tie his hands; he refused, saying, "I am sure of myself;" but on being again urged he mildly held out his hands, and then advancing to the left side of the platform, he cried out with a loud voice, "Frenchmen, I die innocent; I forgive my enemies, and wish my death may be useful to France."

Santerre then ordered a roll of the drums, which drowned his voice, and prevented him from finishing.

"Go, Son of St. Louis, ascend to Heaven!" said his confessor with enthusiasm, and the unfortunate monarch presented his head to the executioner. His body was conveyed to the burying ground of St. Magdalen, and according to the decree of the Convention, consumed in unslacked lime.

Frenchmen! you have been acting a part for these last twenty-four years unnatural to your character; loyalty, honour, and attachment to your Sovereign, have ever been your leading features. Your legitimate monarch is now restored; the joy and enthusiasm expressed by all ranks and descriptions of people at Paris, and of which I was an eye-witness, convince me how sensible you are of this latter blessing.

A due attention to morality, and to the education of youth, are the only means likely to efface the dangerous and pernicious example that your rulers had set for so long a period; and, by devoting yourselves to habits of industry and commerce, you may be the happiest tod most enviable people on earth. I have slightly descanted on parts of the characters of Henry the Fourth and Louis the Sixteenth, from my knowledge of your attachment and devotion to the Bourbons; and if it should appear in this narrative that I have with too much severity spoke of France, you will please to consider that I wrote at a period when your country assumed a fierce, turbulent, and oppressive character, Although your soldiers have been led and worked upon by the very worst of men, yet they always retained their character for generosity and bravery as an enemy.

CHAPTER 52

England

In the course of my walks I met with the Russian General Poltoradski, whom I accompanied to Count Orloff's. The latter addressed me in the politest and kindest manner, alluding to the great obligations his countrymen were under to the British Government, for affording their officers and soldiers relief while prisoners, and complimenting me on the part I had taken. To which I replied that;

> I acted merely as an individual on that occasion, not having any positive authority; but I was satisfied that had I then had the means of a direct communication with his Majesty's ministers, there would have been no bounds to their liberality to so great a people, who had made such sacrifices towards the accomplishment of the wonderful change which had been effected in the state of the world.

I had afterwards the honour of being introduced by Lord Cathcart to the Emperor of Russia, who seemed acquainted with these circumstances, and addressed me with the most affable and obliging attention.

I met General Sebastiani, by accident, on the Boulevards. He informed me .he had heard of my being at Paris, and said, "you must instantly come home with me, to make you sensible of the arrangements I had made for you."

On my arrival at his house I saw ten covers laid for dinner, and among the names written on the plates I perceived my own: "there," said he, "dine or not, no other person shall occupy that place so long as you remain at Paris. My staff consider you as one of themselves; since you left us they have continually talked of you, and a standing toast for some time was your health."

To which I replied;

> really, General, I feel so much flattered that I know not how to express myself. I can only say, that your attention, and that of your staff, who are of the first description of gentlemen, possessing qualities the most rare, has made an impression on me never to be effaced: and I confess I felt myself so much at ease from their extreme politeness, that when among them I frequently launched out into follies and eccentricities that caught their fancy, so that I became more their companion than their prisoner; for we all gave scope to the same fancies, and however limited the means might have been at Grenada, certainly we cannot plead that excuse at Paris.

I regretted not having it in my power that day to dine with the general, as I was engaged to Lord Castlereagh; where I had the honour of meeting the Prince of Orange, with several Dutch, English and foreign gentlemen of distinction. The entertainment was extremely splendid, and such as should be given by the representative of Great Britain. In this instance, I was most agreeably disappointed in Lord Castlereagh; having conceived that from his intense application to parliamentary and other official engagements, it might have been presumed he was not quite *au fait* at such etiquette as his new situation required; but I must do his lordship the justice to observe, that in his solicitous attention to the company, he displayed that ease and affability, united with dignity, which were perfectly characteristic of the high station he was fulfilling, and which reflected infinite honour, both on himself and his country. The conspicuous urbanity of Lady Castlereagh's manners need not my eulogium.

Among the curiosities I saw at Paris, none amazed me more

than the Théâtre Mécanique de Monsieur Pierre, and I recommend it to those particularly who find themselves disposed to pay attention to such works of art.

After quitting Paris I again visited Verdun, to look after some property I had left there, consisting of two houses, wine, furniture, &c. and found; they escaped much better than I could have expected. Indeed, the Cossacks, on whom they bestow every epithet that is possibly bad, are the most inoffensive and harmless beings in the world. The Baskirs and Calmucks are so lazy that they would not give themselves the trouble to plunder. The Baskirs are armed with bows and arrows, which at this period of civilization surprised me.

They were almost naked and miserable in the extreme, both as to themselves and their horses, and extremely ugly. To discern their eyes you must look under them, and their general resemblance one to another is so strong, that you would imagine they were all of the same parents. The same may be observed of those who were selected for England by the Emperor of Russia. In the morning a sort of kettle or machine is sounded, when the troop all assemble at the window of their chiefs where they sing hymns to the Almighty, and in praise of their commander, who is particular as to the muster; and this is all the parade or ceremony required.

One of their chiefs made signs to me signifying they were all his own property, both men and horses. I should conceive them a sad encumbrance to any army. Their horses, which are miserable, go with their heads near the ground, and have a piece of wood for a bit in their mouths. They appeared scarce able to crawl along, and yet suddenly displayed great agility and made very rapid movements. Indeed, ever thing about these people surprised me; they were so unlike whatever I had seen before. I overtook them on their return to Russia, Verdun being the direct line.

I had heard much of the mischief done to the country during the campaign, but was much surprised to find so little, considering the sharp encounters which had taken place, and the towns and country being alternately in possession of the French and the Allies, Some bridges were blown up, and some villages burnt, but nothing of consequence in comparison to what the French merited for their excesses in other countries.

Soon after my arrival in Verdun I had an opportunity of seeing the worthy family of Monsieur Gaud, he having gone on an embassy, with others, to congratulate Louis XVIII. on the restoration of his family. I collected from the general sentiments of the Verdunois, that they were strongly in favour of Napoleon, and hostile to the Bourbons; which, however, were soon changed, by Louis XVIII. sending and judiciously distributing amongst them sixteen white ribbons, and sixteen little pieces of silver, representing a *fleur de lis*, in value about thirty *sous*, or fifteen pence, which I have seen termed in the newspapers, "the Order of the Lilly."

I purchased the *château* at Arnumon, where I formerly resided. It is an ancient building, beautifully situated on the borders of the Meuse, and the walls so thick that small apartments are excavated in their centre. The gardens belonging to the. *château* are very extensive, in addition to which I purchased a tolerable quantity of land. I have besides the entire liberty of the chace, and the right of cutting more wood than I can possibly burn in the course of the year. This estate, where I can bathe and fish in the Meuse, may afford me, I conceive, a pleasant retreat for a few months in the summer season, or whenever I may feel inclined to visit France.

I set out on my journey to England, in wet and rain, which continued three days. My intention was to go through Holland, but I discovered, by letters, that my presence was. required at home; added to which, there would have been a sad inconvenience in passing through Holland, as I understood the accommodations were very bad, and the charges extremely exorbitant.

In going through Sedan I had the curiosity to inspect the fortress, so celebrated for being the place of punishment of those English prisoners who attempted to make their escape from other depôts. Nothing could be more formidable than the place of confinement for these poor fellows, in the citadel or *château*, which is situated nearly in the centre of the town. To arrive at this abode of systematic torture, you have to pass two very extensive covered ways, the latter of which is very steep, and cut through a solid rock.

On the entering, you perceive a cell allotted to each person; no communication being ever permitted one with another. The doors of their prison are double, and secured with bars in all directions. Should anyone escape out of his cell, the wall to descend in the lower part is about one hundred and sixty feet deep; and having once attained that point, he has to climb over prodigious rocks, and walls formed out of immense heights, surrounded by centinels at short and convenient intervals.

For a stranger to look at these precautions, he would suppose it next to an impossibility to escape; but such is the powerful incentive to liberty, that I have seen and known many common soldiers and sailors, who have escaped from these prisons, without even the assistance of money to clear a passage; and almost all of whom, after having surmounted these difficulties, and obtained the summit of their wishes, uniformly committed themselves by some act of intemperance or folly. I recollect an instance worthy reciting of a soldier belonging to the 61st regiment, a native of the north of Ireland, who wrote me a note, wishing to see me at the Porte Chaussée Prison in Verdun. On my going there he observed;

> I am sorry to be so troublesome to your honour, for this is the fifth time I have troubled your honour within these last fifteen months; and three times I have escaped from the citadel of Sedan, If your honour will look at the state of my limbs you will see how they are worn to the bone; and I have, an please your honour's honour, been confined in cells underground; but I have always contrived to make my escape: neither could all the prisons in France contain me, was it not for my own foolishness as soon as I get out. If your honour will but look at the pair of handcuffs, or

bracelets, with which I am now ornamented, you may judge.

Then taking me a little on one side he disengaged himself from these encumbrances with a dexterity which I did not conceive possible, and again replaced his hands in the situation in which they previously were.

Sedan contains a population of about ten thousand inhabitants, and is remarkable for its manufacture of superfine cloths.

Previous to my arrival there. I passed by the town of Mouzon, leaving it a little to the left: it is celebrated for manufacturing the finest cloths in France.

From Sedan I proceeded over a fertile country, but great part of the way along very bad roads, passing though the town of Mezieres, a fortification strong from its flat situation and natural position, although not in very good repair. I slept at a most abominable place called La Capelle, where I met some persons who dealt largely in cambrics, from St. Quintin, and had much conversation concerning that trade. I passed likewise the fortifications of Landrecy and Quesnoy, which were so celebrated during the campaign of the Duke of York and the Prince of Saxe-Cobourg, since which period the science of warfare must be much improved; for had the Allies wasted their time and resources against several fortifications in their progress, Napoleon would in all probability have been at present on the throne of France.

I could not however pass over this country without feeling interested from having beard so much about it, and having marched and countermarched through various parts in Flanders during the Duke of York's campaign. On my arrival at Valenciennes I put up at the Grand Canard, of which I had heard a good account; but was much disappointed, as it was very uncomfortable, with large straggling rooms, and very dirty, I was soon waited on, and invited to dine with Monsieur Fazeau, the banker, and his brother, which invitation I accepted, and in the evening went to a concert of amateurs, or gentlemen performers, at the public rooms, where the music was delightful. Monsieur Fazeau took a leading part in the concert, and performed with the greatest applause.

I was rather surprised to find so many acquaintances in a place which to me was quite new. Among them I was accosted by my old friend, Colonel Cosini, who was the second in command of this garrison, and chief of the engineer department. Colonel Cosini, I have already remarked, was head of the engineer department with General Sebastiani. He was an excellent officer in his line, and from whom I derived much information in Spain. On leaving Valenciennes the landlord was determined to make me pay *comme un véritable Milord*, for my bill was enormous. The best plan I conceived was to pay; but I suggested to my friend Cosini, (as the inhabitants were complaining much of the expenses incurred by having so many soldiers quartered on them) that he must certainly be wealthy.

If we might judge by his mode of making out a bill, and therefore such a burthen, however grievous it might be upon others, must be light to him. The result was, he had forthwith thirty additional soldiers quartered on him, which gratified my spleen, and gave me ample revenge of my landlord, who then begged me to admit of his making a deduction from the bill, which I positively refused, observing that, "*Messieurs les Milords Anglois* had the character of generosity, and I could not think of being the means of depreciating them in the French opinion."

From Valenciennes I proceeded on my journey over a very rich country and paved road, until I arrived at the town of Mons, where I rested for the night. My servants preceded me with the carriage, as I had a great desire to ride over the ground and position of Jemmapes, where Dumourier gained that important victory, which awakened the eyes of Europe in some measure as to the danger to be apprehended from *carmugnoles*, who, until that battle, the grave tacticians and *mustacio'd* chiefs of the North treated with severe sarcasms and sovereign contempt

The French however, have taught the world an awful lesson, as to the imprudence of despising an enemy: and sincerely do I hope that our rulers in England may not, in like manner, hold the Americans too cheap, which may cause a long and disastrous warfare; for I know personally many French officers who have embarked their fortunes in the American cause, although not by the consent of the French Government

From Mons I proceeded the following morning to Brussels. Along the road the peasantry and various persons were inquisitive to know to whom their country was to belong? a question it was not in my power satisfactorily to answer.

On my arrival at Brussels I met many of my old acquaintances in the English army, who were quartered there. My first visit being to the parade, I was highly gratified to see the troops in such excellent order.

There were several English families, and many more expected, most of whom I believe have retired to this part of the world for economy.

Lord Lyndock commanded, whose absence I had to regret, he being then in England, but was expected the following day. I dined with general Fraser, and met many of my old acquaintance. From Brussels I took my departure for Ghent, along a charming road and very rich country. On passing through Alost I had the curiosity to go over the ground on which I was engaged in an action under Lord Moira.

The country was nearly the same, with very little alteration. I recollected every spot, and went to, the position we occupied, even to the. Hedge we had partly cut down to admit of our musketry. From Alost I reached Ghent, being but a short distance, and over a very fine road; and was soon recognised, and waited on by an English gentleman, who had been, long resident here and at Ostend.

There was a Prussian garrison in the city, consisting of about five thousand troops, all well clothed and appointed, in English clothing; one corps in particular I remarked, from being dressed in all respects precisely the same as the 95th regiment. These troops, however, had not a military appearance, being awkward in their discipline, young, and not well set up.

On, the following morning I had an opportunity of seeing

the total of the force under arms, to receive the Emperor of Russia. There was a violent rain, which continued almost the whole of the day, under which the authorities as well as the troops all paraded. The several corporate bodies, &c. marched out, dressed in silk stockings, with bands of curious looking musicians, to congratulate His Majesty on his arrival at Ghent. Although I could not but admire their public spirit, yet I pitied their situation, for the rain poured in torrents on these full drest and highly powdered people.

The Emperor at length arrived, after having, detained them some hours. He received the authorities and corporate bodies in a large tent, erected for the purpose, at the gate entering the town and then mounted on horseback, and galloped through all the streets, preceded by a well appointed detachment of Prussian hussars, amidst the shouts and applauses of a numerous body of people. Alexander took off his hat at intervals, and huzzaed also, although going at speed, in a very severe rain. His Majesty, I understood, immediately took his departure for Antwerp.

I had the curiosity soon after to visit the cathedral, which is a handsome and very noble building, well worthy the notice of any traveller who may visit Ghent. There is one small figure of an angel, cut in marble, on the right side of the altar, which has been much admired for its perfection, and for which more than its weight in gold has been, several times refused. In the course of this day, about twenty-five thousand French troops arrived, on their road from Hamburgh to France, composing part of the Prince d'Ekmuhl's army. I have seldom seen a more soldier-like, or, in all respects, a better appointed body of men, or more calculated for service. Their artillery and all their appointments corresponded, being in excellent order, although after a very fatiguing march.

On leaving the town of Ghent I was accosted by a hearty comfortable looking landlord, who addressed me in bad English, and insisted on my entering his house, which was situated at the extremity of the canal, for the accommodation of canal passengers; his rooms were spacious, commodious, and well fitted up. I promised him that when I again visited Ghent I would stop at his house and smoke a pipe. He insisted on my tasting his Hollands and liquors, which were very good; and, what is rather strange in a Fleming, refused to accept money.

On my arrival at the ancient town of Bruges I found it full of Prussian troops, and it was with difficulty I procured accommodation. The Prussian soldiers indeed are so much complained of, from their exorbitant demands in their quarters, that it has created dissatisfaction bordering on insurrection, they pay nothing, and are extremely nice in their palate, demanding delicacies in addition to their sustenance with a haughty and imperious tone. The landlord of the inn had acted as an assistant commissary in the army in which I served under His Royal Highness, and we had much conversation relative to past events.

I accidently met in the coffee-room a respectable looking gentleman, who offering his services and being communicative, I invited to take some wine and smoke a *segar* after dinner. His conversation turning on the entertainment given to the Emperor of Russia, the King of Prussia, and the other illustrious foreigners, in London, he was anxious to know who were the merchant tailors who gave this grand fête? for it appeared that both he and the French newspapers had blended and confound, the dinner as being given by the merchant tailors, instead of the merchants, bankers, &c. of the city at Merchant Tailors' Hall.

I excited much interest by giving him a description and history of the several corporate bodies in London, with an account of the rights and privileges attached to each; and I observed him particularly interested concerning the tailors. As it was the first time of my life I had heard a tailor described as a fine fellow, I was induced to pump him a little more, when I discovered my friend to be a tailor himself.

In the morning I pursued my journey chiefly along the banks of the canal, until I reached Ostend, the distance not exceeding twelve miles. An English garrison was here, and I was well acquainted with the commandant, who was lieutenant-colonel of the 44th, then composing part of it. He introduced me to a

Prussian general, of Engineers, who was just arrived from England, and was anxious to see the works round the town, which the French certainly have spared neither pains nor expense to render formidable.

The situation in some parts being flat, is much in their favour; they are greatly extended, and the old works entirely destroyed; it would now require a considerable force to defend them. At a handsome bridge close to the town is a very large basin of water, formed by the French, and connected with the Bruges canal, for the purpose of deepening the entrance for shipping. The floods gates are constructed on a very simple and ingenious principle, so that one person with the greatest ease opens or shuts them, and they are worthy a traveller's attention.

When these locks are open the water rushes out with prodigious force, forming a violent torrent and cascade, occasioned by a descent or fall from twenty to twenty-four feet. This goes forward with great rapidity to the sea, sweeping in its course quantities of mud and other obstructions, and has the effect, by this means, of deepening the harbour, or at all events prevents its being choked by sand or mud, which otherwise would accumulate.

A little farther on are the locks that had been destroyed by the expedition commanded by Sir Eyre Coote, but which were now re-established on a better and more solid principle. We passed over a drawbridge, and proceeded across the sand hills to visit the fort lately completed to the eastward of the town, to prevent an enemy making an attack on that side. It must, without doubt, have cost an immense deal, of money, from the difficulty of obtaining a foundation, being built on the sand. It is constructed entirely of brick, and the ditches are extremely deep; it mounts many guns of various calibre, and is a regular pentagon; its casemates, underground-works and magazines, are spacious and commodious, and I think, for its size, it is the most perfect and handsome fortification I ever met with.

It is commanded, however, by several sand hills within musket shot, which would disturb the artillery stationed to work the guns; but I have understood it was the intention of the French to have removed these hills, had they kept this position. Go into any country you please where the French have governed, you find their public works and institutions greatly add to its civilization and improvement.

The commandant invited the general and myself to partake of a mess dinner, to which we, acceded; the object was to amuse the Prussian, who was a polite and well bred man. We had much interesting conversation, but were frequently interrupted with the band of music continually playing; for in English regimental messes the rule is to introduce the band, without consulting whether the musicians are good or bad performers.

To amuse the Prussian still more, a soldier was sent for who had some humour, and was a great adept at singing comic songs. His figure was in his favour, and his face likewise, having lost an eye, and being much marked by the smallpox, and knowingly warped on one side. His songs required a person to be acquainted with slang terms and phrases; but unfortunately the general understood very few words of English, and could not appreciate the merits of these curious notes.

On my departure the Prussian officer accompanied me to my hotel, to smoke a *segar*, where he remarked, although in a polite manner, the whims and curious circumstances of John Bull; and gave me a description of the manner the Sovereigns and the illustrious visitors passed their time in England. What struck him most forcibly was his visit to Woolwich, which he, was much surprised to find so abundantly supplied, after having so long furnished the whole worlds with means of destruction. He much admired the handsome equipages, and the bank; but observed that in public buildings France had greatly the superiority.

From Ostend I pursued my journey along the coast to Dunkirk and Calais; from whence I took my passage to England.

Appendix

LETTERS RESPECTING THE EXPEDITION

No. 1.

Gibraltar, October 9, 1910.—10 a.m.

My Dear Sir,

You will be pleased to consider that the *Sparrowhawk*, which is a fast sailer, leaves this tomorrow at an early hour; she will be at Mirabella by two o'clock with the arms. As there may be no one to receive them, they will be at a loss how to act; pray mention to Colonel Basset the necessity of your being there at that hour, if possible; and that Molina organizes the country so as to protect flanks from Rondo, Antequera, &c. &c.; much depends on it. I expect we shall land near Malaga early on Friday morning at daybreak.

You may see us, and the assistance of Molina will be indispensable with us in going into Malaga, in the direction set forth. He and you must arrange the distribution of the peasantry in the intermediate line between Ronda and Antequera, totally unconnected with, but at the same time corresponding with, our movements.

I am, &c. &c.

(Signed) Blayney, Major-General.

N.B. Twenty-four mules or horses, to assist in the transport of artillery, must be provided. To Captain Miller &c. &c.

No. 2

Topaze at Sea, October 11, 1810.

Sir,

I beg leave to send you two hundred weight of tobacco and three hundred pair of shoes, for the use of the foreigners who accompany the expedition.

You must appoint some person to act as quarter-master serjeant, and to distribute the shoes only to those who want them. You will assure them I place every confidence in their valour and good conduct. I have no doubt of success, and they may rest satisfied their exertions will be rewarded by the British nation.

The French army of Portugal has met with a complete defeat under the command of Marshal Massena; they attacked the British line at every pointy and were everywhere defeated with loss.

I must particularly direct the attention of the foreign troops to the abstaining from plunder. They shall want for nothing that the nature of the service can afford; I therefore expect they may exert a spirit and pride amongst them, so as to keep a watch upon each other's conduct, and prevent my having recourse to unpleasant measures. Any instance of that nature which may happen shall be severely punished; the offender shall be instantly stripped of the British uniform as unworthy of it, his arms taken from him, and left to the mercy of those he has injured. I hope and feel confident there will be no necessity for such an expedient, and, that you will particularly impress upon their minds the confidence I repose in them, which confidence is confirmed by his Excellency Lieutenant General Campbell sending British officers to command them, who have gallantly volunteered their services, and are determined to share their fate.

I have the honour to be,
&c. &c. &c.

(Signed) Blayney, Major-General.

To Major M'Donald.

No. 3

To the Inhabitants of Malaga.

His Excellency Lieutenant-General Colin Campbell, Lieutenant-Governor of Gibraltar, having with the spirit and magnanimity worthy his character, and truly worthy the generosity of the British nation, who keeps fleets and armies always employed merely for the protection of the helpless and oppressed, has, with the tenderness and affection of a parent, sent me with a force to relieve the good people of Malaga from French tyranny.

My instructions and inclinations are to protect your property, relieve you from your sufferings, and respect your laws. As your friend, I must now address you with candour. For ten months you have permitted an insignificant French force, never exceeding twelve hundred men, to keep possession of your capital, when your population exceeded twenty thousand, which conduct forms a striking contrast to those glorious periods of your history, when your ancestors, by perseverance, courage, and constancy, not to be subdued during three hundred years, finally succeeded in expelling the Moors from your territory.

I therefore call upon you in the name of your holy religion, in the glorious and immortal fame which your ancestors acquired, and above all for your self-preservation, to stand forward in support of your own cause. The artillery, shall be directed only against your enemies; the enemies of order and charier. But if you remain tame spectators, and make no exertions in your own defence, I must (although reluctantly) consider your neutrality as inimical, and point the guns against your fair city. All persons who may have come from Gibraltar and enrolled themselves in the ranks of the enemy are graciously pardoned.

All inhabitants who have hitherto borne arms in their support are graciously pardoned, satisfied that nothing but terror and compulsion can induce them to act so unworthy a part.

I therefore wait your decision; and may the Almighty, who always favours the cause of the righteous and just, take you into his holy keeping. Given on board His Majesty's Ship *Topaze*, at —— this day of —— Signed) Blayney, Major-General.

No. 4

In order that there may be no mistakes, but one complete understanding and co-operation between the forces embarked, the following sounds on the bugle must direct the movements of the troops:

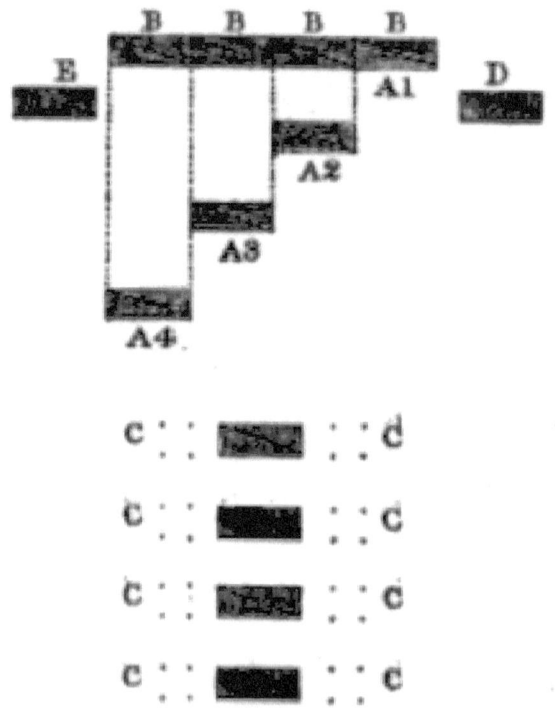

On the signal to advance, the two leading divisions of riflemen form four subdivisions, as A, A, A, A, extended *en échellon*. The third and fourth, or rear subdivisions, to extend from right to left, so that the right of the third subdivision covers the left hand man of division. No. 1, and covers the left flank of the column. The front and leading subdivision covers the right flank of *ditto*, and the second the head of the column. When attacked, the second subdivision advances to support the first on its left, the third and fourth to support those of *ditto*, forming one line, as B, B, B, B.

On the flank of each company of the entire line, are to be told off two file, as steady light troops, which are to guard the flanks of their respective companies, C, C—On the sound to commence firing, all the flankers to the right of companies run forward, and form line, or take advantage of ground to the right of the leading division; all those on the left flank form to the left of the riflemen, as D and E.

The foreign troops push forward in the *éventail*, or fair movement, so as to form line on the left.

The 89th form to the right, taking advantage of ground, and acting in line as nearly as possible. The rifle and light troops only are to be in extended order, the others as usual in regiments for close files. The Spanish regiment of Toledo to form a reserve in rear of the centre, so as to act as the exigency of the occasion may require.

All advances or retreats are to be from the right of companies by files. Thus there are to be only four sounds on the bugle with which the soldiers are to be made acquainted on board ship. They are as follows:

1. Signal to advance.
2. Commence firing.
3. Form line.
4. Retire.

Form line in retreating. Do so in retreating. Steady and intelligent men must be placed on pivot flanks.

The guns will act as occasion may require. If the column should be attacked on the left, the bugle sounds form line, in which case left wheel into line; therefore it is the rear rank acting in front, as they will be often changed, which shews front in all points that can be possibly attacked. If on the right, right wheel into line.

No.5

To His Excellency Lieutenant-General Campbell.

Sir,

It is impossible to relate the misfortune which happened to

the expedition, which you did me the honour to plaice under my command, without concern. On the 15th I had reason to expect an attack, having received information of large reinforcements being on their march, under the command of General Sebastiani. I accordingly gave orders to change our position, so as to have our right to Fiangerolla, and left on a strong ridge of hills, with the sea close to our rear, and both flanks guarded by gunboats; a position I conceived, capable of resisting any effort the enemy could have made.

During this period I went to the rear, to arrange with Captain Hall the gunboats' station; when I heard an attack was made, chiefly directed against the left, where the foreign troops were posted, who fled without resistance. The 89th were in front, employed in procuring provisions, and the enemy possessed themselves of our artillery. I instantly formed the 89th regiment, consisting of only two hundred and eighty rank and file, and proceeded to retake the guns, in which I was most gallantly supported by that corps, and succeeded after a resolute charge; the enemy fled in disorder.

On the left it was cried out, "they are Spaniards;" their dress was precisely the same, and I was cautious of firing until I could ascertain the fact. My horse being previously shot, I could not go by the rear to the left, so as to ascertain it, and was obliged to go in front. During this period, a desperate body closed in from the left, and so heavy a fire ensued, that those around me were mostly killed and wounded; resistance on my part was useless, and I was forced to surrender.

I learned afterwards, with concern, that the guns had again been taken, and the troops forced to retreat. I left them in their possession, and I can see no reason why they were abandoned. Had my misfortune not happened, my intention was to have taken that position instantly, which I hesitate not in saying, would have secured us a safe and, honourable retreat. The information was so various and incorrect, no dependence could be placed on it, neither would it have been prudent further to pursue the object of the expedition, from the vast superiority of the enemy's force.

From General Sebastiani and the French officers I have met with the greatest attention; but. Sir, I shall never again enjoy one happy moment, only in the consolation, that I have done my duty, and that my conduct personally may meet your Excellency's approbation.

     I have the honour to be, &c.
     [Signed] Blayney, Major.-General.
Malaga, 17th October, 1810.

No. 6

     Grenada, 8th November, 1810.

I wrote to your Excellency a hasty account from Malaga, relative to the proceedings of the expedition which you did me the honour of placing under my command; which account was confined to the transactions of the 15th of October only, not being equal (from my sufferings, owing to the bruises I had received when taken, and want of accommodation) to write with that precision which a matter of that nature required.

I avail myself of an escort going to Malaga, to relate to your Excellency the proceedings as nearly as possible.

Having received the Spanish regiment of Toledo on board at Ceuta, after a tedious passage we landed on the 14th of October at Calle de la Morale, a small bay, one league eastward of Marebella, and two distant from Fiangerolla. We proceeded over a difficult and mountainous country, until we came opposite the castle of Fiangerolla. Immediately on my arrival, I sent in a flag of truce, which was refused, and the enemy commenced a heavy fire on our gunboats, sunk one, and killed and wounded many of our soldiers in others; on which I advanced close to the works, with the Germans and 89th, when a warm fire of musketry commenced, supported by grape from the fort.

In this contest, I lament to inform your Excellency that Major Grant,, of the 99th, was mortally wounded (since dead), with several ethers. We succeeded, however, in silencing the guns, so as to admit the boats taking a station. During a severe night of thunder and rain, the artillery, consisting of one thirty-two pound carronade And two twelve pounders and a howitzer with two swivels were landed. Early next morning, a heavy and destructive fire commenced on both sides.

I ascertained by our advanced piquets, that the enemy in the course of the night had received large reinforcements, and I had information of a considerable army being on their march from Malaga, under the command of General Sebastiani; I accordingly, as I had already the honour of mentioning to your Excellency, gave orders to change our position, our right to Fiangerolla, and left on a strong ridge of hills with the sea close to our rear, and both flanks protected by gunboats; a position I conceived capable of resisting any effort the enemy could have made.

I had been arranging a disposition for the gunboats, when I heard an attack was made chiefly directed against the left, where the foreign troops were posted, and the enemy possessed themselves of our artillery. I instantly formed the 89th regiment, consisting of only two hundred and eighty men, and retook the guns with the bayonet. On the left an irregular force advanced, dressed precisely the same as the Spanish troops, and it was called out they were Spaniards. My horse being previously shot, I could not go by the left sufficiently rapid to ascertain the fact, and obliged to go by the front, when a desperate body closed in from the left, and so heavy a fire commenced that those around me were mostly killed and wounded; here a warm contest ensued, chiefly with the bayonet, and I was obliged to surrender, having but nine men remaining on the hill.

I learned afterwards, with concern, that the guns had again been taken, and the troops forced to retreat.

I lament my misfortune the more, Sir, as had it not happened, my intention was to have instantly taken up the position, which I have the confidence to think would have secured a safe and honourable retreat.

The information was so incorrect, no dependence could be placed on it. It is the misfortune of this country that their zeal has a tendency to mislead; what one asserts, the other generally contradicts. .I believe the opinion was, that General Blake was in sufficient force to keep the French in check so as to prevent their leaving Grenada; whereas I have since ascertained, that the advanced post of that army was at Valley Rubro, distant twenty-six Spanish leagues from Grenada; and the headquarters at Murcia, distant fifty- two leagues.

I cannot form an opinion of the impression which the want of success may make on your Excellency, or the public mind; the original intelligence was most favourable, nor could the arrival of General Sebastiani's army have been foreseen. I therefore hope my exertions, though personally unfortunate, from meeting such a superiority of force, compared to those of the British, may meet your Excellency's approbation.

General Sebastiani's conduct to me, and that of his officers, does credit to his nation.

Captains Hope, Hall and Pringle, of the Navy, with Lieutenant Carrol, and the officers commanding the gunboats, performed their part with the zeal and intrepidity which has hitherto distinguished that service.

I have the honour to be,
&c. &c. &c.

Signed) Blayney, Major-General.
To his Excellency Lieut.-General Campbell,
&c. &c. &c.

Ministère De La Guerre—5me Division—Bureau des Prissoniers de Guerre—Représailles

A Monsieur le Colonel Soyer, commondant le Dépôt de Verdun,
Monsieur,   *Paris, 6 Mars, 1812.*

Sa Majesté informée que le gouvernement Anglois a fait mettre le Général Simon, prisonnier de Guerre François en prison, m'a prescrit de faire arêter sur le champ le Lord Blayney. Vous le ferez détenir à la citadelle de Verdun, et vous lui notifierez qu'il répondra sur sa tête de la conduite de son gouvernement envers le Général François. S'il désire écrire à cet égard en Angleterre, ses lettres seront adressées sans retard au Ministre de la Marine pour leur transmission.

Vous me rendrez compte sur le champ de l'exécution de cet ordre.

Recevez, Monsieur, l'assurance de ma considération.
  (Signé) Le Duc de Feltre, Ministre de la Guerre.
  (Pour copie conforme.)—*Le Colonel Baron de Beauchêne, commandant le dépôt des prisonniers de guerre Anglois.*
  (Signé)   Soyer.

Copy of a Letter from Major-General Lord Blayney to the Earl of Liverpool.

My Lord,   March 8, 1812.

I beg leave to inform your Lordship that I am this moment put in close confinement, by order of the French Government, in consequence of the French General Officer, Simon, being arrested by the British, for what cause I have not been informed. The order for my arrestation in part runs thus:—*De faire arrêter sur le champ le Lord Blayney; vous le ferez détenir à la citadelle de Verdun, et lui notifierez qu'il répondra sur sa tête de la conduite de son gouvernement envers le Général François.*

Whatever may be the cause of General Simon's arrest, I hope the British government will be pleased to consider how unjust it is that I should be the victim of any rash or imprudent act on the part of that General.

I therefore submit it to your Lordship's consideration, in hopes that steps may be taken suited to relieve me from my present situation.

                I have the honour to remain, &c. &c.
                (Signed)   Blayney, Major-General.
To the Right Hon. the Earl of Liverpool

Copy of a Letter from Major-General Lord Blayney to Messrs. Coutts and Co.

                Citadel of Verdun, March 12, 1812.
Gentlemen,

As Lord Caledon, or none of my friends, may be in London, I request you will inform them, by letter, that I am now a close prisoner, by order of the French government, and their orders are executed with the utmost rigour.

I wrote a letter to Lord Liverpool, and another to the Duke

of York, at the desire of the French government, (perhaps they have never been forwarded); I therefore beg leave to enclose you a copy, nearly similar to each, which I will thank you to send to His Royal Highness and Lord Liverpool, lest the originals may not have been received; with this observation, which of course I could not send through the Minister of Marine here, that however great my sufferings may be (and I can assure you they are now very severe), that I hope they may never be considered in competition with the dignity and honour of the country.

I have the honour to remain, &c., &c.
(Signed)   Blayney, Major-General.

Copy of a Letter from Major-General Lord Blayney to the Baron de Beauchêsne, Commanding the Depôt of Prisoners of War, at Verdun.

Monsieur le Baron,

Vous avez sans doute remarqué l'observation que Monsieur le Général Lacoste a écrite sur mon passeport; il ne m'appartient pas d'anticiper sur le jugement que vous-même, Monsieur le Baron, porterez sur cette affaire; mais vous voudrez cependant me permettre de vous dire, que la manière dont j'ai été reçu par Monsieur le Général Lacoste ne fait honneur ni à son rang comme officier général ni à son entendement. Il aura pu voir sur mon passeport que comme militaire je suis son égal, et que comme particulier mon rang me mettra bien au-dessus de lui.

A sa violence et sa hauteur je n'ai opposé que le mépris et la compassion qu'a excité en moi une personne qui à un tel point poussoit l'oubli des convenances et de ce qu'il devoit à sa situation. Comme j'ignore de quelle manière tout ceci vous sera représenté, je dois vous observer. Monsieur le Baron, que je ne lui ai pas fait de réplique;. et comme il serait très-possible qu'il cherchât à justifier cette conduite par sa crainte de voir les officiers Anglois communiquent avec les prisonniers Espagnois, je puis vous assurer que je n'ai ni parlé ni eu aucune communication quelconque avec les Messieurs qui sont à Nancy.

J'étois autant plus surpris de cette conduite de Monsieur le Général Lacoste que j'étois plus loin de in'y attendre d'après l'opinion que je m'en étois formé, et que je suis bien assuré qu'elle n'est aucune-

ment d'accord, ni avec les intentions, ni avec les ordres de Sa Majesté l'Empereur.

J' ai l'honneur d'être, &c. &c.
(Signé)   Blayney, Major-Général.
Verdun, le 26 Mai, 1812.

Copy of a Letter from Major-General Lord Blayney to Messrs. Mallett, at Paris.

Verdun, July 23, 1812.

Gentlemen,

Mr. Hall has this day shown me your letter of the 18th instant, relative to the discounting such bills as may be necessary to draw on the British Government, for the several sums which may be necessary to remit to the various depôts; these bills are always drawn in my favour and indorsed by me, although I have hitherto transacted my private business with Messrs. Peregaux and Co., and entertain the highest opinion of their house, at the same time feel grateful for the attentions they have at all times paid to my private concerns since being in France.

My duty in a public capacity is to procure cash for supplies on the most moderate terms possible, so that the British government may see that correct justice is in all respects paid to obtaining it on good terms; therefore in my humble opinion was this money to be negotiated with Messrs. Peregaux and Co. from their having almost entirely the English money concerns to transact, it would lead to a monopoly that the British Government may not think judicious on my part to admit.

I therefore beg leave to inform you as nearly as possible of the sum which may be annually wanted, amounting to about £40,000 sterling (including clothing for the soldiers), which sum you will remit to the different depôts in such manner as Mr. Hall shall advise you; and I am in hopes you will adopt measures with your correspondent at these depots, so that the least possible expense in discount on these remittances may be incurred. The letters of advice shall be placed on the back of the bills in such manner as hitherto has been customary, and is perfectly understood with the agents on whom these bills are drawn.

I have the honour to remain, &c.

(Signed) Blayney, Major-General.

P. S. You will be pleased to observe that this letter relates to the public concern only, as I could not with any propriety withdraw my private concerns from Messrs. Peregaux and Co.

Copy of a Letter from Major-General Lord Blayney to Mr. Olivier, Commandant of the Depôt at Sarre-Louis.

Verdun, le 20 Août 1811.

Monsieur le Commandant,

Je viens de recevoir de Monsieur Penrice la copie de plusieurs extraits de mes lettres pubiées au dépôt sous vos ordres et avec votre approbation.

Permettez-moi, Monsieur le Commandant, de vous témoigner ma reconnaissance de tous les soins que vous vous donnez pour rendre le sort des prisonniers de guerre aussi doux que le permettent les circonstances et l'ordre des choses; j'ai vu avec un sensible plaisir que vous jugez que les lettres j'ai adressées aux prisonniers de guerre à votre dépôt ont pû ou peuvent contribuer au bon ordre et à la tranquillité que vous desirez y maintenir,

Je serois charmé, Monsieur, s'il pût se présenter une occasion de vous être utile et agréable, du moins me plairai-je toujours de vous rendre en tout lieu et en toute circonstance la justice dû à un brave militaire qui comme vous, Monsieur, sait servir son souverain et sa patrie avec honneur, sans oublier ce qu'il doit à l'humanité. C'est très-sincèrement que je vous prie d'agréer les assurances de la parfaite estime avec laquelle j'ai l'honneur d'être,

(Signé) Blayney, Major-Général.

Copy of a Letter from Monsieur Olivier, commanding the Depôt of British Prisoners at Sarre-Louis, to Major-General Lord Blayney.

Sarre-Louisy le 22 Août, 1812.

Mi Lord,

J'ai reçu a la lettre flatteuse que vous avez bieu voulu m'écrire, en date du 20 de ce mois. Je vous prie de croire, qu'en rendant le sort des *prisonniers Anglois aussi doux que le permettent les circonstances, je n'ai suivi que les intentions de mon Souverain et l'impulsion de mon cœur.*

Je dois vous faire connaître, Monsieur le Général, que Monsieur le Lieutenant Penrice m'a beaucoup aider, aussi avons, nous la satisfaction de voir chaque jour une amélioration sensible dans le dépôt sous ma surveillance.

Je suis flatté, Monsieur le Général, que tout ce que je fais pour le bien de vos compatriotes puisse vous être agréable, et votre assentiment est pour moi au delà de tout.

N'ayant jamais eu d'ambition que celle de m'attirer l'estime de tous les honnêtes gens, la vôtre, Monsieur le Général, me flatté beaucoup.

Recevez, je vous prie, l'assurance du profond respect avec laquelle j'ai l'honneur d'être,

  (Signé) Olivier,

Ministere de la Guerre—5eme Division—Bureau des Prissonniere de Guerre.

Copy of a letter from the Duc de Feltre, Minister of War, to the Baron de Beauchêsne, Commandant of the Depôt of English Prisoners of War at Verdun.

Monsieur,

J'ai lieu de croire que Lord Blayney entretien une correspondence administrative dans les dépôts des prisonniers de guerre de sa nation; qu'il réclame des états de situation et de fourniture, &c.; enfin qu'il exerce sans mission les fonctions, d'un commisssaire Britannique. La formation des conseils d'administration dans les dépôts, et l'admission de deux prisonniers de guerre dans chacun de ces conseils ont suffisamment prouvé que le gouvernement Français n'eut l'entière exécution des règlemens; elle sait respecter les droits du malheur, mais l'Empereur en refusant d'admettre un commissaire Anglois autorisé, veut à plus fort raison qu'aucun prisonnier ne s'arroge ses fonctions; vous ferez notifier sur-le-champ à Lord Blayney la défense de continuer des relations aussi contraires aux ordres de Sa Majesté, et vous veillerez à ce qu'il s'y conforme.

    Recevez, Monsieur, &c.
 (Signé) *Le Ministre De La Guerre, Duc de Feltre.*

Pour copie conforme.

Le Colonel, Baron de Beauchêsne, commandant du dépôt des prisonniers de guerre Anglois dans le département de la Meuse.

(Signé)   Soyer.

P. S. Je ne m'oppose pas à ce que les secours venus de la Grande Bretagne et de l'Irlande pour divers prisonniers leur soyent envoyés par Lord Blayney, pourvu que les fonds soyent faits par les familles ou proviennent des souscriptions particulières; mais la distribution ne peut en être faite secrètement et sans le concours de l'autorité Française.

Copy of Letter from Major General Lord Blayney to the Duc de Feltre, Minister of War.

My Lord Duke,

I have this day received the copy of a letter your Excellency wrote to Monsieur le Baron de Beauchêsne, which he did me the favour to enclose. Your Excellency may not be aware of the situation in which the British sailors as well as soldiers (while prisoners) are circumstanced. Their pay is placed in due course to their credit, equally the same as if they were with their corps, and have a just right to claim and receive it from the British Government; therefore, instead of receiving their money on their return to England, they requested I would act as their agent, and draw for them a moiety of the sum due, to purchase tobacco, or such comforts (in addition to the French allowance) which might alleviate their situation; it is only drawing for them their own property; and so far from my acting as a commissary on the part of the British Government, if your Excellency will only peruse the correspondence between me and them on the subject, you will find in this instance that they opposed it, on the principle of the advantage France would derive from the loss of exchange, and the disadvantage to England; and, finally, I represented that, unless they acquiesced, these prisoners would send each separately an order to their friends to receive the money due to them, and that they would individually draw it through that channel, which, when explained, the British Government admitted a portion of their pay being drawn, as your Excellency may perceive by the copy of the Secretary at War's letter to me, and that he corresponded, with me on that subject merely as senior officer on full pay, and not as commissary. I am therefore induced to conclude that the benevolent disposition of his Majesty the Emperor and your Excellency would not prevent the unfortunate men whom the chance of war has placed in your hands, from receiving the miserable sum of six *sous* per day, with perhaps an additional shirt and a pair of shoes; and your Excellency may perceive, on a reference to Messrs. Peregaux and Mallett, bankers, that these bills are drawn on the agents of the regiments, and not on the War Office or Government of Great Britain.

I must refer your Excellency to my correspondence with the commandant at Briançon, and other depôts, to shew that my communication has not been in secret, but open, and I should have addressed your Excellency on this subject, had I conceived it worthy of your Excellency's consideration. I am therefore in hopes my conduct corresponds with the postscript in your Excellency's letter.

I have the honour to remain,
&c. &c. &c.
(Signed)   Blayney, Major-General.

P. S. I am in hopes this explanation will be satisfactory to your Excellency.

Copy of a letter from Captain Dabel and Lieutenant Mosqua, of the Duke of Brunswick's Corps.

Mayence, January 1, 1812.

My Lord,

We do not omit offering you our best wishes at the beginning of the year; we have also this honour of acquainting your Lordship, that the letter dated the 27th *ult.* has enabled us to settle in future our money affairs. Mr. Peregaux in Paris has remitted to us the amount of a bill on our agents in London, sent to him some time ago. The bill for £50, from Monsieur, Antoine, has also been paid to us at the rate of exchange mentioned in the letter of the 27th *ult*. We have always laid under the conviction that the Government whom we have the honour to serve, would not abandon us, and that it was owing to our very limited acquaintance with affairs of that sort, that our helpless situation till now must be ascribed. There is one passage in the above-mentioned letter which strengthens our minds to encounter future undeserved sufferings: the flattering idea that our Protector will employ his interest in our behalf, has infused the hope of a better futurity in our hearts. In vain do we endeavour by writing to express the sentiments of gratitude with which we are animated towards him, who so generously rescued us from misery, and who has restored us again to the society of them of which we had been so long deprived. We remain, with the most profound respect, &c.

(Signed)   Dabel, Captain,
                         Mosqua, Lieut.

To Major, General Lord Blayney.

Copy of a Letter from the Duke of Brunswick Oels to Major-General Lord Blayney.

Brunswick, March 18, 1814.

My Lord,

I have the pleasure to inform your Lordship, that Captain Dabel and Lieutenant Mosqua of my Light Infantry regiment have joined me, and I lose no time to express to you my sincerest and warmest thanks for the kind and favourable protection which you have granted to those gentlemen. I hope they will soon have an opportunity of retaliating the bad treatment which they have experienced from the enemy, and that it may be known to all Germany in what manner these brave men were treated. I shall write today to Messrs.

Greenwood, the agents of my corps, and request them to settle with your Lordship the different sums which were forwarded from you to these officers. In requesting your Lordship to accept of my warmest gratitude,

I have the honour to be,
Your Lordship's obedient servant,
(Signed)   William, Duke of Brunswick.
            Major-General Lord Blayney.

ALSO FROM LEONAUR
AVAILABLE IN SOFTCOVER OR HARDCOVER WITH DUST JACKET

CAPTAIN OF THE 95th (Rifles) *by Jonathan Leach*—An officer of Wellington's Sharpshooters during the Peninsular, South of France and Waterloo Campaigns of the Napoleonic Wars.

BUGLER AND OFFICER OF THE RIFLES *by William Green & Harry Smith* With the 95th (Rifles) during the Peninsular & Waterloo Campaigns of the Napoleonic Wars

BAYONETS, BUGLES AND BONNETS *by James 'Thomas' Todd*—Experiences of hard soldiering with the 71st Foot - the Highland Light Infantry - through many battles of the Napoleonic wars including the Peninsular & Waterloo Campaigns

THE ADVENTURES OF A LIGHT DRAGOON *by George Farmer & G.R. Gleig*—A cavalryman during the Peninsular & Waterloo Campaigns, in captivity & at the siege of Bhurtpore, India

THE COMPLEAT RIFLEMAN HARRIS *by Benjamin Harris as told to & transcribed by Captain Henry Curling*—The adventures of a soldier of the 95th (Rifles) during the Peninsular Campaign of the Napoleonic Wars

WITH WELLINGTON'S LIGHT CAVALRY *by William Tomkinson*—The Experiences of an officer of the 16th Light Dragoons in the Peninsular and Waterloo campaigns of the Napoleonic Wars.

SURTEES OF THE RIFLES *by William Surtees*—A Soldier of the 95th (Rifles) in the Peninsular campaign of the Napoleonic Wars.

ENSIGN BELL IN THE PENINSULAR WAR *by George Bell*—The Experiences of a young British Soldier of the 34th Regiment 'The Cumberland Gentlemen' in the Napoleonic wars.

WITH THE LIGHT DIVISION *by John H. Cooke*—The Experiences of an Officer of the 43rd Light Infantry in the Peninsula and South of France During the Napoleonic Wars

NAPOLEON'S IMPERIAL GUARD: FROM MARENGO TO WATERLOO *by J. T. Headley*—This is the story of Napoleon's Imperial Guard from the bearskin caps of the grenadiers to the flamboyance of their mounted chasseurs, their principal characters and the men who commanded them.

BATTLES & SIEGES OF THE PENINSULAR WAR *by W. H. Fitchett*—Corunna, Busaco, Albuera, Ciudad Rodrigo, Badajos, Salamanca, San Sebastian & Others

AVAILABLE ONLINE AT **www.leonaur.com**
AND OTHER GOOD BOOK STORES

ALSO FROM LEONAUR
AVAILABLE IN SOFTCOVER OR HARDCOVER WITH DUST JACKET

WELLINGTON AND THE PYRENEES CAMPAIGN VOLUME I: FROM VITORIA TO THE BIDASSOA by *F. C. Beatson*—The final phase of the campaign in the Iberian Peninsula.

WELLINGTON AND THE INVASION OF FRANCE VOLUME II: THE BIDASSOA TO THE BATTLE OF THE NIVELLE by *F. C. Beatson*—The second of Beatson's series on the fall of Revolutionary France published by Leonaur, the reader is once again taken into the centre of Wellington's strategic and tactical genius.

WELLINGTON AND THE FALL OF FRANCE VOLUME III: THE GAVES AND THE BATTLE OF ORTHEZ by *F. C. Beatson*—This final chapter of F. C. Beatson's brilliant trilogy shows the 'captain of the age' at his most inspired and makes all three books essential additions to any Peninsular War library.

NAVAL BATTLES OF THE NAPOLEONIC WARS by *W. H. Fitchett*—Cape St. Vincent, the Nile, Cadiz, Copenhagen, Trafalgar & Others

SERGEANT GUILLEMARD: THE MAN WHO SHOT NELSON? by *Robert Guillemard*—A Soldier of the Infantry of the French Army of Napoleon on Campaign Throughout Europe

WITH THE GUARDS ACROSS THE PYRENEES by *Robert Batty*—The Experiences of a British Officer of Wellington's Army During the Battles for the Fall of Napoleonic France, 1813.

A STAFF OFFICER IN THE PENINSULA by *E. W. Buckham*—An Officer of the British Staff Corps Cavalry During the Peninsula Campaign of the Napoleonic Wars

THE LEIPZIG CAMPAIGN: 1813—NAPOLEON AND THE "BATTLE OF THE NATIONS" by *F. N. Maude*—Colonel Maude's analysis of Napoleon's campaign of 1813.

BUGEAUD: A PACK WITH A BATON by *Thomas Robert Bugeaud*—The Early Campaigns of a Soldier of Napoleon's Army Who Would Become a Marshal of France.

TWO LEONAUR ORIGINALS

SERGEANT NICOL by *Daniel Nicol*—The Experiences of a Gordon Highlander During the Napoleonic Wars in Egypt, the Peninsula and France.

WATERLOO RECOLLECTIONS by *Frederick Llewellyn*—Rare First Hand Accounts, Letters, Reports and Retellings from the Campaign of 1815.

AVAILABLE ONLINE AT **www.leonaur.com**
AND OTHER GOOD BOOK STORES

www.ingramcontent.com/pod-product-compliance
Lightning Source LLC
Chambersburg PA
CBHW021955160426
43197CB00007B/137